D0216176

Bipolar Expeditions

Bipolar Expeditions

Mania and Depression in American Culture

EMILY MARTIN

Princeton University Press
Princeton and Oxford

Copyright © 2007 by Princeton University Press
Published by Princeton University Press, 41 William Street,
Princeton, New Jersey 08540
In the United Kingdom: Princeton University Press, 3 Market Place,
Woodstock, Oxfordshire OX20 1SY

All Rights Reserved

Library of Congress Cataloging-in-Publication Data

Martin, Emily.
Bipolar expeditions : mania and depression in American culture / Emily Martin.
p.   cm.
Includes bibliographical references and index.
ISBN-13: 978-0-691-00423-5 (hardcover : alk. paper)
ISBN-10: 0-691-00423-4 (hardcover : alk. paper)
1. Manic-depressive illness—Social aspects—United States. 2. Medical anthropology—
United States. I. Title.
[DNLM: 1. Bipolar Disorder—United States. 2. Anthropology, Cultural—United States.
WM 207 M379b 2007]
RC516.M382 2007
362.196′89500973—dc22
2006036317

British Library Cataloging-in-Publication Data is available

This book has been composed in Electra.

Printed on acid-free paper. ∞

press.princeton.edu

Printed in the United States of America

1   3   5   7   9   10   8   6   4   2

Does the sign-post leave no doubt open about the
way I have to go? Does it shew which direction I am to
take when I have passed it; whether along the road or the
footpath or cross-country? But where is it said which
way I am to follow it; whether in the direction of its finger
or (e.g.) in the opposite one?

—Ludwig Wittgenstein, *Philosophical Investigations*

For my students

Contents

Illustrations

Figures

Tables

Preface: Ethnographic Ways and Means

Studies are outcomes rather than realized objectives.
They are intellectual footprints, not blueprints.
—Herbert Fingarette, *The Self in Transformation*

I have done ethnographic projects before, but none has tapped into my personal experience as deeply as this one did.[1] While I was writing my last book, I experienced a break with reality. Most writers are probably familiar with the self-doubt that plagues the mind while one is hammering out a draft of something new. That kind of self-doubt was a familiar feeling to me too. But this time something different happened: whenever I tried to write, I felt a sinister figure, a cold gray gargoyle, perched tenaciously on my shoulder, looking at what I was writing on the computer screen, and muttering a devastatingly negative commentary about what it read there. Obscene and inescapable, the creature knew me intimately and did not wish me well.[2] This might sound like a parody of academic anxiety, but the experience was anything but funny. I felt trapped, frightened, and out of control. I didn't know whether or not I was going mad, but I did suspect this was not just another episode in the periodic depressions for which I was taking antidepressants. In the weeks that followed, the psychiatrist I consulted concluded that the antidepressants I was taking (prescribed by another psychiatrist) had exacerbated my true underlying mental state—manic depression—which had darkly flowered to the point of psychosis.[3]

A couple of years later, in 1996, I was spending a semester at the Humanities Research Institute in Irvine, California, when I saw an announcement in the local paper for weekly meetings of "manic depression support groups" held at several locations in Orange County. As I began to attend these groups, I realized I might be at the start of a new ethnography. I had already been surprised to find, during my last fieldwork project, that authors of books and magazines for businesspeople were discussing both manic depression (also known as bipolar disorder) and Attention Deficit Hyperactivity Disorder (ADHD), praising these conditions for the creative potential they offered corporations. Now I wondered if I were facing an opportunity for a broadly based ethnographic inquiry into how such a strange juxtaposition could be taking form. I explained to each support group I attended that I was thinking of doing an ethnographic study of manic depression and ADHD, although I had no idea yet what that would mean. The groups made it clear it was not a problem for me to wear two hats—a writer's and a patient's—because I had already met the criteria for admission to the group: I had received the diagnosis of a mood disorder and was on medication under psychiatric care. Their only request was that I not reveal any member's identity. But through looks and gestures the first time I took out pencil and paper, people also made it abundantly clear that they would not tolerate note taking of any kind.

So I faced a challenge. My own condition might provide a route for me to study aspects of mental illness that could not be witnessed in any other way. But fears around the stigma of mental illness would prevent me from using key tools in the craft of ethnography, which involve careful note taking or recording, preferably as events take place. After a long period of uncertainty, I decided to do this ethnography more the way I had done my work in Chinese villages in Taiwan years ago than the way I had done my more recent U.S. fieldwork. I would participate in events and observe them mostly without tape recording and I would consider carefully before requesting interviews. I would take notes on the fly, in the moment whenever possible, or immediately after events were over, if not. My reasons for this are important to clarify. Some were practical: the stigma against mental illness is so great that my knowing someone's phone number and address, which I would need to do a lengthy, confidential interview, could be threatening. People have lost jobs and relationships when such information has gotten into the wrong hands and for this reason participants rarely revealed their last names or addresses in support groups. To understand something like madness, defined as outside "rationality," I would need to venture into unfamiliar territory.[4]

I used the word "madness" in the last sentence intentionally, although the term "mental illness" has the benefit of grouping mental phenomena with physical phenomena, implying optimistically that both have biological causes and potential cures. Without denying the utility of this grouping, I would say that the term "mental illness" also robs the experience of being "mentally ill" of its complex darkness, and it is this darkness that I want to understand better. I knew from my own experience and that of my interlocutors that grappling with the category of madness would require me to find ways of pursuing the "darker forces in human life," as James Baldwin puts it. He was concerned with the repression and denial of "human weight and complexity" to African Americans, but many of his arguments bear full weight against the ways those deemed "mentally ill" are denied the status of the fully human.[5] For Baldwin, the division between blacks and whites was maintained by relegating black men to the status of exotic rarities, thus erecting a separation between blacks and whites that could not be bridged.[6] The stigmas of race and mental illness are certainly not identical, but both draw on terrible reserves of repressed fears and angers.

In my own work and employment, facing the stigma of mental illness has been an ongoing problem. When, as part of fieldwork, I had been trained to lead support groups for people with manic depression, the organization that provided the training strongly encouraged us trainees to start a support group in our own local town or workplace. I was a professor at Princeton at the time and I knew that several of my students were struggling with bipolar disorder.[7] I went to the psychiatrist who was head of the student counseling service and explained what I had been trained to do, offering to facilitate the formation of a group in some small way. She thanked me but explained that students at Princeton did not need such a group. She said that students with those kinds of serious mental problems would simply not be able to function in the intellectually demanding environment at Princeton, so there was no need to form a group. In this social setting, if you say you have manic depression, you may well be categorized as a nonfunctional person, as a less than a fully rational person. I did not tell her that I, too, had the diagnosis because at the time this admission felt too terrible to bring to light. Would I, too, be judged incapable of functioning at Princeton?

Among you who have read this far, or among your nearest and dearest, may be a person who is living under the description of one of the psychological conditions I discuss in this book. Some of you may also be taking psychotropic drugs or undergoing psychotherapy. I want to acknowledge the pain and suffering that can be attendant upon these conditions, as well as the real amelioration that drugs and other therapies can offer, but I also want to understand these conditions in a broader cultural and historical context in order to shed light on the experience of having manic depression. In my life, as in this book, I stand in a doubled position as a person who appreciates the benefits of psychopharmacology and other therapies and who is curious about their historical and cultural significance. I invite readers to do the same.

When I have given lectures on the material in this book at public and private universities, large and small, members of the audience, students as well as faculty, have often felt moved to reveal their diagnosis of manic depression or some other mental disorder. Some have done this very publicly during audience discussions after the lecture, which always made me feel a mixture of delight and dismay: delight because the lecture had opened a space in which someone could make such a difficult admission; dismay because the person, carried away by the moment, might not realize the possible sanctions that could await her. At a seminar at the University of Washington, in front of some of the faculty on his committee, a graduate student revealed that he had been diagnosed with manic depression. Later, at dinner with a small group of faculty, I worried whether I should have forewarned my audience not to make such rash confessions. Susan Jeffords, professor and vice provost, suggested that the audience could have handled the confession better if they had done more than simply listen in anxious silence. When the student revealed his diagnosis of "bipolar disorder," the others present could have acknowledged the vulnerability he had just created for himself and offered to become his local guardians. Until the stigma attached to mental illness eases, which is to say until our cultural understanding of it changes, the best alternative to secrecy and fear is this kind of collective responsibility.

Readers will not find in this book a handbook on how to live with manic depression, although they will find accounts of what it is like to live under the description of manic depression. Readers will not find here accusing fingers pointed at any single one of the experts or techniques that come to bear on our moods today—psychiatrists, patients, pharmaceutical companies, support groups, or drugs—although they will find a description of some disturbing aspects of the emerging landscape on which these and other forces have been interacting over many years to produce the thing we now know as bipolar disorder. There are groups who have mobilized to expose and discredit both psychiatry and the pharmaceutical industry: MadLib, the Alliance for Human Research Protection, and the Antipsychiatry Coalition, among others. Some individuals and groups have decided to opt out of the psychopharmacological world completely. In this ethnography I aim to explore the daily experiences of those who, for better or worse, are participating in the world that psychopharmacology has opened up.

Looking optimistically to the future, I would like to make use of the word "crazy," because its dictionary meanings include: insane, full of cracks or flaws (desirable in certain kinds of pottery glaze), being out of the ordinary, distracted with desire or excitement, and passionately preoccupied. The word "gay" went from a shameful whisper to a proud shout, as homosexual identity became less stigmatized. I would hope that, somewhat differently, the word "crazy" could come to mark the ways that everyone belongs in one way or another—even if only in their dreams—to the realm of the irrational. I am not saying that we are all alike or that some of us are not disabled by our craziness. I am saying that there could be friendly recognition across the sometimes arbitrary line between rational and irrational acts and thoughts, not just in the corporate world but in all walks of life.

With this in mind, proceeds from the publication of this book will go toward support of the Live Crazy Network, http://www.livecrazy.org, a nonprofit organization that maintains an independent Web site for the writings of anyone who wishes to describe and analyze their experiences of the mind—a mind-opening endeavor.

Acknowledgments

Over the ten years of research and writing for this book, I have incurred many debts. I relied on the help of a number of able research assistants, who transcribed interviews, found obscure references, and tracked down endless details. For all this, I am most grateful to Anne Rose, Gabriella Drinovan, Ilka Datig, Rachel Dvorkin, Rachel Lears, Veronica Davidov, and Emily Cohen. Kelly Gillespie's efficient and confident help was a godsend in the process of gathering permissions and preparing illustrations.

In the spirit of collaboration, several people accompanied me on interviews or introduced me to people they knew. I could not have conducted these interviews unless they had vouched for my research. I thank Mimi Dumville, Allison Smith, and Julie Smith for their remarkable generosity in giving their time and their trust to the project.

I had the benefit of much intellectual stimulation from faculty and students at the two universities in which I worked during the last ten years, Princeton University and New York University. For helping me with the important details of bureaucratic life, I thank Carol Zanca, Eileen Bowman, and Jennie Tichenor. I feel fortunate to have many colleagues whose intellectual company was inspiring in the areas of my research and who sharpened my thinking during the course of many conversations over the years: Jim Boon, Joe Dumit, Troy Duster, Faye Ginsburg, David Harvey, David Healy, Elizabeth Lunbeck, Fred Myers, Gananath Obeyesekere, Mary Poovey, Bambi Schieffelin, Erica Schoenberger, Judy Stacey, Rayna Rapp, and Nikolas Rose. Some colleagues also read and commented on the manuscript in detail, in whole or part. For taking valuable time from their own pressing lives and helping me make the book far more cogent and accessible, I owe profound thanks to Richard Chisolm, Richard Cone, Susan Harding, Don Kulick, Liisa Malkki, Leith Mullings, Lorna Rhodes, Louis Sass, Amy Smiley, and Melissa Wright.

For taking on the book when she was editor at Princeton University Press, and giving her superbly talented editorial hand to the manuscript not once but twice since beginning a new career in anthropology, I am grateful to Mary Murrell. Her generous and committed work with the manuscript profoundly improved its coherence. In turn, Fred Appel freely gave me encouragement, as well as sound editorial advice, and played a crucial role in shaping the final version of the manuscript. He also ably shepherded the book through the stages of editing and production at the Press. I also want to thank Natalie Baan at the Press for her warm enthusiasm and her outstanding organizational skills. Jennifer Backer provided meticulous and timely copyediting, as well as encouragement, for which I am grateful.

Because of the sensitivity of being identified with mental illness, I am not able to name many of the people who gave me so much insight into their lives, who allowed me into their organizations and homes to discuss their experiences. I hope they know how much I honor them and their willingness to participate in this research. Knowing them has immeasurably enriched my life. I can thank by name some individuals who helped me conceptualize places I might locate the research and who also provided keys to important doors. Jay Folkes, Charles Gross, William Helfand, John Kallir, Paul McHugh, and Everett Siegel have my lasting gratitude for their remarkable generosity. I will remember Dana Caruso for her courage in sharing the powerful story of her life until its untimely end. The Web site www.livecrazy.org is dedicated to her and to carrying on her efforts to increase knowledge about bipolar disorder. Special thanks go to Jim Ferguson and Liisa Malkki, who allowed me to house-sit for them when they were away for several summers, thus giving me a local residence in Orange County and a lovely place to entertain people I met during fieldwork. I also owe special thanks to C. E. Chaffin for his inspiring poetry and many insightful conversations.

I gratefully acknowledge support from three Princeton Faculty Research grants, a Guggenheim Fellowship, a National Science Foundation grant, and a Spencer Foundation grant. I gained some specialized insight into the advertising industry through a visiting professorship from the Advertising Educational Foundation, which I greatly appreciate. Access to the collections of the History of Medicine Division of the National Library of Medicine was enabled by a summer position, for which I thank Elizabeth Fee.

To my family, who smiled with recognition when I became consumed with this latest project and always believed that something would emerge from it, even when I was not sure, go my deepest thanks. My husband, Richard, knew from the start and accepted with grace that this project would mean tolerating a good measure of emotional upheaval. For cooking delicious meals, finding humor in everyday life, and letting me in on the adventures of their different lives, I thank Richard, Ariel, Jenny, and Yohance. Each in a unique way provided me with inspiration and the belief that active engagement with different forms of injustice can lead to social change. The nonhuman members of my family also helped keep me steady: I thank Rubie (the parrot) for being exuberant but usually staying just this side of mania; I thank Celeste and Ebony (the cats) for being calm but never sliding over into depression.

To those friends who bolstered my confidence during this project, I owe more than my heart can express. Without them this book surely would never have seen the light of day: Meg and Richard Chisolm, Susan Harding, Liisa Malkki, Leith Mullings, Lorna Rhodes, Erica Schoenberger, and Amy Smiley. Joan Bielefeld was my inventive and tireless advocate, helping me find a path through thickets of the mind. Her emotional warmth, acute observations, knowledge of psychopharmaceuticals, and solid good sense saved me over and over.

I also greatly benefited from the responses of colleagues and audiences while I lectured during the years I was writing the manuscript. I acknowledge with appreciation all that I learned at Harvard University, the Massachusetts Institute of Technology, the City University of New York, the University of Washington, the University of Texas, Colby College, the University of British Columbia, the National Library of Medicine (History of Medicine Division), the National University of Ireland, Maynooth, the University of Wisconsin, Denison College, the Centre for Advanced Studies, Berlin, L'École Normale Supérieure, the University of Michigan, the University of Bergen, and the London School of Economics.

Some chapters in this book contain revisions and expansions of previously published material: "The Rationality of Mania," in *Doing Science + Culture*, edited by Roddey Reid and Sharon Traweek (New York: Routledge, 2000), 177–98; "Rationality, Feminism, and Mind," in *Feminism in Twentieth-Century Science, Technology, and Medicine*, edited by Angela N. H. Creager, Elizabeth Lunbeck, and Londa Schiebinger (Chicago: University of Chicago Press, 2001), 214–29; "Moods and Representations of Social Inequality," in *Gender, Race, Class and Health: Intersectional Approaches*, edited by Leith Mullings and Amy Shultz (San Francisco: Jossey Bass, 2005), 60–88; "Project Security," in *Making Threats: Biofears and Environmental Anxieties*, edited by Betsy Hartmann, Banu Subramiam, and Charles Zerner (Lanham, MD: Rowman and Littlefield, 2005), 187–97; and "Cultures of Mania: Towards an Anthropology of Mood," in *The New Politics of Surveillance and Visibility*, edited by Kevin D. Haggerty and Richard V. Ericson (Toronto: University of Toronto Press, 2006), 327–39. Portions of C. E. Chaffin's poems, "Manic-depression" (published in the online journal *Interface*) and "My Testament" (published in the online journal *Poetry Superhighway*) are printed here with permission. A portion of Robert Penn Warren's poem, "Tell Me a Story," is printed with permission, copyright © 1998 by the estate of Robert Penn Warren and reprinted by permission of the William Morris Agency, LLC, on behalf of the author.

More than any other project I have undertaken, my classes with undergraduate and graduate students have informed this book. In seminars at Princeton University and New York University, students subjected the basic texts that engaged me to collective scrutiny and, by arguing with me, gave my ideas greater purchase. The most important courses were Cultures of the Mental, the Anthropology of Personhood, Drugs, Politics and Culture, and the Anthropology of the Unconscious (taught jointly with Don Kulick). To my colleagues and former graduate students who, under the leadership of Karen-Sue Taussig, held a session for my sixtieth birthday at the 2005 American Anthropological Association meetings, I owe one of the happiest afternoons of my life and the courage to finish this book.

Bipolar Expeditions

Manic Depression in America

If I want to be beyond criticism, loved by everyone,
flawless as a gem and incorruptible as platinum,
having a holy hatred of evil and a desperate love of good—
and if I plunge into suicidal melancholy
when I realize how impossible this is,
is it such a bad thing?

—C. E. Chaffin, "My Testament"

American culture today has a strong affinity with manic behavior. Advertisements use the quality of mania to sell products from Macintosh computers to luxury linens, from perfumes by Armani to shoes by Adidas. Manic energy fuels the plots of detective novels, MTV shows, and television dramas such as *ER*; it rings through the lyrics of songs like Jimi Hendrix's "Manic Depression." Serious academic tomes as well as patient advocacy Web sites and professional psychiatry meetings celebrate the creative mania of artists from Vincent van Gogh to Georgia O'Keeffe. During my ethnographic research in the years since 1996, I have found that people in many walks of life in the United States are fascinated by manic behavior and see it as a valuable resource in the ever-accelerating spiral of "productivity." Members of support groups for people with manic depression look to figures like Robin Williams or Jim Carrey as role models because of their manic performances; television regales the general public with the adventures of larger-than-life figures such as the polar explorer Sir Ernest Shackleton because of his manic and heroic feats. Television programs like Jim Cramer's *Mad Money* operate at "hurricane-force," mirroring the manic pace of markets.[1] The high energy associated with manic behavior seems to add to the creative potential of entrepreneurs, business leaders, and entertainers.

CEOs, Hollywood stars, and MTV *The Real World* youths embrace the diagnosis of manic depression, reveling in the creativity of its mania and regretting the immobility of its depression. Frequently, stories about manic depression involve life-and-death risks. One executive, a "manic CEO," delivered his company "from the brink of death to complete dominance in an important technology market." His kinetic energy and frenetic enthusiasm made him "the greatest salesman in the world," and talking to him was "like being on an acid trip."[2] But while manic CEOs are carrying off feats like these in the business world, they are also facing their own brush with death: fearing the public revulsion toward mental illness and reluctant to admit they need treatment because it would be taken as a sign of weakness, they face their inner turmoil privately. Some, like Mark Helmke, first "spend a company into bankruptcy" and then commit suicide.[3] Popular media frequently assert the life-threatening nature of the condition. The *Washington Post*, in an article on the rise in diagnosis of bipolar disorder among children, puts it in a nutshell: "The illness, which is usually diagnosed in adolescence or early adulthood, is a serious and disabling mood disorder that, if untreated, carries an elevated risk of suicide. Sufferers typically cycle between manic highs, in which they can go for days without sleep in the grip of grandiose delusions, and depressive lows, marked by a preoccupation with death and feelings of worthlessness."[4] Too often, the depressive lows swallow up a person's life.

Even in the face of life-and-death risk, popular books like *Emotional Contagion* or *Leading Change* report on the importance of high-energy moods.[5] Since a leader's mood is "literally contagious," his primary task, indeed, his *primal task*, is "emotional leadership." Mood is seen as all important for success: "A leader needs to make sure that not only is he regularly in an optimistic, authentic, high-energy mood, but also that, through his chosen actions, his followers feel and act that way, too."[6] A wide variety of publications directed toward business managers claim that the emotional contagion of high moods can directly affect business success.[7]

In this book, I will explore the cultural understandings and practices that surround mania and manic depression in the United States. How have these understandings and practices emerged from the recent past

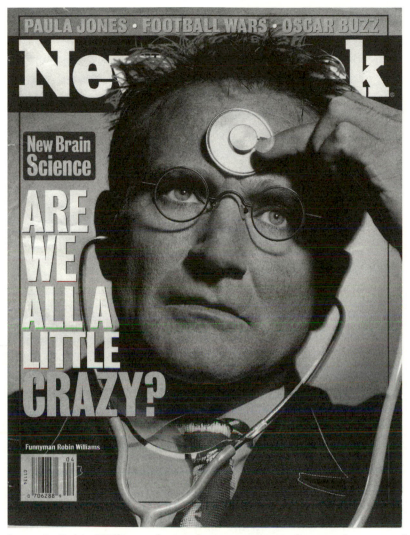

Intro. 1. Robin Williams, depicted as a crazy comedian on the cover of *Newsweek*. *Newsweek*, January 26, 1998. © 1998 *Newsweek*, Inc. All rights reserved. Reprinted by permission. Photo by MosheBrakha.com.

and how were they different in the past? With what American cultural assumptions about life, death, power, weakness, capacity and incapacity, the mind, and the body are they infused? How do these assumptions differ for people in diverse life circumstances and at different ages, for men and women, for people with different racial or ethnic identities? Most crucially, how can we understand contemporary psychiatric and neurological claims to knowledge about mental states in a historical and cultural way when they beg to be taken as new forms of scientific truth and when, for some of us (including me), our status as rational people may be deeply dependent on these claims?

The affinity that contemporary American culture has for highly energetic, "manic" behavior is not simple.[8] On the one hand, in 1998 GQ chose Ted Turner as "man of the year." Because Turner launched several dramatic business successes with the help of his "manic" energy, the magazine described him as "the corporealized spirit of the age."[9] On the other hand, just a few years later, Howard Dean's "manic" behavior wounded him fatally after the 2004 Iowa primary. Some journalists described Dean's behavior as outrageous: "Face plastered with a manic grin, Dean three times screamed out a litany of states he would win, and capped off his sound bite with a barbaric yawp."[10] His behavior was even seen as animal-like: "Dean was as manic as a hamster on a wheel as he rambled on and let out a rebel yell."[11] Dean's fate makes it plain that mania is as much an object of horror as desire. Whatever affinity there is between mania and American culture, it is not harmonious or sympathetic: fear, disgust, and revulsion are the kinds of sentiments that roil the surface when a person flies out of control and "cracks up." Extreme states like mania may fascinate and attract us, but they disquiet us as well.[12] Why was mania good for Ted Turner but bad for Howard Dean? In this book I will try to answer this question by considering how people in the United States understand manic behavior generally and how scientists, therapists, patients, and pharmaceutical employees understand the kind of mania that is part of the specific condition of manic depression.

Is the mania attributed to Ted Turner or Howard Dean the same thing as the mania that is part of manic depression? This question has no simple answer. In my ethnographic research, moving from setting to setting allowed me to observe and listen to patients diagnosed with manic depression, psychiatrists struggling to treat it, pharmaceutical marketers hoping to sell remedies for it, and researchers seeking to understand its causes. None of these different groups would agree on a single answer to the question. Apart from my research proper, my daily life had already shown me that no part of manic depression is seen simply as an asset. Ever since I began to write and speak about bipolar disorder, college students have been telling me how often administrators react with dismay and alarm when they hear a student has been diagnosed with manic depression. At Princeton, where I taught for a number of years, students who are diagnosed with manic depression must often take a lengthy leave and then apply for readmission. Fear— of a student committing suicide, failing academically, socializing excessively—is mixed with the attraction—for writing creatively, studying energetically, socializing exuberantly—that people imagine could come along with the condition. A colleague at a large state university called me for advice about what to do for a graduate student who confided that he had been diagnosed with manic depression. My colleague wondered whether she should inform other faculty, assuming the student gave his permission. Speaking out might cast suspicion on the student's rationality and his academic abilities, but it might also help protect him against undue stress. My colleague felt caught in a vise: the student's manic depression might signal his special creativity but at the same time it would also signal that he suffered from a frightening and dangerous emotional disorder.

Rational and Irrational

Being known as a manic-depressive person throws one's rationality into question. There are high stakes involved in losing one's status as a rational person because everything from one's ability to do one's job, teach one's students, obey the law of the land, or live with one's family can be thrown into doubt.[13] Exploring how rationality is understood today will be one of my main goals in the chapters to come.[14] From classical times to the nineteenth century, madness was defined as the loss of rational, intellectual functions. Plato and Aristotle considered "reason" the defining human characteristic, the means of achieving knowledge, and the prerequisite of ethical freedom. When reason was absent or obliterated, the result was error and evil: the unleashed "passions" would be the source of disorder. However, the passions, as the animal part of humans, served as their source of energy: hence it was important for emotions to be present, albeit reduced and subordinated.[15] The Greeks defined such things as dreams, passion, and poetic intuition, the voices of the insane or of the prophets as irrational. They were not regarded as sources of knowledge of a rational kind, but they were regarded with respect because they came from contact with the supernatural world.[16] There was an interest, in classical Greece, in making a sharp separation between the rational and the irrational: only the rational, male, adult Greek was a full person, a citizen who owned property and cast his vote in the city-state.

Today much of this has changed, but some institutions, like the law, reveal the outline of older dichotomies. Consider a case that appeared in the Florida courts in 1996. Alice Faye Redd was a prominent, well-off citizen who was president of the PTA, the Junior League, and the Garden Club. During Richard Nixon's presidency she was honored as one of ten outstanding young women of America. Her daughter, however, discovered that for nine years Redd had been running a pyramid scheme, involving 103 people (many of them elderly members of her church), who eventually lost $3.6 million. The family, assuming she "must have lost touch with reality," sent her to a mental hospital. There she was diagnosed as "chronic hypomanic personality," a condition, "known as Bipolar 2, in which she was almost always in an elevated mood, needed little sleep, was full of grandiose ideas and was likely to engage in foolish business investments." Meanwhile, prosecutors charged her with racketeering and grand theft, charges she did not contest. Psychiatrists retained by both sides in the case agreed she was suffering from "a form of manic depression that made her seem vivacious and charming, while at the same time twisting her thinking." The psychiatrists selected by the prosecution wrote the judge that she "was operating on a different reality" and that "her ability to appreciate the nature and quality of the acts was impaired."[17]

But the judge could find her insane only if she could not tell the difference between right and wrong.[18] Finding that she was not insane, the judge sentenced her to fifteen years in prison. He argued that her bipolar disorder merely slightly modified her perceptions, like wearing "rose-colored glasses." Rather than making her fail to understand that what she did caused harm, her mania merely caused her to underestimate the harm she was doing to others. In the press coverage of the case, reporters said that people who knew her were fooled by appearance and blind to reality. "Appearance" was that "she seemed normal, a 'superwoman.' . . . She always had a smile and her hair and makeup were as impeccable as her gracious Southern manners."[19] The "reality" was that mental illness was common in the last six generations of her family, as shown by a genealogical chart included in the article.

If Redd were a rational person, then she would be held responsible for her actions and be subject to the law. Her actions would flow from the person she seemed to be, and where her actions were illegal, she would have to pay the price. But if Redd were an irrational person, an afflicted person with unmedicated manic depression who seemed rational but actually lived in a different reality, she would need to be hospitalized, not jailed.[20]

The Alice Faye Redd case shows how oddly in between manic depression is. Like Emil Kraepelin, an early twentieth-century psychiatrist who noted its "peculiar mixture of sense and maniacal activity," the judge placed her in between having sense and being a maniac.[21] If he found her to be a wholly sensible person, he would be denying her hereditary manic depression; if he found her to be a wholly maniacal person, he could not sentence her to prison. The assumption that produces this dilemma is that the normal person is wholly rational. I suggest otherwise: in their everyday lives, most people have various degrees of awareness of reality and of the consequences of their actions, various degrees of "reason" in their decisions and opinions. I have an inkling of this from generations of undergraduates and graduate students in my classes who, given the chance to discuss the presence of the irrational in their daily lives, have a lot to say about their waking experiences of disassociation, free association, flight of ideas, emotional tempests or voids, and so on. These experiences are often fleeting, they do not usually interfere with daily life, and they would not be grounds for a diagnosis of serious psychological illness. But so frightful is the specter of such a diagnosis that most students say they have never admitted their small flights from the rule of reason before. It takes the strong grip of cultural assumptions to suppress evidence of the myriad ways people experience the "irrational"—awake or asleep. If such evidence did enter the picture, what would we do with Redd? Her case pointedly raises the question of whether the notion of an incompletely rational person—someone, I argue, who is like most of us—is compatible with the operation of one of our central institutions.[22]

Although the term "mental illness" implies that Alice Faye Redd could be cured of what is wrong with her, and although new therapies are available that might cure her, the fear of madness still haunts those diagnosed with mental illness. Madness is a strange and horrible thing: who has not felt this? One of the classics of Western literature, *Heart of Darkness*, gave us the image of Colonel Kurtz, a mad soul wandering in a wilderness inhabited by beings he considers barely human, consumed by desire without restraint, operating outside reason.[23] A contemporary anthropological study describes the fear of madness as the terror of looking into the eyes of a mentally ill person and seeing no answering comprehension.[24] A contemporary memoir describes the madness of depression as a descent into darkness with a terrifying loss of lucidity.[25] In the face of such deep terror, my strategy in this book is to open up the terrain between the comfortable rational and the terrifying irrational, allowing more complex kinds of description to emerge. Most of the tidy dichotomies that float in the wake of the separation between rational and irrational (sane/insane, controlled/uncontrolled, responsible/irresponsible, reasonable/unreasonable) are inadequate to the task of capturing complex experiences like living under the description of manic depression.[26]

My focus will be on mania for two reasons. First, far less has been written about mania than depression, perhaps because depressive disor-

ders are more common in the United States than manic depression
(depressive disorders are commonly estimated to be found in 9.5 percent of the population over a twelve-month period, compared to 1.2
percent for manic depression).[27] Second, mania is the part of manic
depression that we will see emerges onto the political economic stage
as an object of desire. My argument is that we need to understand the
meaning of manic behavior by describing what people do with "mania"
and why they do it. In the same way we might try to understand the
meaning of a word in a foreign language by noticing all the ways native
speakers use the word, I have tried to notice all the ways that "mania"
and related concepts and practices are used and interpreted in the different contexts of my fieldwork. The task is complicated because people
cannot be aware of all aspects of their behavior. A great deal of what
people communicate in their words and behavior is inchoate, beyond
articulation in words. For this reason I have taken care to notice aspects
of behavior—sometimes fleeting ones—that involve performance and
style. On the importance of her own performance and style as a dancer,
Isadora Duncan said, "[I]f I could tell you what it meant, there would
be no point in dancing it." The anthropologist Gregory Bateson understood Duncan's remark to mean that communicating her message in
words would falsify it: the use of words would imply that her message
was fully voluntary and consciously understood when it was not.[28]

Fully conscious or not, how another person understands one's actions on a certain occasion may well hinge on such things as the effectiveness of one's performance or one's success in carrying off a style.
These concepts will be central in my accounts of mania because they
allow me to capture nonverbal aspects of meaning and to capture meaning in the moment people are making it.[29] Given the importance of
language in forming our concepts of mental illness—medical diagnosis
and the like—it will be especially important for me to focus on people's
actions as well as their words. Habitual actions, outside discourse, can
persist in social life because they are relatively immune from being
completely overtaken by the terms of discourse. Habitual practices
could be said "to haunt objects and the material world."[30] Hence both
observing everyday actions and tracking the movement of ordinary ob-

jects are ways to glimpse forms of agency that are not entirely captured by the terms of discourse.

These tasks complement the task my students took on: although they were defined as psychologically normal, they were able to produce reams of material about "irrational" experiences in their lives. In this book, I describe the behavior of people living under the description of manic depression, showing that their range of meaning-making, inflected by style, achieved through performance, is easily as complex as it is for those described as psychologically normal. Just what people take manic behavior to be—whether it is rational, irrational, or somewhere in between—is not a given. It is a matter determined by people actively trying to place behavior, words, performance, and style in a field of meanings. To keep this issue foremost, I deliberately use the phrase "living under the description of manic depression (or bipolar disorder)" to refer to people who have received this medical diagnosis. The phrase is meant to reflect the social fact that they have been given a diagnosis. At the same time, it calls attention to another social fact: the diagnosis is only one description of a person among many.

Mania is a concept that is used so differently by people in the same setting that it is almost as if the same word is being used in the sentences of different languages. This makes it a fruitful place to see contemporary changes in the significance that is given to manic behavior. What is happening is not completely new—mania has enduring significance that draws on its early twentieth-century formulation—but the concept is being applied in new domains and used to solve new problems, problems that are specific to the present time and place. While I have just written of "new" problems and domains, I do not pretend that what I will describe in this book is altogether new. It would be more accurate to describe what is happening as a shift of emphasis, a refocusing of the lenses through which we look. Broad notions of self-improvement, cyclic emotion, brain-based mind, and creative insanity have long been abroad in American society. But, as usual, the devil is in the details: my goal is to describe not a completely new set of concepts but rather an intensification of many old concepts that has made it possible for Americans to think about social life and about their psychic lives in new ways.

Brains and Genes

Cultural aspects of knowledge from the brain sciences are not a major focus of this book, largely because this knowledge, though central, did not play a dynamic role in the main settings of my fieldwork. The belief that the brain and its genetic determinants lie behind mental disorders like manic depression was simply assumed by most of the people in my fieldwork, inside and outside medical settings.[31] In the course I took on neuropsychology during my fieldwork, we students dissected our way, week by week, through a sheep's brain. To understand psychological phenomena like attention or perception, we would have to understand the physical workings of the brain. This meant not only knowing the names and locations of brain structures, but also learning how to see them, and to separate them with a knife from the gray, gelatinous mass of brain tissue. In California, where research on brain imaging is a particular focus of university neuroscientists, many scientists I met were involved in ongoing efforts to correlate specific images of brain activity with specific disorders. More generally, there were increasing numbers of media articles picturing the activity of the brain (through PET scans and MRIs) and claiming to correlate brain states and conditions like emotion, addiction, schizophrenia, or criminality.[32] Lately these claims have begun to reach an astonishing degree of specificity. One group reported that Democrats and Republicans had different brain states when they watched campaign commercials.[33] Reflecting an awareness of these news items, people in support groups I attended would quite commonly remark that they had volunteered as subjects in local university or hospital research on brain imaging and bipolar disorder. In group discussions, people often made remarks about having disordered or un-balanced "brain chemistry," which they hoped the drugs they were taking would fix. Since having a physical malady has far more validity in Western culture than having a mental one, people usually greeted new evidence that bipolar disorder is a "brain disease" as welcome news because of the generally accepted belief that physical ailments can be cured and, in the meantime, would be covered by health insurance, disability payments, or compensation claims.

As for the genes that we may regard as responsible for the shape of our particular brains, people in support groups would often bring in newspaper clippings of scientific researchers' efforts to identify genetic and anatomic locations for manic depression. This was invariably done in the hopeful spirit, identical to the spirit in which most such articles are written, that locating the right gene or genes would lead to a specific treatment for the root cause of the problem. Perhaps because genetic research into the causes of manic depression has not yet reached a plausible conclusion, let alone developed therapeutic interventions, concern with this level of understanding among people in my field-work, outside research labs, was at a fairly general, taken-for-granted level. Most people hoped and believed that in time more effective treatments for psychic disorders would come along, and they would act directly, somehow, on genes, the brain, or both.

Although the topic of brains and genes was not often the subject of dispute during the years of my fieldwork, it could still give rise to drama. Some of my interlocutors living under the diagnosis of manic depression told me that given the presumption that the condition has a genetic component, they wondered about having children. The condition might be—whatever its value for creativity and productivity—too painful to risk bringing on one's own. Some knew of the brutal way Kay Jamison (a psychiatrist who has written about her own manic-depressive illness) was advised by her doctor not to have children.[34] Others knew of a scene in Stephen Hinshaw's book about his bipolar father, Virgil Hinshaw: Kay Jamison visited Stephen's medical school class and proposed a hypothetical question. If in the future, a prenatal test were available that could detect a gene that was strongly linked to bipolar disorder, how many would elect to abort if their fetus received a positive diagnosis? Almost all of the twenty-odd medical students, interns, and staff in the room raised their hands.[35] In these cases, fear of mental illness is enough to make manic depression seem incompatible with life.

Many people in my research believed that neurons and neurotransmitters in the brain affected their mental states.[36] In support groups, I frequently heard people discuss their ideas about how low serotonin levels cause depression and how medication can raise the level of serotonin. Although most people treated the brain and its neurotransmitters as stable givens determined by their genetic makeup, they also assumed that drugs could modify the brain and its neurotransmitters.[37] In this book I do not deal extensively with the brain or genes, but I do not mean to imply that brain chemistry is unrelated to a scientific understanding of manic depression or to patients' experience of manic depression. I often heard from my psychiatrist that my problems were related to my neurotransmitters, and I always found this comforting. I took this to mean that my problems were not entirely within my control.

The Drug Factor

It is difficult to estimate with certainty whether the prevalence of mood disorders is increasing, but there is widespread public belief that it is.[38] For those who have access to information and health care, enhancement and modulation of moods through drugs has become as matter-of-fact as driving a sport-utility vehicle down the highway.

The one glimpse I had of the kinds of databases that the pharmaceutical industry has access to showed me that the rates of prescriptions for antidepressants and antipsychotics (increasingly used for mood disorders) had recently increased about two and a half times, from 51,003,000 in 1991 to 133,782,000 in 1998.[39] In 2006, a national survey reported in the *New York Times* found that prescriptions of "potent" antipsychotics for children and adolescents had risen fivefold from 1993 to 2003.[40] To understand the ways in which drugs become available, we will have to confront some forces that seem driven by the profit motive. For example, the Republican administration made determined efforts in 2004 to prevent the lowering of domestic prices for drugs by blocking European countries from exporting cheaper drugs to the United States and by delaying competition from generic drugs.[41] When I was lecturing in Iceland in 2003, I visited a medical conference that had attracted numerous sales representatives from the major pharmaceutical companies. I asked the representatives at one booth why they had come to Iceland, with its small population and lack of direct-to-consumer (DTC) advertising. The reps explained that they

Intro. 2. Refrigerator magnet showing antidepressant and anti-anxiety drugs as highway signs. Courtesy of Ephemera-Inc. © Amy Hill.

expected Iceland to be the first European country to permit DTC advertising. They were there to make connections with fledgling patient support organizations for depression and other conditions, and to support them financially as they have done in the United States. Presumably, people suffering from depression, manic depression, anxiety, panic, and other harrowing conditions will benefit from strengthened organizations that work on their behalf, not to mention from greater access to and information about drugs that can lift the spirit, smooth the brow, and ease despair.

A reader might judge these benefits to be sullied by the commercial motives that propelled the development and promotion of psychotropic drugs in the first place, but even the most aggressive commercial campaign can have intriguing multiple effects. Pharmaceutical marketers are no strangers to the kinds of cultural nuances that surround how mental life is imagined. They are studying these nuances, often with the help of ethnographers on staff in their companies. But they have different aims in mind. For example, there is a sophisticated effort in play to introduce drugs for depression in Japan. This effort began when Solvay Pharmaceuticals and the two Japanese companies that shared rights to sell an antidepressant called Luvox decided it would be necessary to change the language Japanese people used to describe depression. Since the original word, "utso-byo," was associated with severe psychiatric illness, they began to substitute "kokoro no kaze," which loosely means "the soul catching a cold." This phrase, meant to imply that depression is a simple malady whose symptoms can be treated, contributed to sales of Luvox and to efforts to introduce similar drugs, among them Paxil and Zoloft.[42] One effect of the companies' efforts might be to increase the social acceptability of mental disorders, but it is disquieting that the drug comes first and the disorder it is said to cure comes second.

Mania is like a new continent with a distant frontier, whose receding horizon invites exploration and development, promising profits to pioneers. To extend the metaphor, many "developers" have been attracted to the riches of this land, where they have begun to exploit manic behavior as a promising source. Specialized companies actually help corporate work teams learn *how to be* manic. In no case is the development of methods of managing mania a simple matter of exploiting or manipulating people. In order for such management methods to capture public attention and compel action, a cultural proposition about the necessity of continually improving the person must already exist. This proposition builds on the longstanding American tradition of self-help through psychological knowledge,[43] but now greatly intensifies it. No person has an option about pursuing his or her development and the task is never done: the horizon of development is ever receding and the landscape that affects *how* one should develop is continuously changing.

The development of a large new array of drugs to alter and enhance psychological states has changed the psychological environment for everyone, inside and outside the categories of mental illness, although not, of course, for everyone in the same way. The familiar debate over whether a person with mental illness is capable of rationality is changed beyond recognition when people in every corner of society are thinking about enhancing their mental processes and when domains like mania

that were formerly categorized as irrational have become a new continent waiting to be tapped for the sake of greater creativity and innovation, and, ultimately, greater productivity and profit.

A Short History of Manic Depression

Where did the category of "manic depression" come from? Its history
goes back to the ancient Greeks, who thought that the health of the
body was related to the four body humors: blood, phlegm, choler (yellow bile), and black bile. Because one's character and health reflected
whichever of these fluids was preponderant, a person could be sanguine, phlegmatic, choleric (bilious), or melancholic. Some traits that
would look like depression today belonged to the melancholic humor
and some that would look like mania today belonged to the choleric
humor. The Greeks believed that mental derangement could involve
imbalance among the humors, as when melancholy, heated by the
fluxes of the blood, became its opposite, mania. Faced with such an
organic cause, they might attempt to restore humoral balance by bleed-
ing or purging.[44]

In classical thought, the causes of madness were thought to be much
broader than physical imbalance. In Plato's account in the *Phaedrus*,
manias could be caused by inspiration—from God, from poetry, or
from love. A much later text greatly influenced by classical thought,
Robert Burton's *Anatomy of Melancholy* (published in 1621 and still in
print), listed a wide range of causes for melancholy, including faulty
education, stress (he cites too much studying), childhood influences,
heredity, supernatural elements, Satan, the stars, God, a bad nurse,
poverty, and much else.[45] Nor were these causes easy to classify as divine
or demonic: in Christendom, especially, there was a heated debate
about how to tell whether madness in the form of mania was divinely
inspired, a form of spiritual rapture, or demonic, a form of frenzied
lunacy.[46] In mania, because the soul had partly or wholly escaped the
restraint of the body, the result could be sublime (one could be lifted
into a transcendent state) or frightening (one could descend into a bes-
tial, obscene condition).[47]

In later antiquity, some writers began to identify states other than the humors, which contributed to health. Galen wrote about the "non-naturals," which included the passions, and set them alongside the humors. For Galen and other later medieval scholars, keeping the passions in balance was as important for mental and physical health as keeping the humors balanced.[48] However, they still believed that the primary cause of insanity lay within the intellect rather than within the passions. Melancholia, for example, involved loss of acuity of an intellectual sort (a mixture of irrationality and impaired behavior) rather than disordered emotions. A specific emotional state such as sadness or fear was neither a necessary nor a sufficient condition for insanity.[49] The emphasis on the intellect as the domain of sanity—a sound mind as the basis of rationality—reached its apex in the philosophy of Descartes and other seventeenth-century thinkers. In this period, theories of insanity moved away from emphasis on the demons and humors of classical thinking. Enlightenment theorists provided no detailed account of insanity, but left it by default to a defect in the body or to a defective connection between mind and body.[50]

The idea that disorders of the emotions could be responsible for insanity emerged in a halting way. After 1800, adherents of "faculty psychology" began to regard emotions as one of the separate powers of the mind, alongside others such as the will and the intellect.[51] Faculty psychologists acknowledged that there might be disorders of the emotions, or affect, and in line with this, they proposed emotional forms of insanity.[52] But even those most interested in including the emotions as a cause of insanity failed to develop a systematic account of what different forms of emotion meant to those experiencing them.[53] Darwin hindered the chance of developing a more sophisticated understanding of affect because he believed that the emotions were registered so deeply in the organism that no individual experience could account for them. According to Darwin, the emotions were the result of our evolutionary past and revealed our animal origins. Hence, individuals' subjective experiences would not shed much light on their emotions, a view that left by the wayside doctors who tried to understand patients in terms of their individual lives.[54]

In spite of Darwin's impact, under the influence of faculty psychology in the second half of the nineteenth century, mania and melancholia were narrowed down and redefined as "primary disorder[s] of affect and action."[55] These new forms were "combined into the new concept of alternating, periodic, circular or double-form insanity."[56] This process culminated in Emil Kraepelin's concept of "manic-depressive insanity," which included most forms of affective disorders under the same diagnostic umbrella.[57] Drawing on thousands of clinical cases in Germany, Kraepelin reclassified all known mental illnesses into two major categories: dementia praecox (later renamed schizophrenia) and manic depression. In this bold reorganization, referred to as Kraepelin's synthesis, one major category (dementia praecox) was a malady of the intellect; the other (manic depression) a malady of the emotions.[58] He distinguished emotional maladies from intellectual maladies: emotional maladies were periodic, more benign in prognosis, and common in family histories.[59] Since Kraepelin thought of manic depression as a disease, he assumed that eventually a specific cause would be discovered and the invariant course of the disease would be described, just as the specific natural history and pathophysiology of pellagra (vitamin deficiency) and syphilis, both of which were believed to affect the central nervous system, already had been.[60] Kraepelin's synthesis continues to operate with force in contemporary psychiatric taxonomies, shaping the division between cognitive and affective disorders.

The other psychiatric school of thought that developed ideas about the etiology of mania and depression in the early twentieth century was psychoanalysis. In his early writings (1917), Sigmund Freud saw melancholia, an "open wound" that drains the ego until it is "utterly depleted," as a loss or disappointment that was turned inward against the ego. He recognized that some patients alternated between melancholia and mania but could not at that time devise an explanation that satisfied him.[61] By 1923, Freud saw that when melancholia takes hold, it is a result of the person's "excessively strong super-ego," which rages sadistically against the ego and can drive the ego into death, if the ego "does not fend off its tyrant in time by the change round into mania."[62] Mania, therefore, is the ego's defense against the destructive impulses of the super-ego. More influential in England than in Europe or the United States, Melanie Klein developed the notion of the "depressive position," something the healthy psyche achieves in the first year of life. The depressive position, in which the person recognizes herself as separate from others and as a result has to contend with feelings of loss, mourning, and sadness, can give rise to the "manic defense." Out of a wish to avoid the pain of the depressive position, the person uses a sense of omnipotence (manic activity) to master and control the threat. Hence, for Klein, depression and mania could both be part of normal development, though ideally the manic defense would eventually give way to other forms of accommodation to the depressive position.[63]

Alongside these developments in psychiatry, popular representations of mania and manic depression took many turns from the beginning of the twentieth century to the present. From the start of the century until the 1940s, judging from my reading of popular magazines and newspapers in the United States, neither mania nor manic depression was mentioned with any frequency except in relation to a frightening kind of insanity.[64] News stories about people with manic depression described uncontrollable impulses that led to violence or self-destruction. These headlines illustrate the tone: "Maniac Kills Man by Push on Elevated [railway]; Says He Acted on Irresistible Impulse in Causing Death at First Attributed to Fall" (1929)[65]; "Mrs. Fosdick Kills 2 Children and Self; Lawyer's Wife, Deranged for Years, Shoots Daughter, 16, and Son, 10, as They Sleep" (1932).[66] Closer to the 1940s, articles with sensational headlines about deranged maniacs become hard to find. The appearance of the first reports of chemical means to treat mental illness could have been responsible for a reduction in fear of the out-of-control "mentally ill." "Chemistry of Insanity" (1938) describes new therapies using insulin and Metrazol shock therapy and new technology, such as the electroencephalograph, that could reveal different brain electric waves in different forms of mental illness.[67] "New Vistas Opened for Chemical Approach to the Treatment of Mental Illnesses" (1947) and "Chemical's Cure of Insane Is Seen" (1947) describes continuing technological advances in visualizing brain function and evidence of physical differences between normal and "mentally ill" patients' brains.[68]

From the 1940s to the 1960s, the tone in descriptions of manic depression is tinged with sorrow. An episode of the television show *Manhattan* (1960) featured a heroine who was driven to manic depression by her villainous husband.[69] The victim in this episode was seen as helpless, but in other cases, the manic-depressive person was exhorted to improve. In lectures given in New York to Red Cross home nurses to prepare them to care for returning war veterans, manic-depressive patients were described thus: "They don't deviate too much from normal people—except they go too far. They are over-elated. They over-talk, over-act. They cannot settle down to things that are part of daily routine." The cause of this is that these individuals have denied themselves simple pleasures over the years, in favor of working too much. As a result, there is "an accumulation of tension and a final blowing off into a manic-depressive stage." These people need to be shown "how vitally important it is for them to tone down their excessive energy and to give some of it to the enjoyment of simple human pleasures."[70]

I have been able to find only a handful of book-length biographies or autobiographies from the turn of the century to the end of the 1960s that mention the subject's manic depression. By and large, reviews of these books only obliquely, if at all, associate manic depression with talent or virtue. A minor character in a biography of the Robert Pearsall Smith family suffers from manic depression in old age and becomes an "intolerable old man."[71] Lawrence Jayson, the author of an autobiography from 1937 titled *Mania* does not spare the reader accounts of his suffering and subsequent suicide attempts. In this book, unusual for its time, the author juxtaposes the states of mania and depression with his experiences at work, for good or ill. On the one hand, his coworkers try to draw on his "high powered salesmanship" to save an account; on the other, he fears that if he fails, this will precipitate another cycle of depression.

> It had been the failure of just such business deals as the one I had plunged into last night that had precipitated my melancholia and brought me down. Worry. Worry. Anguish about failing business. Watching the market crash. Then, overwhelmed by a fear of falling seriously ill, of having my brain impaired, I had tried to forget by driving myself more fiercely into work.[72]

A more positive view surrounded the biography of John Ruskin by R. H. Wilenski (1933), which was hailed in the press for successfully correlating Ruskin's writing with the state of his mind at the time. He was a "mental invalid all his life," "suffering continuously from the malady known in psychiatric circles as 'manic depression.'"[73] Ruskin was regarded as talented: "He learned as the imaginative genius learns, by suddenly piercing to the heart of a thing and understanding it." But his talent stood somewhat to the side of his illness: "In his manic moods he boasted of his power. Even in his depressed moods he very seldom doubted it. And he really had it."[74] In a similar vein, the publication of the journals of André Gide in 1947 conveyed to the reviewer his "emotional intensity, his alternate ascent to peaks of joy and physical well-being and descent to an avernus [gateway to Hades] of acute depression, nervousness, insomnia and gloom. Amateur psychiatrists would have no trouble finding plenty of evidence of manic depression in these pages . . . [he] was hardly in normal control of his emotions." As with Ruskin, Gide succeeds in spite of, not because of, his manic depression: "But, there can be no doubt, that [he] has one of the most acute minds and one of the most genuine literary talents of his generation."[75] Equally tellingly, when Virginia Woolf's husband, Leonard Woolf, died in 1969, there were some thoughtful articles about his role in her struggles with manic depression, and many references to her "genius." But there was little mention of a link between these two aspects of her life.[76]

By 1970, an atmospheric change had taken hold. The efficacy of lithium carbonate in animal studies led to its use in humans for the treatment of manic depression, and this discovery received major press attention, even before it had received approval for therapeutic use in the United States.[77] As if the existence of a treatment for manic depression in and of itself made the malady seem more approachable or possible to imagine as something more than maniacal insanity, a series of media developments ensued. Lithium as a remedy for manic depression made it into two episodes of a television show, *Maude*, in January 1976. The airing of these shows was controversial because people feared that the public, jumping to the conclusion that all forms of mental illness could be treated by lithium, would ignore lithium's potentially serious side effects.[78] Autobiographies began to describe manic depression as a stimulus to creativity as well as a hurdle to be overcome. In *Josh: My Up and Down, In and Out Life*, Josh Logan, a theater director and producer who won a Pulitzer Prize for *South Pacific*, describes the triumphs of his career despite the two breakdowns he had as a result of his manic depression. In 1976, Ronald Fieve, who, not coincidently, was Josh Logan's psychiatrist, wrote the first widely popular book about manic depression, stressing that it could be treated with lithium. This book, *Moodswing*, also laid the groundwork for future elaborations of the links between the manic phase of manic depression and success in the marketplace. In a filmed interview, Fieve expounds on what he called the "Midas effect": the ability of a manic person to take creative risks, work with enormous energy, and sweep others up along the way often leads to his economic success.[79]

Around this time manic depression came to be used as a general metaphor or framing device for the social conditions of the day. In a 1977 newspaper editorial, "Man's Despair, and Hope," Eric Bentley mused on the "glum" faces of the people he saw across from him on the subway. Their facial expression ranged only from "resignation to rage, from moroseness to aggression." He noted how differently people were depicted on the subway advertisements above their heads: "They picture the same people—ourselves—our fellow Americans, but in an exactly opposite mood. Gone is their manic depression. Come is their fixed elation. Their beautiful teeth proclaim their unmixed happiness. They laugh, they smile, or they show a gravity that is all poise and self-assurance. . . . In short, the ads are populated by optimists, while the seats are occupied by pessimists." Bentley went on to decry both exaggerated optimism and exaggerated depression among U.S. citizens in general, and to call on the moderating effects of an active intelligence to raise mindless (and overly emotional) hopelessness and to lower equally mindless optimism.[80]

By 1980, Kay Jamison had begun to publish her work on creativity and manic depression.[81] In *Touched with Fire*, through careful examination of the content of personal diaries and letters, and patterns of productivity and fallowness, Jamison suggested that the diagnosis of manic depression (she prefers the term "manic-depressive illness") could be retrospectively applied to writers and artists such as Walt

Whitman, Vincent van Gogh, Virginia Woolf, Anne Sexton, and Edgar Allan Poe. Jamison listed over two hundred composers, artists, and writers who arguably had some version of manic depression, from T. S. Eliot and Edna St. Vincent Millay to Georgia O'Keeffe, Edvard Munch, and Jackson Pollock.[82] Her effect on the public representation of mental illness was dramatic. By 1989, a mental illness advocacy group, Mental Illness Foundation, was soliciting contributions from the public in an advertisement featuring a photograph of Abraham Lincoln.[83] The headline read, "You'd be surprised how many people have suffered from mental illness." The text of the ad read, "It is not commonly known how many well-known figures in history suffered from mental illness. Depression. Manic depression. Schizophrenia. Suicide. Among them were Abraham Lincoln. Vincent van Gogh. Nijinski. To the world at large, they were powerful figures, but in the privacy of their own thoughts and feelings, they were at the mercy of mental illness, and suicidal tendencies." The ad did assert the link between creative and powerful people and mental illness, but its main message was still that these great people had to overcome a serious handicap in order to succeed.

It would be hard to exaggerate the impact of Jamison's work, which has been featured in major newspapers, magazines, and documentary films. In 1995 she published an article in *Scientific American*, arguing that the "temperaments and cognitive styles associated with mood disorders can in fact enhance creativity in some individuals."[84] The article singles out a number of famous artists, musicians, and writers who could be considered manic depressive by the evidence in their letters and journals, or in descriptions given by physicians, family, and friends. No less than eighteen of these figures were illustrated with dramatic photographs or self-portraits, which surely enhanced the impact of the article for its readers. Among those pictured were poets Walt Whitman and Sylvia Plath, artists Vincent van Gogh and Paul Gauguin, writers Virginia Woolf and Edgar Allan Poe, and musicians Gustav Mahler and Cole Porter. Since Jamison was well known as the coauthor of a technical reference work on manic depression and as a frequent participant in national meetings of advocacy organizations, her publications on

Manic-Depressive Illness and Creativity

Does some fine madness plague great artists?
Several studies now show that creativity
and mood disorders are linked

by Kay Redfield Jamison

Intro. 3. Icons of artistic creativity from *Scientific American* article by Kay Jamison.

creativity added an additional layer to the esteem in which she was already held.[85]

Her revelation in 1995 that she had the diagnosis of manic-depressive illness added further to her popularity. At one meeting of a manic depression support group in Orange County, the facilitator, Sarah, started off by passing around an issue of the *Saturday Evening Post* containing an article on manic depression by Kay Jamison, together with a program from a concert Jamison organized in southern California to highlight the music of famous manic-depressive composers such as Handel, Schumann, Haydn, and others.[86] Sarah commented that because these artists from the past did not have the benefit of today's medicine, they were so out of control that they made lots of suicide attempts. She also passed around a photo album that she had kept over the years with photographs she had taken of Kay Jamison giving talks at national meetings. This album was very worn from use and filled with Polaroid photos Sarah had taken herself.

The next developments in the revaluation of mania amount to a sea change in the understanding of mood: scientists began to understand the molecular mechanisms involving receptors in the brain as a system of interacting receptors and neurotransmitters. The pharmaceutical industry began to develop a new generation of drugs that could modify the way receptors worked and therefore the ways people experienced moods. For a brief glimpse of the public representation of these developments, we can look at two public health posters from 1984. The first commemorates Julius Axelrod's discovery of the cycle of interactions involving serotonin, a neurotransmitter: the abstract illustration depicts the space in between neurons, known as the synaptic cleft, and shows the newly understood variety of molecules in that space. The other commemorates a National Institutes of Health (NIH) conference held to develop a consensus about how mood disorders could best be treated. The poster portrays three men on the "merry-go-round" of mood disorder, one in the grip of mania, one in the grip of depression, and one somewhere in between. The title of the conference, "Mood Disorders: The Pharmacologic Prevention of Recurrences," indicated that the components of mood disorders at both ends of the scale from depression to mania seemed amenable to a vastly greater degree of management.

In the 1990s, an important shift in popular terminology occurred, one that probably played a significant role in changing how people regard manic depression. Authors of popular books and articles began using the term "bipolar disorder," following the shift from manic depression to bipolar disorder in the DSM-III in 1980.[87] From the 1980s

Intro. 4. Poster from 1984 National Institute of Mental Health Consensus Development Conference showing the ups and downs of mood disorders. Courtesy of National Library of Medicine. Artwork by Robert F. Prien, Ph.D.

to the end of the 1990s, the use of the two terms was equally frequent in U.S. newspapers, but in the years since 1999, "bipolar disorder" has been used nearly three times as often. In August 2002 the major consumer advocacy organization for manic depression and depression, the National Depression and Manic Depression Association (NDMDA), changed its name to Depression and Bipolar Support Alliance (DBSA), specifically to avoid the term "manic depression." They explained on their Web site:

> The decision to change our name came only after long and hard thought. There are many reasons the Board of Directors feels this is important. First, and foremost, our name was long and difficult for most people to remember correctly. Perhaps even more difficult was saying our tongue-tying acronym—National DMDA. In addition, bipolar disorder is no longer called manic depression. Many people are frightened by the term "manic depression" and this keeps them from contacting us for help.[88]

Over the last one hundred years or so, fright over the term "manic depression" has transformed into fascination with the term "bipolar." Sometimes this fascination involves the extraordinary abilities bipolar people apparently have, as demonstrated in the *New Yorker* cartoon that depicts a couple viewing a painting in a museum. One says to the other, "It's good, but it doesn't say bipolar." In other words, if the painter were "crazy," his painting would have more value.

Sometimes whatever the manic end of bipolar represents has come to seem essential for survival, and certainly for success, as long as it is not overdone. As the novelist Tom Wolfe captures this sentiment in *A Man in Full*, the mayor of Atlanta discusses the city's midtown high-rise towers and how they demonstrate that Atlanta wasn't a regional center, but a national one: "He gestured vaguely toward the towers that reached up far above them. 'They did it! Atlanta favors people who are hypomanic—I think that's the term—people like Inman Armholster who are so manic they refuse to pay attention to the odds against them, but not so manic that they are irrational.'"[89]

Kay Jamison prefers the term "manic-depressive illness" to bipolar disorder because it "seems to capture both the nature and the seri-

"It's good, but it doesn't say 'bipolar.'"

Intro. 5. *New Yorker* cartoon associating "bipolar" with outstanding art. Reprinted with permission. *The New Yorker* (2002): 74. © The New Yorker Collection 2002 Tom Cheney from cartoonbank.com. All rights reserved.

ousness of the disease," while "bipolar" seems to her "strangely and powerfully offensive."[90] "Bipolar" "obscure[s] and minimize[s] the illness it is supposed to represent."[91] Anticipating a theme that will emerge at the end of chapter 8, she also finds that the separation of moods implied by the term "bipolar" "perpetuates the notion that depression exists rather tidily segregated on its own pole, while mania clusters off neatly and discreetly on another."[92] In this book I prefer the more old-fashioned term "manic depression" because it leaves open the question whether the condition is to be understood only as an illness or also as a psychological style. But when I describe fieldwork contexts, I follow the usage of my interlocutors.

Manic Depression in Culture

This book follows the history I have just sketched, beginning with the experience of manic depression as a psychological state and then tracing its emergence into a broader cultural field. Closely connected to ideas about the market, manic depression morphs into bipolar disorder and comes to serve as a focal point for collective disquiet about why exhilarating highs and frightful lows seem to be inescapably intertwined in contemporary life.

My primary goal is not to take sides in the debate over whether social causes of mood disorders are more important than biological ones. Rather, I am interested in issues that are simply left out of that debate. I want to offer different kinds of descriptions of the experiences and actions of people said to have manic depression, descriptions that allow such people to belong fully to the human condition rather than to an outer sphere of "irrationality."[93] I want to propose that "the human condition" might include both mania and depression within it. I have been guided by this analogy: consider manic depression to be a hand with a pointing finger. We might want to know about the physical properties of the hand, its muscles, tendons, bones, and how they enable the finger to point. Without those physical structures and relationships, no finger could point. But while the structures are necessary for pointing, they are not sufficient to understand what a pointing finger means. The pointing finger is a gesture that takes its cultural meaning from its use in a particular social context. By looking at mania and depression as "gestures," my aim is to move toward a social theory of irrationality.

Will I be claiming that manic depression is not "real"? Not at all. I will claim that the reality of manic depression lies in more than whatever biological traits may accompany it. The "reality" of manic depression lies in the cultural contexts that give particular meanings to its oscillations and multiplicities. Will I be claiming that people living under the description of manic depression do not need treatment? Not at all. I will claim that whatever suffering attends the condition should be treated by any means possible. But I will also say that manic depression is culturally inflected: its "irrational" heights and depths are entwined in the present-day cultural imagination with economic success and economic failure. This is a central reason, as we will see, why manic depression's triumphs and failures hold very different kinds of promises and threats for those in powerful social positions compared to those in weak ones.

Research Methods

When I began the research for this project, I had only the sketch of a plan. I began with support groups in southern California and was led to psychiatry, neuroscience, the pharmaceutical industry, and the rest out of my interest in following up on what people living under the description of manic depression were experiencing. I thought of these excursions as "expeditions" into large-scale organizations whose activities I could only sample in the most modest way. The description that follows has the coherence of something written after the fact.

Beginning in 1996, I attended seven support groups for manic depression, some on the East Coast and some on the West Coast, as regularly as I could for the better part of five years. For the most part, I observed and participated in ongoing group meetings and social events, and had informal conversations with people I met. Toward the end of my research I interviewed some of the leaders of the groups' sponsoring organizations, in their official capacities.

My ethnography primarily focused on a pair of contrasting urban regions on each coast: the Baltimore metropolitan region in the Northeast (this area has been the base of my ethnographic work in the United States for the last twenty years) and Orange County in southern California. Both regions are suffering the effects of deindustrialization, poverty, and faltering town centers.[94] Baltimore has attempted to recoup its losses by constructing an urban spectacle in a historic harbor to attract tourism and finance capital, but this has arguably increased the concentration of capital in the hands of a few multinational corporations and contributed to poverty in the city.[95] Psychiatry in the region is located in both public and private institutions, including the University of Maryland, Sheppard Pratt Hospital, and The Johns Hopkins Hospital. Although I attended events at all of these institutions, the psychiatry department in one of them, here given the pseudonym Wellingtown Hospital, gave me permission to observe over a long term many of the ordinary contexts in which medical students and residents received training in how to treat patients for mood disorders. Since the department chair confined my activity to that of a medical student, I could attend classes and sit in on rounds (meetings in which doctors and students met with patients whose cases illustrated an important aspect of some psychiatric condition). However, I could not follow patients behind the scenes into the clinic or the community because this would have threatened the patients' confidentiality.

Orange County, in contrast to Baltimore, has become the site for many small and medium-sized firms supporting burgeoning information technologies and the entertainment industry, from Hollywood to Disneyland. Like these industries, psychiatry is also relatively decentralized, diverse, and entrepreneurial, and seeks to create opportunities for feedback from patients.[96] Though Baltimore County and Orange County are roughly comparable in population and income distribution, and are largely "post-suburban,"[97] Baltimore County has a concentrated urban settlement (Baltimore City), which it surrounds and which the state requires it to support financially. Whereas in Baltimore I concentrated on the psychiatric treatment of manic depression, in Orange County I worked with the neuroscientists in the region, who were some of the foremost national experts in brain imaging for manic depression and ADHD.

This geographic reach allowed me to pose comparative questions about personhood and mental illness. For example, in Orange County, on the low end of the social scale, I came upon cases of both ADHD and manic depression being used by recent Mexican immigrants as explanations for their own or their children's poor school performance, despite the high intelligence their family and friends perceived. Although people in support groups frequently stressed that each person was unique, they acted as though the group members' common diagnosis could override any social or ethnic differences. The diagnosis apparently provided a neutral way of explaining differences, as well as a path to success in school or work with the help of medication. An ADHD support group in Orange County (all of whom were white) embraced a new member who was Asian American as being "just like us": all were thought to share a particular chemical makeup that made them unable to tolerate conventional nine-to-five desk jobs. In these cases, individuals were brought together across ethnic lines. On the high end of the social scale, my interlocutors in Orange County saw manic depression as tantamount to a requirement for a career in Hollywood, so common was it known to be in the entertainment industry and so necessary did its manic qualities seem for success in that field. Throughout the project, I was able to see how psychological categories were used in Orange County, as compared to the harsher, more rigidly divided economic environment of the Baltimore region, even though I did not organize the book along those lines. My research concerned manic depression and ADHD in about equal measure. Since the story that emerged turned out to be very complex, I have, for reasons of space, focused this book primarily on manic depression and its contexts. Because I will be able to mention ADHD here only rarely, the longer account of ADHD in its educational, media, work, and legal settings will have to wait for later publications.[98]

The third project location was central New Jersey (in particular the counties of Somerset, Middlesex, and Mercer), through which the Route 1 high-technology corridor passes. With its high concentration of finance, communications, and pharmaceutical companies (Bristol-Meyers Squibb, Johnson and Johnson, Roche, Merck, American Home Products, Warner Lambert, and Hoechst, among others), its highly educated workforce, and its increasing reliance on temporary workers and outsourcing, the area is an East Coast version of Orange County's business environment.[99] In New Jersey, I concentrated my research on interviews with pharmaceutical company representatives and marketers, but it was also in New Jersey at Princeton University that I got basic training in the concepts and laboratory practices of contemporary neuroscience.

In addition to these geographically bounded sites, I traveled wherever I could to attend conferences and gatherings for professionals and patients related to manic depression and ADHD: the annual meetings of the American Psychiatric Association (APA); the meetings of the Neuropsychopharmacology Society; the Childhood and Adult Attention Deficit Disorder Association (CHADD); the Attention Deficit Disorder Association (ADDA); the Depression and Related Affective Disorders Association (DRADA); and the Depression and Manic Depression Association (DMDA). Over several years, I also attended a large variety of classes and seminars concerning work and the psychology of daily life: support groups for downsized workers, workshops and training sessions for management of the workplace, training sessions for workers, support groups for adults with ADHD, seminars in self-esteem, classes for raising children to be productive adults, raising and schooling children with attention deficits, and so on. I collected and analyzed several hundred hours of tape recordings from these events. With people I met in these contexts, I carried out over eighty extensive, semi-structured interviews. To understand the contexts in which psychotropic drugs are produced, marketed, and advertised, I informally interviewed employees in the pharmaceutical industry in sales, marketing, and advertising. I also held a position as "visiting professor" in a major advertising agency.

PART ONE

Manic Depression as Experience

The purpose of part 1 is to explore the experiences of people living under the description of manic depression. This task is difficult because I wish to raise perplexing questions about the terms in which manic depression, and mental illness more generally, are understood. However, people living under its description have themselves usually incorporated these terms into their self-understanding. My strategy is to begin by sorting out the meanings of common terms used to describe manic depression in psychiatric contexts and in daily life (mood, emotion, and motivation, for example). A contextual understanding of these terms is the best route to the counterintuitive perspectives I use in the remaining chapters. When I focus close-up on the daily experiences of the people I came to know during my fieldwork, I will be able to show what such terms capture and what they leave out.

CHAPTER ONE

Personhood and Emotion

Per-son
1. A living human . . . 2. An individual of specified
character: *a person of importance.* 3. The composite of
characteristics that make up an individual personality;
the self. 4. The living body of a human: *searched the
prisoner's person.* 5. Physique and
general appearance. 6. *Law* A human or organization
with legal rights and duties . . . 9. A character or role, as
in a play; a guise: *"Well, in her person, I say I will not
have you"* (Shakespeare).

—*American Heritage Dictionary of the English
Language,* 4th ed., 2000

When one is diagnosed with manic depression, one's status as a rational person is thrown into question. What it means to be rational or irrational depends on what notions of personhood are in play, notions that must be understood in their cultural context.[1] In Western culture since the seventeenth century, a particular kind of person, the "individual," has been the norm. In the writings of John Locke and others, the individual was defined as "essentially the proprietor of his own person or capacities, owing nothing to society for them. The individual was seen neither as a moral whole, nor as part of a larger social whole, but as an owner of himself."[2] He was a being capable of conscious awareness, deliberate choice, and independent volition. His actions were generated from his own desires, desires that grew out of his individual intention to grow, develop, or acquire.[3] In due course, I will make clear what it is about manic depression that seems to challenge this conception of the rational individual person. For the moment, I will say that a manic-depressive person takes these desirable traits to extremes: when depressed the person is profoundly dejected and turned inward, unable to act or love; when manic the person is consumed by his desires and acts on all of them, whether for sex, or money, or power, at once. Freud described the "maniac" just released from the inhibition of depression as someone who runs after his new desires "like a starving man after bread."[4]

Taking things to such extremes seems like being out of control. But is being in control always considered desirable and normal? Historically, the individual "owner of himself" has not always been expected to exert continuous control over his actions. In the United States in the late nineteenth-century, psychic states that might erode the edges of the disciplined and aware self, make its borders permeable to other selves, or allow it to drift into discontiguous psychic spaces were given positive value. In 1889, when William James carried out his "Census of Hallucinations" in the United States, he, his collaborators, and many of the over six thousand Americans interviewed regarded states such as hallucination in a variety of positive ways.[5] However, by the twentieth century, mainstream popular culture in the United States had largely come to denigrate "forms of experience not characterized by self-consciousness."[6] Even experimentation with mind-altering drugs, popular in the 1960s, was generally valued for heightened *self-consciousness* rather than loss of self.

The ideal that a person should be disciplined and self-aware came about partly through the requirements of work in industrial settings and the growth of a consumer society. The moving assembly line with its dedicated machinery enabled efficient mass production and paved the way for profitable mass marketing based on increased consumption of commodities. Corporate organizations were hierarchically structured bureaucracies whose ideal employee was conformist, passive, stable, consistent, and acquiescent.[7] More broadly, scientific planning was brought to bear on all kinds of human groups, yielding rational social organization and rational thought. People and the groups they formed were devoted to development (in a linear way) through time, toward goals that not all could reach, but which all should desire, because they represented the lofty heights of abstract thought.[8] For the adult person, stability and solidity were at a premium. Early in the century, identity was described as something that was "forged": like wrought iron, a person's identity should be strong.[9] This solid sort of identity was akin to the older concept of "character," which was a more or less given quality of the person manifested by working hard and honoring the dictates of duty. However, at the same time, the locus of a person's stability was changing. The term "personality" came into common usage only in the early twentieth century, bringing with it the potential for more flexible self-presentation. In his classic book *The Organization Man*, published in 1956, W. H. Whyte gives satirical advice on how to get a high score on personality tests: always choose the most conventional word in word association tests, so that you will be classified as a person who has normal ways of thinking rather than abnormal emotional ways of thinking.[10] But Whyte's advice contains the possibility for other ways of defining the personality. One could now strategize about presenting one's personality in different ways for different purposes.[11]

In *American Cool*, the historian Peter Stearns argues that Americans experienced a major change in emotional style in the 1920s. In the late nineteenth century, influenced by Victorian values, Americans placed great importance on the intense emotions attached to romantic love and to the passions necessary for great deeds. After the 1920s, the emotional climate shifted to restrained coolness: management was the key across the board—"no emotion should gain control over one's thought processes."[12] Since my argument develops from a recent resurgence of interest in strong emotion-like states, Stearns's argument has particular salience. How exactly might Americans have gotten from the restrained cool that was the ideal in the beginning decades of mass production society to the unrestrained heat that ignites our cultural heroes today?

One explanation lies in an understanding of recent political and economic changes that have begun to make themselves felt in the United States, as elsewhere, changes with important implications for understanding contemporary concepts of the person. The differential internationalization of labor and markets, the growth of the information and service economies, and the abrupt decline of redistributive state services (among other things) have meant that access to the world's wealth has become much more difficult for most people. In the United States, concentration of wealth and income at the top of the social order is more extreme than at any time since the Depression, and poverty has grown correspondingly deeper, despite the persistent myth of social mobility toward the American dream. Successive waves of downsizing have picked off, in addition to the disadvantaged, significant numbers of people from occupations and classes not accustomed to a dramatic fall in their prospects and standard of living.[13] The imperative to become the kind of flexible worker who can succeed in extremely competitive circumstances has intensified, and the stakes for failing have greatly increased. In one sign of the unforgiving nature of increased competition, references to the "survival of the fittest" have increased exponentially in the popular media since the early 1980s.[14]

Everyday experiences of time and space themselves may be shifting, too.[15] Activities that were once localized—education, work, and family life—are now increasingly being spread over space, changing the spatial and social dimensions of human interaction. "Close" and "distant" once applied both to relationships and spatial distance, and usually were coincident. No longer. Space seems to loom larger as it intrudes into relationships (a couple, of necessity, holding two or three jobs, parents and children following available jobs away from their extended family, grown siblings scattering to the four corners of the globe). Simultaneously, space disappears through electronic technologies (cell phones, the Internet) that make time speed up and communication happen instantaneously.[16] The stable time-space grid described in many earlier accounts of the disciplinary control characteristic of factories, prisons, military barracks, mental asylums, or schools since the onset of modernity has altered beyond recognition.[17]

The factory, which has often served as both a laboratory and a conceptual guide for understandings of human behavior, is also changing. The hierarchical factory of the mass production era, with its worker drones and foremen, is being replaced (at least in the elite sectors of the global economy) with new forms: machines that process information and communicate with "self-managed" workers, who are in turn invested with greater decision-making powers. Corporations are flattening hierarchies, downsizing bureaucracies, and enhancing their corporate "culture," becoming nimble and agile in hopes of surviving in rapidly changing markets. Relentlessly, corporations are also sending manufacturing divisions to cheaper labor markets overseas (where most laborers do not have the resources to follow them). To enable these activities, corporations seek organization in the form of fluid networks of alliances, a highly decoupled and dynamic form with great organizational flexibility.

Six million manufacturing jobs have been shed in the United States over the last thirty years, and many workers who lost their jobs have skidded down the socioeconomic hierarchy.[18] As my previous work has shown, workers and managers are expected to meet this threat by "evolving" with the aid of self-study, training courses, and an insistence on self-management when they are lucky enough to be employed inside a corporation, and then aggressive entrepreneurialism during the frequent periods they now expect to spend outside it.[19] Although from the beginnings of capitalism, firms and individuals have had to innovate and improve or decline and perish at the hands of competitors, competition in the present climate has become extremely fierce. Because of policies guided by "neoliberal" ideas, the individual must now creatively pursue his or her own development with the aid of fewer supports than ever before.[20] The role of the state, according to the theory of political economic practices that fosters this climate, is to establish strong private property rights, free markets, and free trade. The state should ensure the free functioning of markets, and expand or extend markets to areas such as education, the environment, or social security. But the state should not provide social safety nets that would protect individuals whom markets exclude or defeat.[21] Corporations, too, are increasing the risks employees must bear, not only by cutting jobs but also by stopping their contributions to the pension plans of the workers who remain.[22]

In this environment, the individual is responsible for his or her own success or failure in a high-stakes and ever-changing set of arenas. The person now seems to be made up of a collection of assets, as if she were the proprietor of herself as a stock portfolio. In the 1990s, there was an increase in "home-based work," based on telecommuting or the "You, Inc." phenomenon.[23] "People need to invest in their development as if they were a corporation," said Anthony Carnevale, chairman of the National Commission for Employment Policy at the Department of Labor.[24] Individuals, like mini-corporations, were supposed to "shapeshift" in their changing environments, accumulating and investing information and resources.[25] There is a sense in which, as the U.S. government withdraws from provisioning individuals, the individual moves from being a citizen, oriented to the interests of the nation, to being a mini-corporation, oriented primarily to its own interests in global flows of capital.[26] In preparation for this endeavor, as I will describe in coming chapters, American children, teenagers, and adults are doing many things to develop their mental capacities in specific ways, taking on self-management practices with or without the help of mind-enhancing drugs.

In one popular formulation of the state of things, Virginia Postrel's *The Future and Its Enemies*, "stasists" will be left behind by "dynamists" who celebrate "emergent, complex messiness . . . an order that is unpredictable, spontaneous and ever shifting, a pattern created by millions of uncoordinated, independent decisions . . . these actions shape a future no one can see, a future that is dynamic and inherently unstable."[27] In the radically atomized world Postrel imagines, there is an imperative for people who are always adapting, scanning the environment, continuously changing in creative and innovative ways, flying from one thing to another, pushing the limits of everything, and doing it all with an intense level of energy devoted to anticipating and investing in the future.[28] High school and college-age children in the United States and globally appear already to be entering this future.[29]

Given this procession of dramatic changes on many social, cultural, affective, economic, and political fronts, what concepts of the person are enabled by and enable these conditions? As the mechanical regularity demanded of the assembly line worker gives way to the ideal of a flexible and constantly changing worker, what will happen to the value previously placed on stability and conformity? A new attitude toward change is emerging: continuous retraining for workers at all levels is becoming normal.[30] Today it is not just that individuals circulate among different jobs or careers, nor just that the conditions of their work change over time. In addition, the individual comes to consist of potentials to be realized and capacities to be fulfilled: self-maximization and self-optimization are the watchwords. Since these potentials and capacities take their shape in relation to the requirements of a continuously changing environment, their content, and even the terms in which they are understood, are also in constant change.

What competent and successful persons are expected to do has changed over time. These changing expectations might even stretch to include the emotions: could the value of emotional coolness character- istic of the early twentieth century be giving way, under conditions of greatly increased capitalist competition, to a focus on emotional *labil- ity*? Coolness is by definition flat and restrained, and might be seen as suited to ordered and stable environments and institutions. Lability in emotional life means movement on the scale of feelings, and might be seen as suited to the ferment and turmoil of entrepreneurial activity. This possibility brings us directly into view of the changeable emotions thought to be characteristic of manic depression and hints at why fasci- nation with manic depression may be increasing.[31] This hint, however, raises more questions than it answers. In psychiatric terms, manic de- pression is a "mood disorder." Rather than taking this at face value, we need to ask: Are moods actually a form of emotions? Does manic depression only involve a disorder of moods or does it more centrally involve a diminution or exaggeration of *motivation*? How exactly could an entrepreneurial climate call forth a revaluation of manic depression, whether it involves moods, motivations, or both? To pursue these ques- tions, I begin with the basics: the changing definitions of emotions, moods, and motivations in their cultural contexts.

What Are Moods?

The standard source for defining psychiatric diagnoses in the United States, the fourth edition of the *Diagnostic and Statistical Manual of Mental Disorders* (DSM-IV), makes a strong link between mood and emotion. Bipolar disorder is a "mood disorder": mood in turn is "A pervasive and sustained emotion that colors the perception of the world."[32] Given this, it is startling to realize that the DSM definitions of mania and depression do not include much obvious reference to emotions. A manic episode is the following: "A distinct period of abnor- mally and persistently elevated, expansive, or irritable mood, lasting at least 1 week (or any duration if hospitalization is necessary)." During this period, three or more of the following symptoms should have been present:

1. inflated self-esteem or grandiosity
2. decreased need for sleep (e.g., feels rested after only three hours of sleep)
3. more talkative than usual or pressure to keep talking
4. flight of ideas or subjective experience that thoughts are racing
5. distractibility (i.e., attention too easily drawn to unimportant or irrelevant external stimuli)
6. increase in goal-directed activity (either socially, at work or school, or sexually) or psychomotor agitation
7. excessive involvement in pleasurable activities that have a high potential for painful consequences (e.g., engaging in unrestrained buying sprees, sexual indiscretions, or foolish business investments).[33]

An episode of major depression involves five or more of the following symptoms during a two-week period:

1. depressed mood, nearly every day during most of the day
2. marked diminished interest or pleasure in all or almost all activities
3. significant weight loss (when not dieting), weight gain, or a change in appetite
4. insomnia or hypersomnia (excess sleep)
5. psychomotor agitation or psychomotor retardation
6. fatigue or loss of energy
7. feelings of worthlessness or inappropriate guilt
8. diminished ability to think or concentrate, or indecisiveness
9. recurrent thoughts of death or recurrent suicidal ideation, a suicide attempt, or a specific plan for committing suicide.[34]

Mania's "elevated mood" might translate into "elation," and "depressed mood" might translate into "sadness"; some of the intense activities in mania might translate into "joy," and the immobility of depression into "despair," but the DSM symptoms do not fit squarely with an ordinary sense of what emotions are. Nor is it clear whether a "mood" is the same thing as an "emotion." We need to understand better what the terms "mood" and "emotion" mean.[35]

In the 1990s, anthropologists turned their attention to the central features of "emotions" in Western languages.[36] They determined that in Western societies people consider emotions to be physiological forces located within the individual. Further, in Western beliefs, a person's emotions constitute his or her sense of uniqueness because they represent a kind of inner truth about the self. Language that describes emotion gets its force from its "putative referentiality," that is, from the assumption that when a person speaks the language of emotion, the emotion is really there.[37] In other words, when I feel an emotion (anger, joy, or fear) and talk about it, what I say has rhetorical force because listeners assume the emotional state (anger, joy, or fear) is genuinely there inside me.

Are mania and depression emotions in this sense? Do they have a "putative referentiality" to an "inner truth about the self"? From the earliest history of the term, mania has taken its core meaning not from reference to an inner truth about the self but from a comparison with its opposite: depression. For the ancient Greeks, health involved equilibrium between opposite states and sickness involved the presence of one extreme or its opposite. The historian Roy Porter points out that in the Greeks' humoral system, "[M]ania implied—almost required— the presence of an equal but opposite pathological state: melancholy. The categories of mania and melancholy—representing hot and cold, wet and dry . . . became ingrained, intellectually, emotionally, and perhaps even aesthetically and subliminally."[38] The humoral conceptions of mania and melancholy that first developed in classical Greece and Rome continued to dominate medical writing through medieval times and the Renaissance, right up to the mid-nineteenth century. Although mania and melancholy were seen as opposites in the humoral system, they were also seen as connected: "Where mania and depression are considered in the historical medical literature, a link is almost always made."[39] Scholars thought mania and depression were linked together, and that they somehow brought forth each other. By the mid-nineteenth century, mania and depression came to be seen as aspects of a single disease, and accordingly this disease was given a new name by French "alienists": *la folie circulaire* (circular insanity). Falret described this in 1854 as an illness in which "this succession of mania and melancholia manifests itself with continuity and in a manner almost regular."[40]

Building on la folie circulaire at the turn of the century, the German psychiatrist Emil Kraepelin, as mentioned earlier, separated "manic-depressive insanity" from dementia praecox (later termed schizophrenia). Kraepelin made moods a key component of both mania and depression: mania involved rapture, "exalted" mood, "unrestrained merriment," or "happiness."[41] Depression involved a "gloomy hopelessness," grief, or "sombre and sad melancholy."[42] But, much like the later DSM, Kraepelin's definition included far more than moods: among the common "psychic symptoms" of mania were disorders of attention (distracted), consciousness (clouded), memory (impaired), train of ideas (digressive), activity (pressured), speech and writing (increased), sexual excitability (heightened), and movements of expression (vivacious).[43] Most interesting, Kraepelin emphasized that all these "morbid forms" were "impossible to keep apart."[44] Instead, one would find "gradual transitions" between states, as well as "mixed forms," combining mania and melancholy in the same person.[45] He asserted that the morbid forms "*not only pass over the one into the other without recognisable boundaries, but that they may even replace each other in one and the same case.*"[46]

From Falret's la folie circulaire through Kraepelin's manic-depressive insanity to the DSM-IV's bipolar disorder, manic depression is an interrelated set of moods and behaviors whose hallmark is intensity. In the entire class of moods such a person experiences, the dial of intensity is turned up much too far. Wherever you look in the landscape of moods or behaviors, you find *too much or too little*. The same person, at different times, is too happy, too sad, too energized, or too immobilized. French, German, and Scottish psychiatric researchers from the mid- to late nineteenth century published photographs of their manic-depressive patients, often choosing pairs of photographs that would show the contrast between each patient's high and low extremes of emotion and behavior.[47] Part of the meaning of mania is that it is the opposite of depression and part of the significance of this opposition is that the extreme states it embraces are sometimes found in the same person alternating with each other.

We can now see one reason why manic depression sits somewhat adjacent to the concept of emotion. Since opposite emotions, such as elation and sadness, or opposite behaviors, such as excitement and inhibition, are present too intensely in the same person, manic depression might be called a "meta" state. It is not a *member* of the class of emotions, but an emotional condition that *contains* classes of particularly intense emotions. The components of manic depression do not simply refer to something truly in the person, as emotions do; rather, they also gain meaning by their relationship to other parts of the person's system of emotions and behaviors. Within this meta-state, moods do not just coexist; they oscillate. The DSM formulates the definition of manic depression in a way that makes its meta-status clear. In the DSM-IV, both depression and mania are kinds of "mood episodes." Mood episodes serve as the building blocks for the diagnosis of a mood disorder. But the DSM handles the building blocks of depression and mania quite differently. Whereas depressive episodes can combine into many types and subtypes of "depressive disorders," mania by itself cannot be the only building block of a mood disorder. As far as the DSM-IV is concerned, mania only occurs as part of "bipolar disorder," where it alternates with depressive episodes. In other words, mania always exists as a part of a system of moods, manic highs followed by depressed lows.

By definition, the manic-depressive person swings from the bright glow of mania to the ugly dark slough of depression. Many people living under the description of manic depression experience being in the grip of an oscillating force. When manic, one feels like one is kindled, blazing, incandescent to the point one fears burning out. When the descent into depression comes, it feels inevitable and without end. To anticipate an argument I make in part 2, the inevitable oscillation of moods in manic depression makes it resonate with the "mania" and "depression" in the markets of today. Both seem alive and regenerative in a sense, because for both the source of renewal seems to lie within: depression's "death" is brought on by mania's "life" and vice versa.

Although there is little consensus among psychologists about how to define and understand emotions, anthropologists have made clear from studies in a variety of cultures that, however defined, emotions are strongly linked to social interactions.[48] To develop this point, I turn to Vincent Crapanzano's trenchant anthropological account of emotions. In Crapanzano's analysis, the grounding of emotions in the psychology of the individual should not be allowed to mask the important role that emotions also have in transactions. How do emotions function within social exchanges? Emotions "help call the context," that is, their presence automatically changes the context in which they occur.[49] This happens because emotions are conventionally taken to be a "manifestation, a symptom, of the condition—the emotion they are said to be describing." Emotions refer so powerfully to the things they name, that to utter the words is to have the emotion: "Their truth and sincerity cannot be questioned, for they point to those perturbations as unquestionably, as nonarbitrarily, as smoke points to fire."[50] When a person expresses the "smoke" of anger or love, this conventionally means that the "fire" of anger or love must actually be there inside him. Those who witness the "smoke" of anger or love understand that the "fire" is there in much the same way they would understand any standard meanings in the English language. But because a person's expression of an emotion such as anger or love is taken to mean that his inner state has changed in an important way, the very expression of such an emotion changes *the context* in which he is interacting with others.[51] His witnesses are now dealing with an altered situation: they are dealing with a person on fire with anger or love.

Because they have to do with a set of moods, each of which is experienced intensely, mood disorders operate in social life in a different way than any one emotion does. When people witness the expression of emotions like anger or love, they are, as Crapanzano argues, *pulled into a changed definition of the context* because they are witnessing something that is genuine by definition. As we have seen, moods in a person with a mood disorder do not function exactly like emotions: participants in a social setting where a component of a mood disorder, such as mania, is expressed may be *pushed out of the context*. This is because the expressions of mania point not only like smoke to an ember glowing truly within—the "smoke" of the person's elation means elation is really inside them—but also like smoke to a burning house: in the context of a mood disorder, the elation may also be taken as a sign that something is awry with the person's entire system of emotional expressions. This is a way of saying that it is important not to oversimplify manic depression as merely the experience of one or another extreme emotion.

Mood and Motivation

If manic depression does not sit easily with our everyday understandings of *emotion*, does it sit more easily with our everyday understandings of *motivation*? Certainly, the DSM hints as much by including "increase in goal-directed activity" in the traits characteristic of a manic episode. How exactly are moods different from emotion? Focusing on everyday language, Clifford Geertz analyzes the differences: moods are above all states we speak of as fleeting: they "go nowhere. They spring from certain circumstances but they are responsive to no ends. Like fogs, they just settle and lift; like scents, suffuse and evaporate."[52] While moods are fleeting, they can also settle down and become, briefly, all-encompassing.[53] In contrast to moods, motives are neither acts nor feelings, but "liabilities to perform particular classes of act or have particular classes of feeling."[54] Unlike moods, which can be fleeting, motivations tend to be enduring. Unlike moods, which can monopolize, motivations tend to coexist. Motives "have a directional cast, they describe a certain overall course, gravitate toward certain, usually temporary, consummations."[55] Multiple motivations can coexist, sometimes in harmony and sometimes in conflict. A person can be motivated to both pursue a career and find a spouse, and find these goals compatible; or a person can be motivated to both pursue a career and nurture a family, and find these goals incompatible.

The DSM connects the characteristics of manic depression closely to everyday understandings of motivation—intensely present in mania and conspicuously absent in depression. For mania, DSM traits connected to motivation include "continuous wakefulness," "excessive involvement in pleasurable activities," or, as mentioned above, "increasingly goal directed activity." For depression, DSM traits related to lack of motivation include "marked diminished interest or pleasure in almost all activities" and "fatigue or loss of energy." These traits make manic depression seem as much like a bundle of "motivations" as a bundle of "moods." In the end, the DSM links manic depression to *both* motivation (purposive and directional) *and* moods (fleeting and all-encompassing). Over time a person with this diagnosis is liable to experience both motivation and moods as too high and then too low: passionate pursuit of one's interests followed by lethargic immobility. I suspect it is the heightened *motivation* people in the United States associate with mania today that accounts for their bemused affection for the condition, at least among certain professionals who think of themselves as competing fiercely for rank and prestige. Whenever I have read the DSM definition of mania to audiences of students and faculty at universities and colleges, it has met with good-natured laughs and chuckles. When I asked why the definition was funny, people would tell me, "Because this manic level of activity sounds like me and a lot of the people I know." Even though the DSM-IV category describes a major psychiatric disorder, people in this particular social setting enjoy recognizing themselves and their friends in mania's energy and passion.

"Motivation" is the part of mania that our economic system places at a premium. The historian Elizabeth Lunbeck believes that the link between mania and enhanced motivation may be a "survival" of a much older way of distinguishing psychological states, focused on the "will."[56] Evidence of this is a document from 1922, "Mood in Relation to Performance." In this early psychological study of thirty-eight men and women, the author found *no* relationship between measures of mood and tests of performance. She hypothesized that her subjects experienced moods as "distractions," but that they were able to overcome such distractions by exerting their will and "increasing the output of energy."[57] At this time people evidently thought the will led directly to performance: moods were minor annoyances that the will could overcome. Although in this study mood and motivation were unconnected, today they surely are. As we will see in part 2, mood and motivation are especially strongly linked when the term "mania" is applied to the market. The psychological category of manic depression now appears to contain one capacity—moods—that directly enhances both individual productivity and the energy of markets and another capacity—depression—that is a liability for the productivity of individuals and markets alike.

Our Manic Affinity

Psychiatrists have often assumed that schizophrenia is characterized by an absence of emotion, and, as we have seen, manic depression is characterized by an excess of emotions. Confounding this simple dichotomy, Louis Sass has argued that the link between schizophrenia and lack of emotionality is misleading. What psychiatrists call "flat affect"—lacking emotion—in schizophrenia actually turns out to be a complex state filled with strong feeling. Despite appearing outwardly emotionally flat, when asked, people with schizophrenia report strong inner feelings. Sass relates this disjunction between outer flatness and inner turmoil to various forms of fragmentation. In one form of fragmentation in schizophrenia, people, their actions, or their things may be perceived as stripped of their recognizable "affordances," the qualities of persons and things that make them useful or significant in social life. For a schizophrenic person, people and things may retain their three-dimensional geometry but lose their everyday meaning: a chair becomes an object of a certain size and shape rather than a thing to sit on; a person becomes a body with certain dimensions rather than a being one might love, hate, or fear.[58] This kind of fragmented state can be incompatible with emotion: if one perceives a three-dimensional shape instead of a person, one forfeits the possibility for "reacting with lust, loathing, or a yearning for peaceful repose."[59] The weakening of common emotional experiences may be behind the perception that people with schizophrenia have flat affect. Contrary to this common perception, accounts of patients attest that "flat affect" does not entail lack of feeling.[60] Instead of emotion, their interior landscape is often filled with free-floating tension, fear, and vague anxiety. These anxious, fearful states can be highly intense, but they lack grounding in shared social experience. In her *Autobiography of a Schizophrenic Girl*, Renee writes that when she looked at her therapist, she saw "a statue, a figure of ice which smiled at me. And this smile, showing her white teeth, frightened me."[61] Sass suggests that this "withdrawal from worldly emotional directedness" can provide a "haven from the frightening unpredictability of external circumstances."[62] This is the heart of the matter. "Withdrawal from worldly emotional directedness" is not simply a matter of suffering pain and becoming numb as a result. Rather, it is a matter of losing one's accustomed way of connecting objects to a context, people to collectivities, or features to a face, and all this produces a state in which emotions become problematic. Inner turmoil, anxious perturbation, and nameless agitation often result.

At this point we can see the historical significance of the timing of Kraepelin's bifurcation between manic depression and schizophrenia.[63] Manic depression emerged as a condition characterized by intense emotion-like states in the context of an engaged (whether timid or exuberant) sociality; schizophrenia emerged as a condition characterized by fragmented, alienated consciousness, isolation from the social, and anxious agitation rather than emotion. This bifurcation allows us to understand how the two conditions relate to late modernity in opposite ways. On the one side, many of the activities that capitalism demands fragment, separate, flatten, and deaden feeling. The psychological hallmark of these experiences would be better called nameless agitation and anxiety, rather than emotion. In fact, as early as the turn of the twentieth century in the United States, "nerve weakness" or neurasthenia was a well-recognized set of symptoms for specifically modern anxieties. The symptoms of neurasthenia could include nervous dyspepsia, insomnia, hysteria, hypochondria, or asthma. Maladies like sick headache, skin rashes, hay fever, premature baldness, inebriety, hot and cold flashes, nervous exhaustion, brain collapse, and forms of "elementary insanity" were thought to be caused by "simple exposure to the hectic pace and excessive stimuli of modern life."[64] As a result, people felt "anxious busyness."[65] Still today, under the neoliberal administrations of the 1980s and 1990s, in tune with a style of government the linguist George Lakoff terms "the strict father," many speeches and policies encourage a worldview that life is fundamentally dangerous.[66] Since evil threatens the world (in the form of irrational terrorism) and the individual (in the form of immoral temptations), the strong leadership of a strict, moral leader is necessary. Some regard this as a bald effort to arouse anxiety and fear because "people kept in a state of constant stress will sacrifice their best instincts and even their real interests for the illusion of safety"—an illusion that a politician posing as a strict father can foster.[67] These anxious states seem akin to the nervous perturbation of schizoid states.

Yet, on the other side of the bifurcation, we are in an era in the United States when markets command a preeminent place and where the economic has come to dominate the social. To flourish, these all-important markets, operating with fierce ruthlessness in more domains than ever before, require emotions: not flattened but intense emotions. The "animal spirits" of entrepreneurs, their vital energies, are increasingly being called forth for the sake of stimulating markets.

In some settings, specialty firms are *teaching* people how to be manic for the sake of greater productivity; the mania they intend to tap flows from the mind and will go forth, so they hope, to unleash creative potential. Harnessing the mania of individuals to stoke the economy is happening in a country with a longstanding expectation that much of a person's worth—not to mention survival—is defined in terms of his or her productivity, where productivity means creating value in ways the market can acknowledge and reward. As the United States' sense of its own power has escalated, so has its sense that vitality flows primarily from its markets and the firms that participate in them. Increasingly, the financial order of things has a degree of autonomy and authority as never before. The United States is a country that sees itself as (and in some ways is) at the center of the global system of power and wealth.[68] In this global system, markets are treated as a "life force," and, paradoxically, people are treated as an ever more disposable source of inefficiency. As the anthropologists Jean and John Comaroff put it, "The spiraling virtuality of fiscal circulation, of the accumulation of wealth purely through exchange . . . enables the speculative side of capitalism to act as if it were entirely independent of human manufacture. The market and its masters, an 'electronic herd' of nomadic deterritorialized investors, appear less and less constrained by the costs or moral economy of concrete labor."[69] In other words, markets are not human, but they are vital—"alive" with "animal spirits"—at the same time as this vital energy is being drained out of actual living people. Experiences of mania, once considered a sign of fearful and disordered irrationality, have come to epitomize the vital energy —found in the psyche rather than the laboring body—which the market needs to keep expanding. This is the heart of the affinity between contemporary American culture and the characteristics of manic depression.

CHAPTER TWO

Performing the "Rationality" of "Irrationality"

The mind is its own place, and in itself
Can make a Heaven of Hell, a Hell of Heaven.

—John Milton, *Paradise Lost*

I n all its forms, "irrationality" is the enemy of "rationality," the enemy of order, stability, and civilization. In this chapter I challenge the integrity of this battle line by showing how the rational and the irrational are not clearly separable. I begin with the point of view of patients diagnosed with a mood disorder.

Patients' Rationality: Double Bookkeeping

The psychologist Louis Sass has brought to light the term "double book-keeping," which psychiatrists use to refer to a schizophrenic patient's ability to "live in two parallel but separate worlds: consensual reality and the realm of their hallucinations and delusions." For example, some schizophrenics who hold firmly to ideas others would call delusions nonetheless "treat these same beliefs with what seems a certain distance or irony." A patient of Eugene Bleuler, an early psychoanalyst, "was well aware that the voices he heard originated in his own ears, for he compared these voices to the sound of the sea that can be heard by placing a shell to one's ear."[1] In his initial formulations of manic depression, Emil Kraepelin seemed to acknowledge a kindred kind of doubled awareness in manic-depressive people. He wrote, "It is just the *peculiar mixture of sense and maniacal activity* . . . which makes them extremely ingenious in finding out means to satisfy their numerous desires, to deceive their surroundings, to procure for themselves all kinds of advantages, to secure the property of others for themselves. They usually soon domineer completely over their fellow-patients, use them for profit, report about them to the physician in technical terms, act as guardian to them, and hold them in check."[2]

The question raised by Sass, Bleuler, and Kraepelin is whether people designated as mentally ill are aware of living in a doubled reality through such "double bookkeeping." If so, the question of whether they are rational becomes problematic, and I often faced this dilemma during my fieldwork. During a meeting of an evening bipolar disorder support group in northern Orange County, Richard, a physician with manic depression, now a writer living on a disability allowance, had briefed me about the regular members of the group and warned me that one member, Kevin, had a brain cyst in addition to his bipolar disorder. Richard thought Kevin's condition might cause him to behave in a bizarre manner. I noticed that this group began its meetings with brief introductions, but then, in contrast to all the other meetings I had attended, people went on to list all their coexisting conditions, sometimes in dizzying numbers.

In a typical example, Marge began by saying, "I am bipolar, I have anxiety and panic attacks, I am an alcoholic, an addict, I have post-traumatic stress disorder, and one more thing . . . oh yes, I have borderline personality."[3] Breaking the pattern, and jarringly out of sync with the rest of the group, Kevin introduced himself by describing some miscellaneous events at his job as a mechanic for an auto shop, providing no clue about any diagnosis of mental disorder. When he finished, Richard leaned over to me and said, "That is the guy who has a cyst on his brain." When the meeting was over, Richard and I joined the others at a nearby restaurant.

After about an hour of eating, drinking coffee, and boisterous—sometimes outrageous, often highly exuberant—talk, Kevin suddenly asked me, "Do I look dead?" Hoping to fall into the spirit of the occasion, I said, "You produce a good illusion." Richard joked, "He is actually an alien." Kevin said to me, "I will never forget you. Are you married?" I nodded. Kevin's friend Paul persisted, "Well, do you fool around then?" At this point I was thoroughly embarrassed and nervous. Were they kidding? Would I offend them no matter what I said? Were they aware of how uncomfortable this conversation made me feel? If I went wrong here, would I be able to return to the group? Or were they simply taking a slightly mischievous delight in my unease? Confirming my dawning sense that Kevin was aiming for my ambiguous status as both a legitimate insider and a suspicious outsider who not only lived on the other side of the country but also intended to write down her own account of the group, he asked, to general hilarity, "Am I your science project?"

By definition the group occupies the space of the "mentally ill" wherever it gathers, and some of its members' behavior in public obviously made other customers wonder what was wrong with them: their raised eyebrows, quizzical looks, and stares indicated that our loud voices, dramatic gestures, and raucous laughter were outside of the norm in a family restaurant. But the sense in which there was double bookkeeping going on is this: Kevin knew that his behavior was outside of the norm, and he knew that I knew that. Having seen Richard speak to me, he may well have guessed I had heard about his brain cyst. He knew that I was studying him, and he knew that I knew he knew that. He could put these various descriptions of behavior into action in rapid succession, faster than I could anticipate what was coming next, shifting from one ledger to another, and from one perspective to another, with great facility and with the effect of keeping me off balance. Watching Kevin was like viewing the alternative "takes" in the raw footage of a movie scene, where Kevin was an improv actor. At first he appeared to be mentally compromised; on closer inspection he revealed himself to be a teasing observer; then he became a mischievous commentator.[4]

Another example of double awareness occurred during an event in the department of psychiatry where I attended classes and seminars as an ethnographer. During the department's weekly Affective Disorder Clinical Rounds, clinical rounds for short, doctors and residents (physicians in postgraduate training) would discuss a particularly interesting and instructive patient currently residing on the inpatient ward. The chosen patient would then be invited to join the group. Rounds were held in the ward's activity room, which was outfitted with upholstered armchairs, a stereo, and a wall of windows overlooking the city. Just before 11 a.m., medical students came in and arranged the armchairs: they set up two chairs at the front of the room, turned slightly toward each other. The rest were arranged in a few rows facing the front and were quickly occupied by medical students, residents, and psychiatrists.

On this day, just before the event started, a large woman in a brightly colored knit dress came in, holding a bag of pretzels, a soda, and a few magazines. I took her to be a patient looking for a quiet spot. Apparently noticing the chairs in rows and the students in white coats, she said, "Oh, you want a lecture? [a short pause] *I'm* lecturing. What would you like? How about 'Manic-Depression as It Manifests Itself in Schizophrenia'?" As she talked, she moved toward the door, and the soda and pretzels she was holding started to spill onto the floor. Pretzels flew out here and there, as she, balancing her soda and magazines, tried to get the door open. The door was heavy and tricky to unlatch, so more pretzels spilled. She made no particular effort to stop the flow of pretzels or pick any of them up and, as a result, every doctor and medical student who came into the room in the next few moments stepped onto the crunchy, slippery mess, looked down, disconcerted, perhaps taking a swipe at the crumbs with the toe of a shoe. It was as if the patient (by definition a person with a disordered mind) had left confounding traces of disorder in the room. She knew the mental disorder of patients like her was about to be studied in this room by doctors, but she reversed the direction of control: *she* announced the lecture and deftly made the entering doctors and students feel disconcerted. Marked as mentally disordered by her patient status, she could not only name psychiatric conditions and give a mocking announcement of a lecture about them, but she could enact a bit of disordered behavior in such a way that it looped back on the proceedings, in a small way perturbing those who came for the purpose of creating scientific order.

Because of the circumscribed role I occupied as a fieldworker, I couldn't ask the patient, but as far as I could tell, this little scene was not part of a planned and rehearsed series of performances by patients to disconcert those attending clinical rounds. In all likelihood, it was a one-off affair. But for this reason, it can serve as a hinge in this chapter between the notion of doubled awareness in those who are conventionally thought to be out of touch with reality and those who are not. People in both categories use performances of many kinds as they par-

ticipate in a broad cultural fascination with mania and manic depression. The linguistic anthropologist Richard Bauman once reflected that
there is a kind of power "inherent in performance," a power that could
work either for enhancement of experience or for "subverting and trans-
forming the status quo." He argues that it is the "special emergent quality of performance" that can make a community's capacity for change
become clear.[5]

Since I will use the concept of performance often in the remaining
chapters of part 1, I want to be clear from the start about why the concept is pertinent to my argument. At the present time, notions of performance and performativity are playing an important role in critiques of
conventional ideas about sex and gender.[6] Introducing the idea that
one's identity as a gendered person is not given in nature but produced
by one's actions has led to a searching critique of taken-for-granted
assumptions. In my account, performance matters in a different way:
performance provides a way, in actions as well as words, for people
cast into the category of the irrational to comment *on* their putative
"irrationality." In so doing, they demonstrate that they *are* rational. In
this chapter I look at a wide variety of performances in which people
hold the category of mania up to one community or another for
thoughtful consideration. Although I use the term "performance" liberally in this chapter, these performances, with the exception of those
with professional actors on a stage or in front of a camera, are barely
formal enough to be worthy of the term. They are held without planning, they are unscripted, spontaneous, and ephemeral, but for all that
they are no less able to provide sharp-witted commentary on living
under the description of manic depression.[7]

Doctors' Rationality: A Closed Circle

When people who are designated "mentally ill" question and perturb
medical categories, they use complex kinds of intentional action: mocking, reframing, or caricaturing. Hopefully even the small examples I
have introduced so far make us reluctant to hold onto the overly simple

notions that "mentally ill" people are unaware of what they are doing and that they are in wholly irrational states of mind. But we also need to look at how people learn and use categories at the center of what we often assume to be rational scientific knowledge. A good entrée into the logic of the system is the pedagogical material used to train aspiring psychiatrists and other mental health professionals. Doctors dramatize medical categories for particular purposes, and in the process they reveal some qualities of the rationality of their scientific mode of thought.

To see one way physicians dramatize the category "manic depression," I turn to a section of a teaching video, *Simulated Psychiatric Profiles*. The psychiatrist who produced this set of VHS tapes, Donald Fidler, a professor at the University of West Virginia, told me that for reasons of patient confidentiality, the people depicted in the video are paid actors. (When I began to teach at New York University, I found out that some students at the Tisch School of the Arts, who are studying method acting, take jobs like these to help finance their education.[8]) The actors prepare for their parts by watching videos of patients diagnosed with DSM conditions interacting with psychiatrists in therapy sessions. As an actor attempts to re-create what he sees in a patient, psychiatrists coach him until his performance captures the DSM definition of the condition closely enough. The set of videos is organized according to the major categories in DSM-III, which was current when this video was made, and each one is divided into sections illustrating the various subtypes in the DSM categories. The videotape of most interest to my research is labeled "Affective Disorders: Mania and Depression," and the following transcript is from the section labeled "Mania I."

> [Patient and psychiatrist are sitting in an interview room.]
> **Psychiatrist:** Hello, I'm Dr. Grey.
> **Patient:** Yeah, well, I'm Dr. Brown today myself, you know, even though you've got green pants [patient touches the doctor's pants]. I got a thesis advisor, his name is Dr. Green, and last time I was in the hospital [while talking, patient is agitated; he begins taking his sweater off.] I had a Dr. Blue . . .
> **Psychiatrist:** Uh huh . . . well, why are you here?

Patient: [continually crossing and uncrossing his legs] Why I am here—well, I'd kinda like to know that myself, you know [still taking his sweater off], you know, is that really the kind of question you want to ask me? I mean, don't you think you should sit up straight, you know, and have a tie, and I don't know about those shoes, Dr. Blues uh, you know, they're kind of bad news for me, at least.

Psychiatrist: Okay, can you tell me why—how—you decided to come here?

Patient: Come here? Well, you know I didn't decide to come here—what are you some kind of fag or what, you know, I mean that's something I usually do with my girlfriend at home alone in bed. [Patient has now taken the sweater off and tied it around his knees.]

Psychiatrist: Uh huh.

Patient: What else do you wanna know? [Patient crosses his legs and fidgets constantly. He continues, talking very rapidly.] . . . What I'd really like to talk about is the fact that I'm having trouble with my girlfriend, okay? I mean, you're a psychiatrist or something, right? So I'm having trouble with my—is that a camera? [Patient points at camera.] Because look, you know, my father's on the English faculty here, you know, and I just don't think that doctors should, should put people on cameras [patient is gesturing emphatically with both hands] and I don't want to be on the cover of *Newsweek* or something, anyway.

Psychiatrist: The camera's not on.

Patient: Okay, well good, that's better—that's a lot better [patient nervously takes his comb out of his shirt pocket and drops it into his lap and then picks it up and combs through his hair once] because if it were I'd comb my hair, okay?

Psychiatrist: Uh huh.

Patient: You know, so, what do you want to know? Don't you have any questions or anything?

Psychiatrist: Yes, can you tell me who decided you should come here?

Patient: Oh yeah, right okay, well I—I dunno, I—I—I could start like one day ago, three days ago, or two weeks. Maybe I better start two weeks ago, okay, 'cause I'm a graduate student, right? And I've been working on my thesis project with my advisor, not that he has much advice to give—you know, much advice or consent—he looks like a senator, but he doesn't have much advice or consent to give me. [Patient is still nervously placing his sweater on his lap, turning it over, and putting his arm through it.] Anyway, so, okay, about two weeks ago I was really excited and I went in and talked to the guy— he's kind of an old guy and he's kind of conservative, but he's really pretty smart [patient is constantly folding and unfolding his sweater and he is agitated—constantly moving in his chair—he literally cannot sit still], so we were talking about my project, okay, and he was even getting excited, 'cause you know he's really kind of a staid guy but even he was getting excited. Then yesterday, okay, so I went in and talked to him again, and he was not nearly as impressed—I don't know we kinda got into a big fight yesterday and I think that maybe what happened is he called up my girlfriend—'cause they know each other and they've met at parties and everything, and we've been living together for a while—not my advisor, okay, just me and my girl-friend—so I think that maybe he talked to her, and—and I don't know I—maybe my roommate's part of it, too [patient is running his hands through his hair], 'cause I think that—maybe—I think maybe my thesis advisor's kind of jealous of what I'm doing, 'cause I've been doing really good work, okay.[9]

Because the patient's behavior is meant to follow the DSM description exactly, this drama has a circular form. Point after point in the checklist of DSM symptoms is illustrated in the patient's behavior: in the segment above we see grandiosity, distractibility, pressure to talk, and racing thoughts. Whereas the patient dramatizations we saw earlier disturb the neat order of assumptions behind categories like these, here the circle of discourse is closed: present and future members of the profession of psychiatry are listening to themselves but not monitoring what is being said. The category of manic depression is meant to be translated directly from the DSM into the actor's depiction, and from there into students' concepts and practices. There is only *one* set of books in this accounting, not two.[10]

We might guess that in practice things are not so simple. Given that method actors are sought for this dramatic performance, it is safe to say that the actors are doing far more than mechanically translating a set of descriptions into behavior. Method actors report drawing on their own personal experience of related if not identical emotional states in making such a character sketch. Nor are the psychiatrists coaching the actors simply doing a mechanical translation. They are trying to reveal the main features singled out by the DSM but also get what they call "the feel" of the patient right. In spite of these complexities, the main goal of such teaching materials is to pass on an intact set of clear working categories to the next cohort of students, not to perturb and question them. This is an important aspect of the quality of scientific rationality, which assumes students need to learn, as a solid foundation, the current state of knowledge. To this end, multiple meanings and ambiguous interpretations are excised as much as possible.

Despite the desire to excise ambiguity, it sneaks through anyway. Right in the midst of his pressured speech, the patient-actor sees the camera and protests. The psychiatrist-actor tells him the camera isn't on, and the patient-actor remarks, in the subjunctive, "if it were." What is being modeled here is quite outside the DSM: the patient accurately perceives something in his environment (the camera) and reasonably worries about his private affairs being exposed. The psychiatrist then models denying the patient's perceptions and allowing him to be filmed without his knowledge. The teaching video has thoroughly exceeded the description of mania in the DSM and has introduced layers of ambiguity: can people be perceptive even when floridly manic? Should psychiatrists deny patients' perceptions even when doing so would serve the ends of scientific rationality? What is being modeled is a psychiatrist who deceives his patient about taking a visual record of the session and a patient who is left to remark (perhaps sarcastically), "because if [the camera] were [on], I'd comb my hair." All the while, he does comb his hair! A lot like Kevin's multiple takes, this patient (as enacted) knew that the psychiatrist knew that he knew the camera was on. In short, although for pedagogical reasons, the video is meant to have only one set of books, a second set of books slips through like a shadow.

The Bipolar Experience: Multiplicity

In the series of manic performances I consider next, meanings are multiplied rather than excised; multiple beings seem to coexist in the same person to such an extent that they cause interruptions in the person's sense of self. I begin with a kind of comedic performance that is often described as "manic," in a dramatic rather than a pathological sense, to draw out the characteristic features of multiplicity in mania. Here is a glimpse of Robin Williams in a very fast-paced, improvisational comedy routine that took place in a San Francisco nightclub in the 1980s, done to the accompaniment of continuous peals of laughter from the audience.

> **Williams:** [takes sip of wine] My god, woman! [Williams moves quickly toward the audience and steps off the stage to admire the fur coat of a patron seated at a table.] Where did you get this coat? My god, Nanook of Marin! [audience is laughing] My god! [Williams takes the coat and steps back onstage.] This is lovely—look at this thing, right now there's a whole lot of animals going, "Shit is it cold. . . . Jeezus!" [Williams makes a gesture of protecting himself from the cold—arms around himself—audience cheers and laughs. He looks at the garment label and feels the texture of the fur.] Made from kittens around the world . . . let me try this on. [Williams begins putting the coat on through his arm.] I won't get the smell in there— you take it home tonight and the animals'll be goin' [makes a noise to indicate animal sounds]—hee hee hoo hoo oh! [As he notices that the underneath of the arms is another color,] I guess you couldn't afford the bottom part. [Williams puts the coat around his shoulders.] I feel like Liberace right now—"Oh, just leave me the candelabra, Samuel, just leave me the candelabra." Wonderful. [He sighs.] Williams's wearing the lovely pants from Hefty Bag. [Williams parades around the stage holding the sides of his pants, which are made of a shiny, thin, latex-like, black material.] La da dee dah. [Williams hums.] . . . I love this—this is the type of coat you can go [Williams allows the coat to slide off his shoulders onto the floor as he puts his head up in a stuck-up fashion to imitate a high-society woman],

"Andre, park the car." Or I could play Elephant Man [Williams puts the coat over his face with the arm sticking out in front] going, "I'm not an animal . . . I'm a comedian!"[11]

If we compare these two performances—the actor's simulation of the grad student's mania as described in the DSM and Robin Williams's manic performance—what we notice is that Robin Williams and the actor both appear to be persons with a crowd of people inside them, all jostling for control at once. Aggressive, mocking, conciliatory, humorous, challenging, bragging, suspicious, hostile, expansive, open, belligerent, rejecting, fearful—what stance is not enacted? Although Williams controls his display of multiplicity for comedic reasons, and the actor for pedagogical reasons, they both capture the forms of linguistic expression common among people living under the description of manic depression: ideas are "excessively and immoderately combined and elaborated," with a "playful, mirthful, and breezy quality" that leads them to intrude incongruous ideas into conversation.[12]

Such internal multiplicity has long been considered central to the manic condition. As Kraepelin describes it in his classic account of mania,

> Impulses crowd one upon the other and the coherence of activity is gradually lost. . . . [H]is pressure of activity may finally resolve itself into a variegated sequence of volitional actions ever new and quickly changing, in which no common aim can be recognised any longer, but they come and go as they are born of the moment. The patient sings, chatters, dances, romps about, does gymnastics, beats time, claps his hands, scolds, threatens, and makes a disturbance, throws everything down on the floor, undresses, decorates himself in a wonderful way, screams and screeches, laughs or cries ungovernably, makes faces, assumes theatrical attitudes, recites with wild passionate gestures. But, however abrupt and disconnected this curious behaviour is, it is still always made up of fractional parts of actions, which stand in some sort of relation to purposeful ideas or to emotions; it is a case of movements of expression, unrestrained jokes, attacks on people, amusement, courtship, and the like.[13]

Internal multiplicity may be central to what makes manic depression belong to the irrational, because behavior that seems to indicate there is a crowd of different people inside one person disturbs some common assumptions about normality. Historians have shown that by the early nineteenth century, the prevailing opinion in the United States was that a person should have a certain unity, as if some central organizing force—one's self, one's identity—were in charge. This idea depended on a concept of self-control possessed by the individual. Each individual possessed a rational mental apparatus located inside the brain and this apparatus was a battleground on which the mind's rationality and will fought to control the "uncivilized" animal impulses of the body.[14] Without a central organizing principle, the person became a bundle of frighteningly unpredictable impulses. Instead of following a coherent plan of action, the person went in many directions at once; instead of subordinating the passions to the governing intellect and will, the person gave them uncontrolled reign.

Persons without a controlling principle were fearsome, as were uncontrolled groups of persons. When the order and control conferred on groups of people by the structure of a school, an army, or a factory was absent, a "crowd" was the result. At the turn of the twentieth century the French writer Le Bon described the fear of crowds graphically: "Isolated, he may be a cultivated individual; in a crowd, he is a barbarian— that is, a creature acting by instinct. He possesses the spontaneity, the violence, the ferocity, and also the enthusiasm and heroism of primitive beings."[15] Le Bon participated in the Eurocentrism and racism of his day in likening crowd behavior to "primitive" behavior. But he was also pointing to what apparently can happen when the borders of the controlled, rational, cultivated individual break down: caught up in a crowd, individuals become highly suggestible and lose their ability to reason.[16] In a crowd, many people meld into one "person," the crowd, and the crowd goes out of control. In manic depression, the elements are different but the result is similar: one person becomes a "crowd," and each of the different persons in the "crowd" can go out of control in turn. I stress that the kind of "crowd" at issue in manic depression is not the same as the technically defined condition multiple personality disorder. It is something more like a style of self-presentation or manner of engaging with the world that covers such a wide range of emotions and energy levels over time that it evokes the idea of more than one person at the ready. More often than not, in this kind of multiplicity, the person is all too aware of the other guises at hand. In fact, people report that sometimes they almost deliberately stoke manic energy out of fear of an encroaching depression or out of a desire to "ride the tiger" of an energy-filled mania.[17] Teddy Roosevelt, said to be "haunted, if not ruled, by melancholy," observed in a letter to a friend, "depression rarely sits behind a rider whose pace is fast enough."[18]

In my fieldwork, I observed many contexts in which medical students, learning to identify various forms of mental illness, encountered multiplicity in manic-depressive patients. For example, in this incident from clinical rounds, a resident described a patient as having become a different person. Dr. Dean chaired as a resident presented Mr. Nielson's case, summarizing information from the patient's medical records and from interviews with him and others. After a childhood full of family conflict,

> Mr. Nielson graduated high school, went into the army, and left with an honorable discharge. He belongs to an evangelical church, and now lives with a family from the church in Baltimore. His work is waterproofing basements, which involves heavy labor, carrying many bags of cement.
>
> *Last fall, he became a different person:* he started feeling sad and withdrawn and thinking of suicide. One time, he put his belongings in the trash, wrote a suicide note, put a noose around his neck, but then ran out of steam. He sleeps twelve or more hours at night and then a couple more during the day. He feels a weight on his head, like a stone. He has difficulty concentrating. He feels he doesn't know what is real. He also has anhedonia [the absence of pleasure from acts that would normally be pleasurable] and doesn't do things he enjoys, like drawing, playing golf, or ringing doors [proselytizing] for the church. He says his stinking brain has gone downhill. He shows compulsive traits such as checking doors over and over, apologizing over and over, and he has been experiencing panic attacks. He got 27 out of 30 on his mini mental [a standard test of mental acuity].

He is hearing voices, and they say, "You should kill yourself, you are a bad person, you are so stupid."

He has been on the ward since yesterday; the current plan is to try ECT [electroconvulsive therapy].

Stooped over, Mr. Nielson walked into the room slowly, head hanging down with a dejected expression. He was very thin, and his longish hair looked unwashed and uncombed.

Dr. Dean: How are you feeling today?
Mr. Nielson: I don't want to live, I don't know how to get out of this.
Dr. Dean: Is it sad?
Mr. Nielson: It is like a weight on my head, in my brain.
Dr. Dean: Do you think something is wrong with your health?
Mr. Nielson: Yes.
Dr. Dean: Like what? Like HIV?
Mr. Nielson: Yes. I have lost thirty pounds. I have panic attacks where I am sure the basement I am working in will be caving in. My heart races, I have sweats, it feels like I will die.

For all of Dr. Dean's gentle efforts to draw him out, Mr. Nielson was silent or monosyllabic during most of the interview. In this case, we only know that Mr. Nielson "became a different person" because of the medical history. Although Mr. Nielson's behavior in rounds belonged only to the depressed end of the mood spectrum, the resident's case history clearly revealed that in the past he had been a dramatically different person.

In a second example from rounds, the patient articulated her own multiplicity, which began after she accidentally fell and hit the back of her head.

It is like I have an extra sister, I watch myself being eaten by the disease. I am getting barely Bs and Cs while *the real me* knows I could get As. I am bad, no, worse, I am better than bad, but I am never good. There is a window of productivity—there are some hours when I can do errands, even though when I do them I am still crying. Then I have to drop into bed again. *I want my life back.* Everything feels heavy. Everyone gets better but me. Others have lost parents or were abused and so they have a reason to be depressed. But I don't. I had a very happy childhood, a great family.

Two beings coexist inside this patient: herself and her "extra sister." Watching her "extra sister" do poorly in school, she yearns to become the "real me" who is a good student. Only then would she have her "life back."

In support groups, people frequently described both becoming a different person and, at the same time, missing the person they once were. In these cases, one person gives way to a different person while the original person, present in the same body, remains helpless and frustrated—aware of the change but unable to do anything about it. In an evening meeting in Orange County, Brenda, a woman who was there for the first time, told me before the meeting that she was desperately depressed because she had tried various drugs for a year, to no avail. When the meeting began, she was the first to speak.

> *I miss my self, I miss my personality.* I was once a bubbly, happy outgoing person, then I got depressed, then I went on Paxil and herbs and I was doing well, I felt then like *I had my self back.* Then I had to go off the Paxil because of the side effects, and since then I have been depressed.

Brenda lost her self, got it back, and then, having lost it again, she now misses her self. In a Baltimore group, Caroline also spoke of losing her self as she descended into depression: "It is like breaking apart, like falling into a thousand pieces, like dying inside, [to the group] *you* know what I mean."

The Bipolar Experience: Interruption

In these last few examples, a false, depressed person seems to replace the real person at a single point in time. Because my fieldwork focused on manic depression rather than major depression, I more often heard people describe feeling like they had more than one person inside at the *same* time or swiftly alternating with each other. This brings us to the second characteristic feature of mania—interruption. The conception of the ideal person in U.S. culture involves constancy: the person may develop or improve over time, but such changes are seen as manifesting more of the person's original self rather than revealing a new self. As the anthropologist Atwood Gaines puts it, "Constancy is a positive attribute. It is an assumed characteristic of the normal self."[19] Given this cultural assumption, if the constancy of the person seems lost, personhood itself seems interrupted. In one support group, Jane, who sometimes acted as the group facilitator, asked to speak.

> Everything was going fine this week. At work I passed a clerical test, and I was feeling good about that. I had started going to a singles' over-fifty group, and a couple of older men had called. I assure you there was no reason, there was no reason, none at all. I was feeling life is good. I was also looking forward to going out with friends last night, and visiting Thousand Oaks to see other friends over Easter. But a few days ago I woke up in a depression. Now I only want to sleep. I am still going to work, and acting normally then, but all the rest of the time I sleep. I know now I cannot have normal relationships. I cannot have them because there will always be—*this interruption*—and normal people do not understand. No matter what they say, normal people do not understand. Suppose I had already been dating someone and this happened, what could I do or say? If I told him . . . people do not understand, and it would end it to say I am mentally ill. I know it is chemical, it is the chemicals starting in . . . I feel hopeless, useless, loveless.

Jane was distressed because her self, which she assumed must have a certain coherence over time to be intelligible to another person, kept on being interrupted. Tom, a regular member of the group as well as a former leader of the organization, tried to soften Jane's belief that her "interruptions" made her unable to have "normal" relationships. He reframed her story by leaving out her reference to having an interrupted self and describing her problems as ordinary: "'Normal' people are not so different. 'Normal' people also have problems, and also have bad relationships." Whereas Jane took the ruptures she experienced as a sign of deep abnormality, Tom urged her to recognize that everyone experiences ruptures in the continuity of the person from time to time.[20]

Looking back over a long adulthood of such interruptions leads John, a Vietnam vet, group leader, and writer, to speak of being different people at different times. We had been talking over a leisurely meal in a small restaurant.

> When I find I am getting stressful, when the demons are bursting out, I feel pressure building from the inside. The world is not pressing in, you are percolating, your inside temperature is rising to an earthquake, and you have a molten core. Now you are getting down to Dante, the molten core, and there is lava spewing forth. I was Jonathan for a while, the poet. Then I adopted that as a name, a name to write by, and I lived by that for a while. I became John Dante Prescott, that was kind of nice, and so I went through the years. After I was born, I had four different names: I was born John Robin Prescott. At five, I became John Frank Randall, because the father who adopted me was Frank Randall.
>
> When I came back after the manic depression in 1970–71, I became John Abraham Prescott, so my initials were the same as my sister. I was going with a Jewish girl, so that's the Abraham. Then I became John Dante Prescott. I promised my grandmother I would be a Prescott. Having four names, it works for the stages of my life. It is like being born again, and each of those people who died are friends, still incorporated within me, even though I couldn't do the things I did when I was them.

John undergoes the interruptions in his self sequentially, and, as with Jane and the other examples above, his different ways of being coexist— as he puts it, like friends who died.

Sometimes a person will apparently embody multiple ways of being simultaneously. Members of a California support group often commented on how beautiful they considered one of their regular members, Terry, to be. She was very tall and thin, with fine, golden, shoulder-length hair, sculpted chin, and large eyes. When she smiled she looked like a movie star and she smiled frequently. When she talked, her face became animated, but—and this was the disjunction—her words did not match. At one meeting, she spoke of her extreme pain.

I am aloof, as usual, and I really don't ever know what I feel. [Flash of a brilliant smile.] I am in trouble at work, and this has upset me a lot, though I am trying to want what God wants for me at work. I struggle with alcoholism, drug addiction, and now it is so bad I physically can't drink alcohol. I bought a bottle of champagne but couldn't even swallow it, so I ended up pouring it down the drain. I am not willing to turn myself over to AA and get a sponsor, I am just not ready to follow that, and I guess I feel overwhelmed by them.

She gave the impression of having a huge, pent-up, tightly controlled rage, somehow poised between her inner anguish and her outer radiance. When I returned to visit the leader of this group a few months later, he told me the group had been disbanded. Terry had killed herself during the winter, and other conflicts in the group had grown unmanageable in the wake of her suicide.

While this group was still together, Ann, an athletically youthful woman in her fifties, spoke intensely about her dread and fear of an approaching manic episode, describing it as an outside force that threatened to take over her self.

The last time I had [a manic episode] it ended in a hospitalization. At that time my Christian neighbors who talked about Satan and said they were praying for me influenced me. I ended up throwing furniture out of the house because I thought Satan was in it. I had visions of Satan. Now I am facing a trip to Las Vegas and I feel something similar is going on. The neighbors are praying for me again. It feels like an irresistible force, like it is inevitable, like I will pretty soon get so tired of fighting it, I will give up. I want to break all the rules, just throw them to the wind. There is an irresistible force pushing me to do the irrational. My doctor isn't much help; he just sits there fascinated, saying, "Tell me more," but you can tell he is titillated.

Ann describes mania as if an outside force that takes over her self was possessing her. She fights but eventually gives up and, possessed by the manic force, begins to act like an irrational person. In Ann's case, the crowd inside is composed of two entities, herself and the manic force.

In another Orange County group, Gerta also talked about the condition of manic depression as a force that takes her over. It disturbs her when her friend greets her descriptions of how she feels with, "Oh, I know just what you mean, I feel the same way."

> This just refocuses the conversation over on her. But it isn't the same, she doesn't know what it is like. It is more extreme and it is frightening. It is a lifelong sentence. When somebody has an ordinary illness, even something serious like cancer, they want to look into it, they want to find out more, they want to explore that territory. But with bipolar, *you* don't find out about *it*, *it* finds *you*, it finds you, it finds you.

In her memoir, Kay Jamison eloquently describes the feeling of bifurcation that she experienced in manic depression: "Which of the me's is me? The wild, impulsive, chaotic, energetic, crazy one? Or the shy, withdrawn, desperate, suicidal, doomed, and tired one?"[21] When a single person encompasses within herself such extremes of emotion and behavior, she exceeds the limits of "rationality." I am arguing that recognizing the multiplicity and interruption often experienced in manic depression makes the judgment that it is an irrational state more comprehensible. Given common cultural assumptions that the normal person has a controlled and constant self, how could it be judged any other way? Paradoxically, when we understand the reasons for finding manic depression irrational, we simultaneously gain an interpretation (based on grasping the experiences of multiplicity and interruption) that might make us question how "normal" the controlled, constant self really is.[22]

The multiplicity we are discussing here needs to be considered in light of the regenerative character of manic depression we discussed in chapter 1. The inextricableness of manic depression's highs and lows, the unnerving experience of mania always being twinned to depression and depression twinned to mania, also entails multiplicity. Both forms of multiplicity may draw on specifically Protestant notions that good and bad are inextricable: heaven implies hell; God, Satan; the saved, the lost; and perfection, sin. In my fieldwork, John was not the only one who spoke of manic depression as Dante's heaven and hell: Richard also told me that when he is manic he sees the world engaged in a great battle of good versus evil, as in C. S. Lewis's *Chronicles of Narnia*.

He can see the conspiracy of evil, the works of the devil and of God. Others living under the description of manic depression told me that their Protestant neighbors often thought they were inhabited by diabolical forces and in chapter 5 we will meet Mary, whose neighbors helped her cast out the devil they believed possessed her.

Pulling all these threads together, Jane told her California support group that she relied on Christian inspirational literature to help her through the first five minutes of feeling suicidal. Later that evening, when the group reconvened at a diner, she added, "Once in a Christian bookstore I found a section on manic depression which said manic depression was Satanic! The manic person was doing it on purpose, there was no evidence there was any biological aspect to it. My mother and I objected, and the shop clerk said she would 'red flag' the book." John sympathized with Jane: "Those Apollonian Christians can't stand the Dionysian manic depressives!" Reflecting his knowledge that mania was once considered possession and that possession was not always considered negatively, he added, "But we were once the shamans after all!" Christian views of life and death are relevant here, not in a strict doctrinal sense, but in the sense that American culture is imbued with them. They are part of the deep background that flows into the social life surrounding the multiplicity and interruption of manic depression.[23]

Sounding a Second Voice

People who experience themselves as containing multiple centers of action could be said to be capable of performing many different roles. In support group meetings, I initially found it startling that what seemed to be deliberate enactments of manic behavior occurred quite frequently. At one evening meeting, a group was sitting around a table watching a video called *Dark Glasses and Kaleidoscopes*, produced by Abbott Laboratories, the makers of Depakote, a new drug found to be effective in the treatment of manic depression.

As they watched the video, people in the support group were dismissive or hostile, criticizing and mocking the film's optimistic promise that if you take your medications, your life will be so normal that you can have a job or a profession, even if you are diagnosed with manic depression. Some of their comments were: "That's an ideal world!"; "It's bullshit that medications can be fixed to keep you 'just right'"; "Yeah, you can work in a profession as long as you don't tell your employer [you have manic depression]"; "Go ahead and call the 1-800 number as long as you can block a tracer on the call." There was all-around scoffing and scorn when the video showed a person with manic depression saying, "Losing the ability to monitor my own behavior is what having manic depression is." Depakote, according to the video, restores that ability and allows the person to adapt to ordinary life.

When the video ended, one man began to turn the tables on the video's story by changing the definition of who needs to be medicated: "You know what I always say, the whole world needs a dose of lithium." Someone else chimed in, "Yeah, put it in the water, put it in the air!" The next moment, a man who had come to meetings week after week, but who always sat quietly, saying nothing, with a gloomy expression and dejected appearance, said, "I usually don't say anything at all, I have been silent here for weeks and weeks, but tonight I realize I can't hold it all in. I have to let it out." Then he launched into a string of shockingly barbed and funny jokes. Startled, everyone looked around the table hesitantly. Smiles bloomed as a rapid "eye flash"—eye contact that moved rapidly around the group—signaled the start of a hilarious session of joke telling that took up the entire rest of the two-hour meeting.[24] Every now and then someone would say plaintively, but obviously not really seriously, "What are we doing? What if someone wants to share?!?" Virtually every person there told raunchy, gross, lewd, or insulting jokes about Catholics, Jews, Poles, blondes, wives, the elderly, or the pope. Everyone shrieked with laughter and frenetic energy built and built. Food and soft drinks cascaded over the room and people gave up their seats in a tidy circle to lounge on tables, chairs, and the floor.[25]

How might we understand this? Given that everyone in the room had been diagnosed with a major psychiatric illness, and was thus categorized as irrational, this event might be understood as a commentary *about* putatively irrational conditions themselves. Since self-awareness is a central ingredient of rationality in the Western tradition, if people can give an impromptu performance *about* the definition of rationality, the question of their "irrationality" becomes more complex. To the extent they are aware of the irrational conditions attributed to them, they possess a key attribute of rationality.[26]

Additionally, we might say the support group reaction to the film was a critical commentary on the current understanding of manic depression: a carnivalesque reversal of the established order. By reversing the usual decorum of the support group, in which each person sits quietly in a chair, speaking only when invited by the moderator, the group reversed the can-do theme of the video. In contrast to the video's message, most group members were not working regularly and subsisted on disability payments. They frequently experienced employment or other discrimination when their status as "mentally ill" was known, and they learned from these experiences that revealing the diagnosis of manic depression was risky. Their comments provided an opposing narrative to the overly optimistic estimate of the drug's effectiveness the video portrayed.

Yet another description of the event would be that the group displayed the view of manic depression in the video a second time.[27] The Abbott-sponsored story of mania in the video is the "first voice." The first voice becomes a passive tool in the hands of the group when they sound a "second voice" in their own story of mania. The Abbott Laboratories story is thus shown to be a specific world produced in particular circumstances: one in which Abbott's Depakote manages moods perfectly and everyone has a job. The Abbott video depicts a world in which the condition of manic depression means the person cannot monitor his own behavior, cannot reflect consciously on his own behavior, without the aid of a drug. In being at least somewhat self-conscious and purposeful, the behavior of the support group members runs against the grain of the lack of self-awareness manic depressives are supposed to have. The enactment at the meeting shows that manic-depressive persons, with or without drugs, and certainly without increasing their medication just then, are people with enough self-awareness to deliberately enact mania. Their enactment, fit to the specifics of the time and place, is a well-tailored communication *about* mania, instead of an instance of out-and-out mania. Seeing this self-awareness, even in the midst of an event any casual observer would describe as manic, returns us to the issue with which I opened this chapter: if there can be self-awareness (and therefore "rationality"), even in the midst of strange experiences of multiplicity, the sharp line between the "rational" and the "irrational" begins to waver.

Other moments in which people sounded a "second voice" occurred frequently in my fieldwork. At the yearly August picnic for all the support groups in Orange County, signs were posted at many places around the public park, directing visitors to the DMDA (Depression and Manic Depression Association) picnic. The acronym was never spelled out, but several people commented that they were self-conscious about being publicly identifiable. At one point, the small cluster of people I was standing with discussed the possibility that the stigma against manic depression came from confusing manic depressives with schizophrenics. One person thought many people did not realize that manic depression, unlike schizophrenia, has medications that can keep it under control. At this moment, an "eye flash" occurred, initiating an impromptu enactment of mania in which everyone spoke loudly and extremely fast, jumped from one topic to another, gestured dramatically, glanced around vivaciously, laughing all the while. One woman made us all dissolve into shrieks of laughter when she interjected, "Yeah, and we drool, too," as she somehow contrived to let strings of saliva drip from the corner of her mouth.[28]

This was not the same cast of characters who enacted mania in the support group meeting, but they also had a lightning fast response to the claim that manic depressives can only act normally with the help of medication. By deliberately enacting manic behavior, the group showed the limits of the medication they were all most likely taking to control manic behavior. The small drama ended when the woman who drooled commented, "Actually, my *medicine* does make me drool, but only a little," thus breaking the simple formula of manic-depressive person plus medication equals normal behavior. In her display, manic-depressive person plus medication equals the abnormal behavior of drooling.

Angela Vickers enacted a small performance of mania as a speaker at the national meetings of the DMDA, attended by patients, doctors, researchers, and advocates. She told the audience that although she had professional credentials in law, she had also received the diagnosis of manic depression. She began to study law because her manic depression had cost her custody of her children: "On the one side the court saw a wealthy businessman, and on the other a psychotic wife." Studying law in order to bring about reforms so that this kind of discrimination would not happen to others, she remembered encountering discrimination in the classroom. One law professor remarked, "Watch out for those manic depressives, they *look* so normal." Her own doctor warned her, "Keep your condition quiet; you will never be seen as the same again." But this was a level of complicity with discrimination she told us she could not accept. To make her point, she said, "I am a Vivien Leigh variety of manic depressive," and launched into a tiny drama with some similarities to the support group's disorderly meeting. While enacting many features of manic behavior—eyes burning, head tossing, arms waving, hands gesturing—she called out, "I am not crazy, I am not crazy, I am not crazy!" The audience nodded and laughed along with her, understanding her message: like Vivien Leigh, my style is dramatic, and in the right context, such as this conference or the courtroom, it can be effective.

But still more can be gleaned from this material. Events fit the definition of verbal performance in Richard Bauman's definition, when they involve a performer who assumes responsibility "to an audience for the way in which communication is carried out, above and beyond its referential content. . . . [T]hus conceived, performance is a mode of language use, a way of speaking."[29] By this definition, it might appear that I have mistakenly described the events from my fieldwork as "performances." There is not usually an audience separate from the performers, and there is certainly no formal way in which the "performances," if such they are, could be evaluated in Bauman's terms. I want to evoke a more modest notion of performance, with the help of anthropologist Donald Brenneis's description of the Indian *pancayat* in Fiji. The goal of a dramatic performance among Indians in Fiji is not to act out the feeling or mood itself, but to act out the "conditions that excite that mood and the responses that follow from it."[30] In contrast to usual Western notions, in which the locus of emotion (or moods) is in the individual, a theory from classical Hindu poetics called *rasa-bhava* locates nonindividualized moods in events. "Moods" or, as they are also called, "flavors" are seen as "impersonal, universal sentiments." In addition, feelings seem not to be viewed as internal states; instead, the local Hindu word for emotion is the "same as that for gesture or display." Rasa-bhava theory also values the nonindividualized mood— rasa—more highly than whatever personal feelings are associated with it. Hence performers strive to produce a shared emotional experience for the audience rather than to express themselves.[31]

Brenneis's description enlarges the capacities we can see in the ephemeral enactments of mania I described. Each of them starts with an "eye flash" of recognition that races around the group, an eye-to-eye signal of knowing anticipation, a gestural equivalent to a film director's call, "Action!" The following enactment places "mania" squarely in a social setting, in the intersubjective space among group members who, in a passing moment, seize their chance to comment on the state of their moods. That they do so socially moves the focus away from the inside, where Western common sense places the psyche. For those living under the description of manic depression, the inside site of emotion is where what is wrong with them is said to be, and for which they have trouble finding a legitimating form of description, apart from medical discourse. The force of these performances is that they enact a nonindividualized mood—as Fijians depict rasa—and give this enactment legitimacy in the social space of their meetings.

With this modest concept of performance in hand, let us return briefly to the incidents I discussed earlier in this chapter. In the support group meeting and at the picnic, people deeply marginalized by being classified as "irrational" were by definition not expected to be capable of producing commentary *about* the classifications that marginalized them. Their commentaries occurred in out-of-the-way places, they were fleeting and one-off in form, and they arose spontaneously out of the materials and experiences immediately at hand. They could be called social experiences "in solution" rather than "precipitated." They were forms of action critical of the dominant understanding of mental illness, even though they were not expressed in the dominant language about mental illness.[32] Such experiences blur the sharp division between the rational and irrational by revealing how much of social life and imagination lies somewhere in between. If the groups' reactions had been "precipitated," they might have consisted of a clear, formal statement like, "Manic depressive people are rational enough to manage themselves." Remaining "in solution," their impromptu dramatic sketches nonetheless created ripostes to the idea that people living under the description of manic depression cannot control themselves. Once we see their actions as performances, as artifice, then we do not have to see them as involuntary signs of madness caused by natural or biological forces that people are helpless to control. At the least, we can see their actions lying somewhere in between these poles. To the extent that we can see these events as performances, we gain a way of seeing mania as a state people can actively produce under the right conditions, rather than as a state that overpowers a person entirely. If acts, however spontaneous, have a certain deliberate quality, why should we not think of them as rational?

Equally important, seen as performances, such events also open spaces where questions about the collective and social aspects of any display of mania might be asked. Were the support groups feeling their way toward a view of manic depression from their own perspective? Their actions had a performative cast, where the cast was toward the "meta," toward actions whose import was to comment on the whole class of phenomena they were displaying. In a sense the groups were displaying a message to themselves—they were both acting and observing—and in a sense the audience, albeit not literally present, was made up of those who espouse the conventional understanding of manic depression. Thinking about events through the concept of performance helps us see how the lines between the rational and the irrational quake and shift.

Style and Manic Performances

The concept of performance becomes more powerful when it is combined with the concept of "style." With "style," individual variation and unconscious thought enter the picture. To capture the double meanings at the core of the ways "style" has been used in art criticism, Carlo Ginzburg explicates a pun made by a theologian, Paolo Sarpi, in 1607. Sarpi was excommunicated by the church for his heretical views and then, some months later, five men armed with daggers assaulted him. He whispered to the physician brought to his aid that his wounds had been made "stylo Romanae curiae." The pun lay in the word "stylo" or "style," which meant both "'by the knife of the Roman Curia' and 'by the legal procedure [literally the pen] of the Roman Curia.'"[33] Ginzburg takes this pun as his starting point to show that " 'style' often has been used as a cutting device, as a weapon, and as a self-defining category."[34] As a category in the arts, style could refer to both the persisting, distinguishing qualities of a school or tradition of art and the particular, individually variable quality of a specific artist's work.[35] Early in the nineteenth century, John Flaxman described how ubiquitous individually conferred style was: he thought even a "savage" could "superadd to the elegance of form an additional decoration in relief on the surface of the instrument, a wave line, a zig-zag, or the tie of a band, imitating such simple objects as his wants and occupations render familiar to his observation."[36] The other side of the meaning of "style"—uniformity over time—came to have dark associations with race and national character, culminating in its use by National Socialists to distinguish "pure" German culture from Jewish or other "impure" forms.[37] Running throughout scholarly debate about both senses of style is the question whether style is produced consciously or unconsciously. Art historians have clearly recognized that style can be consciously deployed, as when the Assyrian state built statues with massive arms and torsos to depict their massive power.[38] But, in a contemporary example, cultural critics have recognized unconscious factors in styles that consumers develop by means of commercial goods. Consumers may be only partially conscious of the larger cultural values that affect how they attach complex affective experiences to commodities.[39]

The tension between conscious and unconscious thought and imagination is also involved in how style is thought to work in language. In anthropological linguistics, style is a concept valued for the way it confounds easy distinctions between unconscious patterns and conscious choice.[40] Styles of language or dress can be by turns "extremely self-conscious," designed for display of a particular identity, or simply part of timeworn habit.[41] In his early, classic work in linguistics, Roman Jakobson analyzed the structure of many forms of aphasia (speech defects caused by brain damage) and saw all forms of aphasic alteration in speech, including child language, as fully part of language. Even though different types of aphasia were structured at a deep, unconscious level, Jakobson thought that the differences among kinds of aphasia could also be called differences of style.[42] Whatever type of aphasia a person displays, he "exhibits his personal style, his verbal predilections and preferences."[43] Of the variety of aphasic disturbances, in effect, Jakobson held that every aphasia has its own style.[44] Jakobson saw the aphasic as losing particular aspects of language ability, but in the face of the immense variety of ways language can be spoken and written, he thought it would be a mistake to assume any particular loss would result in lack of competence: "The changes in an aphasic's speech are not mere losses, but also replacements."[45] By looking across the whole field of a person's language, a particular loss could be seen as compensated by an idiosyncratic but functional style.[46]

In sum, style contains both separation and incorporation, both enduring uniformity and individual variation, both conscious and unconscious thought. It is both patterned aesthetically and it escapes our efforts to describe its patterns fully.[47] The work of the French phenomenologist Merleau-Ponty could be taken to argue that it is the visceral aspect of human experience that lends style its ineffability. Merleau-Ponty's everyday examples make the point most forcibly while serving as a bridge back to this chapter's earlier performances of mania.

> The acquisition of a habit is indeed the grasping of a significance, but it is the motor grasping of a motor significance. Now what precisely does this mean? A woman may, without any calculation, keep a safe distance between the feather in her hat and things which might break it off. She feels where the feather is just as we feel where our hand is. If I am in the habit of driving a car, I enter a narrow opening and see that I can "get through" without comparing the width of the opening with that of the wings, just as I go through a doorway without checking the width of the doorway against that of my body . . . to get

used to a hat, a car or a stick is to be transplanted into them, or conversely, to incorporate them into the bulk of our own body. Habit expresses our power of dilating our being-in-the-world, or changing our existence by appropriating fresh instruments.[48]

I want to borrow Merleau-Ponty's way of describing habitual patterns of action in relation to the body "as an expressive space."[49] A person's finger movements, hand gestures, and body bearing are united by a certain style: the style results from her performance of her body, and none other; it is marked by her style, and none other.[50]

There is this kind of *style*—both individual and social—in what I have been calling performances of mania.[51] For mania, style enters in each particular individual's way of expanding his or her body in the world, reaching out in broad gestures, standing tall, speaking loudly, moving vigorously. Manic gestures take their meaning by contrast to depressed gestures: shrinking the body, containing the body in a close space, becoming silent, immobile, still. The concept of performance allows us to see that these ways of being can be at least in part learned and enacted. The concept of style allows us to imagine that they may be less rote and wooden enactments of a script than vibrant and lively (or contained and downcast) interpretations done with unmistakable individual flair. Let me be clear: I am not saying being manic (or depressed) is simply a learned habit. Nor am I saying such an action is entirely consciously chosen behavior. I am saying that being manic does not fit easily at either end of opposites like conscious/unconscious, habitual/novel; compelled/chosen; or innate/learned. We need languages such as Merleau-Ponty's to describe the terrain between these poles.

I will now return to the manic performances I discussed earlier, this time with the notions of performance and style in hand. At first gloss, Robin Williams's comedy seems to be a paradigmatic case of performance that builds on a traditional comedic style. In the tradition of Jonathan Winters and Don Rickles, he would have worked for his particular way of making comedy through apprenticeship, discipline, and training. Looked at this way, it is conventional. But at the same time, most people would probably agree there is something inimitable about

Robin Williams: could you mistake him for anyone else? Here we need the concept of style to capture the unique way Williams maintains a high level of energy, spinning out threads of connection among the objects he handles and the things he says and hears through a kind of slipping: a word leads to an association with another word, then an object; an object is put to one use, then another and another; everything is pushed and wrung to yield meaning after meaning.[52]

In the training video, the actor's depiction of manic behavior as defined by the DSM is certainly also a result of training for control of gesture, speech, expression, posture, and tone of voice, among other things. The actual words the actor spoke probably, in fact, followed a written script. But, to pass muster as an educational video, the actor would have had to master what psychiatrists call "the feel" of manic depression as he moved from depictions of anger, fear, and paranoia to grandiosity. If a viewer judged his performance to be a rather flat rendition of manic depression (many do), this might be because the actor had mastered his lines well enough to give a performance, but had not understood manic depression well enough to have performed it with style. If he had performed it with style, we would have seen the actor's particular personality refracted through the exaggerated exuberance of mania.[53]

When we look back at all the instances I have presented so far of mania performed by people with the diagnosis of manic depression — in the support group meeting, at the DMDA picnic, in conference lectures—we could say that they have been training for these performances during all the manic episodes they have witnessed in others or experienced themselves. But just as with Robin Williams, training for a performance is not the same as performing with style. Each of these occasions, whether collective or individual, provides a chance that fleeting, contingent circumstances and individual personalities could enliven the performance with style. We could say that, after Jakobson, "Every mania has its own style."

Describing manic behavior in terms of performance and style helps mania escape the narrow confines of pathology. Seen as a style and materialized as performance, mania can join hands with many ordinary practices and some extraordinary ones. But inevitably in the contemporary world, as this "style" materializes, it becomes more visible and ever more vulnerable to being captured and redescribed as a treatable condition. It comes to be seen as a pathology that is fixable or a brain condition that can be optimized. Of course, this may be a development that people desire because mania, like depression, can cause great suffering. No one would wish to deny healing for a condition that causes suffering. In due course I will be asking what kind of healing psychotropic medication offers. One thing is certain, as we will see in later chapters: pharmaceutical commodification, like the stylo, the knife of the Roman curia, separates and isolates mental conditions. Through this taxonomic process, they come to seem less like "styles" that are both socially patterned and individually inventive and more like fixed biological brain states. Where appropriate, isn't it more compelling to see mania as a performance "in solution" and manic performers as artisans of their experience?

CHAPTER THREE

Managing Mania and Depression

That is the secret delight and security of hell, that
it is not to be informed on, that it is protected from
speech, that it just is, but cannot be public in the
newspaper, be brought by any word to critical
knowledge, wherefore precisely the words
"subterranean," "cellar," "thick walls," "soundlessness,"
"forgottenness," "hopelessness," are the poor
weak symbols.

—Thomas Mann, *Doctor Faustus*

The people I introduced in the previous chapter were neither help-
lessly mired in mania nor so medicated that they were incapable
of displaying mania. Rather, they were able to perform mania in a situa-
tionally appropriate way, commenting through meta-action on the condition itself. As I sketched in the book's introduction, at the heart of the
degradation often felt by those diagnosed with mental illness is the loss
of one or more of the central components of personhood as it has been
understood in Western societies since the seventeenth century. These
components included being an autonomous individual who had control over his body, his capacities, and his property.[1] The person was
thought to exercise control through his *will*, a capacity that would enable him to choose his thoughts and actions.[2] Full and unqualified
personhood was thought to be found only in adult men, namely, in
"men of reason." Their property-less dependents, such as women, children, servants, or slaves, did not possess the capacity to be full persons.
From the seventeenth century, too, the "mad" were relegated to the
ranks of the "irrational," separated by an abyss from men of reason.

My goal, in close readings of daily events experienced by people
deemed "mad," is to examine the abyss that still conventionally divides

the rational from the irrational. This is not to detract from the gains in recognition of their human worthiness the "mad" have made in the intervening centuries. Andrew Scull argues elegantly that in the eighteenth century, the "mad" were seen ontologically as little more than beasts. Because their reason, the faculty common to all humans, was deranged, they were regarded and treated as brutes.[3] This conception of madness changed dramatically in the nineteenth century with the introduction of moral treatments, such as orderly living arrangements, disciplined work, and exercise, which would lead, under the proper wholesome and edifying conditions, to a cure. The "mad," their irreducible humanity still intact, could regain their reason. Any lunatic's rational qualities could be restored to him "so that he could once more function as a sober, rational citizen."[4] Though Scull argues persuasively that this was a change in "the cultural meaning of madness," there was still a long way to go before the mad were treated as equal to any other citizen.[5] This abyss remains today: a diagnosis of major mental illness, in practice, if not in law, often disqualifies a person from high-security clearance, from employment of various kinds, from political office, from insurance coverage, and from college enrollment. Some kind of terrible abyss is still thought to divide "normal people" from the "mentally ill." This difference made necessary (and welcome) the principles that the Office of the United Nations High Commissioner for Human Rights issued in 1991 for the protection of people with mental illness and for the improvement of mental health care. Among the principles was this fundamental freedom and right: "All persons with a mental illness, or who are being treated as such persons, shall be treated with humanity and respect for the inherent dignity of the human person."

I want to fill this abyss with complex social experiences that contain degrees of autonomous and deliberate action, so that the fearful darkness of this space will lighten. As we saw in chapter 2, the support groups' deliberate enactments of mania could be seen as demonstrations that being manic is something one could choose to do, and hence that people with manic depression possess volition—a key attribute of personhood. In this chapter I continue this inquiry, focusing in particular on whether people living under the description of manic depression are capable of self-management.

I begin by looking at what happens when a person living under the description of manic depression takes psychotropic drugs. Since autonomy is a key aspect of personhood, whether or not a person who takes a psychotropic drug retains his or her autonomy is an important question. Is the cost of relying on a drug for achieving rationality that the drug is seen as substituting for the autonomous action of the self by becoming the person's "manager"? If so, would this leave the medicated person "rational" in form but lacking self-generated action, one of the key substantive features of personhood in the Western cultural context? This is why it matters who is the "manager" of the manic depression. Is it the drug, acting autonomously inside the person, or is it the person who takes the drug? In support groups, facilitators discouraged detailed discussion of drugs because no doctors were present to provide qualified medical advice. Nonetheless members traded a good amount of information about side effects, combination effects, long-term effects, dosages, brands, and like matters before and after meetings. Brief though these conversations were, they were usually based on the assumption that (at least ideally) a person rather than a drug played the role of manager. People urged each other to notice signs of elevating or descending moods before they became severe, to keep doctors apprised of ongoing changes in life circumstances so that medications could be adjusted, to gather information about the comparative side effects and benefits of various drugs, and to assiduously develop structured life habits (diet, exercise, sleep, mood charting, or recreation) that help optimize moods.

Doctors often shared this desire for patients to monitor themselves. Publications well known among support group members, such as psychiatrist Peter Whybrow's *A Mood Apart*, describe the importance of self-monitoring in manic depression. Whybrow enacted the thoughts of a hypothetical patient for me in an interview.

> If I look back over the last week, I've had increasing shortened sleep, my energy is beginning to pick up, I'm thinking faster, and I'm interrupting people. There's no reason why a thoughtful person can't say, "That's the beginning of the mania—I'm going to increase my lithium, and I'm going to insist that I stay in bed even though I'm not asleep,

for seven hours. I'm not going to go out tonight and stay out until two a.m.," and so on. So individuals then become their own gatekeepers.

Whybrow is imagining the patient detecting the early symptoms of a manic episode and taking measures, medicinal and behavioral, to prevent it from entering the "gate," that is, becoming full-blown.

In contrast to their reticence in support groups, people use Internet newsgroups devoted to manic depression to delve into the effects of drugs and drug interactions, comparing their experience and knowledge. In this context, many people clearly see the manic-depressive person as the "manager" of the shifting cocktails of drugs that have become the preferred mode of treatment for their condition. For example, one writer responds to a message in a newsgroup on manic depression from a person who is considering not taking her medication anymore in the following way:

First of all I understand how in times of distress and frustration your drug therapies are seemingly useless and pointless. However if you were only diagnosed in May of this year you couldn't possibly have tried even a majority of AD's [antidepressants] because many if not most require a 4–6 week optimization period. Others require increases in titration in 2 week intervals after assessment. I've been through about 14 different AD's over the past 3 years and I've still got tons I haven't checked out. The point is that don't give up on thinking you'll find the right cocktail blend for you no matter how concerned and impatient you are for results. Bipolar isn't like a normal situational anxiety that is often medicated by tranquillizers. We're talking about finding the right control and balance of Serotonin, Norepinephrine, Dopamine. That all takes time and can be masked and distorted by the use of other over the counter meds, alcohol, [and] caffeine, not to mention other social drugs.[6]

This message, another example from an Internet newsgroup, responds to a person who had an unfortunate experience with her psychiatrist.

A person can have a biochemical imbalance, but that doesn't mean that the rest of the world is sane. For me, getting my biochemistry stabilized makes it easier to cope with an insane world. That doesn't mean it numbs me to the reality of how messed up my environment is. On the contrary, it gives me the stability to cope with it, and the energy and focus to do what I can. I have my own biases too. For years, I subscribed to the "willpower, not pillpower" theory. Somehow, I thought it made me less of a person to be a "mental patient on mood stabilizers." I blamed all my problems on a bad environment and a messed-up personality. I hated myself for not being able to control my moods no matter how hard I tried, and it seemed like just as I had things under control, for no reason at all I'd lose control again. One therapist implored me to see a psychiatrist, saying, "If willpower alone could have cured you, you would've been cured years ago." I had to get to the point where I lost my career, my friends, and almost my life before I finally saw a pdoc [psychiatrist]. I am so glad I did now. I no longer see myself as less of a person for being on meds. I feel stronger than ever. I'm lucky now. I have a pdoc (middle aged male) who respects me as a human being and sees me as a competent, talented person, not just a mental patient. When I told him I was doing my own research on BP [bipolar], and networking with local support groups, he asked *me* for the resources. But I still take my medication which he prescribes. I do not see myself as "dependent" on him. I see myself as taking responsibility for myself by taking my medication as prescribed, being honest with my pdoc about my symptoms, and doing what I can to control my symptoms and live a full life.[7]

And this newsgroup posting responds to a question about a particular medication.

I've been on Neurontin for two years now. I asked to try it for both mood stabilization and to help control chronic pain. It is one of the things in my arsenal that helps keep my emotions on a more even keel. I ramped up to 3600 mg of Neurontin—that was best for the pain, but it was not so good for my mood. So, I backed down to 2400 mg/day—which works best for me. But, it did not do enough for my mood. So I added 10 grams of cold pressed flax seed oil/day. I was already taking trazodone and lithium. The combination of all of them and massive doses of all b-vitamins has brought me a *long* way to better control of my emotions and my behavior. Neurontin has a half life of 6 hours—so it should be dosed every six hours for mood stabilization—otherwise—you will see no benefit from it. IOW [in other words] Neurontin does not build levels in your body like other medications. I will not give up Neurontin—it has been a godsend for me. I get a bit shaky or clumsy sometimes, but well worth it for the benefits.[8]

In these messages, the writers try to convince their correspondents to continue taking medication by arguing that a person on drugs for manic depression does not lose control to either the drugs or the prescribing doctor. A person can remain in control, active and responsible: in the terms introduced here, the person can retain full personhood and agency through the ability to make autonomous, rational choices about which drugs to take.

In my fieldwork, in settings other than support groups, I observed professional psychiatrists or psychologists striving to help "mentally ill" patients retain or recover the hallmarks of full personhood and rationality, especially the ability to carry out self-monitoring. However, their efforts were often somewhat ambivalent, reflecting both the easy slippage across the line between rationality and irrationality and the great social distance between doctor and patient. At one conference I attended annually during my fieldwork, the meetings of the patient advocacy organization, NDMDA, researchers, clinicians, advocates, and patients lectured, listened, and held discussions on different aspects of manic depression. Many lecturers had understandable problems finding a voice that could include everyone in the audience. In one lecture, Charles Nemeroff, an eminent psychiatrist who does research on manic depression, began by including patients with manic depression in the audience in his remarks: "How do you live with a tiger in your tank? You have to balance denial and comfort against terror of the beast. We all end up with foibles and weaknesses we have to deal with." But he then marked a clear line between himself, other researchers, and drug developers, on the one hand, and patients with manic depression, on the other. His point of reference shifted to make it clear there was a line across which he was talking. People on the other side of the line did not have just ordinary foibles and weaknesses: they needed an alliance with psychiatrists who could "know" and manage their illness.

> What is it like to have a disorder where you are energized when you don't want to be, where your idle is too high, and then where you come close to despair for reasons that are not clear? You know that eventually you will get a combination of three or four meds that will work for you. But what is different about manic depression is that it is always changing over time. Unlike depression where you only need to step on the gas, manic depression needs both brakes and gas.

Up to this point, Nemeroff had been speaking in a way that included the people living under the description of manic depression who were present in his audience. In the next few sentences, he made abrupt shifts that excluded them, included them, and then excluded them again. Excluding: "Too often the plunge has already happened when we [doctors] are trying to manage it." Including: "So you need a health care ally." And then excluding again: "My family is used to patients calling all the damn time. How else can you take care of these people? We need the understanding that they may have a fuller cup when well [i.e., they may operate at a higher level] than most people. So the stakes are higher in treating them." He asserted that people on the other side of the line needed to have drugs residing inside them to achieve even a modicum of rational self-monitoring.

> When drugs are well established, a partnership can be established, in which the patient is granted partial and temporary control over himself. Self-knowledge is critical and this is why therapy is moving into psychological education. Knowledge is power! These meetings are for that purpose: not to help doctors dictate to patients from on high, but to help patients collaborate with their providers. They are to facilitate self-control and self-actualization. I try to move quickly to ways patients can even adjust their own dose of medications—for example, high-powered attorneys who have to try a case in court might want to have less medication onboard that day. If I have worked with them long enough and have trust in them, they can be in control of their medications for that day. This enhances their sense of control.

Dr. Nemeroff was speaking to an audience that included a good mix of physicians, patients, and patient advocates, so it is no wonder his point of view shifted. That he could shift between himself and his manic-depressive patients so frequently indicates the line may be easier to move than we think.

The two patient advocacy organizations I studied, which were to varying degrees run by people with the diagnosis of manic depression, provided rich ground for considering whether people assigned to the "irrational" space of mental illness were thought to be capable of managing their own or others' behavior. In both organizations, the facilitators of weekly support groups were self-selected members who underwent specific training provided by the organization. I took the elaborate course of training offered in Baltimore during my fieldwork. In the training sessions, there was often explicit commentary on the unruliness of manic depressives, their need—at times—for management by others. From a leader (with the diagnosis of manic depression) who had come back for a refresher course:

> I have learned over time. It used to be total chaos, more than one person talking at a time, and there I am not doing anything about it, or it's all jokes and then all of a sudden someone is crying. You get three or four manics at one time. I will tell you the whole skill of moderating is get the manics to shut up and the depressives to talk, but they censored me on this! If you are manic, you gotta shut up, because if you are manic you can't shut yourself up.

This leader is positioned in between: he is charged with managing a group of people who are deemed unmanageable because of a diagnosis he shares, and like Dr. Nemeroff he has to keep moving the line between those who need management and those who do not.

In an interview with me, the county president of the California patient advocacy organization, DMDA, explicitly cited the common association between manic depression and unmanageable disorder as the reason "ours is an organization that was created primarily by the patients themselves." She explained,

> Our chapter here got started because four or five psychiatrists from this area went to a psychiatric convention and that was where [they

heard] the national DMDA was getting started. They thought it was a terrific idea, so they came back here and talked among themselves. Then they just picked a day and told their patients to come if they were interested. Right from the beginning it was very important that DMDA remain a patient organization because there was a kind of pride that it was the only organization of this kind that was patient-organized and run. So we were making a statement that, "Yes, we have this illness but we can function."

Thereafter, on the West Coast, psychiatrists immediately handed over control of the organization to patients.

But on the East Coast, Ray DePaulo, the psychiatrist who primarily helped launch the other advocacy organization, the Depression and Related Affective Disorders Association (DRADA), hesitated to do this. DePaulo, whose main research is on bipolar genetics, told me that the idea to form an organization came after he gave a talk on bipolar disorder to another organization, the National Alliance for the Mentally Ill (NAMI), which mostly concerns itself with the needs of schizophrenics and their families. Eighty families came to his talk, hungry for more information about bipolar disorder. He explained, "They had been trying to read the psychological and psychiatric literature themselves." Stimulated by his talk, a wealthy local businesswoman whose son was bipolar gave the initial seed grant for a new organization. At first DePaulo imagined they would model their organization on the West Coast DMDA, but he came to doubt that DMDA's insistence on being patient-run would work: "You know how they only have patients, no doctors or professionals? We couldn't work with them." So DRADA came to be organized independently and along different lines. Even so, one early donor and organizer shared some of the qualities DePaulo worried about in DMDA members: "She was one of those hyperenergized people, definitely on the irritable edge of things, not quite managing the hyper side. She would call you eight times a day. There was this energy and passion. At first her husband would keep her under control. But when he retired, then they both got irritable." Eventually, appointing a board and enlisting the organizational help of a social worker resolved this start-up problem. DRADA has thrived and now has chapters in several states in the Northeast, as well as strong links between its membership and psychiatric research projects.

In this East Coast organization, manic depression appeared to be inimical to the particular kind of order required of bureaucratic organizations. Bureaucratic order, as Max Weber observed, is quintessentially rational: "Bureaucracy has a 'rational' character: rules, means, ends, and matter-of-factness dominate its bearing."[9] DMDA and DRADA have taken up different aspects of the rationality thrown into question by the diagnosis of manic depression. DMDA wants to show that manic-depressive people are competent and can run a bureaucratic organization rationally, in classic Weberian terms. DRADA prefers to let professional managers run the organization and ensure a greater chance that manic-depressive people will have input into and benefit from scientific research.

Situations where people labeled "irrational" perform "rationally" throw into light both the arbitrariness of the categories rational and irrational and the fuzziness of the line between them. A skeptic could reply that people living under the description of manic depression simply move back and forth from lucidity to confusion, but in doing so they do not disturb the line between the categories rational and irrational. An event from my fieldwork, in which members of a manic depression support group in California were asked by a doctor to vouchsafe passage to a schizophrenic man, illustrates acutely that their position does disturb the line between the categories rational and irrational.

The group met in the early evening, in a classroom provided by a hospital on the coast. The meeting had begun some time ago when Sam, a man I had been told by other members was really appropriately diagnosed as schizophrenic, not manic depressive, came in. From earlier meetings, I knew that he inevitably disturbed the group's routine and that the facilitator had tried unsuccessfully to get him to attend a NAMI group, which is oriented more toward schizophrenia. As Sam came in and sat down, we could all see he had a significant cut on his head. He was mopping up the blood with handfuls of tissues. He told us he had wrecked his van; in fact he had totaled it by hitting a ceiling beam in the garage and his head had then broken the windshield. He showed us his letter to the president in Washington, and began to describe his plans to deliver it in person, but a nurse and an orderly with a wheelchair burst in to take him to the emergency room. A while later the nurse returned to ask someone from the group to go speak to Dr. Torrance in the emergency room in order to "assess" Sam.

Five of us, Erica, Larry, Michelle, John, and I, went down to the emergency room to find Sam. Dr. Torrance came out to the waiting room with Sam, and stood with us in a circle. Dr. Torrance was very young, in his late twenties, earnest in manner, and dressed in green scrubs. He said to Sam, "Can we talk openly? Is there anything I shouldn't mention? Is it all right to talk freely, just like on the fourth floor [the psychiatric ward]?" Sam assented. Dr. Torrance told us Sam's head was fine, there was no problem from his injury: "I am only concerned because I want to feel good about releasing him into a safe situation. We have had a good talk, he's obviously highly intelligent, but you may know he just got out of the hospital yesterday, and I am concerned about him being on a cross-country trip on a presidential mission right now. Maybe a night with his brother until he can get on his feet and get the car fixed, but that means getting him to Mission Viejo." Erica said she had her car and could give him a ride there. "The brother," Dr. Torrance went on, "says Sam can stay there, but reluctantly, since he just got him off on his own and this will start up the whole cycle again." Dr. Torrance then went silent and looked around at all of us with wide eyes. I imagined him realizing that he had just asked a group of people from a manic depression support group to help him assess the status of and take responsibility for a schizophrenic person. He then asked us repeatedly if he could trust us to take care of Sam, to look after him well, and be sure Sam got to his brother's house.

All of us were now caught in a kind of double bind: if we were crazy, we couldn't assess and care for Sam, but if we were not then maybe Sam wasn't either. Not knowing what else to do, we all, including Dr. Torrance, trooped off to the garage to assess the damage from the accident. The car was an old VW van with a homemade camper built into the body. The van was once painted red but there was no shine left, and the dented aluminum panels of the ancient camper were all askew.

The accident had broken the windshield on the driver's side and bashed in the passenger side roof. Apparently the vehicle was too high for the roof beams of the garage. The support group discussed how best to get Sam to his brother's house, going over where to leave the van, how to map the route, and whether Erica was the best person to drive him. Erica, now the chosen driver, asked Sam repeatedly if he had what he needed for the night—things like his toothbrush, a jacket, and so forth. At this, Sam went in and out of the camper several times, each time struggling with a door that would neither open nor close readily, but never seemed to find his overnight supplies. Finally he emerged from the camper grinning, carrying a large fruit basket full of fresh oranges, which he explained he had picked at an orchard earlier in the day. With a quirky smile, he enthusiastically offered the oranges around. Amid our laughter and disbelief at this nonsequitur, Sam said, pointing to his van's bumper, "Look at my sign, my sister got it for me." The sign was a bumper sticker that read, "If you haven't changed your mind lately, maybe you don't have one."

The dizzying switches in this small event kept us all off balance. How would anyone decide who exactly was capable of being in charge here? The doctor, after all, was handing over responsibility for Sam to a bunch of manic depressives. The manic depressives, for their part, understood what Sam needed but, no strangers to rapidly shifting states of mind, were still having trouble keeping up with Sam's U-turns. There seemed to be no way out because we were all caught in a contradiction: if each of us had to be either rational or irrational with no space in between, clearly the doctor would be the only rational person. The rest of us would be irrational. But then the doctor's decision to hand Sam over to manic depressives would clearly be irrational! Worse, the manic-depressive group's behavior was practical and goal directed, hence apparently rational, even though the group members' diagnoses made them irrational by definition. Of course, one way out of this paradox is to imagine that the manic depressives were all perfectly managed by their medications, and their medications in turn perfectly managed by their doctors. The doctor could be assumed to be perfectly rational without the aid of any medications. That would leave Sam, probably unmedicated, as the only one out of control. Framing this situation in terms of a hierarchy of management—doctors control the drugs, drugs control the patients—allows us to escape the paradox, but at a cost. Such a framing would leave out the cultural heart of the matter, the complexities that make Sam's situation compelling and interesting. What Sam, Whybrow, Nemeroff, DMDA, and DRADA show us is that psychiatrists, patient advocates, and people living under the description of manic depression constantly (like anyone else) move back and forth across the arbitrary line between the rational and the irrational.

CHAPTER FOUR

I Now Pronounce You Manic Depressive

Kissing the picture of a loved one. This is obviously
not based on a belief that it will have a definite
effect on the object which the picture represents. It
aims at some satisfaction and it achieves it. Or rather,
it does not *aim* at anything; we act in this way and
then feel satisfied. The description
[Darstellung] of a wish is, *eo ipso*, the description
of its fulfillment.
—Ludwig Wittgenstein, *Remarks on Frazer's
Golden Bough*

How do people adapt their sense of themselves as persons when they receive the diagnosis of manic depression? Although the form of DSM-IV categories—the orderly, nested, numerically coded organization we saw on display in the teaching video—would seem to speak for their unambiguousness and clarity, in practice they are anything but. Nor do psychiatrists who have the authority to apply these terms to other people always find the process straightforward. What the terms mean, how they should be applied, and even whether doctor or patient will get to apply them are all matters of contention.[1] In this chapter, we will see the creativity that patients and physicians bring to how DSM terms are used. The issues play out differently in the various medical contexts of my fieldwork in Baltimore, in the pseudonymous Wellingtown Hospital. Wellingtown is a large teaching hospital, and audiences for weekly Affective Disorder Clinical Rounds are largely made up of physicians and medical students. The patients have all been admitted as inpatients on one ward or another. Rounds serve a teaching function not only for medical students, interns, and residents learning as apprentices how diagnoses are made, but also for more senior physicians refining their knowledge. A senior physician chooses cases for rounds that will illustrate some aspect of a condition particularly clearly: for example, whether a patient has major depression or bipolar disorder; or whether a patient is experiencing hallucinations or not. Even with the guidance of the medical resident who presents the patient's medical history and the careful interviewing done by a senior physician, each case produces a welter of complex events and experiences. The goal of rounds is didactic: to produce at least small islands of clarity out of the complexity of a patient's life, so that in practice a psychiatrist can decide on the diagnosis that will allow the most appropriate treatment.

My purpose in describing these rounds is to illustrate the inventive interactions between physicians and patients in what has been called a "contact zone," a space where people with different kinds of power and perspectives negotiate cultural meanings.[2] Because the perspective I take in this chapter is limited to rounds as specific events, what I am able to say cannot represent the full depth and quality of understanding that psychiatrists, nurses, and other medical staff bring to bear on diagnosis and teaching. Others, such as the anthropologist T. M. Luhrmann, have described the poignant dilemmas faced by psychiatrists determined to help patients empathically, especially when they are hampered by the constraints of managed care.[3]

The events I witnessed in rounds evoked for me the term "ground-sea," an archaic West Indian name for a "swell of the ocean, which occurs in calm weather and without obvious cause, breaking on the shore in heavy roaring billows."[4] A distant storm, out of sight, is often the cause of a ground-sea. In the academic context of rounds, the sober and calm demeanor of both faculty and students and the staid presence of the imperturbable DSM-IV make for the appearance of calm weather. But as the following cases show, distant storms are indeed sending heavy, roaring waves to break on this shore. As we will be able to see by the end of the chapter, the distant storm in question arises from social distinctions in the wider society—based on race and class— that bring disquiet into the medical setting. The disquiet is the distant storm whose force we will finally glimpse. The cases that follow are either from psychiatry grand rounds, in which a patient and his or her case are discussed formally before a large audience in an auditorium, or from Affective Disorders Clinical Rounds, the more informal weekly teaching sessions in a small classroom described in chapter 2. The eight cases I describe (two sessions of grand rounds, six sessions of clinical rounds) are arranged loosely in order of their complexity, and accordingly I will have the most to say about the last case.

(1) I'm in a Hole

In this grand rounds, a young doctor, a resident, began by reviewing the patient's medical history. Called "presenting the case," this narration followed a standard form (abbreviated here), which students learn to follow in medical school.[5]

> This is a forty-six-year-old white, divorced woman with a two-year history of depression, who has recently been suicidal. Her father was treated here, too, and he urged her to come. She has a military family background and has moved frequently. Her father was depressed and her mother was alcoholic. [Here he described in some detail the many jobs she has had.] She had thirteen years of psychotherapy with no drugs, then after that took many drugs, including Zoloft, Klonopin, Restoril, and Xanax: she was so doped, she had to quit her job. She became suicidal and took to drinking to lessen her pain. She had restrained herself from committing suicide because of the pain it would cause her father and sister, but drinking lessened this concern. She searched the Internet for suicide methods, including some from Kevorkian.
>
> At Wellingtown Hospital, her therapist diagnosed her as bipolar because of her rapid speech and high energy level: she said her nerve endings were alive, she felt high as a kite, and her mind was going a thousand miles an hour. Her ex-husband said she was babbling. Her therapist changed her meds to Depakote and Prozac, then to Depakote, Serzone, and Nortriptyline. At present, she is stable.

After this description, a senior physician, Dr. Murray, took over the session as the patient herself, introduced as Ms. Peterson, was escorted in from a side door. She was seated in one of two armchairs on the stage, side by side, facing the audience, but angled slightly toward each other. Dr. Murray interviewed her, by turns sympathetically and prob-ingly. He thanked her sincerely for coming. Most of his questions fo-cused on her experience of being depressed, as in this brief excerpt.

> **Dr. Murray:** You have been depressed for so long, and you've been through so much, it must seem a long haul. I am glad you have been good, you've followed your doctor's advice, and you seem still willing to try. When you are depressed, what is different?
>
> **Ms. Peterson:** Depression is a whole world: I am in a hole; all around me is dark. I can't make the smallest decision, so the simplest thing, like taking a shower, is horrible.
>
> **Dr. Murray:** Does it really seem darker or is that just a metaphor?
>
> **Ms. Peterson:** There is constant negative self-talk. There is no hope. I feel scared and overwhelmed.

After about twenty minutes, Dr. Murray ended the interview politely, accompanied Ms. Peterson to the door, and then led a discussion with the audience about the importance of continual efforts to adjust and modify the combination of drugs she was taking. This case was rela-tively uncomplicated. There were no perceptible disagreements among doctors about her diagnosis or about how to treat her depression. The patient, quietly and sweetly, offered her succinct and telling descrip-tions of the experience of depression without questioning her diagnosis or its treatment.

(2) I Thought I Was Normal When I Was Speedy

At a grand rounds event I attended later, the medical history presented by a resident went this way:

> Ms. Vincent is a forty-something-year-old African American woman, separated from her husband. She has a history of cocaine abuse and was admitted in a bipolar state. Her father was alcoholic, her sister was once admitted with hallucinations, and her brother may be a schizophrenic. All family members are [drug] abusers and there is a family history of suicide. . . . Her work has included being a model and working for a design agency. She was a business manager at one point and she is a college graduate.

She has a six-year-old child who is now in Texas protective services. Ms. Vincent was jailed for second-degree manslaughter (a man beat her and she killed him to defend herself), so the child was put in foster care.

In 1998 she was diagnosed as bipolar by Health Care for the Homeless. At age eleven she was hypomanic; at age sixteen she had postpartum depression. She has a long history with many episodes. (You wonder why they didn't notice that she has this bright energy! It is a driven kind of energy.)

She had peculiar hallucinations. She saw herself jump in front of a train. Once before she had seen herself jump out of a window. She admitted herself to the Wellingtown inpatient ward and was given Zyprexa and lithium. She was very cooperative. She tended to be depressed in the morning and revved up in the evening. She was then discharged to the Wellingtown day hospital [a clinic that patients visit daily without overnight stays] but seemed downcast, and under that downcast mood was animation. She felt ugly inside, like she must have done something wrong. She has a fear of the dark and agoraphobia and she understands that she has a mood disorder. Because the Zyprexa caused side effects that bothered her, it was discontinued. Effexor was begun instead and lithium was continued. She was still depressed, but on Effexor she has had only one day of hypomania. She has gotten gradually more depressed and she is fearful of being hurt. They have now raised her dose and today she is somewhat hypomanic. She has been completely reliable in coming into the day hospital. Even on the snow day when the hospital was closed, she showed up, and she was the only patient to do so. Her goal is to get back to Texas and get her daughter back.

Dr. Murray summarized this as "a case of chronic and refractory illness." Ms. Vincent, a tall and solidly built woman, stately and dignified, was then ushered in. She was the only African American person in the room. Dr. Murray sat in a chair turned slightly toward her and began.

Dr. Murray: How are you feeling today?
Ms. Vincent: Speedy, high.
Dr. Murray: Is it pleasant?

Ms. Vincent: No.

Dr. Murray: What is speeding? Your thoughts? Your actions?

Ms. Vincent: My hand movements and all are fast. I can't keep still.

Dr. Murray: Do you feel bad about yourself?

Ms. Vincent: No.

Dr. Murray: Are you depressed?

Ms. Vincent: I don't feel suicidal, I feel real sad.

Dr. Murray: Is it worse than being speedy?

Ms. Vincent: It scares me.

Dr. Murray: Why?

Ms. Vincent: I can't control myself.

Dr. Murray: What is it like when you're well, when you're yourself?

Ms. Vincent: I don't know. I just found out I'm sick. I thought I was normal when I was speedy.

Dr. Murray: Did you see in the hospital that you were different?

Ms. Vincent: I saw the difference.

Dr. Murray: Did the medications help?

Ms. Vincent: Until they found out the medications have to keep changing. I just want the medications to make me normal, and to make me not be depressed.

Dr. Murray: How long has it been since you were on an even keel?

Ms. Vincent: I cannot remember.

Dr. Murray: Does this upset your estimation of yourself? There must have been times when you were on an even keel and you felt okay. When were those?

Ms. Vincent: In 1995 and 1996 in Texas, but I was speeding all the time.

Dr. Murray: It would be a problem to decide when your ability was normal. You're a bright and lively person, but we wouldn't want to confuse that with being speedy. Can you remember times when you were doing OK? When you could keep a job? When you could control yourself? What kind of state is it when you can go to work?

Ms. Vincent: I am responsible even when speeding. So as I said I thought this was normal.

Dr. Murray: A lot of people go pretty fast! What is your state now?

Ms. Vincent: I'm speeding but normal.

Dr. Murray: So too much speeding gets to be abnormal? How was your weekend?

Ms. Vincent: It was a good one. I was with friends and I slept over with them.

Dr. Murray: I understand they raised your medications some.

Ms. Vincent: Because I had hallucinations. I was in my third-floor apartment and I saw myself going up to the window. I was wide awake. It was like my body left me. I came to the hospital, but I was scared of it and of the security guards.

Dr. Murray: Are you convinced to take your medications?

Ms. Vincent: I'm not going to attempt suicide today.

Dr. Murray: I hope you don't ever do it.

Ms. Vincent: I have Prisoners' Aid, and they are helping with my medical, legal, and housing expenses. Psychological aid is part of the treatment.

Dr. Murray: Life—we are for it.

Dr. Murray thanked the patient and she went out of the room. Turning to the audience, he said, "*That* was an awkward interview. I think we could get some idea about her 'speediness.' She is quite a lively person, but she is dangerous to herself. She has experienced the disruption of a lifetime. You can see the deterioration of the person this illness brings out. It's not clear what she means by her 'normal' state and we have to work on this."

Of the fifty minutes devoted to grand rounds, the time given to detailing the patient's medical history is comparable to or even exceeds the time given to interviewing the patient. The history frames the interview, both questions and responses. Within this frame, the interview is intended to bring out the experiential aspects of the illness. The patient is there to tell the audience "what it is like" to be depressed or manic. But the setting of grand rounds is no doubt intimidating for the patient. The auditorium has seats for hundreds of people, arranged in steeply tiered rows that look down on the stage. Often, the gender and/or race of the patients (many of whom are African American because the hospital's cachement area is an African American neighborhood) place them at an additional disadvantage vis-à-vis the audience and interviewer (almost all of whom are white). In this hierarchical setting, patients may elaborate on their experiences, but they are not likely to question how doctors apply the categories of illness themselves. It is remarkable that even hints of questioning appeared in these events, such as Ms. Vincent's effort to say that she regarded her "speeding" as normal, and only her depression as in need of treatment. Dr. Murray preferred to have her see her "speeding" as abnormal, and in need of increased medication.

In the teaching event called clinical rounds, the physical layout is certainly less intimidating than the one in grand rounds: the room is the size of a large living room and the chairs are arranged informally in a circle. Below I describe six cases presented in clinical rounds during my fieldwork, which will illustrate interactions between doctors and patients that involve considerable ambiguity and contestation.

(3) What Is the Diagnosis?

A resident presented the first case, which serves to illustrate the complex social, physical, and emotional conditions that bring people to this tertiary care hospital in the inner city.

> Ms. Simmons is a thirty-two-year-old unmarried African American female who works as a paralegal. She has audio hallucinations and difficulty thinking clearly. In her family history, her father was manic depressive and he was a murder victim. Her mother was depressed. Her brother died of cerebral hemorrhage. Two other maternal relatives were schizophrenic. She experienced sexual abuse from ages seven to fourteen from her cousins. Her sexual preference is homosexual. Her religion—she mentioned Buddhism.
>
> In her medical history, she has asthma and is a chronic steroid user. She has an inherited condition that involves a seizure disorder. As for medications, she is now on Depakote and Mellaril, but she has been on many others—she has tried them all. In her psychiatric history, she has had twenty-five admissions. In kindergarten she was diagnosed

with ADHD and given Ritalin. At age seventeen she entered Jackson Hospital [pseudonym for a local residential psychiatric hospital].

As far as her previous diagnosis goes, there has been much debate over whether she has Bipolar 2 or schizoaffective disorder. For a time, she had trouble with paraphilias [nontypical sexual interests] involving kids aged two to five. [Dr. Dean: Did she act on them?] Apparently not, they were just fantasies. She did take Depo-Provera. She has had bulimia, and there is also a possible borderline diagnosis. She has done some self-injury. She has had many suicidal gestures, and has been given over fifty ECTs. Drugs she has taken include Haldol, Mellaril, Risperdal, and Depakote.

For the last two months she has expressed fear of the outside. She can't go to the supermarket and she fears people are laughing at her. She thought her coworkers would call her names if she went to work. During this time she also experienced less need for sleep and racing thoughts. She quit her job and then began to have delusions about her uncle and grandmother, with whom she lived. She thought they were involved in witchcraft and were plotting against her because of their homophobia.

We stopped the Mellaril and with this change in medication she looks much better. [This opens a door into a disagreement among the staff about the patient's condition. Dr. Morrison breaks in: Yes, but what is the real reason she looks better? The real reason is she wants to go home. Her motivation is strong to look good enough to get out because she does not like to be in hospital, once she gets in. She spent a long time in Jackson Hospital when she was younger. She has said she has to be home to pay the rent, even though it is clear she could mail the check. The only possibility she admits is that she must be there physically to do it.]

At this point, Ms. Simmons was accompanied into the room. She wore a short Afro and a casual T-shirt and jeans. Her manner was subdued but she was responsive to Dr. Dean's gentle but persistent questions. After thanking her and explaining that the group is made up of students and researchers interested in understanding what her experiences are like so that they can develop improved treatments, the interview began.

Dr. Dean: What brought you in?

Ms. Simmons: I couldn't go out even to get to the grocery store. At work I got the sense the others were talking about me. It is a law office, legal aid. They talked about everyone else, and they were also talking and laughing about me.

Dr. Dean: Are things looking better now that you are here?

Ms. Simmons: Yes, I got back my sense of "why would they be talking about me?" But I also hear the voices of my cousins.

Dr. Dean: Where are the voices?

Ms. Simmons: They are my own thoughts.

Dr. Dean: Where are they?—Here? There? Up? Down?

Ms. Simmons: They are mine but it is Andrew [her cousin]! It is this insidious giggling. I have had a fear of dying, I feel sure I am going to die. But I am not suicidal. My depression is I can't get going. To talk is hard, the worst. If I could go to work and there would not have to be any talking, that would be ideal. If I take antidepressants, they make me manic, irritable, and angry to the point of violence. I can't be around people.

Dr. Dean: Why did you choose to come to Wellingtown Hospital?

Ms. Simmons: I knew you used the new medicines.

Dr. Dean ended the interview here, expressed the group's appreciation, and walked her to the door. Turning to the group, he led us through the intricacies of diagnosis.

Dr. Dean: How do we know she is not just shy and introverted? The voices—are they hallucinations?

Student: Not as Jaspers describes it.

Dr. Dean tried to help the student recall exactly what Karl Jaspers, whose classic early twentieth-century accounts of abnormal psychic phenomena are required reading for students in the department, had written.

Dr. Dean: A true hallucination is a perception without a stimulus. But she describes the voices as being among her thoughts. Jaspers has two lists, each with six questions—can you recall them?

Student: Someone help me out here!

Dr. Dean: Jaspers says if an experience is not a perceptual experience then it is just thought. We have expressions for this: my conscience was talking to me; I saw it in my mind's eye.

The difference between image and perception is that you can locate a perception in space and it has properties like clarity. You can't be persuaded it is not there. Jaspers calls this indubitability. It is also important whether the phenomenon is received passively or actively. If passively, it is an object independent of our will; if actively, you have to do something to conjure it up. She gave a mixed description just now. [To the students:] *You* try to see which it is most like.

Jaspers also defines "pseudo hallucinations," which are inside your head. Outside your head in external objective space is "real." Ms. Simmons knows this lingo and so says the voices come to her through her ears, but when asked, she cannot locate them in space. People say that on medication, the voices get farther away, less clear, or they go inside the head. She has pseudo hallucinations or vivid images. Her feeling of being criticized is typical of depression.

What is at issue here is teaching medical students to distinguish the defining characteristics of psychiatric conditions, such as true versus pseudo hallucinations. Dr. Dean led them to see that Ms. Simmons's hallucinations were "pseudo hallucinations," which lent credence to the diagnosis of manic depression and cast doubt on another diagnosis such as schizophrenia. Her fear of others talking about her was laid at the feet of her depression, adding further credence to the manic-depressive diagnosis rather than something like paranoid psychosis. Ms. Simmons described her experience, but when what she said was inconsistent with Jaspers's categories, her description was discounted. Partly as a result, she came across as a difficult and manipulative patient, wanting the latest medications Wellingtown Hospital had to offer, but not willing to stay long enough to be treated properly. Taking all the episodes of her hospitalization into account, some of the doctors concluded that she deliberately tried to sound more psychotic than she really was in order to merit serious medical attention.

(4) Who Is Manic?

Dr. Morrison, wearing a bow tie as usual, presided while a resident presented the patient.

> We have Mr. Czermanski, a twenty-eight-year-old Slavic male with no psychiatric history. He comes from the state of Moldovia, which is part of the former Soviet Union. He worked as a librarian there, and had incidents of verbal aggression. He and his wife are living in Ronald McDonald house in Baltimore while their three-year-old undergoes a spinal fusion. The daughter is in a body cast. He has no medical or psychiatric history. One month ago he became religious and began to have revelations. He was getting messages from the television and saw films in his head. He had ideas about suicide but said he would not act on them because of his wife and child. He shows pressured speech, he is irritable, and he had a delusion that he was a psychoanalyst. On admission, he was tangential in speech, had loose associations, and was hard to follow. He is not very willing to take meds.

Dr. Morrison said Mr. Czermanski's wife might be coming in with him, and he arranged a second chair for her. They entered together, both young, lithe, and thin, with broad faces and open, interested expressions. After Mr. Czermanski sat down, he immediately shook his head, pointing to his mouth. His wife explained in articulate English that his tongue was swollen, and thus he couldn't talk very well.

> **Dr. Morrison:** But just this morning it was OK—when did this happen?
> **Mrs. Czermanski:** This afternoon.
> **Dr. Morrison:** We will look into that.
> **Mrs. Czermanski:** Back in Moldavia, he had a kind of conversion experience, where he saw a lot of ethical issues clearly, and I liked this, because he was thinking just as I did about a lot of issues. Then when he was here for our daughter's operation, he was not making sense. Since starting the Zyprexa, only yesterday, he is improved I think. He does make more sense today.
> **Dr. Morrison:** Mr. Czermanski, what do you hope to get out of being here?

Mr. Czermanski: Your bow tie! I want *all* your bow ties. [Laughter.]
Dr. Morrison: What do you think is wrong? Why would you say you are here?
Mr. Czermanski: I don't know.
Dr. Morrison: Have you heard of mania? Do you think you have mania?
Mr. Czermanski: *You* have mania! You have bow tie mania!!

Shortly, in the wake of the group's laughter over this remark (in which he sheepishly joined), Dr. Morrison turned his attention to Mr. Czermanski's swollen tongue and decided he needed to be accompanied out to the clinic to be treated for it. Perhaps because of his foreign nationality, his educated and professional status, or his exuberant mania, Mr. Czermanski managed, if only briefly and humorously, to turn the tables between the diagnoser and the diagnosed. Mr. Czermanski entered the room in the midst of a manic episode with a probable diagnosis of bipolar disorder. Part of being in such a state is being out of touch with reality, exaggerating one's abilities and one's importance. That is, the person is not aware of reality, including his own mania. But Mr. Czermanski startles the group into laughter because he shows he is aware of reality, including the reality that his doctor, the diagnostician of his mania, so frequently wears jaunty bow ties that he could be said to have a mania for them. When Mr. Czermanski turned the tables, he did not reverse the power relations between doctor and patient: these were left intact, as Dr. Morrison made clear by sending Mr. Czermanski out to the clinic. What Mr. Czermanski did was capture Dr. Morrison in the ordinary rules of the social game: faced with the presence of the audience, who implicitly understood the etiquette of the situation, he had to laugh at the joke or show himself to be a person with no sense of humor.[6]

(5) What Is Bipolar 2b?

Dr. Lerner presiding, a resident presents the case.

Mr. Lawrence is a twenty-one-year-old single African American male. He has been irritable and volatile. In his family history his mother is bipolar; he had a paternal uncle with bipolar who committed suicide and an aunt who committed suicide. He was born at full term and met his milestones. He comes from a poor family: his parents are divorced and after they separated he stayed with his father. He went to public school, and was in the gifted and talented program. In school he got into fistfights, had difficulty holding down jobs, and difficulty following rules because he felt otherwise he would become a conformist. Past medications include lithium, Prozac, and Celexa. He is now on Depakote and Zoloft, with a trial of Prozac.

He reports getting messages from the television, and that someone understands him and is talking to him directly through the television. He is not keen on mood stability or management and he is not very compliant. But he definitely wanted the ECT he was given in the past. He has had eleven ECT courses so far, ten unilateral, one bilateral.

He tends to spend six months up and six down, manic and then depressed, and he says he is a different person in each period. Not long ago, he believed the world would end, but he made no plans. When asked, "What is missing?" he said, "My soul." When asked, "Why don't you take your meds?" He replied, "I would miss my hypomanic states." He has a lot of "push to speak," and some delusions, such as believing the year 1999 really signifies the satanic number 666.

At this point, the patient, Mr. Lawrence, a slim, neatly dressed, very alert young man, came in. There were the usual introductions, explanations, and thanks. Dr. Lerner asked him open-ended questions about what it was like to be depressed or manic. He described his depression at length, and then, in the following excerpt, his mania.

Mr. Lawrence: When you are hypomanic, it is the greatest feeling in the world. It is all about brain chemistry. Cocaine gives you a high by changing the chemistry in the brain, but mine changes by itself. I describe myself as Mr. Hookup because I know how to get freebies.
Dr. Lerner: Are you very persuasive?
Mr. Lawrence: Yes, I can sell anything, I worked in sales, I sold vacuum cleaners, and I mess with a lot of women.

Dr. Lerner: You told your psychiatrist you had periods of greatness, when you can do no wrong?

Mr. Lawrence: Yes.

Dr. Lerner: Did someone tell you that you were bipolar?

Mr. Lawrence: No one said I was bipolar. I started reading books myself, like Kay Jamison's. I also read *Moodswing*. It hit so on the point, I diagnosed myself: I am Bipolar 2b. It is hard to deal with jobs, when the whole world is nothing but consistency and you are not.

The group then suddenly realized the hour was almost up and that this discussion had gone on much longer than the usual half hour or so. Dr. Lerner thanked the patient with feeling and assured him the group would try hard to shed more light on his treatment. When the patient had left, the group began a hurried discussion with many simultaneous remarks.

Dr. Lerner: Is he Bipolar 1 or 2? Are there psychotic beliefs?

A second psychiatrist: Is he really depressed? He loved mania so much. . . .

A third psychiatrist: I think he has hyperthymic temperament, it is hard driving and it fits him. He gives such a good description of depression. But because he has this up quality, it does produce a little cognitive dissonance.

Student: What is Bipolar 2b anyway?

The rounds ended on this question, confused and unresolved, as students rushed out of the room for their next class. I was confused, too, until I looked it up and discovered that actually there is no category Bipolar 2b in the DSM-IV. Usually in rounds, the patient is asked about his or her experiences and the doctors discuss the correct diagnosis after the patient goes out. Here the patient described his own experiences as usual, but then went on to diagnose himself using the DSM. He even elaborated the categories in the book to produce a new subcategory and thus extended the rational order of the classification system. This event upset the usual role of diagnosis as a "ritual of disclosure" and so left the group in some disarray. Ordinarily, the occasion of diagnosis would legitimate the physicians' and medical system's authority because scientific knowledge and technology would disclose the hidden cause of illness.[7] Here the ritual was derailed. The group lost its usual focus and organization during this rounds, something that is all the more remarkable in light of the hierarchy that was palpable, in this case, between the mostly white doctors and medical students employed or enrolled in this prestigious medical center and an African American man, living without the benefit of many resources, in the same city.

(6) I Ain't Gonna Mess with It Backwards

Resident: Ms. Miller is a sixty-two-year-old married African American woman. She was admitted one month ago with bipolar disorder, sent to the day hospital, and then she was readmitted here. Her father and mother are deceased from heart attacks, but neither had mental illness. Her niece is schizophrenic. She grew up in Baltimore in a poor family and she is now on disability [Social Security Disability Insurance (SSDI)] because of mental illness. She was recently married. There are some indications the husband is abusive. She has two kids, one of whom died by suicide. She is a Jehovah's Witness, very involved in her religion. There has been some alcohol abuse in the past. [Here the resident describes her many hospitalizations.]

In June 2000 she had a psychotic episode. She was paranoid, religiously grandiose, very talkative, agitated, and manic. Then she was begun on Zyprexa and lithium.

In the day hospital this time she was delirious and manic. It was hard to treat all this as an outpatient, so readmission was recommended. On readmission, she had formal thought disorder. Asked what year it was, she said, "The fourth." But it was the fourth of the month.

We thought the delirium was from the lithium or drug interaction. So we stopped all but the Zyprexa. She refused an EEG [electroencephalogram] because she said it would mess up her hair and her brain. This case is interesting because of the various competing categories: manic depression versus schizophrenia and mania versus delirium.

At this point Ms. Miller was escorted into the room. She was dressed in a neat blue sweat suit and running shoes. Her long, braided hair hung straight down, all but covering her eyes. Dr. Dean thanked her for coming and explained that the group wanted to learn from patients and hoped to improve treatment of her condition.

Ms. Miller: I didn't want to come.

Dr. Dean: How do you feel?

Ms. Miller: Fine.

Dr. Dean: Not confused?

Ms. Miller: No, my normal self.

Dr. Dean: Do you drink?

Ms. Miller: Only in moderation.

Dr. Dean: Do you want to go home?

Ms. Miller: I sure would. I am not good with crowds of people, like here.

Dr. Dean: You are active in Jehovah's Witness, and there are crowds there, right?

Ms. Miller: Yes, I was able to accept those crowds. I was born out in field service, so my best spot is on the corner.

Dr. Dean: How is your temperament, your mood? Are you pretty even-keeled?

Ms. Miller: I am moody today. My moods are a little off. I am not sad, I *put* myself in a happy mood.

Dr. Dean: What have you been doing?

Ms. Miller: OT [occupational therapy]. It is terrible! Oh!! [seeing the OT therapist in the room] I didn't see you sitting over there.

Dr. Dean: I am going to name three things: baseball, airplane, cactus. Can you remember?

Ms. Miller: Baseball . . . I can't do the other two.

Dr. Dean: Can you spell "cloud"?

Ms. Miller: I'm not good at spelling.

Dr. Dean: Try.

Ms. Miller: "C, L, O, D."

Dr. Dean: That's "clod." Try "cloud."

Ms. Miller: No.

Dr. Dean: Can you spell it backwards?

Ms. Miller: I ain't gonna mess with it backwards.

Dr. Dean: Just try.

Ms. Miller: You better figure it out for yourself then.

Dr. Dean: Can you recall the three items?

Ms. Miller: No.

Dr. Dean: Can you recall them?

Ms. Miller: No.

Dr. Dean: You have been in treatment for some thirty years?

Ms. Miller: Yes, the first breakdown was terrible. I was real upset. I didn't get no good treatment, they brought me to the seclusion room and pinned me to the mat. It was not explained to me what it was all about. I just wanted to talk to my husband first.

At this time, the floor was opened to questions from others.

Dr. Murray: Are you enthused about Jehovah today?

Ms. Miller: I am not doing that no more.

Dr. Murray: How many times a day do you pray?

Ms. Miller: That's an interesting question. About three times.

Dr. Murray: Do you do any food rituals?

Ms. Miller: No.

Dr. Murray: How are you feeling now?

Ms. Miller: Lively.

Dr. Murray: How is your thinking? Clear?

Ms. Miller: To me it is.

The interview ended at this point, and, after Dr. Dean thanked Ms. Miller and a student accompanied her out, the discussion continued.

Dr. Neal: At her 1992 admission she was off the wall. She invoked Jehovah, would not eat, was paranoid about the food, and finally she had to be put in the quiet room. She was pacing the halls and frequently up during the night.

Resident presenting the case earlier, who wears a yarmulke: The extent of her praying would not be unusual even among the people I associate with, who practice Judaism.

Dr. Dean: Is she trying to put her mania under a bushel to get discharged?

The students were asked to distinguish disorientation from attention. Disorientation involves being delirious, whereas lack of attention involves memory. The group decides that she was not disoriented but did have trouble recalling things, even though she could pay attention to some extent.

Of the many countervailing currents in this event, I will mention only a few. On one side lies the legitimacy of religious practice, which is often at odds with the routines of daily life; on the other lies the worry that her religious practices line up with other extreme aspects of her behavior to indicate a serious psychological condition. On one side is her feeling that previous treatment was not explained to her and she felt coerced (together with her preference not to be at this event at all); on the other is the staff's concern that she was subdued because she was out of control and that being presented at rounds might lead to some new ideas about how to treat her. On the one side is her resistance to taking a test based on schoolroom activities, knowing that her mental state will be assessed on the basis of it; on the other is the doctors' need to find out if her thought process is disordered so they can recommend appropriate medication. What is at stake here, among other things, is which side of the DSM distinction between cognitive and emotional disorder she belongs on, or where in between. The rounds presentation is a moment in an ongoing discussion among the staff about whether she is manic depressive (and so best treated with lithium, as well as an antipsychotic like Zyprexa), schizophrenic (and best treated with an antipsychotic alone), or, alternatively, whether her psychosis was caused by the combination of drugs she had been taking on admission.

(7) Maybe He Is a Normal Variant

Resident: Mr. Anderson is an economics professor at a university in a nearby state. He is Bipolar 1, not presently controlled by medication. He is a rapid cycler. He is married, but it is a conflicted marriage, and his wife is narcissistic and whiny. He was on lithium for twenty years and did well. Then he got renal insufficiency, evidently from the lithium, and was told by his nephrologist to go off the lithium. Then he was all over the place. He was sexually inappropriate with students at a party while drinking, and experienced a general decrease of his social inhibitions. He has tried Depakote, Neurontin, Seroquel, and Tegretol.

His teaching became poor, he was nasty in class, and he pushed at the desk in anger, which students found intimidating. He would break into song in the middle of lecturing (and he teaches one of the core courses). There were student complaints. As of this January, he was relieved of his teaching duties. He is a renowned economist, and he has written textbooks. When he was up, he experienced higher spending than usual, low impulsivity, irritability, and pressured speech. When he was down, he needed increased sleep and he experienced anhedonia. The cycles were every four to five months to hourly.

Mr. Anderson came in, looking drawn and gray, with a shaggy beard. Wearing a casual plaid shirt, jeans, and a cardigan, he walked with a shambling, erratic gait and jerky limbs.

Dr. Dean: How are you doing today?
Mr. Anderson: I am where I want to be—I am getting better so I can function in a productive way. I went off lithium in 1996. Since then, things have been erratic, I have had trouble sleeping, I've been waking early and feeling irritable, talking fast, with slurred speech; I've been making mistakes, getting mixed up at the blackboard, but I have great energy and I think I am superman. I am committing myself to grand research projects and big research problems.

My department upgraded the curriculum, and this put my courses out of date. My math is not good enough to handle the newer techniques, and this causes me great anxiety. One of the students complained I put a question on the exam I myself had not been able to answer during class, but I thought that was OK, that students should figure things out for themselves. This happened when I was manic. When I am depressed, I sleep a lot, and come to class unprepared. I talk slowly and I don't meet my duties.

Dr. Dean: Do you feel normal?

Mr. Anderson: No, not since stopping the lithium. Since being off the lithium, I would say I have been more manic.

Dr. Dean: Do you have any delusions?

Mr. Anderson: That I am competent to do what I can't, to work with mathematical models I don't have training for. I put articles on the syllabus I don't understand.

Dr. Dean: This is not a delusion, but overconfidence. What is the worst thing about the depressions?

Mr. Anderson: When I got the letter from the department saying I was out of the classroom. I had lost my job, and was really down.

Dr. Dean: Do you experience rapid cycling?

[Mr. Anderson describes in some detail the variation in the lengths of his moods.]

Dr. Dean: Do you go through a normal state there for a minute in between?

Mr. Anderson: That would be the smallest time, and it is the only time I feel normal.

Dr. Dean: Can you bring the moods on? Can you change your mood?

Mr. Anderson launched into a long and involved but coherent narrative about his experiences working in industry and his decision to move to academia. Dr. Dean tried unsuccessfully to interrupt him a couple of times. After the interview ended, Dr. Dean turned to the group.

Dr. Dean: Was this an easy diagnosis to make? [The first two students he called on hesitated and could offer no answers.] We need some help for our friends here. How would we describe his speech? What is pressured speech?

Student: The person can't get the words out?

Dr. Dean: No, it is the opposite, you cannot interrupt. You can't get a word in. He qualifies. He goes off on tangents and doesn't answer the question. You could use the word "circumlocution" if he eventually gets back, but I despaired of him ever getting back several times.

Is it a thought disorder? We look at his syntax and semantics. Is the syntax loose, is he distracted? And his semantics—is he appropriate?

Students had trouble answering these questions, but Dr. Dean summed up the consensus that Mr. Anderson did not have thought disorder.

Dr. Dean: Maybe he is a normal variant. His condition is especially common among professors. This is a gray zone.

Dr. Jones: It is not clear-cut. His pattern is not at all uncommon, especially among writers and artists.

In this case, since several criteria of schizophrenia or schizoaffective disorder were lacking (delusions and thought disorders), the physicians in the room focused on the diagnosis of bipolar disorder. Since he had many positive signs of manic depression, the treatment recommended at the end of rounds was restarting a low dose of lithium, in hopes that the renal problems would not recur. Nonetheless, Mr. Anderson was placed in a "gray zone" between mental illness and mental health, perhaps because the doctors identified with the patient and his brilliant youth, followed by his faltering middle age. His moodiness, his occasional overreaching of his knowledge, and his travails moving between academia and industry might have been all too familiar. A certain generosity might also have been flowing from Mr. Anderson's gratitude for the medical treatment he received at Wellingtown Hospital and his open expression of insight into the pathological features of his condition.

(8) I'm a Twenty-Year-Old College Student with a 3.75 GPA and I Am Not Crazy

Dr. Paulson presiding, a resident presents the case.

This is a twenty-year-old African American male admitted in the emergency room at Riverside Hospital [pseudonym for a recently built medical complex in Baltimore] with a strong suicidal gesture: he said he wanted to blow off his head with a gun, and he actually did have a gun. He grew up in Newark, where his parents were drug dealers and users. He had a pattern of working at a lot of jobs, at times five at once. He has been in jail, once for a number of years, and he is a college student. His personal history: he was born by C-section, drank bleach at eight months of age and was hospitalized then. Life was poor and chaotic, but he stood out. He was outgoing like all the kids, but he was sensitive, and he would stay inside and study. Assiduous and studious, he did very well at school. But he did get into fights, from age fourteen on, and was jailed for fighting several times. Two years ago he was admitted to State College, in the business program. He kept very busy, often staying up until 2 a.m., during his first year. Now he is home for the summer and has a summer job as an intern at an investment bank, the first job of any substance he has ever had.

One week before admission, he had a dose of Angel Dust [PCP]: unknown to him it was in the marijuana he smoked. In college for the first two years he was on the dean's list. Then there was a downturn because he felt his family didn't visit him and therefore must not love him. After that he only got Cs. He has also been anxious and overactive. He would try to do ten things at once.

Last Tuesday, his family saw an abrupt change. He was very tearful, very labile, and paranoid. He thought the neighbors were going to kill him so he bought a pistol and kept it nearby. (As an aside: this is part of his reality—people do get killed in his neighborhood.) The family called him crazy. He came to Baltimore to see a friend, and at that point he bought *another* gun. Frightened, he called 911 himself. He came into the Riverside emergency room out of control. At one point he ran out naked, and he was then put into the seclusion room. He showed rapid speech, tangential speech; he was labile, tearful, and grandiose. He talked about how he would be rich, a famous rap star. He heard God's voice.

On admission here, I saw someone who was clearly manic. I assessed him as a twenty-year-old with underlying illness who had become floridly manic with all these stressors. Complaining of pain, he was examined and diagnosed with severe testicular torsion, and so he had to have a testicle removed. Now he is close to normal, but he is still intrusive—you can't interrupt him. The reason we brought him in here is to get help with whether his condition is PCP-induced or caused by an underlying illness.

Mr. Burton came in, accompanied by his mother and grandmother. As he entered the room, he looked around at all the people sitting there in white coats, and said, "Hello, I am Keith Burton." Sitting down, mother on one side and grandmother on the other, he said, "I'm a twenty-year-old college student with a 3.75 GPA and I am not crazy." Without missing a beat, Dr. Paulson began the interview.

Dr. Paulson: How are you feeling today?

Mr. Burton: Great.

Dr. Paulson: How did it happen that you called 911?

Mr. Burton: I loved my family and I missed them in Florida, so I came back north. After I got here, my grandmother kicked me out. She said I was crazy to drop out of college, so I told her next time you speak to me I will be calling from a mental institution.

Dr. Paulson: Do you remember the question I just asked you?

Mr. Burton: I came to Baltimore, saw my friend, and called 911 emergency. They took me to Riverside Hospital where they injected me with three needles, because they said I had to be calmed down, but I was terrified, I didn't know what it was.

Dr. Paulson: Were you scared?

Mr. Burton: No, it was really that I was terrified. I wanted to call my mother, because no one even knew where I was, and I didn't know what the needle was. Now I have needle marks all over and I don't even shoot drugs. After the fourth needle, I again wanted to call my mother and father, but they wouldn't let me, so I ran. I was terrified. They called security on me, restrained me. But I still got shot. Now I am back to my old self.

Dr. Paulson: Is anything not quite back?

Mr. Burton: Well, my testicle is gone. But I feel great, great.

Dr. Paulson: How is your energy?

Mr. Burton: Great, I have like an extra little boost.

Dr. Paulson: What's that like?

Mr. Burton: I have more insight now. My mind goes faster than I can articulate it. That Riverside Hospital, I will never go back there again.

Dr. Paulson: How do you feel about your self?

Mr. Burton: Great! My whole self has had a boost. I have a job at the bank, I am going to invest in Phillip Morris, quit my job, and just watch my stock rise. I took the job to learn stocks, and I have learned them in a month. The head of the company says just invest in this stock, you will see. Like you were asking me if I remember the question you asked me, of course I remembered it, I just had to start back a little bit so I could make it clear.

Dr. Paulson: So you are feeling pretty good?

Mr. Burton: My future's so bright you gotta wear shades!

Dr. Paulson: When else do you feel like this?

Mr. Burton: When I come home from college to my family. I am so happy to see my mother, grandmother. [He gives them each a hug and a kiss.]

Dr. Paulson: So last semester you lost interest in school?

Mr. Burton: During Christmas break I didn't want to leave, I cried when I left. I should have known it was wrong to leave.

Dr. Paulson: How were you sleeping?

Mr. Burton: I was up early, and then later I would take a nap, then do homework. I would go to bed at 1 or 2 a.m.

Dr. Paulson: Eating?

Mr. Burton: I eat five meals a day.

Dr. Paulson: Were you eating less or more than usual?

Mr. Burton: I eat five meals a day, and of course I have to work out.

Dr. Paulson: What about your thoughts about the gun? Did you ever have those thoughts before?

Mr. Burton: I could have hurt myself a long time ago.

Dr. Paulson: Did you have those thoughts before?

Mr. Burton: No, it was the PCP. When I was younger, the worst part was not having control. It was pretty decent, except for not having my father living with me. My mother is chemically dependent. I am going to make sure she stays sober. I was the oldest, and when my mom was on a mission, that is what I call it when she goes after drugs, I was in charge of the kids, five or six of them, all these kids, feeding them, dressing them, getting them ready for school. The social services finally took all of us.

Dr. Paulson asked the mother and grandmother whether he seemed normal. They said, "He has all this stress on him. He had too much responsibility as a child. With all that he had on his head when he was younger, then he gets to college and it is overload."

The interview came to a close, and Mr. Burton went around the room on his way out, making eye contact and shaking hands with each one of us, saying, "I have never seen so many doctors in one place in my life."

Dr. Paulson began the discussion: "His speech was tangential and circumstantial. I think he would have gone on and on if I had not redirected." Turning to the medical students, he asked, "Was he manic?"

> **A medical student:** He was overly dramatic, making himself known to us like that.
> **A second medical student:** Also making such a point of kissing his mother and grandmother.
> **A third medical student:** But he did have pressured speech.
> **Dr. Paulson:** Does he have manic syndrome?
> **Another medical student:** He seemed contrived.
> At this Dr. Jones interjected: He had a gun!
> **Dr. Paulson:** Let's see, are there any other students here . . . how about you?
> **An occupational health student:** I am in occupational health.
> **Dr. Paulson:** That counts! What do you see? Was he manic?
> **Occupational health student:** I know how he feels, he worries about grades and the rest of college, he is homesick, and with all that stress on him.

No one responded directly to this, so Dr. Paulson summarized, "I think he has bipolar disorder."

In striking contrast to Mr. Anderson, Keith Burton did not end up in an unclear gray zone as a "normal variant," a person whose behavior is typical of creative researchers, writers, and artists. In Keith's rounds, a set of life categories met a set of medical categories head on. Mr. Burton and his family wanted recognition of his difficult childhood and the responsibilities he had had to bear early on, his intelligence and success in college, his promising job, and his love for his family. His "craziness" consisted in his leaving college out of stress and homesickness. All these issues are contained to a greater or lesser extent in the resident's initial presentation, which makes the important point that the medical case history and the patient's narrative do share common ground.

The medical students saw him as overly dramatic, contriving to demonstrate his affection toward his relatives and his collegial status with respect to the doctors. They saw a *performance* of mania, which meant to them that it was not legitimate. As I argued in chapter 2, a deliberate dramatic quality could be considered part of mania, but in this context, because of Keith's control over his performance, the students wanted to define his condition as less than mania, as ill faith, not illness. The occupational health student identified with his life as a college student far from home and saw a normal reaction to stress. The doctors looked past these descriptions and saw him as under stress, to be sure, but more important, they saw him clearly experiencing by turns suicidal depression and florid mania. Medication, which could be life-saving, would be required at all costs. One might say the medical students reacted to him as a peer, competitively; the occupational health student reacted to him as a peer, sympathetically; and the doctors reacted to him as a patient, one who, despite his denials, must be protected from the consequences of his extreme states. The professionalization of the students required, however, that they learned to think of Mr. Burton as a patient with an illness, if doing so would help him.

From the rounds physicians' point of view, there was agreement that Keith Burton's case and Mr. Anderson's were distinctly different, the one a clear case of bipolar disorder and the other in a gray area. I would not want to debate the medical wisdom of this distinction, but I do want to turn to some less obvious aspects of Mr. Burton's case that complicate his clear diagnosis. As I mentioned earlier, there were forces hovering around this rounds that brought to my mind the image of a ground-sea. The term "repression" comes to mind here, not only in the sense that Freud used it, referring to something internal to the psyche, but also in a social sense. For example, Keith's testicle—which caused him great pain and had to be surgically removed—was dramatically absent in rounds. As Keith says, it was missing: not only from his body but also from the conversation. Since there surely would be other contexts, equally social, where the profound loss of a testicle could be discussed, why was it not discussed in rounds?

To suggest an answer, I turn to Mr. Burton's physical gestures of affection toward his mother and grandmother. The doctors and medical students did not see this behavior as evidence of Keith's ability to function socially. Still less did they see his direct eye contact, firm handshake, and respectful personal greeting as a part of polite behavior for persons of substance in African American culture. Rather, his behavior clearly made them uncomfortable and provided evidence that Keith was "overly dramatic." These signs of affection were an intrusion into the effort to describe in medical terms what was wrong with Keith as an individual. But Keith broke out of the silence and away from the carefully controlled answers he was supposed to make to questions. A young black man who survived urban crime and drugs was now in college with a job headed for Wall Street, his future so bright he had to wear shades. The doctors, all white, might have been experiencing estrangement from his racial identity and his history, but they might also have been experiencing fear of his energy and power. He seemed to contain both too much life and too much death; his presence was disquieting.

Comparing Mr. Anderson and Mr. Burton, there were certainly legitimate medical reasons for giving Mr. Burton the unambiguous diagnosis of bipolar disorder: his posssession of guns not least among them. But the two cases shared elements, too. Both men struggled with mood as well as motivation. For both, motivation soared stratospherically and then faltered when self-doubt and depression struck. For both, mood cycles led to difficulty functioning well. (Recall that Mr. Anderson was relieved of his teaching duties.) Anticipating my discussion of the racialized dimensions of mania in chapter 9, the two men provide a hint of the strong connection between white identity and manic potency. Mr. Anderson can be seen as a successful (white) professor with foibles: his exuberance is overconfidence rather than mania. Mr. Burton can only be seen as a faltering (black) student: his exuberance can only be seen as manic in a disordered and "mentally ill" sense, not in an effective and powerful sense. The sharp lines we imagine separate the rational from the irrational produce a bind here: Mr. Anderson, being white, can be manic, potent, and rational at the same time; Mr. Burton, being black, can be manic, but in becoming manic he loses his potency and his "rationality." The disallowed combination is to be manic, powerful, and black all at once. This bind is not a product of medical categories alone, but of medical categories working in combination with cultural categories that define race in relation to human capacity in historically specific ways. Finally, I can return to Mr. Burton's lost testicle. This literal wound—no doubt a topic of fear and horror to all the men in the room—was evidently unspeakable. There is no way of knowing for sure, but it is possible that the silence over this loss, the quintessence of an emasculating loss, came about because this wound lay too close to the other forms of emasculation going on in rounds at the same time.

Subjection and Rationality

Speak as he might, Keith remains subjected to medical authority. In contemporary critical theory, "subjection" is a technical term, one that can help us understand Keith's position. As part of the process of becoming a person of a certain kind, one becomes subordinated to power while simultaneously becoming a "subject." For example, in philosopher Judith Butler's apt example, the announcement at a baby's birth, "It's a girl!" brings into being a subject who must, "to qualify and remain a viable subject," embody the norms of femininity by "citing" or performing social norms that are required as part of becoming a woman. The convention in Euro-American societies that a person is one of two genders means there are only two choices—it's a boy or it's a girl: other possibilities must be excluded. This powerful process is circular: in order to become a person who can act in the world, one must be granted a legitimate social position (say, that of a girl); one's actions, to be socially legitimate, must work to fulfill the norms of that social position (femininity).[8] Paradoxically, as Michel Foucault made clear, our existence as subjects, as agents, depends on the existence of discourses outside us over which we have no choice.[9] Norms *appear* to come from *outside*, pressing down upon and subordinating the subject, but in fact one can only become a subject with the capacity to act in the world through those very norms. A social norm operates *inside* the person where it "assumes a psychic form that constitutes the subject's self-identity."[10] The circle closes if a subject's enactment of a norm consolidates the norm's apparently unchangeable reality. The circle opens if the subject feels at odds with the norm and takes action to subvert it. "Subjectivity" involves both whatever places a person occupies in the system of categories the culture provides, and whatever senses of identity the person has about those places.

The case that concerns me, the designation of rationality or irrationality, is not necessarily raised for every person the way gender is. One does not announce at birth, "It's a rational human being!" But when one's rationality does become an issue, through one's own experience or the observations of others, the disciplines of psychiatry and biomedicine offer a set of categories of health and illness in terms of which a person can be described, for example, as "manic depressive." When this term was applied to me, I came to identify myself as "a manic-depressive person," thus incorporating the tenets of this knowledge inside myself. But the circularity between norms and subject formation that Butler and Foucault stress leads to an uneasy conclusion in the case of mental illness. Since the category manic depression denotes an irrational condition, I appear to be trapped in a circular process that robs me of the ability to be a subject at all: once I occupy the subject position of the irrational, my actions will always be interpreted as irrational, no matter how much I protest.

To understand such a trap ethnographically, we need accounts of social life that refer not only to language but also to actions, ideas, dreams, institutions, roles, objects, exchanges, memories, expressions, gestures, and a multitude of other socially inflected practices.[11] If we broaden and deepen the social contexts in which we explore subjectivity, we will discover gaps, slips, and sidelines similar to those Freud found in the psyche, famously calling their emanations "the psychopathology of everyday life." Being able to see such gaps is important because they contain places where subjection fails to hold. Butler acknowledges that because a person's enactment of a norm such as femininity never completely instantiates the norm itself, institutions and authorities must make repeated efforts to shore up the norm and strengthen its hold. Just as the gender norms are, in Butler's phrase, "haunted by their own inefficacy,"[12] I would argue that the rational norm is haunted by signs of incompleteness, inconsistency, and conflict.

We can describe social practices in such a way that these kinds of gaps and slippages take social rather than psychic form. Discursive psychology, an approach to the analysis of language in its social context, conceptualizes mental traits and dispositions as accomplishments that we achieve through social interaction. The argument is that we can understand psychological phenomena as brought about through social, linguistic activity instead of through private, inner processes within the individual. Accordingly, discursive psychologists argue that psychology should be based on the study of this outward activity rather than on hypothetical, and essentially unobservable, inner states.[13] The sociologist Avery Gordon has pointed to the important role of repressed, mysterious forces that have no obvious cause yet have great impact on social life. These forces could be seen not as inborn urges beyond or outside language but instead as a constitutive resource of language, the social facts we do not want to recognize pushing into awareness.[14] This would mean that dark, repressed forces in human life need not be hidden only in the psyche: they may be hidden within public social processes including language. Concealment could take place socially, through social interdictions against bringing certain social practices, identities, or roles together in the same context. Even the emergence of a particular subjectivity may be shaped by "certain absences, certain other enunciations that cannot or must not be expressed."[15] We might call this kind of concealment social rather than psychic repression. We might expect the interdictions involved to draw on common forms of social bias, for example on discrimination by race, sex, or class.

The sociolinguist Don Kulick provides a telling analysis of "social repression" as it works to produce gendered subjectivities. Kulick argues that sexual subject positions are crucially structured by "enunciations that cannot or must not be expressed."[16] A person who is socially a "'heterosexual woman' is supposed to say 'no' [to male desire for sex]—this is part of what produces a *female sexual subject*. A person who is socially a 'heterosexual man' is supposed to *not* say 'no' [to female desire for sex]—this is what produces a *male sexual subject*."[17] When a "gay man" approaches a "straight man" with a request for sex, the "straight man" is placed in a position he often feels to be intolerable. Having elicited the gay man's desire puts him in an impossible position. If he says "yes" he will be in the subject position of a gay man; if he says "no" he will be in the subject position of a woman. When a straight man feels degraded by being forced into the subject position of either a gay man or a woman, that is when violence often breaks out against the gay man. These various subjectivities—gay, straight, man, woman—are shaped by social rules that prevent particular behaviors from being brought together.[18]

The case Kulick analyzes is quite different from rounds, because saying "no" to the categories of the doctors (though the speaker may wish otherwise) is *not* part of a system of "nos" (as in the case of Kulick's analysis) that people actively use to produce the subjectivity they desire. On the contrary, saying "no" to a medical diagnosis is often taken by doctors to indicate that the speaker is "mentally ill." Indeed studies in psychiatry explicitly regard "poor insight," defined as disagreeing with the psychiatric diagnosis one is given, as diagnostic of mental illness.[19] The set of possible medical meanings for a person living under the description of mental illness is limited in such a way that efforts to refuse and resist are redefined as illness. In Mr. Burton's rounds, his attempts to describe his intentions and motives were met with a diagnosis of mental illness. He presented himself as an upright young man, well mannered and well loved by his family, who had already had significant successes at school and in work. His exposure to PCP caused him to become paranoid and suicidal and to obtain a gun; he reacted to an overload of past and present stress by leaving college. He realized he was in trouble and called for help, whereupon, in the Riverside emergency room, he was terrified because he was completely alone and threatened with injections he mistrusted.[20] In the psychiatric description, in contrast, depression and anxiety led to changes in his daily habits, his ability to study, and his ability to tolerate being away from home. Depression also played a part in his suicidal and paranoid thoughts and his purchase of guns. PCP was granted a possible role, but overall Mr. Burton displayed a pattern of depression followed by mania: on admission his tangential speech and grandiosity indicated he was in florid mania. Because of the psychiatrists' knowledge and authority, there is no question that their descriptions will become operative in the hospital. Mr. Burton in effect tried to say "no" to the subject position of a person with bipolar disorder, but once he was defined as bipolar by the doctors, his effort was taken as additional evidence of his irrationality.

There is an important element of "performativity" in Mr. Burton's rounds, as there is in the other rounds and in the small, mocking performances I described in chapter 2. In the words of the philosopher J. L. Austin, "performativity" means that "There is something which is *at the moment of uttering being done by the person uttering.*"[21] When a judge of the appropriate kind says the words, "I now pronounce you man and wife," the uttering of the words brings about, performs, the state of marriage. For the couple, two new subject positions, a "husband" and a "wife," come into being.[22] Because the rounds physicians are by definition the ones with the knowledge and authority to diagnosis mental illness, their words—Mr. Burton has bipolar disorder—performatively bring about a new subject position for him: he becomes a person living under the description of bipolar disorder. The other form of subjectivity that often struggles (but fails) to emerge in rounds is the rational subject, one who has self-knowledge and agency and, most important, the ability to make sense of unfolding events. Paradoxically, from the point of view of the person being diagnosed, saying "no" to the categories of mental illness, though the speaker may wish otherwise, is often taken to mean, constitutively, that the speaker is "mentally ill" and hence not capable of being a proper "subject" at all.

Patients in rounds, in striving to articulate an oppositional stance to the medical categories, are expressing a positive desire for a number of things: some wish for a kind of subjectivity and agency that would allow them to refuse to be described in pathological psychiatric terms because their individual cases do not fit it (Mr. Burton, who declared he wasn't crazy); some wish for a kind of subjectivity that would empower them to refuse the legitimacy of psychological tests (Ms. Miller, who wouldn't spell "cloud" backward); others wish for a kind of subjectivity that would enable them to make their definitions of normal and functional stick (Ms. Vincent, who thought she was normal when she was speedy).

These are probably only a few of the wishes and desires contained in these events, all of which go to make up one of the main forces pushing the waves in the ground-sea: the assertion of these patients' subjectivities in a place where the medical model provides little room for it.

In the final analysis, the medical taxonomy used by the doctors naturally enough wins out in the context of rounds, despite patients' occasional efforts to refuse diagnostic tests or to turn the diagnoses back on the doctors. The patients are literally on the hospital grounds, where doctors control almost completely the medications prescribed, the length of stay offered, and the reports filed. In addition, most patients want and need the doctors' goodwill and accumulated experience, which would, if the appropriate diagnosis could be matched with a tolerable treatment, ease their suffering. Many patients have been in this very hospital before and at least sometimes say that they benefited from their treatment. What I intend to illuminate through these brief glimpses into ongoing and complex processes are the many facets of the struggles patients engage in to demonstrate that the pathological irrationality entailed by their psychological condition does not encompass their personhood entirely. I also hope it is possible to see that the medical categories themselves have looseness in them, as any taxonomic system would—fuzzy borders and conditions that overlap with each other—which students can only learn to apply through analysis of cases. This system does not come with clear, unambiguous rules about how its terms should be applied.

I will end with one caveat. The father of performativity theory, J. L. Austin, clearly distinguished cases in which language was performative from cases in which it was not. Characteristically, the criteria of the difference lay in "the circumstances of the utterance":[23] "Thus we may say 'coming from *him*, I took it as an order, not as a request.' "[24] "From *him*" might mean the person could compel obedience or punish disobedience because of his social position or his willingness to use force. Clear cases of performativity in Austin's sense, which can be called "strong illocutionary force," must be distinguished from others, which might only have "weak illocutionary force."[25] "I now pronounce you man and wife," when said by a judge, a religious official, or the captain of a ship, constitutes the performative act of marriage, but pronounced by anyone else does not. "It's a girl!" pronounced by medical staff at a birth, and followed up by a written record, constitutes the performative act of "girling," but, pronounced by the parents, the statement could not, unless the parents by chance had the authority to fill out a birth certificate.[26]

For acts with weak illocutionary force, the sense in which they are intended may be more aptly described as expressing a wish than as making a change in the world. This is the case for much of the backtalk by patients in rounds. No matter what anyone wishes, if the doctors say you are manic depressive and write that down in your chart, then that is what you are, in contexts in which medical authority operates. The territory over which medical authority operates is so vast that however powerful the wish to be classified otherwise, more often than not such a wish is without much effect on the world. But, nonetheless, expressing a wish expresses something about the person who says it: it manifests, however weakly, an aspect of a person's subjectivity: "The description of a wish is, *eo ipso*, the description of its fulfillment." Keith Burton's kisses might, on this account, be understood as the expression of his wish that his attachment to his kin could become part of his medical description and be taken seriously as a real motive in the world. This could not be. Even so, expressing such a wish can be understood in Wittgenstein's words as a "description of its fulfillment." One might hope that such expressions could be more effective in the world than wishes, but this would require medical knowledge to incorporate patients' social environments in a much more profound way. Short of that, we could hope that (within settings like clinical rounds) the efforts of patients like Mr. Burton to influence the medical understanding of their cases could come to be treated as a resource, motivated not by a desire to refuse a diagnosis but to enrich its meaning.

CHAPTER FIVE

Inside the Diagnosis

To dwell means to leave traces. In the interior,
these are accentuated.
—Walter Benjamin, *The Arcades Project*

When I sat in on medical rounds, I knew I was in territory where medical authority would largely be able to form and control the terms of debate. Keith Burton and the others could try to refuse or divert this authority, and they could frequently apply medical terms in novel ways suited to their own purposes. But in the end there was no question who determined the diagnosis and the treatment. In contrast, roaming around among manic depression support groups, I often fancied myself in a sort of ethnographic wilderness, far on the outskirts of medical authority. I thought of fieldwork among the "mentally ill" (even though the condition is no stranger in my personal life) as being in an "elsewhere" or among "others." I imagined myself capturing the intricate sentiments of those cast outside the range of reason and "good sense," documenting their words of wisdom about emotions, moods, or other psychological states that would rescue them from irrationality and throw the category of rationality into question. In fact, my fieldwork showed something I did not expect: when describing their mental states in support group meetings (outside the context of rounds), people most often stayed within the narrow confines of categories—such as "bipolar disorder" or "depression"—whose terms are set by medical conventions such as the DSM and held in place by their required role in insurance claims, among other things. To my surprise, I found that people in support groups used standard medical terms without further elaboration, frustrating my hope of finding a rich, individually and culturally nuanced language about interior states.

DSM Categories as "Text-Atoms"

Work on the DSM as we know it today began in 1974, after the American Psychiatric Association (APA) appointed Robert Spitzer head of a task force to develop "precisely defined, symptom-based disease entities" for psychiatric illnesses:[1] "The ideal, if not the practice, of medicine demanded measurement systems in which symptoms were direct indicators of underlying disease entities, precise classification systems, and clear criteria of therapeutic effectiveness."[2] DSM-III, published in 1980, was a radical change from DSM-II, which was oriented toward dynamic (psychoanalytic) concepts. Psychiatrists who wished to ally with the norms of biomedicine now saw the contents of DSM-II as vague, opaque, imprecise, and unfalsifiable.[3] In accord with the goal of precise classification, in addition to names of conditions, such as "bipolar disorder," DSM-III and the current edition, DSM-IV, have numerical designations. For example, my own condition is designated by the code "296.7"; "296" is the code for most conditions under the DSM-IV category "mood disorders," including Bipolar 1 Disorder and Major Depressive Disorder. A fourth and fifth digit can be added to the code after the decimal to indicate the nature of the most recent episode (e.g., 296.4 would specify that the most recent episode was "manic" or "hypomanic"). A fifth digit indicates the severity of the most recent episode (e.g., 296.43 would specify that the manic episode was "severe without psychotic features"). If only one number is added, 7 in my case, it means that the nature and severity of the most recent episode are not being specified. The system may seem arcane, but it is also potent. Since mental health care providers and patients must list DSM-IV codes on bills and claim forms before insurance companies and state or federal programs will reimburse them or issue support payments, many people have become generally familiar with the language of the DSM-IV. Generally speaking, since only physicians and other mental health professionals need to know the DSM numeric codes, most people do not use this level of abstraction in describing their conditions in support groups.[4]

The reason DSM categories are so prominent is embedded in the history of reimbursement for psychiatric care. In the first half of the century, patients who could afford it usually paid for psychotherapy out-of-pocket, but by the 1960s, insurance companies had begun to cover part of the cost. During the 1970s, the federal program Medicaid became another source of payment for therapy. When third-party payers as powerful as the federal government and insurance companies entered this scene, their interests began to affect what doctors who wished their patients to be reimbursed had to do. They had to use the system of categories developed in accordance with a scientific model—one that was made up of presumably clearly identifiable, discrete disease categories. Using this set of categories has become an "obligatory passage point" for anyone who wishes to tap into the funds of third-party payers.[5] Rules and regulations of various institutions have made the DSM-IV into the only deep channel that leads to the port of payment for mental health care.[6]

The DSM categories are highly abstract "text-atoms," each of which condenses the detailed contexts of daily life in which people experience moods of all sorts. The term comes from the sociolinguists Michael Silverstein and Greg Urban, who point out, "To turn something into a text is to seem to give it a decontextualized structure and meaning, that is, a form and meaning that are imaginable apart from the spatiotemporal and other frames in which they can be said to occur."[7] There is a certain power in such "text-atoms" and in their abstract precision. In support groups people often encountered, or were deliberately taught, a new vocabulary for what they were experiencing. Finding a language for experiences that you could not name and that you did not know were shared can bring relief from feelings of isolation. At an East Coast support group meeting, an African American couple came for the first time. Caroline introduced herself as manic depressive; her husband identified himself as there to support her. She said she liked hearing people in the group use the word "episode" to refer to times they were manic or depressed. She hadn't known what to say of her own manias or depressions, other than that she was "sick," a term that didn't seem right to her. With relief, she embraced "episode" as a way of demarcating her special moods.

At other times, DSM terms can help groups clarify the range of experiences they have. At a West Coast meeting, Sam, the man discussed in chapter 3 who had the accident with his van, came with his sister Rosalind. He showed the group a letter he had been writing to the secretary general of the United Nations arguing that weapons should only be produced as they are needed, not stockpiled for the future. This would be, he said, "a new mind-set for the millennium." After describing the contents of the letter, Sam read some sections from his diary that recounted his days of writing, his moment of reckoning when, rereading the draft, he decided it was worthless, and his descent into depression. Despairingly, he said, "This letter has been in the works for eleven years." Sam and his sister left at the end of the meeting, but a group of six or seven other members went to a nearby restaurant. Sam and his letter were the subjects of much discussion: some thought he was drinking and off his medicine; others focused on his personality, which they felt led him to tell others what to do in a very forceful and domineering way; still others thought he didn't belong in the group because his letter showed he was schizophrenic and not manic depressive. "Ha," said Jane, "haven't you ever read the DSM? Under its description of manic depression, it says manic patients are likely to throw their weight around where they have no knowledge or authority, exactly like Sam writing letters to the UN."

Then there are the times that a term from the DSM, throwing the rationality of the person it describes into question, can embroil a group in serious conflict. At another meeting of the same group, Jane came in late wearing a tight T-shirt that revealed her bulging abdomen. She exuded youth and energy with her bright round cheeks and short punky hair.

> Well, if you haven't noticed it yet you probably can see now that I am pregnant. I just couldn't hide it anymore. It was getting obvious, so I am dressed to let it hang out. I just felt so guilty over the abortion, I had to replace that child. Yesterday I visited a ten-million-dollar estate, and they are going to hire me as nanny and housekeeper because I have a lot of experience with kids. I will live on the estate, in my own house, which the owner has outfitted with a brand-new inte-

rior, including a flat screen TV. I will get a car for my own use, and I chose a Mercedes convertible. (They have seven Mercedes, so I had a choice.) The job sounded so perfect that I was hesitant to tell them I was pregnant, but when I did, they were actually pleased, because it meant I am looking for something long term. They just found out they can't have more children, and my child would make a good playmate for their four-year-old. Of course my child will always be mine, that will be made clear and legal. But I will stay there for six years, raise my child, and they will also support my college education while I am there.

In the stunned silence that followed this, another member of the group, Michelle, declared Jane manic and therefore unreliable.

Jane, I know from my own experience that once I didn't tell a very close friend about a cancer test result I had and I am still paying for that. It was very painful and not worth it. It is better to tell the truth, to just stick with the truth. I am not saying I don't believe you. You just sound a little manic-y to me.

Erica directed even stronger comments to Jane: "I don't believe you. I was in the hospital with you when you had your pregnancy and HIV tests, and the pregnancy test was negative." At this point, Jane interjected, "And it turns out my HIV test is now negative, it only came back positive before because they sent the wrong blood to be tested." Erica was incredulous: "You mean they tested you positive for HIV and negative for pregnancy and now it turns out the tests are both wrong, you are really negative for HIV and pregnant?! I don't believe you, that is not possible." At this point conflict heated up fast: a couple of people tried to tell Jane they were glad she was HIV negative, while Erica and Michelle kept repeating that Jane was not believable, but manic. Jane's face turned bright red and she ran out into the hall. In a moment, it seemed everyone in the room was shouting, cursing, rushing out the door and back in again. John, the group's facilitator, tried to calm the group down, again by using DSM categories, but stressing the continuum that runs between them: "Everything is on a scale without sharp breaks, there's schizophrenic, schizoaffective, manic depressive, and so on. Where they are just depends where the elbow nudges them along to. The important thing is to realize we are all human, and that sometimes unfortunately gets lost." Like Mr. Lawrence in the last chapter, John is owning the DSM categories, using them for his own purposes. For physicians, what matters are the differences among categories; for John, in his capacity of leader of the group, what matters are the commonalities among categories. Stressing the commonalities was his strategy for keeping the group from flying apart.

These are only a few of the many times I saw DSM terms playing an active role in support groups. For a long time it didn't occur to me that alongside the use of DSM terms, no one was describing experientially what their emotional states were like. Looking back on my fieldwork, I now see that an event I participated in early on could have shown me this, if only I had been able to take it in. The event was a regular meeting of a West Coast support group. It was my first time there, so I briefly explained my diagnosis, my fieldwork, and my hopes to write about manic depression. The group was welcoming and asked if I wanted to say anything else. As a newcomer, imagining that such groups sat around discussing their interior states all the time, I plunged in.

> I have very vivid visual images and wonder if anyone else has these? [A group member responded, "Like what?"] Well, recently a professor from Europe visited the institute where I work to give a lecture. I was sitting in the audience with a graduate student who has worked with me, when, to our mutual astonishment, the lecturer began to read word for word several paragraphs of a paper I had published as if it were her own writing. I began to feel a strong sense of unreality, and slowly the visual field in front of my eyes became rent as if it were a movie screen being ripped and torn in several places. What I could see through the torn sections was only a black abyss. I knew that the image came from my own mind, but it was so vivid I felt very frightened. The image lasted for over two days, and then slowly faded.

Looking around the room, I saw a lot of very attentive but hard-to-read faces. I said, "You are all looking at me as if I were crazy!" Laughter and humorous protestations followed this, and to ease my embarrassment, the group facilitator explained, "It's just that you told a good story."

After the meeting was over, two people sought me out to say that although they had had similar experiences, they would never have discussed them in the group. One man took me aside in an outdoor gazebo.

> I didn't want to say anything in there, because they might think I was smoking the funny stuff, but I have visions, too. I have had them all my life. The way to deal with them is through your dreams. You ask your dreams what they mean and your dreams will tell you. Life is a process of education, and dreams and visions are teaching us. I have precognitive dreams, educational dreams, and others, too. More than once I have been warned in advance about something. I work for the railroad, I am an engineer. . . . I bet several other people in the room have had the same kinds of experiences, they just don't want to talk about it. I could lose my job if anyone knew.

I now think the group's reaction to my experience came out of their surprise: I was describing the details of a puzzling interior state instead of simply naming it with a standard term and, moreover, I was revealing something that made me vulnerable to loss—of my employment, driving privileges, or professional credibility.

Why would members of support groups avoid describing their psychological states even to each other? One possible reason is that they fear leaks of information that could harm them. But appearing at the meeting at all means, by the criteria for admission, that one has a diagnosis of depression or manic depression. One does not have to say a single word to be exposed to possibly harmful leaks. Another possibility is that the DSM acts as a cloak against further scrutiny. Nikolas Rose writes about forms of psychological knowledge as *"techniques for the disciplining of human difference."*[8] He refers to the way psychological tests of all kinds—for intelligence, personality, or cognition—as well as psychological surveys or systematic observations at work, school, or home "individualiz[e] humans through classifying them, calibrating their capacities and conducts, inscribing and recording their attributes

and deficiencies, managing and utilizing their individuality and vari-
ability."[9] Once people are given a scientific label for their pathological
condition, they can use that label as protection against further scrutiny.
The terms "Bipolar 2" or "Major Depression Disorder" can bounce
from one person to another without calling for examination and so
allow people to keep their interior landscape closed to comparison,
correction, or calibration against the norm. Instead of acting as agents
of their own internalized knowledge, they may be cloaking themselves
using the very terms of scientific knowledge. DSM terms, as I suggested
earlier, act something like an atomic table of elements for mental illness; they aim to describe the whole universe of mental illness, and
every condition can therefore presumably be given a place to belong
within it. Using the terms is a shorthand others can be assumed to
understand, and this assumption may make further explanation of what
lies within actual individual experience seem unnecessary. In this
sense, the DSM would act as a shield against revealing more intimate
psychic experiences.

A legitimate objection to this line of argument is that there is no
testing or surveying going on in support groups, and (except by the
accident of a member being a psychologist) there are no experts present
capable of such studies. The only people present are "the classified,"
individuals who have already been the subject of questions, tests, and
observations to determine exactly what form of mental pathology they
have. It is possible that my presence could have felt like the intrusion
of a scientific observer. But I made every effort to be unobtrusive: I
never took notes in meetings and rarely asked anyone questions. With
the occasional exception of a few facilitators, I did not do interviews
with people from support groups. Furthermore, by the end of the research I was in frequent social interaction with members of many
groups, going out to restaurants and movies, and communicating by
phone and e-mail. To every extent possible, I behaved like any other
member of these groups. More tellingly, when I was new to each group,
I would often sit through most of one or two meetings before the facilitator gave me a chance to explain myself. Yet I observed no difference
in the pattern of not disclosing interior states between these first meet-

ings and the last meetings I attended some years later. Whether or not people experience the "atomic" character of the DSM acting as a shield against intrusion, I can report that as one participant-observer studying mental states, who attended many meetings hoping for material that would let me interpret and compare interior emotions, I felt foiled by language that both blocked and shielded what I wanted to find out.

However, there is another reason why elaborate descriptions of interior states in support group meetings might have seemed lacking to me. Compared to other support group members, I was probably overtrained to scrutinize my interior emotions. Through the luxury of health insurance from a university medical plan, I had already had years of regular one-on-one conversations with psychiatrists and social workers who taught me how to recognize and describe the nuances of my psychological experiences. Support group members varied widely in how much they had been exposed to this kind of training: although some thought of their bipolarity in psychological terms, many saw it simply as a chemical brain imbalance that could be managed best by psychotropic drugs. For many people, then, scrutiny of their psychic states might have been rather meaningless and uninteresting.

This point begs a larger question, however. To the extent DSM categories act as a shield for people's inner psychic states, the pervasive use of the DSM categories might work to prevent people from realizing the social importance of exploring their inner states. Exploration of inner experience has the potential to challenge the uniform and bureaucratic language of the DSM. Insofar as people use DSM categories *instead of* exploring the phenomena of their experience firsthand, they may have only the illusion of communicating with other people what it is like to be, say, manic. What are the sensory dimensions of the experience — olfactory, tactile, visual, or auditory sensations? How is the experience embedded in its context? In the person's unique history? At the least, what support group members are able to communicate through the DSM categories is only a small part of what they might well have experienced in their individual lives. Recovering this kind of experience in the social setting of the support group might be a way to complement the functions of DSM categories with another kind of knowledge.[10]

The Work of Support Groups

If elaborate accounts of interiority are not the norm, then what kinds of work do support groups typically accomplish? No two support group meetings are alike, but most take up the same set of social tasks. For the most part, these tasks are not exotic: they struck me as similar to ordinary informal group interactions in workplaces, schools, and neighborhoods in the United States. In almost all support group meetings, to a greater or lesser extent, *people create new social connections that last over time*. The usual format of the support group is that one person at a time tells the others what has happened to him since the last meeting or since he last attended a meeting, while the others listen. After a few minutes of this, anyone else in the group may chime in with a question or comment. There is usually a designated facilitator who has received training in maintaining this minimal order. Attendance at meetings is quite variable, but more often than not, each person who speaks will hear from someone who remembers what he or she said last time. At one meeting, Tom described his worries about his daughter, whom he suspected was manifesting signs of bipolar disorder because she totaled a car and then ran out into heavy traffic in an apparent suicide attempt. Rebecca remembered that this daughter had rebuffed and denied Tom's efforts to suggest that she seek medical treatment. Deborah wondered if Tom had discussed the genetic component of the disease and gently brought out the fact that though Tom believed this was relevant, he had not talked directly to his daughter about it. Jeff then took up another common task of such groups: *asserting that other people share one's individual experience*. Jeff sympathized with Tom's concern over his daughter, but advised on the basis of his experience that "since you can't control your children, you have to accept that and not get dragged down. If the child is in denial, as this daughter is, there is not much you can do." In these small ways, a fabric of relatedness is created for people over time. Other people remember them; other people understand their experiences in light of life stories they have told in the past; other people have experienced something similar.

Another common job of the groups is *bringing up relevant informa-tion that can help solve practical problems.* The groups' job in this re-gard is enormous because of the number of technical and social prob-lems in which members' lives are embroiled. How to find a doctor who will accept Medicare or Medi-Cal? How to find a job that will accept one's mood bipolarities or accommodate one's low tolerance for stress? How to know whether a symptom is a normal side effect of medication or a sign of a serious health problem? How to anticipate the effects of more and more complex combinations of drugs? Since there is great volatility in the life circumstances of any individual living under the description of bipolar disorder, conventional class and other social dis-tinctions are less of a barrier to conversation than one might think. A person who gave up a blue-collar job to live on disability will not hesi-tate to advise another person who has just lost her executive position and her house. A person who once held a high-ranking job will not hesitate to advise another person who is struggling on welfare to gain a minimal credential in early childhood education. Sometimes the knowledge that groups produce is practical and straightforward, but even so, it is often offered with sophisticated understanding of the vagar-ies of a person's bipolar characteristics. Charles, whose boss had fired him from his high-powered job as a consultant, had explained at an earlier meeting that though he had loved the energy this job required, it also had also drawn him into the heights of mania. With the help of supportive comments from the group, he could now say, "I have a job I feel is less than I am capable of, but I see that I am getting up, going to work, doing the work, so, hey, I acknowledge the good in that."

Even more specifically related to the group's shared psychiatric diag-nosis, group members *tolerate strikingly unusual behavior, up to a point.* A young woman who jangled her keys on the table the whole time she talked, a man who sat in inert dejection, face completely hidden, a woman who constantly interrupted others, another who told her story with such striking intensity that she took far more time than was cus-tomary, a man who repeated the same lengthy complaints about his boss in the same words week after week: these and many other odd behaviors were common in groups and mostly occurred without com-ment. At any time, the facilitator or someone else might object, correct, or simply describe the unusual behavior, and sometimes conflict would erupt when this happened. But even though there were limits, no one knew when they would be called into play or how they would be received. The limits felt soft and flexible, rather than hard and rigid, but this also lent them uncertainty. For me, this uncertainty tinged the meetings with considerable dramatic tension despite the mundane content of many interactions.

Group members also *tolerate descriptions of extreme behavior in an unruffled manner*, as if their own experiences of similar behavior have made such behavior routine and manageable. For example, Ann, whom we met in chapter 2, a woman in her fifties, told about her dread and fear of an approaching manic episode as she was facing a trip to Las Vegas. The last time she had one it ended in a hospitalization. A group member suggested Ann use writing in her journal to address her anger directly. She seemed to accept this idea thoughtfully, saying she did write in her journal, but not explicitly about her anger. That seemed like a good idea to her and with that the group moved on. Later, after Jane described her deep, immobilizing depression, Ann joked, "What do you suppose would happen if the two of us went to Las Vegas together, the manic and the depressed?"

At another meeting, Ruth said she was spending impulsively, and kept getting more and more tattoos. Today she is upset because she has an infection in one of the recent tattoos. She is behind on the rent and is starting to pawn stuff so she can buy gas to get around. She can't go to a swap meet anymore because she can't just look around without buying anything, as she would have in the past. She went off her lithium because it made her hair fall out: of course she had to go off it! She has promised her family she won't go to the mall. She is not getting depressed over these restrictions; she is just afraid she will get out of control. Ignoring her lapse in taking lithium, Felicity, the group facilitator, said, "What about the 'stop' technique, have you tried that? You just firmly say 'stop' to yourself, if need be many times, if need be very loudly. If you do this, the mind has to work harder to keep being manic." Ruth thought this was a fine idea, promised to try it, and the group moved on.

Something about the matter-of-fact acceptance, the joking, and the mundane remedies is soothing. Perhaps these experiences aren't so horrific after all. Perhaps they can be talked about conversationally, and managed in ordinary ways. But at the same time, groups *insist on action when a person's life or health is seriously at risk.* Julia tells the group she was recently released from the hospital but has only two more days' medication. She couldn't get a follow-up medical appointment for a couple of weeks. Aaron lets her have it: "This is urgent, this is an acute situation. You go into the emergency room and tell them what the situation is and you do not leave until you have what you need. Just do not leave without enough medication to last you." Unlike Ruth's temporary lapse in taking lithium, which the group ignores for the moment, running out of medication after a hospitalization is treated as an emergency. The same would go for any hint of suicidal thinking or behavior.

The process of creating a fabric of relatedness among group members begins on a person's first visit to a group, when one is invited (but not required) to speak. The introductory stories people tell are often stories of sequential diagnosis, of movement through a series of diagnoses expressed in the terms of the DSM. What is my diagnosis today? What earlier diagnoses have I had and why were they abandoned? What medication or therapy followed each diagnosis? My own story, summarized in the introduction, was modeled on those I heard others tell and honed by my visits to numerous groups. It was a story I would not be able to tell in any other setting, except perhaps a psychiatrist's office. In the support groups, no one found it cause for shock or disbelief, and no one doubted I needed all the therapy I was getting. This reaction was unique in my experience and gave a particular flavor, an individuality, to the social relations built with members of the group. Moving as such stories do from one DSM diagnosis to another recapitulates a map of the terrain that a person has moved through in time. In general people tend to present each new diagnosis as a therapist's best effort to capture the whole picture he or she has of the patient in a shorthand form that will be a map, a guide, to treatment (which is exactly the goal of the capturing and naming that students are learning to do in rounds). But if there are frequent or numerous changes in diagnosis, people often express doubt that the right diagnosis will ever be found or that the medical profession has adequate treatments for them. What group members affirm is less the rightness of any particular diagnosis than the difficulty of the terrain over which successive DSM terms map a path. No solution is found easily, no medication lasts forever, and no one is ever cured of a mood disorder.

Support groups can be seen as a kind of enclosed social space that allows particular forms of intimate sociality. Under the impact of the stigma of mental illness, people often have to accept many social losses: a less well-paying and satisfying job; less continuous support from family members and friends; less ability to maintain relationships of all kinds. The continuous presence of the support group—even with its loose and changeable membership—can serve as a softly furnished haven. The traces people leave of themselves in this space are deposited in the memories of other members and retrieved, now and then, over time. The DSM terms, which I described earlier as protective cloaks, could perhaps be understood better as soft fabric, antimacassars, whose function in the interior space of the support group is to capture the evidence that a person was in the group and to soak up the traces of her social existence.[11] The social framework of knowledge and authority that gives validity to the DSM categories reaches out to embrace the patient and enfold him or her in a legitimate—if limited—social fabric. Even if the fabric is a taxonomy of *pathological* conditions, at least it lies within the realm of *vital* social relationships.

Performativity, Intention, and Diagnosis

In chapter 4 I discussed the performative aspects of psychiatric diagnoses like manic depression.[12] When a physician states that a person has a condition like manic depression, he is harnessing the social authority of his medical degree, training, and experience, and perhaps his colleagues' consensus. Simply by naming the patient's condition, he brings the condition about in the sense that the hospital staff, the family doctor, family members, and the patient himself are likely to take actions on the basis of his statement. These actions give the diagnosis social reality. The authority behind the act of naming means that the person will be treated as if he or she had the condition; this is the sense in which the act of diagnosis is performative. The power dynamics of this can be rather oppressive, if one has any doubt about the merit or efficacy of the treatment, or wishes to take an alternative view of the diagnosis and to *act* upon the alternative view.

Is there any way around the performative effect of a diagnosis? If language uttered by a properly constituted authority—a doctor, say—performatively makes a person described as manic depressive *just be* manic depressive, then how can the person so named redescribe him- or herself? Short of going to medical school and returning to the scene of diagnosis to quarrel with the original description, what room for effective speech could there be? Although J. L. Austin was more interested in the conditions under which a speech act could bring about an effect than in the particular conventions (such as heterosexual marriage) that speech acts assumed and protected, recent analyses of performative speech have enhanced our understanding of how active the interaction between performatives and social institutions can be. Judith Butler argues that if a performative succeeds, it does so by covering over the conventionality of the social rules it depends on: "not because an intention successfully governs the action of speech, but only because that action echoes prior actions, and *accumulates the force of authority through the repetition or citation of a prior and authoritative set of practices*. It is not simply that the speech act takes place *within* a practice, but that the act is itself a ritualized practice. What this means, then, is that a performative 'works' to the extent that it *draws on and covers over the constitutive conventions by which it is mobilized*."[13] But constitutive conventions can be challenged. In hate speech, if the person who was insulted takes up the insult and redeploys it for other purposes, "speaking words without prior authorization," the conventions that enabled the hate speech in the first place can be exposed and threatened. Because the redeployment is part of a "labor of self-definition" it is thus "unmoored from prior context" and loses its performative force. For example, the performative "it's a girl" "girls" the baby at her birth.[14] But a future "labor of self-definition" allows the possibility that the individual so "girled" may later enact speech and behavior that challenge and modify that effect—the "girl" may performatively produce herself as a boy, or some other gendered identity.[15]

The ground this appealing scenario leaves unexplored is the traditional ground of cultural anthropology.[16] Can a single individual create a social context with social meaning? Can we speak of a redeployment on the basis of a one-off gesture? Do not such acts depend on a context at least coming into being, an interest group, an identity group, meetings, organizations, publications, support groups, named entities, or at least informal associates who could corroborate an alternative description? In fact, in the case of mood disorders many such organizations and associations are flourishing.[17] In his book about depression, *Speaking of Sadness*, David Karp found that his American interviewees experienced the lack of language they had to describe depression as a profound loss, and that this loss increased their isolation.[18] We might imagine this loss being repaired by social movements that would enable those diagnosed as "mentally ill" to use DSM terms in their own ways or to speak in terms other than the DSMs. In such a context we might see the *emergence* of performativity in conjunction with the mobilization of new social movements and groups.[19]

The crux of the difficulty with this scenario (practically speaking) is that mental illness, as a particular kind of stigmatized condition, is erroneously taken to rob the person it is attached to of her rationality, and therefore of her ability to make sensible observations about the world. Cast into an alien sphere, apparently removed from what is essentially human, how can such a person perform a "labor of self-definition"? Until this daunting situation changes, people in support groups for manic depression can continue to shelter behind and rest upon the soft fabric of the DSM categories.

CHAPTER SIX

Pharmaceutical Personalities

This is the idea of "person" (*personne*), the idea of
"self" (*moi*). . . . Each one of us finds it natural,
clearly determined in the depths of his
consciousness, completely furnished with the
fundaments of the morality which flows from it. For
this simplistic view of its history and present value we
must substitute a more precise view.
—Marcel Mauss, "A Category of the Human Mind"

Drugs are inanimate products that cannot literally speak, think, or feel. Nonetheless, pharmaceutical marketers and advertisers attempt to invest psychotropic drugs with attributes that make it possible to think of them as "persons," as if they were social beings with individual personalities and the ability to have nurturing relationships with the patients who take them. However, patients who take these drugs do not necessarily relate to them as friendly living "persons" who take up residence inside them. Patients are as likely to think of drugs as biological tools, whose potency lies in their specific line of action on something in their brains, and whose harmful side effects might need to be moderated by complex cocktails of different drugs.[1] Despite the friendly imagery of advertising, both patients and pharmaceutical marketers and advertisers invest psychotropic drugs with deeply ambivalent meanings. Psychotropic drugs can help us, so it would seem, but they cannot do so without harming us at the same time.

Marketing a Psychotropic Drug

From my interviews with pharmaceutical employees, I learned that developing a personality for the drug begins early in the production phase.

Two executives from the research and production departments of the same company told me with considerable exasperation how demanding and detailed the concerns of marketers about developing a drug's personality could be.

> Marketers worry about having every possible dose form: tablets in different strengths, a liquid form for pediatrics. They want a form that is aesthetically pleasing, looks good, tastes good, and is not too big. Color is important to them also: you never use red for psychotropic drugs! It is said to be bad for psychological or psychiatric problems, signifying danger. Black and gray mean death. Sometimes blue is bad because it can mean poison and can be seen as cold. But then again, light blue or green can be good when you want calm, soothing colors. Kids' taste buds are different from adults, and different cultures have different associations with tastes. A wintergreen flavor we once used is associated in France with the scent of toilet bowl cleaners!

From the point of view of research and production personnel, the preoccupation of sales, marketing, and advertising personnel with the aesthetics of the tablet was understandable but frustrating. Their own work on the drug's chemical formulation was like building the "body" of the drug, and the rest was its "dress." They would cooperate in making this "dress" comforting and comfortable, stylish and aesthetically pleasing, even though the effort seemed superficial to them in comparison with building the body of the tablet itself.

An e-mail from Sarah Taylor, who is widely experienced in pharmaceutical marketing, summarized the importance of investing drugs with specific personality traits, which could, in due course, be combined with each other.

> The antidepressants in particular have capitalized on [different] effects or lack thereof in their competitive branding campaigns. "All the efficacy without losing sleep, sex, etc." One psychiatric group (at Mass General, Boston) even offers their patients a "menu of reasonable choices." This is a descriptive "menu" of all the antidepressants they could prescribe along with a description of the various side effect and efficacy profiles. This is as close to selecting a pill based on its personality as I can think of. Psychiatrists have reacted to these brand-

ing campaigns in a curious way. Instead of prescribing one antidepressant or the other, they combine the drugs into their favorite "cocktails." In LA, one drug combination became so popular it is called the Hollywood cocktail. It's popular because it utilizes Serzone (somewhat sedating, yet without weight gain, sexual dysfunction, or sleep loss) and Effexor (activating, pep you up so you can "get out of bed in the morning"). This hypermanagement of symptomology to a state that is better than normal or baseline seems like a new kind of medicine to me. In the case of the Hollywood cocktail, the psychs [psychiatrists] are actually inducing a sort of mania or hyper-alertness (at least compared to the person's previous state).

Physicians' readiness to combine the character traits of drugs to optimize a patient's mental state should alert us that however person-like they may seem, drugs are not exactly like persons. Their personality traits are more thing-like than person-like because they can be bought and sold and combined on demand in many ways, more like the parts of a motor or the ingredients of a cake than the personality traits of people. Acknowledging this, an ad in a trade magazine for pharmaceutical marketing shows a plumber installing brands inside a person's head with a wrench.

Because marketers and advertisers make serious efforts to imbue drugs with person-like traits, they quite reasonably also try to foster person-like relationships between drugs and the doctors who prescribe them or the patients who take them. Through the important role of the pharmaceutical sales representative in marketing drugs, a great deal of drug advertising aims to build aesthetic and emotional links with doctors. Here, I will keep my focus on patients by discussing how some ads try to reach through the doctor to the patient. Margaret Connor told me about her experiences as a copywriter for an ad agency: "Pharmaceutical ads use artistic themes because psychiatrists are artistic and this would appeal to them. For Lithium-P,[2] we did a four-month calendar on a poster featuring a portrait of Beethoven and there was even a card you could send in to get a CD of the Ninth Symphony." But she felt this kind of appeal would not be appropriate for consumers.

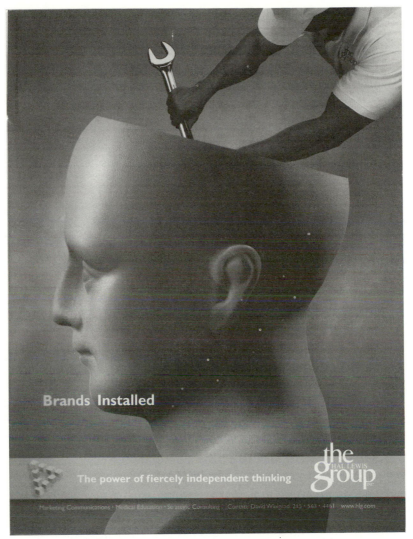

Brands Installed

The power of fiercely independent thinking

the
HAL LEWIS
group INC.

Marketing Communications · Medical Education · Strategic Consulting   Contact: David Windgrad 215 · 563 · 4451   www.hlg.com

6.1. In this ad from a pharmaceutical marketing trade magazine, a plumber installs brand-name drugs directly in the brain. Reprinted with permission. *Guide to Pharmaceutical Marketing Services, MedAd News* 21 (September 2002): 29. Courtesy of the Hal Lewis Group, Inc. All rights reserved.

For example, a client wanted Van Gogh on the cover of a brochure for patients. But you know he committed suicide at the age of thirty-seven! I resisted because [this would make] it sound like you take the drug or you are going to die like he did. In the end, although I resisted, they used the picture, but I did manage to soften the wording.

Margaret also thought it was an ethical problem to put creativity so in the forefront of the ad, because fear of losing creativity is one of the main reasons bipolar patients resist taking Lithium-P: "Why take the drug if you lose that? People enjoy the highs, they feel invincible, they get a lot of work done. We also don't want to scare people off (consumers, that is) about the side effects. So the letter that goes to doctors with the calendar is clear and blunt about side effects, while the consumer materials mute them."

I asked where the idea for Beethoven and Van Gogh came from.

From reading Kay Jamison's book on genius manic depressives, Schumann, Van Gogh, Poe. Then we had another author (I guess he was a jealous academic) ask us why not use his book, which is on military leaders and manic depression, so they did one with Napoleon, with quotes from [military heroes] but they couldn't use Stalin and Hitler. They issued these for three years—they were wonderful!

Later, Jack Levy, medical director of an advertising agency, explained the general principle behind the effort: borrowed interest. Inside the mailing tube with the calendar would be a paragraph on the famous figure and then a full Lithium-P sell: "An example of borrowed interest would be using Cal Ripkin in an ad for a beta blocker. Cal doesn't take the drug, but we borrow his long duration and hope it sticks to the drug."

From her perspective as a production manager, Katherine Holmes talked about how ads are tailored to patients who belong to different populations. Katherine illustrated how pharmaceutical advertisers share general cultural notions about particular mental conditions and funnel them back into materials designed to promote relationships between drugs and populations of patients.

The same drugs are used, but the populations are very different. Schizophrenia tends to be downwardly mobile. I mean when people get it, they could be from any background. But once you get it, you could end up homeless, with no job—people just cannot function. So the average schizophrenic will end up either in a hospital or without a job somewhere living on minimum wage. I mean there are a few, rare cases of people that are teachers, but it's not your average. Whereas with manic depression—those are creative people who are successful, and you wouldn't even know that they [were taking medication or had] the disease. So it's a very high-functioning group of people, which I think makes it even harder to treat them because they are smart, they are creative, and they don't like to take their medication. When they are on the high part of it they create, they produce, they do things, wonderful things. And it's just when they are in the depressive part that things are really bad.

The main "beam" [focus] of the creative for our drug was very artistic—the idea was [to move the patient] from chaos to control. Those aren't the words we used, but the ad would show a page with just a scribble on it and then it would turn into musical notes. And so the idea was that your mind goes from being confused and everything, to kind of understanding, and then up to creative.

Katherine went on to explain how these advertising materials build on the widespread cultural connection between manic depression and creativity.

A lot of the stuff that the advocacy organizations do is around arts—they have art shows. I think there's definitely an understanding that it is a creative person who might have that disorder. I don't think the agency exactly views the disorder as a good thing. Maybe it's more that we should realize it's just OK. Like with depression it's totally open: Mike Wallace is on Zoloft [for depression] and that's not at the level of being abnormal. Depression does have a very dark side, but I think manic depression still really has that other side to it. I'd use the word "crazy" but . . . you know, it's high energy, things are happening.

In devising ads for drugs used to treat manic depression, advertising designers take for granted cultural associations between manic depression and creative energy. The drugs they design for this condition must promise neither too much dampening, which would lead to loss of creativity, nor too little, which would leave the patient's chaotic thinking intact.

The Rationality of Consumers

Between 1998 and 2001, when I was doing fieldwork on the pharmaceutical industry, it was undergoing some important changes that bore on its ability to build relationships with consumers. First, DTC advertising had begun in earnest in 1997. Draft promotional guidelines from the FDA's Division of Drug Marketing, Advertising and Communications (DDMAC) in August of that year permitted pharmaceutical companies to advertise the benefits of prescription drugs by brand as long as they also made clear the product's most important negative effects.[3] The marketing and advertising budgets of the pharmaceuticals subsequently increased through 2000, adding fuel to critics' claims that high prescription drug costs resulted from pharmaceutical advertising.[4]

Second, new FDA guidelines now allowed products to be directly linked to brand names. Early in my research, Sam Giosa, a physician who works as medical director for an advertising agency, explained to me,

> Previously, the FDA legislated that the pharmaceutical companies could use ads to show the drug name or the condition it treated, but they could never link the two. If they did, they had to present the entire product information statement. This would take so much time on TV and cost so much that the companies didn't want to do it. They could link them in print, but they had to include the whole product fine print about side effects, etc. Now there is a trial period where they are allowed to link the two, if they make a "major statement" at the end, so the public won't be misled.[5]

In part because of DTC advertising, the market for psychotropic drugs grew rapidly. In the United States, sales reached $2.5 billion in 1990, $6.6 billion in 1995, about $7.6 billion in 1996, and then over $15 billion in 1999.[6] Academic studies documented that the proportion of visits to a doctor in which a psychotropic medication was prescribed increased from 5.1 percent to 6.5 percent between 1985 and 1994, an increase that can be accounted for by the three new Selective Serotonin Reuptake Inhibitors (SSRIs): fluoxetine in 1988, sertraline in 1991, and paroxetine in 1992.[7]

DTC ads are intended to tap into consumers' emotions, but what happens when the consumer's emotions are disordered? Can a manic-depressive person, say, be a good consumer? On the one hand, we might think that people labeled "irrational" by virtue of mental illness would be considered ripe targets for these ads. Since irrationality is often defined as emotions getting beyond the control of reason, "irrational" people might seem especially susceptible to advertising's emotional appeal.[8] On the other hand, however, the point of the ads is to get the consumer to consume: to decide he needs the drug, to seek a doctor who will prescribe it, and so on. "Irrational" people might not seem reliable in following through all the way to the act of consumption. When I asked my pharmaceutical interlocutors about this puzzle, they were as confounded as I was.

> **Katherine Holmes:** It's something that I think all the drugs that have indications for mental illness have to consider, especially the antidepressants. Depression is more common and the patients are generally more functioning than, let's say, a schizophrenic or a bipolar. The patients, it's hard to reach them, since they are not really necessarily aware of what they are doing, they are not going to respond to . . . [Her voice trails off.] Prozac is trying to do direct-to-consumer [marketing] for their drug, and Zoloft is considering it. It doesn't seem like they've really been that successful. So it's more like public relations than it is like direct advertising to these people because I think . . . it's just . . . [hesitating] because of their illness they're not necessarily . . . they're not going to respond and go ask their doctor for the medication.

Emily Martin: Is that partly an issue of noncompliance? (When patients do not take drugs a doctor has prescribed for them?)

Katherine Holmes: Right, I used to work on that issue, too. Yeah, a lot of this is much more educating the doctors and the caregivers, the families around these people, than it is the person, because these people sometimes really cannot . . . it's not even . . . like if you presented them with a 1-800 number? [Shrugs.]

Jason Marshall, who worked as a sales rep at the beginning of his career in marketing, talks about the difficulties of advertising to patients for Drug S, used for schizophrenia and bipolar disorder.

Emily Martin: Did the company do any DTC advertising?

Jason Marshall: No, there was no DTC for Drug S. I'm just taking a guess about why that was, but first of all it's not a huge market. Psychiatric disorders in general and especially schizophrenia can't be more than a couple million patients. Most of the DTC advertising you see is for physical disorders, which are very common, so it's easy, you know, if you are doing Propicea, because 20 percent of the audience could experience baldness. To advertise directly to people with psychosis . . . [He trailed off with a dubious expression.]

Or you *can* specifically target people with schizophrenia, but that's probably not a good way to advertise something . . . and I'll be willing to bet that as much as doctors are upset about direct-to-consumer advertising with products for asthma and hypertension, they'll be *very* upset with us if we tried to influence a patient with a psychiatric disorder.

Jane Fuller has worked on a number of ad campaigns for psychotropic drugs and so I asked her whether advertising for psychotropic drugs is ever directed to patients who are deemed mentally ill. She thought that doing so would be contradictory because such patients might not have enough self-awareness to act on their own behalf by seeking the drug. But she thought that if a patient took the drug and began to feel better, he or she would "engage," and might begin to complain about weight gain or sexual side effects. With increased awareness, such a patient might be able to behave like a good consumer, that is, behave rationally, and actively seek out the best drug on the market.

The advent of DTC advertising has brought the uneasy and volatile status of the mentally ill directly into the advertising process. A patient who is not regarded as functioning rationally enough to be an appropriate target for a drug ad might still be able to "feel better" with the aid of the drug. Earlier in this chapter we saw how pharmaceutical employees imagine indirect relationships with patients by reaching through the materials provided to doctors. Now we can see that forms of advertising sent directly to the mass of consumers fall short of people who are thought to be "less aware." The relationships in question are almost always one step removed from actual patients, but they live vividly in the imagination of pharmaceutical employees. People with some forms of mental illness are thought to lie outside even this imagined social landscape.

Living with Drugs

If drugs, like other commodities, are given the particular kinds of life I have just described through marketing and advertising, how do people who take the drugs make sense of this thing that now literally takes up residence inside them? Does the drug seem alive to them the way a person or a spirit would be? Does the personality advertisers intend to create for the drug take hold in their imaginations?

Before tackling these questions, we must remember that since psychotropic drugs are a commodity and, as such, carry a price, everything we say about them should be framed in political economic terms. Who can afford to buy them? Who has knowledge to use them? Who has access to physicians or others who can monitor their effects and suggest adjustments? In the United States, these basic questions are determined mostly by where one is in the hierarchy of resources. Whether one is encouraged or required to take psychotropic drugs in a welfare office, never offered the choice in a remote rural or underserved inner-city setting, given them in a one-off way by a doctor in a clinic, or carefully monitored over months or years of minute adjustment: these are more often matters of what one can afford and what one is in a position to know than what one prefers. At the high end of the scale, a psychiatrist in New York City told me that her patients take cell phone calls during their consultations with her about their psychotropic medications. Overhearing them say proudly, "I am with my psychopharmacologist," she commented, "I feel like a Prada bag; everyone has to do this to be up to the minute."

One's standing in the hierarchy can also change over time. As health benefits run out, a job ends, savings evaporate, or the like, a person can drift down the scale. Kiki described this succinctly on a Web newsgroup: "Well—I saw my otherwise wonderful PDOC [psychiatrist] today for a reg. session to discuss meds and my symptoms, etc. In the past I would have liked to have seen her 1x week for meds and therapy, but she is not on my HMO's panel and I cannot afford $175/week—so I see her for meds ($90) and disability management about every three weeks since 4/30."[9] Kiki would prefer a therapeutic hour every week, but she can only afford fifteen minutes every three weeks.

In my many visits to support groups, the vast majority of people spoke of fifteen-minute appointments with county doctors once a month, where the doctor could do little more than just renew prescriptions. Hilary told one support group that she saw a doctor at a clinic who spent at most two minutes talking to her, and then "it is on to the next patient. She must see thousands of patients in a day; it is like you are on an assembly line." This situation is no more the choice of doctors than patients. Speakers at conferences I attended for psychiatrists and for patient support groups alike regarded these kinds of constraints on physicians' ability to treat patients as deplorable.

As we have seen, one main goal of DTC drug advertising is to invest the drug with a personality. When people talk about the experience of taking drugs, however, the drug frequently does not survive with its own intended identity intact. Rather, the drug goes in the person, and a new person results. A woman spoke out at a support group I attended.

> I am Hanna and I am manic depressive. I am a rapid cycler; I am either up or down, and I am not much in the middle, or at normal (if you want to call that normal). I realize I expected the pills to

manage the manic depression, and now I see *I* need to manage it at all levels, including the spiritual. *I* need to learn more, to exercise more, to be active not passive. My shift in thinking is due to taking Depakote—it is like a new suit of clothes! I am a snake who has shed its skin, I am all new and shiny.

In another support group, Gail, a very thin woman in her thirties, whose long, dark hair shadowed her face, had been through four years of a lot of therapy and medications, all of which "came to nothing." Worse than that, the medications she was given made her literally sick, to the point of vomiting. She had just been to see a new doctor who started her on a new drug, Tegretol, and she was feeling hopeful. But in spite of her hopes for the drug, she stated most emphatically that her social relations with other people were more important than the drug in moderating her behavior: "I go to these groups because I have a network of friends in them. I don't want to depend too much on my fiancé to do things for me. Instead I would rather have feedback from my friends *and* my fiancé, because this would allow me to 'modulate my own behavior.'"

Gail's emphasis on her network of friends and family does not mean drugs can come and go from people's lives without perturbation. Linda said she had gone for a second opinion to another doctor, who, the support group facilitator assured her, was a very good psychopharmacologist. This doctor told Linda the medications she was taking were terrible for her. He was so certain these drugs would not deal with her anxiety that he recommended she should taper them off and start a new combination of drugs. Linda was upset by this and told the group, "I want my old personality back. I know I look terrible, and I feel I am looking worse and worse. I am really alone, I don't know whether I lost the phone numbers of the group or just couldn't bring myself to call." As she talked, several people passed her their numbers written on little slips of paper.

Marcy, a graduate student who initiated contact with me and traveled from another state in order to tell her story, described her deep dislike of switching drugs because switching changes one's identity and threatens the "magic" of the original drug.

If I take a new drug, even a new brand name of the same drug, like a different version of the same drug, I have to reshape my entire identity, like now I am not that person who took Depakote. If I have to go and take lithium, then I have to come up with an identity that takes lithium, and that's a lot of work for me, that's something I have to get used to, and so I have an aversion to doing it. It's the work of producing a new identity, it's like integrating something new into your old identity. This is a lot of work, and for what? It takes away from the magic of the first drug. And if the first one worked for you, then it has magical properties. You can only be cured if your medicine has a power beyond being medicine, well, beyond being a drug. What makes it a medicine instead of a drug are the magical properties that I associate with it.

Marcy's notion of "magic" made the drug sound like an impersonal force, but occasionally, others spoke of specific properties of the drug that seemed to give it human-like qualities. For example, at an East Coast support group meeting, Georgia said she told her doctor she wanted to take Zoloft because (holding out her hand as if to cup the pill)

it was like a little robin's egg, it has that blue color and it represents hope. Later the doctor added lithium. Still I was knocked down by depression every spring. Now I am on what my doctor calls an "iron-clad defense" against manic depression: two mood stabilizers, lithium and Depakote, and two antidepressants, Wellbutrin and Zoloft. My friend said, "Oh, I wish he hadn't said that, 'iron-clad defense,'" because it implies the defense could give way. It might break.

In this instance, which stands out from the usual way people spoke of their drugs, Georgia does see Zoloft as alive, like a little robin's egg filled with hope, but before long its hope fades as she finds it to be inadequate by itself to handle her needs.

Although most prescription drugs advertised directly to consumers have a rather amorphous identity in the eyes of patients, lithium, which is not advertised to patients, is granted so much consistent agency that it does have a kind of personality, albeit one with both positive and negative sides. On the positive side, many people felt that lithium was the most "natural" of all the psychotropic drugs, explaining, "It's just a salt." Others referred to the mood-steadying effects of lithium as a boon. Sometimes people mentioned the lyrics of songs such as Sting's "Lithium Sunset," in which lithium folds "obsidian darkness" into its "yellow light."

Lithium is surrounded by ambivalence. For all that some people appreciate how it can lift depression and dampen mania, others resist it more ferociously than any other drug that psychiatrists prescribe. Widespread informal consensus labels lithium the drug that elicits far more "failure to comply" than any other. Partly this is because lithium's side effects—on the liver and thyroid—are well known. But partly it is because people are loath to have the pleasures of a rising mood taken away from them.[10] "I'd rather stand in front of a moving train than tell my psychiatrist I am manic, because I know she will make me take more lithium" was a not uncommon sentiment in my fieldwork. Kay Jamison explains that people who are not manic depressive cannot understand why there is such resistance to lithium, which promises you can "be normal": "But if you have had stars at your feet and the rings of planets through your hands, [and] are used to sleeping only four or five hours a night . . . it is a very real adjustment to blend into a three-piece-suit schedule, which, while comfortable to many, is new, restrictive, seemingly less productive, and maddeningly less intoxicating."[11] As Jamison writes, manic depression "destroys the basis of rational thought."[12] If lithium restores it, then it is highly significant that some patients who have experienced being "irrational" refuse lithium precisely because it restores rationality, despite the agonies that manic depression can produce. Lithium is seen as a kind of stern schoolmaster, enforcing the rules and stopping the fun. Like a stern schoolmaster, it cannot be escaped without detection. Patients who take lithium under the care of a physician are required to have periodic blood tests that assess the level of lithium in the blood, in part to detect possible toxic effects. If you aren't taking your lithium as prescribed, your physician will know that, without a doubt. No other psychotropic drug can be easily assessed in this way, leaving lithium as the only one patients must take or be found out.

There is another dimension to the reluctance to take lithium that has come into play recently. In my fieldwork, some people insisted that the specificity in the design of recent psychotropic drugs adds to their potency. Marcy continued to explain her aversion to lithium, but added this twist at the end.

> **Marcy:** One of the reasons they might have given me the Depakote was that I *really* reacted to the lithium thing, like "I am not taking that, lithium is poison." I mean, it's one thing to be ingesting a controlled substance; it's another thing to take poison, and to me lithium was poison because I knew that a high enough dose of it would definitely kill me. Even now, I will never take lithium. Even though I understand that based on the dosage it might actually be safer than taking Depakote, I still would prefer the Depakote. I associate very negative things with lithium and I for some reason can't handle the idea.
> **Emily Martin:** Does the fact that Depakote is a new drug, produced by new technology, make it more powerful in the way you think about it?
> **Marcy:** It's not more powerful, but taking it has less stigma.
> **Emily Martin:** Less stigma?
> **Marcy:** Yes, less stigma and also more of this, like, specificity. It's more specific. It's tailor-made for me and my disorder, it's tailor-made for me and my disease *and only for me and my disease* and using my drug to treat some other thing takes away from — once again — the magical specificity property that it's going to uniquely help me.

Specificity was a trait many people valued in their drugs, a trait that they thought enabled the drug to produce one but not another particular mental capacity or state.[13] At a support group meeting, Nicole, a petite, fortyish woman, said that she was off for the summer from her job as a guidance counselor for the public schools. Her doctor had her taking drugs five times a day. She had the bottles all lined up on the counter with her pillbox and it was quite something to get it all straight. Because of her continuing depression, the doctor had added an additional dose of antidepressant, Effexor, at 4:00. The last drug she takes before bed is another antidepressant, Seroquel: "I like the last dose of the day best of all, that is the Seroquel. I like the calm, drowsy feeling it gives me, and I sleep very, very well. But now I am having trouble making decisions. Before I never had this problem—like at restaurants I would always know what I wanted to eat. But now I am thinking I need some pill added to help with my decision making." Seroquel does a good job making her calm and drowsy before sleep, so it makes sense that there might be another drug to help her make decisions.

Larry, a young, nattily dressed man with a gentle southern accent, told another group that he had gone back on lithium and was "going up." "You know, now that I am taking lithium again, I am going up. Tegretol sent me down, you know." John, the group facilitator, asked if he was worried about getting too high and manic. Larry said, "I have Risperdal to take if that happens." John agreed: "If you feel mania, or have racing thoughts, you just pop a Risperdal and it brings you right down."

The Web is another place to see how people describe the qualities of drugs, and on the Web there is no disapproval, as there is in support groups, of discussing specific drugs and dosages. Postings on Web newsgroups for bipolar disorder make it immediately apparent how many people are taking complex bundles, "cocktails," of drugs that they try to adjust to ease new symptoms, side effects, or drug interactions. Here are some extracts from newsgroup postings:

On side effects:

Well, after getting sun blisters on Trileptal and double vision as well, my doctor and I have decided to try Topamax once a day to start and a Klonopin at night. I was on Seroquel for sleep but since I had no paranoia or hallucinations, it really wasn't necessary and Klonopin can act as a secondary mood stabilizer anyway. Wish me luck all, this is my 5th cocktail, hopefully it will work. My mind is racing so much and I am so angry, I feel like I'm losing it all.[14]

On recalcitrant symptoms:

I'm new, here's an intro.
I have been diagnosed with bipolar for about 3 years now, before that they were just diagnosing me with mood disorder, chronic depression, anxiety, and personality disorder.

My current meds are:

> Wellbutrin SR = 300 mg daily
> Lorazepam = .5 2× daily
> Topamax = 200 mg daily (just reduced from 400 mg daily)
> Depakote = 250 mg AM
> Depakote ER = 1000 mg PM
> Lithium = 600 mg daily

We're currently playing with my meds again trying to get me stable once more, I'm a rapid cycler, and had a pretty quick cycle into high and then dropped out to a long lasting low that caused some problems.[15]

On side effects and recalcitrant symptoms:

From: selene

Subject: cocktail hour

dearest armchair psychopharmacologists, < i mean that as a compliment > can anyone make any recommendations for my new drug blend? i'm going in to see my pdoc. tomorrow and want to have an idea of what i'd like to try next. of course, i'll listen to her recommendation first . . . but i know we dedicate a lot of time to research around here, and consequently i value such well-read, if unofficial, input! i'm thinking about Neurontin and Effexor . . . here's my chemical resume: started Tegretol (400 mg/day) 3 weeks ago; got unusual red spots on my skin 2 weeks in, discontinued use as instructed by my doctor. also started Wellbutrin at that time—a tiny dose, only 75 mg per day. when i stopped the Tegretol, i continued on with the Wellbutrin. i have not lapsed into hypomania, and am, in fact, quite classically depressed. this is manifesting in a very physical way, more than usual—i feel ok emotionally, but have no motivation to leave the house, tidy up the place, or to do anything but the barest essentials with my time. i feel fuzzy in that i don't even know where to start, i felt much, much clearer before the Wellbutrin—i've been dulled! i have therefore stopped the Wellbutrin. if it seems as though i didn't give the Wellbutrin a fair chance, please note that i took it several years ago, with little/no result. past drugs i've given a fair chance and that haven't worked: lithium, Prozac, Norpramin, Depakote (had a reaction). but i suppose i can't be too choosy, since there's only Neurontin and Lamictal left.[16]

Much in these narratives resonated with my own experiences. At the time, I was taking lithium, Focalin (a form of methylphenidate, the active ingredient of Ritalin, prescribed for ADHD), and Lexapro, an SSRI. Because of my complaints about the side effects of Lexapro—emotional numbness and loss of libido—my psychiatrist convinced me to try Lamictal, an antiseizure drug that doctors had begun to use for manic depression. Depending on how I did on Lamictal, I might be able to get off the Lexapro. Graduating from lithium, Focalin, and an SSRI to lithium, Focalin, and Lamictal frightened me badly. My own prejudices were revealed: I was scared of sharing a medication with people suffering from even more stigmatized conditions than mine—epilepsy, brain damage—and I was scared of the side effects. My doctor told me with some urgency that if I broke out with a rash I should stop the medication and immediately call her. On the CVS pharmacy information sheet, I read: "Rarely, serious (sometimes fatal) skin rashes have occurred while using this medication. These rashes (e.g., Stevens-Johnson [SJ] syndrome) are more common in children . . . even after stopping this medication, it is still possible for the rash to cause permanent or life-threatening scarring along with other problems." To me this seemed a bit more dire than a "rash." On the Web I discovered that there is a foundation for SJ syndrome, and I learned (and saw horrifying pictures of) what it entails.

> Painful blistering of the skin and mucous membrane involvement.
> In many cases preceded with flu-like symptoms and high fever.
> As it evolves the skin literally sloughs off.
> Ocular involvement includes severe conjunctivitis, iritis, palpebral edema, conjunctival and corneal blisters and erosions, and corneal perforation.

In a way I was glad I didn't know what some of these things were. Wanting to be free of Lexapro, and aware that I was fortunate to have superb medical care—a caring psychiatrist, an insurance plan, and Internet access—I began taking Lamictal. Its effects were miraculous.

Some months into taking it, I credited the drug with an immense easing of symptoms of depression, anxiety, and obsessiveness, without the emotional flattening of the SSRI. That left me with just the fear of side effects, and the fact that every few weeks a strange lesion opened up on my face and bled. I was assured this was not "the rash," but no one knew what it was. The lesions embodied ambiguity: were they the result of Lamictal, my fevered imagination, or something else? In any case, I was disconcerted at having escaped one set of side effects only to struggle with another.

In my fieldwork, the strategy of combining drugs into cocktails in pursuit of fewer side effects and fewer symptoms was a commonplace topic during informal discussions among doctors. I did not have access to ongoing clinical sessions where doctors discussed and adjusted medications with patients. Although it was less than ideal for the purpose, I was able to get some hints about the ways physicians talk about managing patients on drugs through Web forums set up (by pharmaceutical companies) for doctors to raise questions about medicating their patients.[17] The pharmaceutical company that produces the drug sponsors the Web forum and it is usually company sales reps who give out passwords to doctors they hope will prescribe the drug. This is one way companies hope to foster off-label uses of their drug. One site to which I gained access through a generous person in a publications company (a pharmaceutical corporation had subcontracted the maintenance of the Web site to this company) showed me the extent to which postings from doctors were concerned about the intricate details of particular patients' overall health, the appropriateness of particular drugs, and how to meet patients' needs through elaborate combinations of drugs. For reasons of confidentiality, I call the drug that is the focus of the Web site "Drug R."

The selection of postings below illustrates a common theme: patients commonly take a great many medications at once and their doctors write to the forum for advice about how to deal with cascading side effects. This doctor describes a patient experiencing significant thirst: "I'm treating a woman in her 40's for depression and panic disorder. She may have a subtle bipolar illness. She is currently on lithium carbonate 1500 mg a day, Drug R 45 mg a day, Depakote 625 mg a day,

Klonopin 0.5 mg TID [three times a day] and Pamelor 50 mg a day. 1/
27/00." Another describes a similarly complex regimen that is still not
handling the patient's depression: "Male 37 years old with previous
documented sexual abuse as a child, current diagnoses: DID [Disasso-
ciative Identity Disorder], ADHD, PTSD [Post-Traumatic Stress Disor-
der], bipolar II with refractory depression . . . current meds: lithium
1200 mg, Lamictal 200 mg, Effexor 450 mg, Drug R 45 mg, Cytomel
.25 mcg, Ritalin 80 mg." When the patient recently became hypomanic, the doctor decreased his Effexor, Ritalin, and Drug R, but in
three days, he again had the "most malignant depression I have ever
treated." Not all postings received a response, but this one did. The
consulting online doctor replied, "With this understandable and heroic
combination of meds, what to do? I suggest adding another mood stabilizer (Depakote or an atypical antipsychotic Olanzapine). 5/12/2000."
When drugs are causing problems, the solution is more drugs.

One doctor asks about a patient whose depression Effexor has relieved but who now experiences anxiety, insomnia, and agitation. He
wonders about augmenting the Effexor with Drug R. The on-call expert replies that the combination is used more and more often in similar circumstances "with anecdotal success," but that there are no controlled studies of safety and efficacy. He suggests a conservative starting
dosage of Drug R. Another doctor asks for suggestions for ways of coun-
teracting a patient's weight gain and sexual dysfunction while on
SSRIs as well as Effexor and Drug R. He has tried augmenting with
Wellbutrin and Buspar, but seeks additional advice. The expert suggests a number of options: switch to a low sexual dysfunction, weight-
neutral antidepressant (Wellbutrin or Serzone); try adding Viagra; try
Gingko, even though there are no controlled data; try dose reduction,
though you may lose therapeutic benefits; prevent the weight gain
through diet and exercise, though this is easier said than done; add
weight loss agents, such as Orlistat, though there are no controlled
studies and it may block the absorption of the antidepressant; try
weight loss agent Topamax, though it has a high incidence of CNS
(central nervous system) side effects.

Another doctor asks for information regarding menstrual irregulari-
ties in her thirty-three-year-old patient taking Drug R, which has eased

her depression. In addition the doctor wonders how to handle the side effect of insomnia, which occurred when he increased the dose of Drug R to a level adequate to handle the depression. The doctor had used Ambien, to induce sleep on a temporary basis, but worries about harm from adding an atypical antidepressant with sedative properties such as trazodone to Drug R. The expert suggests several possibilities: split the total dose of Drug R with a lower dose at night; combine Drug R with trazodone, which has had no complications in his experience; even better, combine Drug R with an over-the-counter antihistamine such as Benadryl; or combine Drug R with a low dose of Zyprexa at night.

As a patient I have experienced how strategies like these are translated into written instructions. At the onset of a rapid descent into depression, with insomnia and anxiety (I had been taking lithium [450 mg] and Celexa [10 mg] at the time), my doctor wrote the additional measures I should take on a prescription pad.

1. bed at 10 p.m.
2. take Ambien at bedtime
3. try Dexedrine 5 mg in a.m.; can go to 20 mg by 5 mg increments
4. Ativan, try .25 mg in afternoon before anxiety sets in and in middle of night try .25 or .5 mg.

One week later, with not much improvement, I got another set of written instructions to *add* to the previous ones.

1. take Ativan, .5 mg 4 times a day, a.m., noon, early p.m., and late p.m.
2. take Ativan again .5 mg during middle of night
3. increase Celexa to 20 mg

Doctors and patients develop more and more elaborate combinations of drugs as they try to solve the side effects or symptoms of one by the action of another.[18] The need to take so many drugs, and to monitor their relational effects, might have the effect of diluting any sense that each drug has a particular personality. Each drug is more like a precise instrument than a living being. Gone from this picture are the complex associations possessed by old drugs like lithium. Marcy prefers "the magical specificity property" of Depakote, but she may have to give up the "yellow light" of Sting's "Lithium Sunset."

When I started this research, perhaps seduced by the marketing literature I had read, I imagined that people would invest their drugs with personalities and form some kind of relationship with them, perhaps seeing them as encouraging companions, calming presences, or strong protectors. My expectations led me to look hard for such relationships. What I actually found was that patients personify new, high-tech drugs only weakly, and do not usually invest them with elaborate symbolic value of a person-like sort. Both doctors and patients see drugs as precision instruments that would excise suffering if they could only find the right combination. It is as if there is a dearth of appealing metaphors to capture what it is like to live with a drug inside you. Let me suggest one: when drugs lift depression or calm mania they could be seen as teachers, modeling new habits. Medications need not be seen as a management tool, a view that inevitably raises the question whether the patient or the doctor is in charge of the medication, but as something we might call "co-performers." This terminology casts them as something like agents inside the person who enable the performance of calm, of energy, of organization, or, if needed, of stability. Medications could be regarded as teachers who enable the person to experience such states. Can a precision instrument that is only slightly personified perform or teach? I think the answer is yes. A training board for a windsurfer, a walker for a stroke patient: these are among the simple but precisely engineered devices that guide and steer people as they learn new skills. Could not drugs be regarded in this light?

The accounts above are permeated with ambivalence—simultaneous and contradictory feelings of attraction and repulsion. The drugs help me, they hurt me; they ease one kind of pain and intensify another; and they take away one painful symptom but add a new one. It was to my astonishment, then, that I witnessed a display at the 2000 APA, which depicted the worry patients feel (some of which is surely legitimate) as a literal form of paranoia. This display, liberally branded with the logo of Risperdal, a major prescription antipsychotic from Janssen Pharmaceutica, was a virtual reality set-up called "Virtual Hallucinations." People stood in line reading an information card explaining what

was to come. Meanwhile, overhead, a video on continuous loop featured a man diagnosed with schizophrenia telling us that the experience we were about to have was true to life. Eventually I reached the
head of the line, went to my assigned station, and put on my head-
phones and helmet. This gear would provide the sight and sound for
me to experience a virtual world. The attendant instructed me, "When
you enter the pharmacy, look around, and keep looking around to find
the pharmacist." As the virtual scene unfolded, I understood that I was
a patient who needed her antipsychotic medication, but my prescription had run out. So my friend, a woman, had brought me to the pharmacy to get a refill. My friend and I entered the pharmacy door. Just
inside, the friend turned around and said, "I'll be back soon; you will
be all right, won't you?" She then vanished rapidly out of sight into the
back of the store. The virtual reality narrator directed me to look around
for the pharmacist. I saw people in the aisles who seemed to be there
one minute and gone the next. The sound was echoing and distorted.
Objects and people sped through space in a blur. Voices came from
everywhere, and sometimes specifically from the people I saw. A
woman in the aisle looked at me suspiciously with a hateful expression.
As I made my way to the back of the line to wait for my prescription,
the virtual reality narrator provided the script of my thoughts: "The
pharmacist does not want me to have the pills; he is going to do something terrible; he is going to call the insurance company and this will
put me in danger. Who can tell what the consequence might be?" I felt
frightened and wanted to flee. As I watched him prepare my medication, the pill bottle turned into a bottle of poison with a skull and crossbones on it. The dissonant music and disturbing special effects made
this terrifying prospect the dramatic culmination of the experience.

The intended message of the display was that paranoia is a well-
known symptom of some psychotic conditions and that the drugs that
the virtual pharmacist was preparing can alleviate this symptom. The
patient, however, could have been frightened by any number of strange
things that happened in the virtual scene. What the patient feared most
intensely was the pharmacist and the drugs he was preparing. This startling development echoes back to Mr. Burton's rounds, where social
knowledge—repressed in rounds but erupting from a hidden place—

pushes through. The obvious message is that the patient has irrational, paranoid fears of the pharmacist. But the obvious message overlays another darker one: the reason the patient fears the pharmacist and his drugs is because the drugs are poison! The association between feelings of paranoia and schizophrenia comes right out of the DSM: what is extraordinary is that Janssen Pharmaceutica, surely despite its own interests, portrayed a prescription antipsychotic (a product they manufacture) as a bottle of poison. When even powerful pharmaceutical corporations cannot stop themselves from imagining that the psychotropic drugs they produce are poisons, we can better understand why the people in this chapter who decide to consume such drugs also regard them with ambivalence.

PART TWO

Mania as a Resource

The purpose of part 2 is to consider how psychotropic drugs and manic depression are imagined on an almost mythical scale. This giant landscape will be replete with larger-than-life images in advertisements and media, and with the activities of powerful institutions like corporations and markets. Although we leave behind the close-up views of pharmaceutical employees, physicians, and patients living under the description of manic depression, we need to remember the uncertainty and ambivalence revealed in part 1. Even international markets and global corporations have come into being through the activities of employees, practitioners, and patients whose actions and notions are imbued with uncertainty.

In the U.S. economic system, there is a premium on measuring and tracking any valuable resource, and that includes moods. The activities of charting and recording moods make moods and their potential benefits or detriments visible and quantifiable. Norms for moods have gone up the scale from "moderate" toward "hot." Anyone living under the description of manic depression—as well as anyone who partakes in the powerful aura of a manic style—learns they have the capacity to be "hot" and the potential to parlay this capacity into a valuable commodity in the market. But being "hot" means walking high up on an "edge." Walking high up on an "edge" means fearing the inevitability of a fall into the abyss of "cold" depression.

CHAPTER SEVEN

Taking the Measure of Moods and Motivations

Numbers are the product of counting. *Quantities*
are the product of measurement. This means that
numbers can conceivably be accurate because there is a
discontinuity between each integer and the next.
Between *two* and *three*, there is a jump. In the case of
quantity, there is no such jump; and because jump is
missing in the world of quantity, it is
impossible for any quantity to be exact. You can have
exactly three tomatoes. You can never have
exactly three gallons of water. Always quantity
is approximate.

—Gregory Bateson, *Mind and Nature:*
A Necessary Unity

As we move from the small-scale daily experiences of people to the larger-scale phenomena of markets and popular media, a bridging concept is Raymond Williams's "structures of feeling."[1] Structures of feeling are actively felt sensibilities that can be vague rather than explicit, informally sensed rather than formally codified. Comedians who use manic energy to draw audiences into hilarious laughter, support groups who turn to an enactment of mania to demonstrate the volitional aspects of going manic, a doctor who uneasily relies on a group of manic depressives to care for a schizophrenic man—all these fleeting events draw on a sense that mania is linked to something powerful, not just to something disordered. Small scale and amorphous they may be, structures of feeling can still play a important part in producing larger-scale phenomena. For example, as we saw in the last chapter, the sensibilities of pharmaceutical advertisers about creativity and manic depression play a role in developing ads that end up as part of mass media. In turn, as we will see in the second half of the book, larger institutional forces flowing from markets and media act back on the everyday sensibilities of the people we met in the first half.

Americans living under the description of manic depression today are often encouraged to keep a "mood chart" in order to manage their manias and depressions. Filling out a mood chart—a small act of individual discipline—can have dramatic effects. When many people fill out the same charts or register their moods on a numerical scale, they make their distinct experiences comparable. When people assign a number to a mood, they are paving the way for statistics that describe the moods of a population and their changes over time. Through the social technology of the mood chart, manic depression emerges from the psychology of individuals onto the scene of national and global concerns with the rationality and productivity of populations.

The practice of mood charting is part of a long tradition dating back to the eighteenth century, when charts were used to manage the daily ups and downs of moods. The Philadelphia physician Benjamin Rush devised a "moral thermometer," published in a popular health magazine in 1833, that enabled people to register changes from "unfeeling," "cold," or "sullen" on the low end to "hot," "passionate," or "ungovernable" on the high end. Rush intended the moral thermometer to regulate people's "tempers" in accord with the dictates of the temperance movement of that time.

At the end of this chapter, I will return to Rush's chart for comparison with the multitude of contemporary charts I came across in my fieldwork. One example is "Amy's self-rated mood chart," found in a popular contemporary handbook on managing bipolar disorder.[2] This chart is a grid that fits on one page of the book, with a row for each day of the month. The left part of the chart is devoted to records of medication and the right part to mood. There are columns for daily notes such as "friend's wedding" or "dog got sick; went to hospital," and columns to indicate "irritability," "anxiety," and hours of sleep. The range of moods is from "elevated" to "depressed," and, strikingly, times when one is "able to work" or "not able to work" are distinguished for both elevated and depressed moods. This chart connects working and not working, productivity and unproductivity, with the individual's moods. This con-

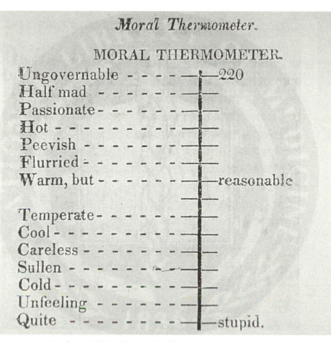

Moral Thermometer.

MORAL THERMOMETER.

Ungovernable - - - - —|—220
Half mad - - - - - - —|—
Passionate - - - - - - —|—
Hot - - - - - - - - —|—
Peevish - - - - - - - —|—
Flurried - - - - - - - —|—
Warm, but - - - - - - —|—reasonable

Temperate - - - - - - —|—
Cool - - - - - - - - - —|—
Careless - - - - - - - —|—
Sullen - - - - - - - - —|—
Cold - - - - - - - - - —|—
Unfeeling - - - - - - —|—
Quite - - - - - - - - —|—stupid.

7.1. Benjamin Rush's 1833 "Moral Thermometer" showing a range of mental states as hot and cold temperatures. © Benjamin Rush, "Moral Thermometer." *Journal of Health and Recreation* 4, no. 1 (1833): 5. Courtesy of National Library of Medicine.

nection reiterates in another form the link we have seen several times before between moods and motivation.

Mood charts such as Amy's encourage people to manage their psychological states rationally so they can work productively. The conviction that psychological management is rational came out of the early history of the disciplines of psychiatry, psychology, and psychoanalysis. These disciplines came to think that persons, as individuals, could achieve desirable goals such as authority, tranquility, sanity, virtue, or efficiency by governing their own subjectivity. To govern themselves, individuals would need to collect information about their subjectivity in any number of forms, from written reports to drawings, from charts to statistics.[3] As the person scrutinized and recorded his inner states, he would become more aware that he was a separate individual who bore the responsibility for self-government.[4] Today, a person who keeps a mood chart is translating inside, subjective experience into outside, socially visible forms.[5] The practices of introspection and record keeping we have come to take for granted build a strong identity at the individual level, both general (I am a self-regulating calculating, rational person) and specific (these are my mood patterns, and this is how I respond to my specific medications).

Once a person writes her subjective information down in some form, she can manage it in new ways. If she collects her information on a chart whose categories are widely used, she can compare her inner states to another person's. The chart creates a sense that everyone experiences the same kinds of moods, though they may experience them in different combinations and intensities. Comparisons on a common scale are not only invited; they rush to the forefront as charts proliferate. It is as if moods have been thrown into what Marx called the "great social retort."[6] The "retort" boils out particular flavors and leaves only measurable abstract qualities, such as degrees of sanity, modernity, or rationality.

If a person collects her information on a chart that has a numerical scale, still more elaborate forms of management open up. She can now track her moods numerically over time and ascertain whether, by the year, month, or day, her moods are averaging higher or lower. As her moods become represented by a numerical value, they become commensurable with the moods of others.[7] If she provides numerical information about her moods to her doctor or a public health specialist, she may contribute to statistical measures of the national or global mood. These forms of record keeping create standardized measures for private, interior states, standardized measures that enable new kinds of measurement of populations.[8]

To gain greater historical perspective on contemporary mood charts, I turn to Emil Kraepelin's charts of moods in *Manic-Depressive Insanity and Paranoia*, originally published in 1921 and reprinted in color in 2002. For Kraepelin, there were a limited number of types of mood states within the general category manic depression. Each was marked with a special graphic or shade of color: mania, hypomania, raving mania, and manic stupor (all in shades of red), light depression, heavy depression, depression with flight of ideas, and depressive excitement (all in shades of blue).[9] But the many charts he included in the book demonstrate that Kraepelin recognized the immense variety of ways individuals with manic depression cycled through mood states. He argued that others' efforts to lump groups of individuals into subtypes of the illness were futile: "[T]he multiplicity of the courses taken by manic-depressive insanity . . . is absolutely inexhaustible. The cases reported only show that there can be no talk of even an approximate regularity in the course, as has formerly been frequently assumed on the ground of certain isolated observations."[10] For Kraepelin, the time scale was in years (numbered on the left side of the chart), subdivided only into months and portions of months (labeled across the top of the chart). So compact was the chart that the entire lifetime of a person could be contained on one single page.

Doctors familiar with patients in a clinical setting compiled the condensed information in Kraepelin's charts over many years. Patients themselves had no role in writing down their symptoms: rather, doctors kept careful records of patients' health, from how much they weighed to how neatly they could write.

Kraepelin saw manic-depressive insanity as a disease that had a natural, inevitable progression. He regarded it as a "natural disease entity"[11] whose characteristics he and his associates discovered through clinical record keeping of "countless" patients.[12] He devised a special form called the "Zählkarten"[13] to categorize information on each patient. Although masses of data were collected and studied, there is no evidence that Kraepelin quantified this data to present it in the form of graphs or charts summarizing many patients. Nor did he use mathematical forms of representation to show, say, the rise and fall of mood in individual patients over time. His charts only showed the many ways subtypes of moods succeeded one another in different individuals.

According to Kraepelin, although the progression of manic-depressive insanity could be charted, ordinarily no cure would be possible for patients admitted to institutions: he said most were "forever lost."[14] The only hope would come from prevention: in Kraepelin's view, at least one-third of all mental illnesses had causes he regarded as preventable, such as alcoholism, syphilis, traumatic injury, or addiction to morphine and cocaine.[15] In spite of the gloomy prospects for

Alter	Januar	Febr.	März	April	Mai	Juni	Juli	August	Sept.	Okt.	Nov.	
30												
40												
					X	X X X X X X X X X X X X X X X X X X						X X
50	X X											
60					X X							

7.2. A 1921 mood chart representing a patient's mood changes month by month over more than three decades. Reprinted with permission. E. Kraepelin, *Manic-Depressive Insanity and Paranoia*. 1921. Bristol, England: Thoemmes Press, 2002. © 2002 (1921) Emil Kraepelin.

his patients, Kraepelin's charts, as well as his descriptions, showed the possibility for patients to enjoy prolonged and frequent disease-free periods. Kraepelin called these remissions "long lucid intervals"[16] when patients were "able to reenter the family, to employ themselves profitably, and to return to their profession."[17] On his charts, these intervals are shown as white spaces.

Today, in contrast to Kraepelin's time, individuals keep their own mood charts. The charts appear in popular books, magazines, doctors' offices, and on the Web. Many groups interested in manic depression explicitly encourage their use. For example, the Web site for the Harvard Bipolar Research group provides a sample chart already filled in and a blank chart you can download and print out for your own use.

The Web site for the patient advocacy group, the Depression and Bipolar Support Alliance, provides a sample chart, a chart for downloading, and a page of detailed instructions. The pharmaceutical company Lilly gives consumers a Web page with a slider to register where one is in the range of moods, and a button to click if one wants to see one's moods over time as a graph. The federally funded NIMH Web site presents visitors with a complex chart accompanied by extensive instructions.[18]

In addition, various kinds of charts have been developed for parents to use at home and for teachers to use in the classroom. With one device, children use markers to color in which cartoon face best represents their moods, from sad to frantic; with another device, children place plastic stickers on a "Mood Tree." The designer of the Mood Tree, Rosalyn Newport-Olsen, LCSW, explained to me that children (or in other versions adolescents or adults) place plastic stickers on the Mood Tree to "illustrate their symptoms when they are occurring and to what degree." She designed the device to be nonthreatening to the patient and to facilitate communication between therapist and patient: "[T]he Mood Tree's visible and tactile appeal makes it useful [for] those unable or unwilling to stay with graphics charting."[19]

These techniques are marketed to the parents of children who display behavior problems in the home or classroom. Most recently, a diary is being marketed directly to children who have no particular behavior problems. *The Judy Moody Mood Journal,* a spin-off from a series of popular books about a temperamental third grade girl, encourages children to keep track of their moods, following the character, Judy Moody, who is "always in a mood." The diary has a "Dial-a-Mood-Meter" built into the cover: you can spin the pointer to see which of ten moods (from "moody blues" to "mischievous") it will come to rest upon.[20] As children are taught to keep records of their interior states, they are being taught to take individual responsibility for managing those states. The record keeping of moods thus extends from children whose moods cause problems at school or home to (potentially) all children.

As in Kraepelin's charts, contemporary charts record a range of psychological states. But in contemporary charts, only simple, everyday feelings and behaviors are listed (anger, sadness, irritability, tiredness,

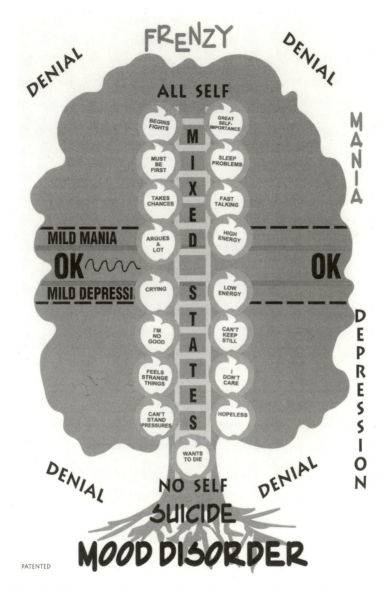

7.3. Children or adults can indicate the state of their moods by moving plastic stickers around the Mood Tree. Reprinted with permission. The Mood Tree, designed by Rosalyn Newport-Olsen, MSW, LCSW. http://www.moodtree.com.

7.4. Cover of *The Judy Moody Mood Journal* with an arrow on a dial that points to different moods when it is spun. Text copyright © 2003 by Megan McDonald. Illustrations copyright © 2003 by Peter H. Reynolds. Judy Moody font copyright © 2003 by Peter H. Reynolds. Reproduced by permission of the publisher, Candlewick Press, Inc.

hunger, and so forth), rather than technically defined complexes of traits (Kraepelin's "manic stupor"). The traits charted, it is assumed, are knowable by the individual directly. Do I feel sadness? Elation? Do I experience energy? Fatigue? The charts do not require trained observers of the sort Kraepelin needed.

Compared to Kraepelin's charts, the contemporary mood chart has undergone a certain elaboration. In Kraepelin's case, an individual's entire life span could be described on one page; today, one page usually contains the details of only a single day. Each day, in turn, can be divided into periods of hours and minutes and each quality or activity can be registered practically by the minute. Self-scrutiny can thus be carried out at a finer level of detail. I can record, and worry about, my mood variations minute by minute. From details *by the year* to details *by the hour* is a speedup of more than 10,000-fold.

The biggest difference between then and now is that contemporary charts invariably contain a place to record the means of ameliorating mood disorders. All charts I have seen have a section, often occupying nearly half of the chart, for recording what medicines the person takes as well as how much and when they take them throughout the day. Medications are carefully plotted in relation to symptoms so that the mood pattern can be adjusted up or down. A software company has devised a program, Mood Monitor, which allows patients to fill out charts on their home computers while the doctor keeps tabs on their condition remotely. The program calculates summary data from moods juxtaposed to medications, and doctors adjust medications as necessary. On the company's Web site, a doctor writes, "I have used Mood Monitor® in my clinical practice and am very impressed. I have long found that bipolar patients are unable to accurately measure their moods and other parameters between sessions. With Mood Monitor, I can see at a glance how their moods are varying as well as how the patient is sleeping. This allows me to make adjustments in medications with more confidence." Even without a doctor's involvement, people in support groups frequently said that representing their moods on a chart over time allowed them to see more clearly exactly what differences medications make. A Web author who makes his mood chart available on line agrees: "I've found that minor changes in medication can make big changes in how I felt, so tracking dosages was useful. And, embarrassing as it was, tracking when I didn't take medicines was useful, too."[21]

Although the contemporary chart seems to offer more hope of improvement through medication than does Kraepelin's, one effect of the detailed moment-by-moment scrutiny is to emphasize the abnormal. People could mark their moods and other states right along the middle axis of the chart, along "normal," but, in fact, they seldom do. What counts as "normal" can occupy as little as one point on the chart, as on the Harvard Bipolar Research Program home page — and this point can be easy to miss. Also, as one charting regular asked me, "Who wants to be a zero?" While for some the zero of normality is tinged negatively, for others the whole chart is negative territory. At a lecture I gave at the University of Texas, Austin, I showed several slides of Kraepelin's mood charts, coded, as I already described, in shades of red for mania, shades of blue for depression, and white for lucid intervals. A woman in the audience, identifying herself as a person from the Austin community diagnosed with bipolar disorder, commented, "Thank you for giving me the white spaces. I am going to go home and just be in a white space." This woman evidently felt relief at being able to visualize "the white spaces" — places where her moods were not disordered and she did not have to monitor them constantly.

In support groups, I observed directly how difficult it is to occupy the zero point as long as one has the diagnosis of a mood disorder. Groups often followed the practice of beginning each meeting by going around the room for brief introductions. Each person would state his or her first name and then, using a kind of oral mood chart, give a number on a scale from −5 to +5, indicating a range of moods from very depressed to very manic. "I'm Jan and I'm +3," "I'm Dave and I'm −2," and so on. Only people with a diagnosis of manic depression attended most meetings, and I never heard anyone choose zero. But one time a woman who attended regularly brought along her husband, who does not have the diagnosis of manic depression. He listened as each person gave his or her name and score. When it was his turn he said uncertainly, "I'm Brad and I guess I must be zero." In sum, everyone can see himself somewhere on the chart and (unless he is a zero) he can see how his emotional states could be moderated by psychotropic medications. Being zero, being normal, placed Brad orthogonal to the chart and out of reach of its demand for self-surveillance.

Mood Hygiene

In a popular book about manic depression, keeping a mood chart is said to be part of "mood hygiene." Francis Mondimore includes a picture of Hygeia, the Greek goddess of health, who, in this context, stands for "Practices and habits that promote good control of mood symptoms in persons with bipolar disorder." In the context of the image of Hygeia, Mondimore points out that research shows "just how important preventive measures can be for improving symptom control in bipolar disorder."[22] This is a powerful image because it is well known (and Mondimore emphatically reminds us) how efficacious hygienic practices (cleaning water, sweeping houses, and washing bodies) were in the reduction of mortality and morbidity that took place in the early twentieth century. But this is also an odd image. Hygiene reduces physical disease by eliminating *pathogens*. What is the hygiene of moods meant to reduce or eliminate? Are the surges and dips above and below the line of "normal" meant to be reduced? If this were to happen, would emotions, feelings, and sentiments in general be reduced? Would it be more "hygienic" if they were reduced to almost nothing? In Mondimore's book, these questions are left unanswered.

To push these questions further, I turn back to a book from 1978: *Mood Disorders: The World's Major Public Health Problem*. Why might "mood disorders" have been considered a public health problem in 1978? The main reason this book cites is that "[d]epression is a public health problem because it is frequent, causes distress and suffering for many patients and their families, and results in severe socioeconomic losses."[23] The link between mood and productivity in the workplace was well entrenched in North America by the end of World War II. An early 1950s public health education film made clear the link between depression and decreased ability to work. Called *Feelings of Depression*, the film tells the story of John, a depressed young man who believes he is failing at his job, and more seriously, believes his company itself is on the brink of failure.[24] The notion that mood disorders were a public health problem was doubtless fueled by the development of a new form of antidepression medication. Frank Ayd, coeditor of the 1978 book, ran Merck's clinical trials for their antidepressant Elavil. Merck bought 50,000 copies of another book Ayd wrote, *Recognizing the Depressed Patient*, and distributed them worldwide. This played a significant role in Elavil's success: "Merck not only sold amitriptyline, it sold an idea. Amitriptyline became the first of the antidepressants to sell in substantial amounts."[25]

More recent items in the media continue to associate "moods," especially depression, with lack of productivity or inability to work. A public health poster from 1991 captioned "Not everyone who is depressed is this visible" depicts a scene of a contemporary open office space in which several (presumably depressed) workers are shown as immobile white plaster statues. In 2001, the business news reported that Bank One, concerned about productivity losses because of depression among its employees, instituted programs to encourage education, screening, and treatment. But the outcome for the bank was that the number of employees taking disability leaves for depression skyrocketed.[26] In 2003, a widely reported study, "Cost of Lost Productive Work Time among U.S. Workers with Depression" (funded by Eli Lilly, manufacturer of the antidepressant Prozac), found that depression costs employers $31 billion per year in lost productive time.[27] Since this study also discovered that use of antidepressants among depressed workers was low, it made the dotted lines between taking antidepressants and increasing productivity easy to connect. Similar lines were connected in the spate of articles in print media, the Web, and on television looking at links between moods like depression and the inability to leave the welfare rolls by means of finding a job.[28] In a *60 Minutes* story on welfare and depression, Lesley Stahl begins,

> One reason there are still five million people on welfare is that "a huge number of them are depressed, not just suffering from a case of the blues, but seriously medically depressed. It's an epidemic of depression among America's poor."

Dr. Kessler of Harvard's School of Public Health estimates between a third and a half of people still on welfare are clinically depressed.

Dr. Carl Bell (of a mental clinic in Chicago): The state of Illinois, bless their heart, finally figured out that maybe the people who were going to be left on welfare were people with psychiatric disorders, and so maybe somebody ought to be here screening for that and referring people for treatment.

Lesley Stahl: So people come in for welfare, for their checks, to make their applications, and if somebody is there that perhaps spots these symptoms . . .

Dr. Bell: You can screen them out—everybody can get a very simple screening form—find out who's got what, and then treat them.[29]

It goes without saying that welfare recipients should be able to reap the same benefits of the latest medication and therapies for depression as economically better-off citizens. But how do we separate those who would be depressed whether rich or poor and those who are depressed *because* they are poor? Screening alone will not do the job.

In the *60 Minutes* scenario, the participants imagine that it would be best for depression to simply disappear. Of course, no one would wish to perpetuate the suffering caused by the despair and paralysis of depression. Least of all would pharmaceutical advertisements, which frequently imply that depression can be eradicated, and that its eradication would be a good thing.[30] On behalf of Prozac and Serafem, Lilly urges you to "Get your life back" (from the depression that has taken it away) and after treatment to remove the depression, declares, "Welcome back!" On behalf of Zoloft, Pfizer exhorts, "When you know more about what is wrong, you can help make it right." Taking Zoloft will correct the "chemical imbalance of serotonin in the brain," which, it is suggested, is the physical signature of depression. In *Against Depression*, Peter Kramer warns us not to romanticize depression as a form of "heroic melancholy," but instead treat it as a disease we can cure. Although I would agree that the suffering caused by depression should not be endowed with virtue, I want to call attention to the socially based reasons why we want to eliminate some moods but keep others. Kramer exempts mania and hypomania from elimination because "they may drive productivity in many fields."[31] Once again, mania is valuable because of its association with motivation and productivity.

Practices of screening populations to detect undesirable mental states have now gone far beyond welfare offices. Heralded through the Bush administration's New Freedom Commission on Mental Health and given a test run as the Texas Medical Algorithm Project (TMAP), systematic screening has already been instituted as official policy in more than ten states. The program is slated for national use. Pennsylvania has run into trouble because Allen Jones, a self-identified whistle blower, publicized the connections between the pharmaceutical industry, the specific, brand-name drugs Pennsylvania placed on its formulary (the list of drugs physicians must choose from), and the financial interests of numerous state and federal officials. My point is not that we should deny the best mental health care—including drugs—for everyone, but that cultural values in favor of productive moods can be tied in a troubling way to economic interests.[32]

With depression eliminated, the way would be open to cultivate a kind of manic energy stripped of its moodiness. Indeed, self-help experts have marketed explicit programs to help achieve this end. Through many best-selling books and television programs, Barbara Sher advocates a program of self-improvement in which moods are considered a distraction. Moods are important to identify so they do not get in the way of the real goal: building motivation. She writes, "You can't ignore your emotions. They're strong and primitive and must be dealt with."[33] But moods and emotions are to be identified and swept away (as if by Hygeia's broom) so that your "hidden motivators" and "untapped energy sources" can be unleashed, even when, as her Web site states, "you are in a lousy mood."[34]

Although mood charts are mostly for people who are afflicted by their moods and need to know them in order to control them by practicing mood hygiene, the word "hygiene" should be a tip-off to us that *selections* are being made among mood states. Just as at the turn of the twentieth century when "unhygienic" behavior was discouraged and "hygienic" behavior was encouraged, the notion is that as depression withers away altogether, the wild, raw mania of the manic depressive can be tamed or optimized, the better to enable individuals to succeed and economies to grow. Key agents in this picture are the growing numbers of psychopharmaceutical drugs. They are what allow contemporary doctors to give a patient a diagnosis of mood disorder and treat it, rather than (as in earlier historical periods) lay the patient's problems at the feet of her temperament or character.[35] This transformation has certain benefits, not least that drugs can be effective and patients can feel less personally responsible for their condition. A newspaper article by a doctor praises the transformation because it unmasks "cheerful character" as "hypomania" (a mild form of mania) and "gloomy temperament" as "hypomania's dark twin 'dysthymia' [a mild form of depression]."[36] In the unmasking, these conditions are rendered treatable. But they are also rendered as conditions that are greatly more susceptible to whatever cultural ideals are in play. It becomes thinkable to manage and adjust moods and motivations in directions that are apparently necessary for survival in the fierce economy of the present. We will see in chapters 8 and 9 how mania (with its intense motivation) gathers attention from the workplace and the "marketplace": I will argue that mania's connection with strong motivation is part of what lies behind our current sense that it is something that can be harnessed as an asset in the workplace.

Concern for the control of mood disorders has even spread beyond the national borders of the United States. In 2001, the World Health Organization (WHO) declared mental illness the main global health crisis of the year. Chief among WHO's concerns were two: the loss of productivity to the world's economies because of depressed mood; and making effective pharmacological treatments more widely available. For their part, the pharmaceutical industry, by the 1990s in possession of a greater range of drug treatments, clearly envisioned the market for these drugs on a global scale, and began to speak of the "global Central Nervous System therapeutics market" estimated at approximately $44 billion.[37]

A number of factors are coming together here: dissemination of mood charts for individuals to track their moods on a daily or hourly basis; a strong link between mood and productivity; and interest in increasing the recognition and treatment of mood disorders across the globe. The modest technology of mood charting has had an important role to play in the claim, first made in 1978 and reiterated often since, that mood disorders are a threat to the health of populations—mood disorders are a public health crisis. For people who feel compromised by their moods, this attention is welcome because it acknowledges the extent of the problem and legitimates its significant impact on life. My argument is that in the process of coming into being, the public health crisis in moods has changed the way people experience their moods. Increasingly, there seems to be one universal set of mood categories that everyone experiences. Through the simple act of recording their moods in terms of these categories, people form the habit of thinking in terms of a standardized taxonomy of mood.[38] As they become more and more aware of their moods at a detailed level, they are likely to feel greater personal responsibility for practicing good mood hygiene. Thus, subjectivity changes. These changes have contradictory aspects. On the one hand, moods gain more and more concreteness as real things in nature, with a biochemical basis. On the other hand, people come to feel more and more responsible for manipulating their environments (lifestyles) and their affective constitutions, through biochemical means if necessary. Affective "nature" is not a given any longer; it is raw material needing management.[39] Nothing less is involved in personal, national, and global success and failure. New habits of recording moods in turn enable governments, public health agencies, and pharmaceutical corporations to compile national and global statistics. These statistics then play their part in convincing organizations like the WHO or state and federal agencies in the United States to target the link between depression and productivity, as we saw in chapter 1. Something very small in scale (keeping a daily record of one's moods) becomes something very big in scale (global statistics that link mood and productivity), which can then loop back and change subjectivity yet again.[40]

Evading Mood Charts

The sociologist Peter Miller has argued that accounting schemes like mood charts are virtually impossible to resist. If people refuse to use one scheme, they will be provided with a new, improved version. Consultants and others will use their complaints to identify the shortcomings of the original calculating technology in order to develop a new one without those shortcomings: "The aspiration to render individuals and spaces calculable seems to engender a constant process of adjudication on the vices and virtues of this technique or that."[41] In small ways, however, people do try to modify calculating technologies themselves. For example, since the publishing capacities of the Web open the door to individual creativity, some individually designed mood charts have the potential to do more than reinscribe the same calculations in a more efficient or effective form.

A chart on a Web site published by Jinnah Mohammed includes large amounts of information about his particular life, undercutting the depersonalized and abstract qualities of most charts. The more specific his information is, the less readily it can be reduced to a number and compared to information from others. Jinnah's chart also separates measures of mood from measures of functionality, opening multiple axes on which he can compare different aspects of his condition. The additional axis has the potential to increase the surveillance of the chart over Jinnah's life, but at the same time it opens the possibility of challenging how standard DSM categories link moods and productivity. In the DSM, moods on either end of the manic depression scale are abnormal. By charting functionality as well as moods Jinnah discovers that he can be functional while his moods are abnormal, thus opening the possibility that he could reject the DSM's assumptions. However, he does not go this way. Instead, he concludes he is never normal: "I have used the charts to show my family that when they thought I was normal (i.e., functional), I wasn't emotionally stable. It came as quite a shock to them often because they couldn't detect anything wrong with me. . . . [The chart allowed me] to realize I had no periods of normality."[42] In the end, Jinnah Mohammed's charting bears out Peter Miller's general point: the more of his life the chart makes visible, the more he feels he does not fit the "norm."

From another point of view, doing the accounting defined as self-management might be considered a strike in favor of one's capacity to be a rational person. Charting one's moods could be seen as demonstrating one's rationality—and this in itself could constitute a form of resistance to being categorized as irrational. From this point of view let us reconsider Amy's mood chart. What is being measured here? What is the something that goes up and down, or gets a numerical designation? Moods? Feelings? Energy? Will? Whatever it is, it comes from a private, individual, interior space. The chart converts specific experiences into abstractions through numeric measurement (Marx's "retort"), but it also makes these experiences social along the way.[43] When one is categorized as "mentally ill" and hence outside the realm of the fully human, having one's private experience count as part of the social holds great significance. The individual uniqueness of experience might be lost in the homogenizing process of abstraction, but in return the private moods of an individual take the form of their opposite, moods that are widely shared. For people with pathological mood disorders, this is a move toward feeling human. This might be why people with mood disorders frequently say that charting their moods in and of itself makes them feel better. Even though, like Jinnah, charting might increase the range of their moods that appear abnormal, charting also makes them like everyone else, managing their moods through keeping records of diet, exercise, and medication.

From Temperate to Hot

I have made a case that compared to Kraepelin's charts, contemporary mood charts encourage self-monitoring because they are kept by patients, subdivided into many categories, liable to eliminate any space for the "normal," and oriented to the relationship between drugs and moods. They, however, may have something in common with Rush's earlier version, the moral thermometer. Rush and his followers explicitly recommended that household members assiduously record information about themselves, though the matrix they provided was indeed less complex than today's charts. In the popular magazine that reprinted the chart, readers were exhorted to enter "in a journal every variation observed in their own tempers" and thus be able to look back over time "to see what measure of improvement has been gained in a given period."[44] Then as today, keeping a written record was a way of providing individuals with a path to self-improvement.

The inventor of the thermometer is persuaded that if ladies and gentlemen, young as well as old, were to use the instrument according to the directions which accompany it, they would find their own happiness increase, and their acquaintance more desirous at all times of their company; neither has he the least doubt, but husbands and wives, parents and children, masters and servants, would find their lives become gradually much more easy and happy by a proper attention to it. N.B. the scale had better be hung up out of reach.

A part of the early temperance movement in the United States, the intent of Rush's moral thermometer was to monitor the effects of consuming spirits and limit their consumption.[45] Like the mood charts of today, the moral thermometer gave individuals a set of categories they could use to describe their states of mind, but it was not attached to broader kinds of summary measures. It had no numerical grid and therefore moods could not be graphed over time, nor could they be collected and compared statistically.

The main contrast between then and now is the ideal temperature on the moral thermometer. We might want to say that for Rush, the structure of feeling of his time was "temperate."

An individual . . . was enabled to effect such a reformation in himself, that for many months on a stretch his temper and habits remained *temperate*, or rose only to the degree marked *warm but reasonable*. A gentleman . . . effected so complete a change in his disposition, by an alteration of his food, that he assured the writer a variation in the moral Thermometer higher than warm or lower than cool was to him an uncommon occurrence.[46]

In contrast, as we will see in the next two chapters, the ideal temperature, the structure of feeling for today, has come to be somewhere between "passionate" and "hot." The small-scale technology of the mood chart allows individual acts of self-surveillance to be collected into large-scale statistics that watch for the rising or falling temperature of moods on a global scale.

CHAPTER EIGHT

Revaluing Mania

It is one of the great ironies of Western culture that
we revere and socially applaud sustained creativity,
drive, and infectious enthusiasm but fail to
recognize these qualities as close cousins of the
disorganization and suspicion that accompany them
in mania and are stigmatized as maniacal madness.
— Peter Whybrow, *A Mood Apart*

In contemporary Euro-American culture there is a pervasive imperative to experience emotion. Ubiquitous advertisements incite our
desire and demand that we engage our strongest feelings. Managers of
employees and creators of ad campaigns learn detailed, practical ways
of arousing and harnessing emotion to increase productivity and increase market share. As we will see, no less an economist than John
Maynard Keynes wrote that the market itself depended on the arousal
of our "animal spirits."[1] Yet, as I mentioned in the introduction, people
in the late twentieth and twenty-first centuries are also profoundly anxious and hence characteristically preoccupied with emotionally flat
conditions—detachment and alienation. The flattening and deadening
of the emotions is a pervasive theme in art, architecture, film, and daily
life.[2] In other words, at present, emotion is both flattened and incited
at the same time. This chapter in the story of manic depression will
take place on the terrain of this strange disjunction. If emotions seem
necessary for the operation of strong markets, yet they seem frightening
when experienced under a pall of intense anxiety, what cultural gloss
will be given to a disorder understood as an excess of emotion? Will
manic-depressive people seem like a scarce resource, a valuable terrain
for exploration and colonization?[3] Will they be less frightening to the
extent their "good" emotions, their manias, can be isolated, fostered,
and optimized? In beginning to answer these questions, my primary

method is to trace changes in the ways in which intense emotionality has been valued or denigrated over time, and for whom. We will need to move back and forth over the line separating people living under the description of manic depression from people who may never have received such a diagnosis but who either think of themselves or appear to others to be "manic" in some sense.

Sociality and Conformity

We will find that the cultural logic of the category of manic depression and its media representation are different. We saw that "moods" are somewhat oblique to the category of "emotion," and that although manic depression is called a "mood" disorder, it has as much to do with "motivation" as "mood." We also saw that although manic depression shares the general characteristics of emotions, its peculiarity is that it is an interrelated, oscillating set of emotions. Most crucially for this chapter, we saw that mania and depression are strongly linked to sociality. This link is important because it opens a way to challenge the popular assumption that mania entails creativity.

To see this, I will look at the link between mania, depression, and sociality more closely, drawing on insights from psychiatrists who have paid close attention to the experiences of people living under the description of manic depression who are their patients. The early twentieth-century German psychiatrist Ernst Kretschmer referred to manic depressives' "harmonious sense of union both with the world and within themselves," which makes them "sociable, immediate, and relatively undivided in their being."[4] Kretschmer found such a patient when in mild mania to be "the emotional man, the good mixer, who is outspoken, easily moved, and perpetually being influenced afresh. He likes meeting any new person and is at once his friend." Even when melancholic, such an "emotional man" has a "non-moralising warm understanding of alien peculiarities" and a "good-natured unassumingness" that makes his company "so pleasant in personal relations."[5] Like his near contemporary, Emil Kraepelin, Kretschmer understood the manic-depressive person's sociability as the opposite of the schizophrenic person's asociability: introverted and isolated, a schizophrenic person was seen as detached from other people and removed from social interaction. In broad strokes, a manic-depressive mode of being was closely attuned to social norms, while, in sharp contrast, a schizoid way of being did not conform to social expectations.[6] Elizabeth Lunbeck has shown that in the early twentieth century, psychiatrists generally reacted favorably to the sociability of patients they diagnosed as manic depressive. As psychiatrists of the time told it,

> the story of the manic depressive was lively, often raucously so, and entertaining. Such individuals engaged the world around them head-on, often wreaking havoc at home and driving their relations mad . . . but they did so with a verve that drew admiration. Their signal characteristics—loquacity, excitability, intense sociability, and mordant wit—differed from those of normal individuals only by virtue of their excess.[7]

It is, of course, exactly *excess* that distinguishes mania from ordinary exuberance. The psychiatrist Alfred Kraus explains manic sociability as an "expansion" of identity. In order to expand her identity in every direction, to achieve a "harmonizing 'oneness' of ego and world," the manic person tends to disregard any limitation on her social roles from other people: her family members, her business associates, or other drivers on the road. The give and take that would be part of ordinary social interactions gets lost.[8] Put another way, in a manic state, a person will hear and amplify the positive reactions from other people and ignore the rest; in a depressed state, she will do the opposite. These forms of sociability are exaggerated in different directions, but they need not seem bizarre to other people. In 1922, E. E. Southard (a psychiatrist at the Boston Psychopathic Hospital) supposed that "every one of us is of manic-depressive stripe."[9] He explained that most of the symptoms are easily understood "because they are exaggerations of the normal feelings rather than new or 'different' or 'peculiar' reactions." As a result, Southard found that "one's 'empathic index' is usually high toward such patients."[10]

Seeing the contrast between manic depression and schizophrenia in this way leads to a startling realization: despite the contemporary belief that manic states can be a source of innovation and creativity, manic depression is actually a malady of social conformity. As Alfred Kraus puts it, the style of interaction of a manic depressive patient involves a "great willingness to fulfill the other person's expectations, in order to bring himself to a peaceful conformity with the other." Their "great sociability" as well as their "high degree of conformity with the world around them" comes from an "attitude of unified human solidarity, avoiding at all cost any threat to this solidarity by anything like non-conformity."[11] In a depressive phase, the person is overly identified with the opinions of others and overly concerned to submit to whatever social norms will gain the approval of others.[12] The person is so sensitive to the opinions of others that he is apt to plunge into despair in the face of others' rejection or disapproval.[13] In the view of some psychoanalysts, depression is such an intolerable condition to sustain that manic-depressive people periodically escape into mania as a defense. On this view, mania serves as an attempt to escape the dependence on the approval of others characteristic of depression when that dependence becomes unbearable. As I mentioned in the introduction, early psychoanalysts such as Melanie Klein explicitly understood the psychodynamics of mania as a defense against the depressive position.

But mania is not usually experienced as the simple opposite of depression's confining dependence on others: in mania one is still connected to others, buoyed by the positive opinions of others, and pleased by every form of heightened social engagement with others. In mania people are said to spend money recklessly, start new businesses, and engage in excessive amounts of activity. This manic activity may be frenetic and somewhat self-absorbed, but it is highly social, too. Kretschmer described this sociability eloquently: in hypomania (a state just short of full-blown mania) a person feels "the overwhelming joy in giving presents and causing pleasure to other people. This hypomanic self-feeling is not an abrupt setting up of the individual's own personality against an outside world, which is regarded with hatred or indifference, but a 'live and let live,' an evenly balanced swimming in comfort for one's self and the world, an almost ludicrous conviction in the value of one's own personality."[14] As we saw in chapter 1, the emotions are constitutively linked with sociality; mania's sociality in turn is strongly connected with emotions. It follows logically that the socially engaged character of manic depression, its "evenly balanced swimming in comfort for one's self and the world" or its eliciting of a high "empathic index," is linked to its emotionality. In contrast, the socially removed character of schizophrenia would seem to be logically linked to its emotional flatness. What manner of creativity could manic depressive people produce, given their heightened sensitivity to social norms? Because they are so attuned to social expectations, are they less apt to break the bounds of convention creatively than to produce—albeit energetically—within the confines of convention?

In an important critique, Louis Sass questions the current assumption that manic depression is linked to creativity. He argues that this assumption is based on a narrow and historically specific definition of creativity, which became prominent in the Romantic movement of the late eighteenth and early nineteenth centuries. The kind of creativity the romantics prized involved the ability to escape from self-consciousness and to liberate the powerful forces of emotions. Poets like Wordsworth and Coleridge are prime examples.[15] By this specific definition, the traits we have just seen are often associated with people living under the description of manic depression—a sense of unity between the self and the world overflowing with emotional energy—would indeed seem to point toward creativity. But, as Sass makes clear, other definitions of creativity are possible. In fact, contrary to current assumptions, schizophrenia may point toward a more profound form of creativity than manic depression. Because they are socially removed rather than constantly socially enmeshed, people diagnosed with schizophrenia could be capable of a more radical creativity that is less attuned to social norms.[16] In comparison, Sass concludes, "Perhaps mania and melancholia should be seen, then, not as a source of radical innovation so much as of a heightening and subtle transmutation of modes of perception that remain reasonably familiar to the majority of other people in the culture."[17] In the rest of this chapter, I describe the conceptions of creativity that people associate with manic depression in popular culture and in support groups. These conceptions will help us understand what happens when the particular form of creativity that is unleashed in mania takes hold in a culture where markets dominate much of social life, a topic I turn to in chapter 9.

Manic Depression and Creativity Today

Since the 1990s, accounts of manic depression have been virtually flooding the press, the best-seller lists, and the airwaves. Manic depression has fueled the plot of a series of detective novels (A *Child of Silence* and others by Abigail Padgett), a prison escape novel (*Green River Rising*), a southern novel (*Sights Unseen*), movies (*About a Boy, Pollock*), and plots of television programs (*The X Files, ER, Six Feet Under*). Manic depression has been featured in specials on MTV ("True Life: I'm Bipolar"), A&E ("Biography of Margot Kidder"), and PBS ("A Brilliant Madness"); it has played an important role in several memoirs (Patty Duke's A *Brilliant Madness*, Katharine Graham's *Personal History*, Jane Pauley's *Skywriting: A Life Out of the Blue*, and Spalding Gray's *Life Interrupted: The Unfinished Monologue*).[18]

Certainly the frequent presence of manic depression in the media does not tell us much about the public's attitude toward it. But part of manic depression, the mania, clearly has a positive gloss. In daily life today, the term mania can be paired with almost anything or activity that people ardently desire. Among the fifty-three million uses of the term "mania" a standard search engine recently found on the Web are innumerable inventive forms of mania: "cicada mania," "monster mania," "muffin mania," "calculator mania," "cursor mania," "pop-o-mania," and "beer coaster mania." Walking through my neighborhood in lower Manhattan, I easily came upon other examples: Cheeze Mania (a snack food), Egg Mania (a computer game for children), Automania, Perfumania, CONDOMania, and Shoemania (retail stores).[19] The term "mania" also figures more and more prominently in advertising campaigns: for athletic shoes ("It's my mania" by Adidas), perfumes ("Mania" by Armani for women and for men), jewelry ("Talismania" by Lladró), and luxury linens (Hermès and Garnet Hill). These uses of the term "mania" suggest it is regarded in a positive light.

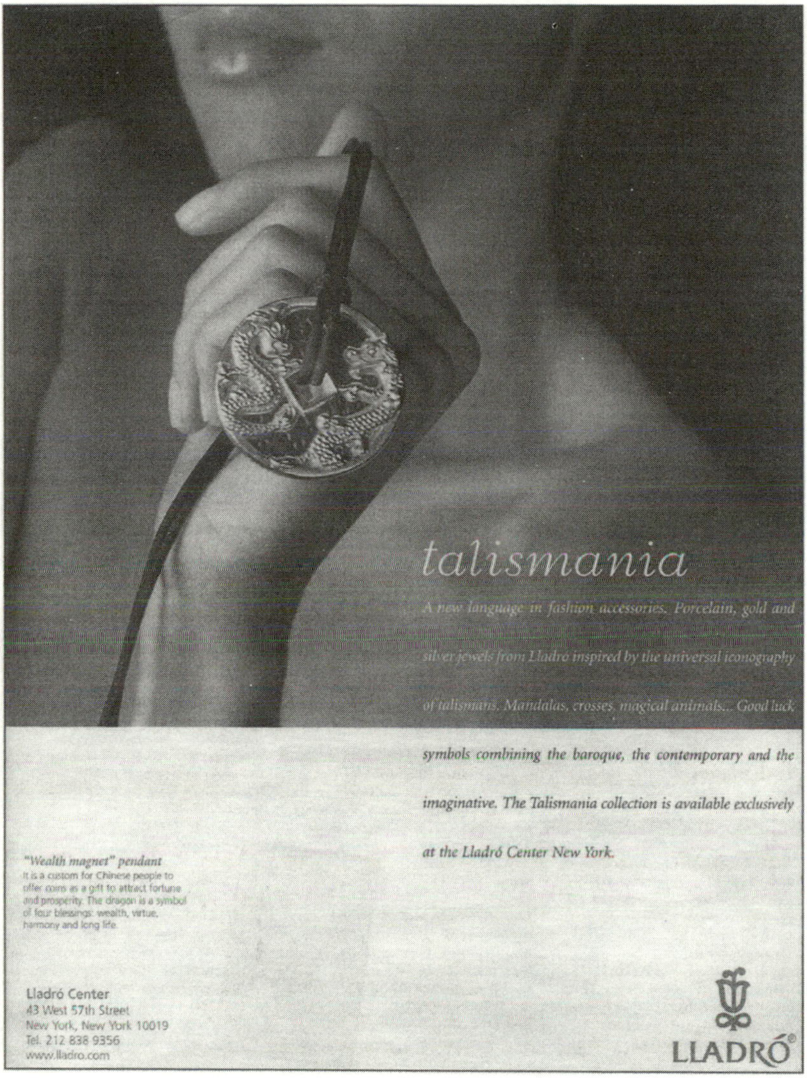

talismania

A new language in fashion accessories. Porcelain, gold and silver jewels from Lladro inspired by the universal iconography of talismans. Mandalas, crosses, magical animals... Good luck symbols combining the baroque, the contemporary and the imaginative. The Talismania collection is available exclusively at the Lladró Center New York.

"Wealth magnet" pendant
It is a custom for Chinese people to offer coins as a gift to attract fortune and prosperity. The dragon is a symbol of four blessings: wealth, virtue, harmony and long life.

Lladró Center
43 West 57th Street
New York, New York 10019
Tel. 212 838 9356
www.lladro.com

LLADRÓ®

8.1. Lladró advertises a collection of fashion accessories called "Talismania." Reprinted with permission, *Gotham* 4, no. 3 (2004): 93. Copyright © Lladró Commercial, S.A.

Manic depression is in the process of redefinition from being simply a disability to being an asset. This new way of looking at manic depression ignores as much about manic depression as it illuminates; however, it is still important to ask why the claim is being made so frequently at the present moment. In many books and Internet sites there are lists of famous and influential people (often including Jamison's examples) whose diaries, letters, and other writings indicate their manic depression played a role in the enormously creative contributions they made to society.[20] In support groups, I found that references to celebrities who have identified themselves as manic depressives were common. In Orange County, where the entertainment industries are a major employer, it was not uncommon for support group members to have had direct experience with these larger than life manic depressives. At one California support group meeting, I had just described my surprise at how calmly a small group of my colleagues had taken the news of my own diagnosis. George, a large-bellied, tall, exuberant man wearing shorts and a Hawaiian shirt, said he would tell the other side of the story—how the condition can also be stigmatizing despite its association with famous people.

> A while ago I told a couple of guys I work with about my manic depression. I thought I could trust them with the information, but I was wrong. They started nudging each other, making remarks. I felt I could do nothing, because whatever way I showed my anger, it would be laid at the feet of my manic depression. Later I was telling a friend about this, and he said, "Do you mind if I do something?" I said, "No." So my friend took one of the first two guys out in the alley and beat him black and blue. I have to admit I felt only the smallest qualm over the incident.

After describing how important this friend's loyalty had been to him, George remembered something else he felt gave strength to people like himself: "Do you know both Robin Williams and Jim Carrey have said they are manic depressive? I heard Robin Williams say it himself, on the movie set. I was there because I also work for the [entertainment] industry." Hearing successful movie stars name their manic-depressive diagnosis openly gave George hope that the kind of stigma he had experienced might one day be eliminated.

Other people told me they felt that persisting negative images of mental illness in the media could be offset by media accounts of manic-depressive heroes. Ann complained to her support group that after her diagnosis two years ago, she had seen four different TV episodes in one weekend that depicted manic depressives as homicidal, suicidal, or worse. She observed, "This is what is behind the fear of the mentally ill, when really we're not that different." But at the county-wide support group picnic a couple of weeks later, I told Ann I was interested in her discussion of television coverage. She and a few others began an animated conversation about both positive and negative images in the media, which she summarized.

> Jim Carrey—you can just tell he is bipolar. I read an article about him that mentioned he is taking Prozac, so I suspect he is bipolar. All these famous people should come out with the truth about their condition. It would really help everyone else.

In the meantime, famous artists from the past said to have had manic depression can be enlisted to help overcome stigma. At a NDMDA meeting, a speaker exhorted the audience to tell others that we work in a civil rights movement for the mentally ill: "We should say this at cocktail parties and put stickers saying 'mental health advocate' on any name tag we wear. Whenever we meet a possibly helpful contact, we should send a thank you note on cards with art by Vincent van Gogh, Abraham Lincoln, or Georgia O'Keeffe."

The association between artistic creativity and the diagnosis of manic depression also saturated professional psychiatry meetings I attended. At the 2000 American Psychiatric Association meetings, Solvay Pharmaceuticals sponsored a major dinner symposium, with speakers on manic depression including Kay Jamison and her coauthor, Fred Goodwin. The poster for the event, widely displayed, showed an illustration of a tortured Beethoven, one of the musicians cited as a genius manic depressive in Jamison's work. Music by Beethoven played during the before-dinner appetizer and wine service. At the same meeting, the extensive exhibit area for one major psychopharmaceutical used in the treatment of manic depression featured a real, live artist who worked on a painting throughout the conference. As I describe the scene in my field notes,

> Randy Cohen was installed at the Zyprexa exhibit. He occupied a large (20′ × 30′) area with a canvas (about 8′ × 10′) in the middle of the Lilly Pharmaceuticals exhibit, which occupied about 1000 square feet. He worked on a collage during most of the days of the meeting. On the floor in front of the canvas was a welter of materials: papers, glues, paints, fabrics, and fibers. There were also brochures about his art, and a poster on an easel describing his work. He himself was sitting on a high stool taking a break. We chatted. He is taking Zyprexa and it has helped him a great deal. At his first appointment with his current doctor, the doctor said that all his bipolar patients are taking Zyprexa as part of a double-blind study. So Randy agreed, signed up to participate in the study, and ended up getting much better. He agreed to pose for a photo next to his collage.

By the time of the 2002 APA, the level of display in the pharmaceutical exhibit area was greatly diminished in a response to growing criticism of extravagance in the face of rising drug prices. By this time, an exhibit as elaborate as the one that included Randy Cohen was only a fond memory, and a representative from another pharmaceutical company told me he missed seeing Randy because it had been gratifying to witness the improvement in him as he took Zyprexa over several years. Less overt references to the link between manic depression and creativity were still apparent. Posters showing successful treatment by antidepressant Celexa showed mellow women painting pictures in domestic settings. And even in the face of an agreement to reduce expenses in marketing, one pharmaceutical company, Organon, had an enormous pile of sand trucked into the convention hall, out of which craftsmen sculpted a life-sized replica of Benjamin Franklin. This sculpture intrigued me. I understood the obvious reference to Franklin's role in the history of Philadelphia, the location of the 2002 APA.

But whereas the link between Randy Cohen's artistic creativity and Zyprexa was unmistakable and explicit, the link between the sand sculpture and the convention, not to mention Remeron, the particular

8.2. A worker is putting the finishing touches on a sand sculpture of Benjamin Franklin at the 2002 American Psychiatric Association meeting in Philadelphia. In addition to Franklin's contribution to Philadelphia's history, he has become a symbol of productive entrepreneurial hyperactivity. The drug Remeron, whose name is sculpted into the statue's base, is a remedy for depression. Photo by Emily Martin, 2002.

antidepressant whose name was sculpted into Ben Franklin's pedestal, was mystifying to everyone I asked. I do not know if anyone was aware that in the popular literature on ADHD, Ben Franklin was at the time being used as an example of success by virtue of his manic and hyper temperament. That literature frequently attributed the success of people like Benjamin Franklin, Winston Churchill, Bill Clinton, and Thomas Edison to the "Edison Effect," which correlates creativity with such a temperament.[21] A few years later, on the occasion of Benjamin Franklin's three-hundredth birthday, there were prominent statements about his "hypomania," based on his "bold curiosity, brash risk-taking, raw ingenuity."[22]

So compellingly desirable are the depictions of mania in support groups and conventions that being manic depressive almost parts company with pathology. In this sense, which I discussed in chapter 2, "mania" could be called "manic style," a style that draws on the "mania" in manic depression, but ignores a great deal of what people experience when they are manic and when they are depressed. Despite all that it ignores, exemplars of manic style are appearing on all sides, from Robin Williams and Jim Carrey, to *Seinfeld*'s Cosmo Kramer and Virgin Inc.'s Richard Branson. Before his suicide, the actor and writer Spalding Gray was featured in a Rockport ad sprawled in a chair, hair standing out electrically, claiming, "I'm comfortable with my madness." Ted Turner is described in the magazine GQ as the "corporealized spirit of the age" and he appears in the *Saturday Evening Post* in a pair of commanding photographs. In one he is a businessman, lecturing soberly behind a podium with a corporate logo and in the other he is a wild-eyed ship's captain, fiercely gripping the wheel at the helm of his yacht. The caption to the photographs notes that Turner's competition should be warned: he has stopped taking his lithium (and so might well be about to launch a manic—and profitable—new venture).[23]

How do people who have the diagnosis of manic depression feel about the manias they experience, in a cultural context in which mania is celebrated in the media? Many people frankly appreciate their manias. In one California support group, I commented that the dampening effect of my medications sometimes made me yearn for the experience of mania. Mike leapt to respond.

> Everyone always talks about the bad side of the illness, but now I am experiencing hypomania and it is good, I feel just incredibly good. When I worked at a luxury hotel on the coast, I remember, I was in charge, ordering "hot and cold running" limousines. A concierge, a Japanese American guy, said, "You know, you really have a gift." I feel it really is a gift, it is productive. I have a shrink who doesn't automatically get out the prescription pad, and that's good.

Sweeping the troubling aspects of his condition under his elation, Mike continued.

> I don't need much sleep at night but when I need to sleep it comes over me suddenly and totally. Once [falling asleep at the wheel] I

sideswiped seven parked cars in a row, but I was only going around thirty miles per hour so no one was hurt badly. I am passionate about the wonderful way I feel; there is nothing bad about it, and it's just a good, productive thing. I feel good about myself.

Referring specifically to the media, people in support groups frequently told me how important celebrated manics were for their morale. Early in my research, I visited an officer of the California patient advocacy organization whose support groups I was attending regularly. Mary and her husband, Ron, responded eagerly to my question about the number of famous people in entertainment and business who were making their diagnosis of manic depression public.

Mary: There are a lot of people with the illness who know that mania has some positive aspects. If you could just control it. If you could just keep it a little bit high but not too high. Manics are, when they are just hypomanic, really fun to be around. They are charismatic, they've got this great personality, and they are outgoing, effervescent. . . .

Ron: They have creativity, productivity.

Mary: Some people who have a lot of that in their illness don't like taking their medications. Then they go off their medications because they want to feel that way and they feel the medications are putting a lid on them and they don't like that. For me personally, I don't have a lot of mania in my illness—some but not a lot—I have more hypomania than anything else. And I'm very depressed, so the medication brings me up to feeling really good compared to what I did feel. So I don't have the tendency to not want to take my medication. It's not putting a lid on me.

Ron: The people that are hypomanic like being hypomanic, and feeling regular to them is drugged down. To people who are depressed, they will do anything to avoid that depth of depression and they are more compliant with their medication.

Mary: The stars and the people who have come out saying that they are manic depressive: I'm not at all surprised because this illness does seem to be linked to intelligence. People with this illness have a higher IQ on average. People are more creative and they do have more energy, so it makes perfect sense to me that they would be writers and poets and actors and actresses and CEOs. It just makes sense.

Mania or, more accurately, mania in mild hypomanic form, is extremely seductive, not least because it seems to offer capacities that lend themselves to success in the contemporary business and entertainment worlds: continuous wakefulness, boundless energy, high motivation, and productivity. Even for those who have been unable to parlay these experiences into lasting fame and fortune, thinking of others who have done so can be inspiring. There is something enthralling about experiencing life as filled with a dizzying number of possibilities, there for the taking.

However intoxicating hypomanic states are, most people in support groups realize that not everyone will be able to ride mania to fame and fortune. By far the greatest majority of stories I heard about mania, hypomania, or depression were stories of pain, loss, and suffering. Enrico told his California support group,

> I fall mostly on the manic side, and I'm seldom depressed—I know that is unusual. I do take my meds. In the past I have gone through a lot of money, you might say it was "a few dollars." I would just spend whatever I had. Now I know if I have three dollars, I should just save half of it. My wife of seventeen years left me—I guess she couldn't take me anymore. I asked my doctor which was worse, the manic side or the depressed side, and he said, "Both."

Gender and Manic Depression

Are the desirable characteristics of mania accessible to men and women alike? Up until the nineteenth century, mania was frequently represented as both frightening and masculine: "Mad people, especially those deemed to be suffering from mania, were often portrayed . . . as wild, raging animals insensitive to normal feelings and experiences such as cold and hunger." The wild figure of the mad person often had a masculine face.[24] By the early twentieth century, the way manic depression was associated with gender categories had changed, so much so that far more women were diagnosed with manic depression than men, by some estimates twice as many. Elizabeth Lunbeck suggests that gender was encoded in the very category itself: the most salient characteristics doctors saw in the manic patient were those associated in other contexts with an unbounded, out-of-control femininity that was at once frightening and alluring.[25] Men diagnosed with manic depression appeared to their doctors, relatives, and friends much like women: excitable, distractible, and talkative, their conduct governed less by rational considerations than by plays of fancy.[26] More generally, in American mores since the post–Civil War period, a volatile temperament in adult women was a handicap for success in standard social roles and the normative definitions of femininity. For example, in Louisa May Alcott's novel *Moods*, Alcott's father, Amos Bronson Alcott, wrote in his letters that the volatile temperaments of his wife and daughter were "dangerous and unnatural."[27] In contrast, Lunbeck points out, dementia praecox (later renamed schizophrenia) was coded male. Its "stolidity, stupidity and catatonia . . . were merely the extreme, pathological manifestations of men's naturally more stable nature, just as the periodicity that characterized the manic mimicked in a more marked form the natural periodicity of women."[28]

Today the gender differences for manic depression and depression have shifted. Statistics show that "manic-depressive illness . . . is equally prevalent across gender[s]," while major depression, with its immobility and numbness, is more common among women than men.[29] We are beginning to observe the inception of the *male manic*, seen as powerful and effective *despite* or, more exactly, *because of* his instability and "irrationality." Far from being feminized and denigrated as he was early in the twentieth century, the male manic now seems filled with potency. In Kay Jamison's words, "[M]anic states . . . seem to be more the provenance of men: restless, fiery, aggressive, volatile, energetic, risk taking, grandiose and visionary, and impatient with the status quo."[30]

This change would leave the female manic no better-off. In the course of her career in psychiatry, Jamison notes that the extremes of mania did not sit easily with being a woman: especially when the passion of mania "tipped over into too much anger[,] [i]t did not seem consistent with being the kind of gentle, well-bred woman I had been brought up to admire and, indeed, continue to admire."[31] The energetic force of mania makes it difficult for a woman to pull off being manic while keeping her female identity. In my fieldwork, Marcy described her experience of the incompatibility between being manic and being a woman.

> For me the diagnosis [of manic depression] felt like a disorder because I'm used to moving through the world in this very unhindered kind of way. Suddenly it was like I could not satisfy anyone. Everything I did was somehow less than what they had gotten from me in the past. I could not meet other people's needs at all. If I had been born with an X and a Y [chromosome], maybe none of this would have happened, because my own sensitivity to not meeting other people's needs is what finally got me upset enough to find my way into the doctor's office. Not meeting other people's needs is so unpleasant for me that I had to put a stop to that any way I could. I would have taken any drugs that they gave me if I thought that they would make this go away. The Depakote actually did; the Depakote made me more tolerable for other people and that was fine with me. I did kind of think that the energy was particularly offensive to many people in a woman and they didn't really know why.

When she was manic, Marcy found herself unable to interact with other people like a good daughter, wife, or girlfriend should, aiming to satisfy the other's needs. Mania's kind of social engagement has a specific quality: it is a one-way outpouring of energy (perceived as masculine in style) rather than a two-way exchange (perceived as feminine in style).

Race and Manic Depression

In addition to gender reversals around manic depression, there have also been some shifts in how racial categories are aligned with the condition. Mania has often been negatively associated with the irrational, out-of-control, overly emotional, racially marked, nonwhite person; today it can be positively associated with the electrified, jubilant, hyperenergized, racially unmarked (white) person. As background to this shift, the historian John Corrigan found in his study of nineteenth-century American business culture that African American emotionality was constructed as outside the range of "acceptable or even human emotionality."[32] African Americans were seen as impulsive, volatile, and prone to extreme emotional outbursts, while at the same time (and paradoxically) lacking human emotion and feeling.[33] In the history of American expressive culture of the early twentieth century, "the primitive" marked an out-of-control and uninhibited energy culturally associated with the female, on the one hand, and the African American, on the other. Aesthetic primitivism in the 1920s could rest on "a stereotype of blackness contrived to erect white subjective potency."[34] White authors wrote about jazz at that time in the United States as a product of effects "at a level of human experience lower and more fundamental— 'deeper,' in one sense—than culture."[35] In 1919 a Swiss commentator described the power of jazz as emanating from a kind of ritual possession, placing possession "within a European dichotomy that strictly separates it from reason, allowing the 'depth' of these musicians to become associated with the power of nature and the thrill of barbarism."[36] In the early decades of the twentieth century, out-of-control emotional energy was associated with "primitive" racial others on the fringes of the human.

Writing in this time period, Marie Cardinal also portrays jazz as an out-of-control force in her autobiography, *The Words to Say It*. Cardinal was a white French girl who grew up in Algeria. She described how she descended into madness upon hearing an intensely emotional trumpet song played by Louis Armstrong in Paris.

> My first anxiety attack occurred during a Louis Armstrong concert. I was nineteen or twenty. Armstrong was going to improvise with his trumpet, to build a whole composition in which each note would be important and would contain within itself the essence of the whole. I was not disappointed: the atmosphere warmed up very fast. . . . The sounds of the trumpet sometimes piled up together, fusing a new musical base, a sort of matrix which gave birth to one precise, unique note, tracing a sound whose path was almost painful, so absolutely

necessary had its equilibrium and duration become; it tore at the nerves of those who followed it.

My heart began to accelerate, becoming more important than the music, shaking the bars of my rib cage, compressing my lungs so the air could no longer enter them. Gripped by panic at the idea of dying there in the middle of spasms, stomping feet, and the crowd howling, I ran into the street like someone possessed.[37]

Toni Morrison writes that she remembers smiling when reading this passage, in part because Cardinal's recollection of the music had such immediacy, and "partly because of what leaped into my mind: what on earth was Louie playing that night? What was there in his music that drove this sensitive young girl hyperventilating into the street," feeling "like someone possessed"? Morrison muses on the "way black people ignite critical moments of discovery or change or emphasis in literature not written by them" and the "consequences of jazz—its visceral, emotional, and intellectual impact on the listener," which in this case tipped Cardinal from sanity to madness, from rationality to "irrationality."[38]

Illuminating Morrison's points further, Phillip Rack, a psychiatrist who observed and treated West Indian immigrants in England in the 1960s and 1970s, wrote about psychiatric diagnosis for Afro-Caribbeans. Rack described a syndrome called "West Indian Psychosis," said to be found among people of Afro-Caribbean descent characterized by "excitement and over-activity, with pressure of thought and speech . . . bizarre behaviour . . . violence . . . talk [which is] fragmented or incoherent."[39] This diagnosis was usually taken to be an attack of an endogenous psychosis, but Rack argues that "when an African, Afro-Caribbean, or Asian patient behaves in a manner that would, in a British patient, point to a diagnosis of mania [which was included in West Indian Psychosis], the practitioner should keep in mind the possibility that this is a stress reaction, and not an attack of an endogenous psychosis."[40] Rack suggests it is perhaps hard for clinicians to see a stress reaction instead of an endogenous psychosis because of certain preconceptions. The stereotype of the "wild West Indian" or "the image of the big wild, dangerous black man or woman" is deep in the minds of many white people, partly because some West Indian speech styles sound to English ears "sharp, intense, abrupt, and hard-edged, with sudden changes of pitch, coupled with an ebullience of manner that suggests intense emotion or extraversion. Also there is a great deal of genuine anger, frustration, and bitterness among certain sections of the Afro-Caribbean community in Britain, and it causes acts of violence that attract a great deal of media coverage."[41] Rack is implying that psychosis (here including mania) fits more comfortably with racialized blackness than it does with racialized whiteness. Hence, clinicians should bear in mind that their preconceptions may lead them to diagnose psychosis where a stress reaction would be more accurate.

In my fieldwork, nonwhite members of support groups expressed outrage similar to Morrison's and Rack's when faced with both the description of manic depression and racist treatment. Enrico explained,

> I'm coming to this group for anger management. I get extremely angry at any comments about "the help," anything like that; maybe I am oversensitive, but in a job interview once, they referred to me as a "green bean." At first I just thought that meant inexperienced, but later I found out that it is a term for an ignorant Mexican. I don't know what to do with the anger. I play sports, and after that incident, I played racquetball so long and hard the ball broke into pieces. Is this the best way? I think maybe I should take up boxing. I also mistrust those little boxes they want you to fill in on the employment application. Ethnic categories! Who's interested in that? If I put "Mexican," they will think I don't speak English!

The group took this very seriously and discussed which state agency would be the best place to report a discrimination complaint. The editor of the regional association newsletter, *The Roller Coaster Times*, happened to be present and she promised to publish the address and phone number of the correct state agency in the next issue of the newsletter. But the more telling point is that some people may be less willing to tolerate extreme emotions from a woman or man of color than from a white man in a position of power. As the sociologist Pam Jackson remarked to me, "A white man can act crazy like Ted Turner, but if a black man acted like that he would be arrested." There are celebrated African American comedians who are described as "manic"—Eddie

Murphy, for one—but unlike white comedians, they are not found on popular lists of famous manic depressives.[42] Not surprisingly, African American CEOs celebrated for their manic style are nonexistent.

Manic Depression as an "Asset"

With her memoir, *An Unquiet Mind,* Jamison reveals her own diagnosis of manic depression and gives us a powerful phenomenological description of the condition. Here is her eloquent account of the exhilaration and despair that can be part of mood disorders: "I now move more easily with the fluctuating tides of energy, ideas, and enthusiasms that I remain so subject to. . . . My high moods and hopes having ridden briefly in the top car of the Ferris wheel will, as suddenly as they came, plummet into a black and gray and tired heap . . . then at some unknown time, the electrifying carnival will come back into my mind."[43] Just as Jamison conveys the pain of depression, the disastrous consequences of mania, and the danger of suicide associated with manic depression, she also describes appealingly the thought processes of mania: "Fluency, rapidity, and flexibility of thought, on the one hand, and the ability to combine ideas or categories of thought in order to form new and original connections on the other . . . rapid, fluid, and divergent thought."[44] Thought is rapid and flighty, jumping blithely from one thing to another.[45] For Jamison, manic depression entails a "distorted" sense of time and space: "delusions" abound in the manic phase. Objects seem to merge, to flow into each other. Shapes shift. Any ordinary thing can change into something else and then something else again.[46]

As rapidly as they are described, however, these distortions are becoming assets in accordance with new realities instead of irrational delusions. In general, the qualities praised seem to fit perfectly with the kind of person I described in chapter 1 as highly desirable in corporate America: adaptive, scanning the environment, continuously changing in innovative ways, a creative chameleon. If there is an increasing demand for restless change and continuous development of the person at all times, in many realms, then manic depression might readily come to be regarded as normal—even ideal—for the human condition under these historically specific circumstances.

How does inhabiting such a space of flux come to seem desirable? Many people I spoke with struggled with this question. In an interview, Peter Whybrow, UCLA psychiatrist and author of accessible and influential books on bipolar disorder, *A Mood Apart* and *Mania in America*, explained to me his view of how manic traits come to seem desirable.

> **Peter Whybrow:** I'm convinced that we have tended to deny the social value of [manic and depressive] behaviors. It's only when they go over the top and create a sort of idle self or a socially destructive self that everybody throws up their arms and says, "Ah, this is terrible," and then stigmatizes [mania or depression]. In a peculiar way, this distinguishes manic depression from exactly the same behavior that doesn't reach quite these heights for some reason. My own sense is that there's a part of American culture that feeds that.
>
> **Emily Martin:** Feeds the stigmatization?
>
> **Peter Whybrow:** No, feeds the escalation. In fact, in the book [*Mania in America*], although I don't make it explicit, the implication is that there's something in "immigrant hubris" that's close to manic hubris. [Early immigrants to the United States were gripped by the conviction they could rise up the social and economic ladder if they poured energy into their work.] For manics today, if you're sleeping four hours a night, having rapid, somewhat bizarre thoughts, on-the-edge ideas and a few other things, you are considered to be helpful in moving an Internet company into the stratosphere . . . and conning a lot of people into giving you a lot of money. That is becoming very advantageous. On the other hand, if I end up saying not "I can build this Internet company and you should give me money because I'm going to make you a millionaire" but just "what I say is significant enough that it's going to change the world" (there is a subtle difference of meaning here!), you immediately are seen as a madman as opposed to an entrepreneur.

"I'm going to change the world with my little company I'm making." Look at Steve Case, CEO of America Online or Jeffrey Bezos, CEO of Amazon.com. When they're asked what they're doing, they say, "We want to change the world."

Well, you get somebody who's in the early stages of mania who says they want to change the world, there's no difference except the context within which they say that. One of them says, "I'm going to change the world through building this new marketing thing, which we call e-commerce," and the other says, "I'm going to change the world because I'm chosen, and I have a better vision than everybody else." The second person goes into the asylum and the first person goes into the Fortune 500. Yet there is no real difference in the early stages of what they're saying.

The perception that mania has market value was expressed even by people I met who have not reaped fame and fortune in their manic depressive lives. John, a Vietnam veteran who has been a California support group leader for some years, thought deeply about this issue. He summarized his dynamic philosophy of life.

Adapt, adapt, change, change, change. You can't catch a firefly: you might catch its corpse, but not the firefly itself. Human beings always have to make decisions based on incomplete information. The idea, though, is to remain practical, remain open, [to have] the ability to accept something new and conditions that are new, because the world is always changing. Many times having a spike [of manic energy] gives you a new perspective, an impetus to creativity. You can see ahead even if you have to go sideways. It is an environment for creativity. If you totally eliminated the spikes, you would diminish creativity over time. The experience of having spikes is a plus and a minus. The perspective is that having gone through a battle, you are a veteran. Just like the shamans of old, you should be praised for having survived it. There is value in it, like going through battle; we exalt our veterans and at the same time we have to go on to peace-time. Manic depression is the same as war in a way because it's the war of all sides seeing something different. Even going psychotic is like being a casualty. [You might be wounded, but not fatally.] You can recover and have a good life, but it is still a battle. The value of it is you have seen some vistas, you've been there and you've survived. You've seen something, and that experience should be neither exalted nor put down.

Having spikes is busting through boxes. I don't have a word for it; we would need to find an image or a metaphor. It's not linear at all.

John is elaborating on ideals of energy and creativity that are held out for our enticement in the culture in a general way, not on his own life-threatening experiences while he has been manic or depressed. In John's case, as for many others living under the description of manic depression, the condition can often be a source of profound suffering. However, John believes that there is social value in being able to shift his manic energy sideways, like a firefly, and to dart in new directions through its glow.

Marcy saw social value in the way her manic states allowed her to experience life as if it were an episode of *Sex and the City*, experiences she thought many women would envy. She began by describing what happened when she was "racing."

> I was getting a lot of response from men, too much. I mean I was not answering my phone after a while. Whatever kind of energy I was giving off, I had men making passes at me. It really shocked me because I felt that they were making passes at me which were completely uninvited and how dare they extend into my personal space. *They* were irritating me. I was single for the first time in four years, but this was beyond anything that any of my friends who were single appeared to be experiencing and beyond anything I've ever experienced in my entire life. These men would approach me who seemed like perfectly normal people. They were convinced that I had sent them a signal and I am looking at them going, "Well, you're very mistaken because there was no signal."

Although she noted her women friends' admiration, and could not help being amazed at her ability to attract men, Marcy expressed ambivalence about not being able to control the pace of either her thoughts or her social interactions.

John and Marcy are feeling the effect of powerful forces that are turning mania into a social asset. Depictions of Robin Williams as a stand-up comedian or Ted Turner as a CEO—both paired with the label "manic depressive"—are part of the movement of the category mania from an impediment to something that gives pleasure, brings rewards, and, in its inventiveness, produces forms of value.[47] John's creative spikes and Marcy's racing states have their dangers, but they also hold the promise of a precious vitality.

As mania becomes valuable intellectual and emotional property, it may also, as we have seen for John and Marcy, elicit fear. Are two kinds of mania emerging, as it were, a "good" kind, harnessed by Robin Williams and Ted Turner, and a "bad" kind to which most sufferers of manic depression are relegated? In the troubles that followed his "barbaric yawp," did Howard Dean stumble into a place where he exemplified both kinds? In this case, even if the value given to the irrational experience of mania increases, validity would yet again be denied to the "mentally ill," and in fact their stigmatization might increase. After all, if those living under the description of manic depression have, by definition, the ability to be manic or hyperactive, and if that ability comes to be seen as an important key to success, then why are they so often social and economic failures? Or, will the presence of a *manic style* in popular culture reduce the stigmatization of manic depression? Now that he is widely thought of as manic depressive, could Robin Williams's performances as a stand-up comedian contribute to moving the category mania altogether away from the stigmatized, because his performances give pleasure, bring rewards, and, in their inventiveness, produce forms of value? Do his funny, madcap antics enhance the growing perception that mania is valuable intellectual property? He may be creative *at a cost to himself*, but in a manner his society values.

A Mental State as a "Thing"

In my fieldwork, I was often struck by how pharmaceutical development, marketing, and advertising strive to move mania and depression away from being thought of as context-dependent experiences and toward being thought of as stable and thing-like. Movement toward thing-like status makes mania and depression seem possible to identify, manipulate, and optimize through the technology of psychotropic drugs and through taxonomic apparatuses. At the 2000 APA, I met a young doctor who practiced in a well-known hospital near Hollywood. We were at a dinner sponsored by Solvay Pharmaceuticals, maker of Luvox, a drug prescribed for depression and anxiety. When he heard about my research, he became quite interested and offered me this experience.

> Where I work, we get a lot of Hollywood comedians coming in. They are manic depressives. There are two important things about this: first, they do not want their condition publicized, and second, their managers always get involved in the details of their treatment. The managers want the mania treated just so. They do not want it floridly out of control, but they also absolutely do not want it damped down too much.

He felt he was being called upon to *optimize* the patients' moods (for particular professions and for the particular kinds of creativity each requires) through proper management of their drugs. His comment made me realize that drugs I was taking were being optimized for my profession, too: not so much lithium that my hands shook when I wrote on the blackboard; not so much Lexapro that my mind slowed down and stopped generating ideas during a class; not so little Focalin that my attention wandered constantly and I couldn't write articles and books; not so little Lamictal that I got depressed and became unproductive altogether. A little like the Hollywood comedians, I was in the fortunate position of being able to afford expensive, expert advice about all this and working in a profession I valued. I began to feel uneasy about the prospect of extending the optimization of psychotropic drugs to suit other kinds of employment. What would happen if optimizing states of mind were extended, through health insurance, say, or perhaps as a condition of employment, to people who work in physically demanding jobs, for long hours, low pay, and little hope of advancement? To people who work in retail jobs demanding continuous emotional work (make the customer smile!), for long hours, low pay, and little hope of advancement? Or to soldiers on combat duty?[48]

Mulling over these questions, I wandered into the Wyeth Ayerst product display area for the drug Effexor, named "Wellness Park" on an enormous banner. I struck up a conversation with a sales representative from Florida, who had taken some anthropology courses in college. We chatted about the displays, many of which showed the same smiling woman in three photographs, the first faded out, the second normally exposed, and the third vividly colored. "We are trying to achieve a higher standard in care for depression," she offered, to explain the vivid coloring in the third photograph. Effexor will help patients be *better than they were even when they were not depressed.* Doctors need to have higher expectations for their patients and this is what the three photos of the smiling woman show, that none of them is depressed anymore, *but there are higher degrees of life satisfaction, performance, and functioning.* She then referred me "upstairs" to a pharmacist who could answer more questions and give me technical literature. I found a spiral staircase, which wound about a life-sized artificial tree trunk along the way. The many, luxuriantly leaved boughs of this tree shaded the whole display area and gave concrete meaning to the "Wellness Park" theme. There was a heart carved into the bark of the tree enclosing chemical symbols for serotonin and for another neurotransmitter, norepinephrine, which represent the two pathways Effexor works on in the brain.

Upstairs in the tree house, I was offered a seat on the other side of a desk from a pharmacist. In response to my question about the significance of the three photographs, he said,

> The FDA grants efficacy for depression when studies find people are 50 percent less depressed on the HAMD scale [a standard measurement of depression] than before treatment. This is defined as a "response." But Effexor gives even *more* response than that, and we have termed this "remission." Remission means return to a virtually asymptomatic state.

He showed me a brochure in which Effexor is said to lead to "more complete and sustained improvement" and then a reprint from the *Journal of Clinical Psychology* called, "Why Settle for Silver When You Can Go for Gold?" The reprint stated that remission, not "response only," will yield "energy, zest, and social drive." In the pharmacist's words,

> The science of depression is to reach a higher standard. The higher standard can be attained through Effexor because it has a dual mech-

anism, like the old antidepressants, the tricyclics, which had both a serotonin reuptake inhibitor and a norepinephrine reuptake inhibitor. Those drugs worked very, very well, except for their severe side effects. With the dual mechanism and without the side effects, Effexor works better than the other antidepressants which are only SSRIs.

This has implications for the patient—can he go back to work? And it has an economic impact—will people be more productive?

Driving home the theme that people once suffering from depression can be better than normal, the display area contained many posters and brochures of laughing people with the claim, "I got my playfulness back." There were also numerous video projectors shining words on screens: "smile," "giggle," "love," and "fun." You could even get your own picture taken under the artificial boughs of the tree, which would be framed and sent to you through the mail. A couple of months later, my own picture arrived in a handsome frame, showing my image digitally inserted into a scene of a phone booth crammed with people, alongside a sign reading, "I got my playfulness back, at this year's APA." The ads promote the idea that depression can be replaced with something like ebullience through the action of a drug. The state of, say, playfulness, is good for the person's and the economy's productivity, and it is so much the same thing for everyone that the same visual scenario can be used to frame any individual's image. The call for people to shift from depression toward the manic end of the scale takes a one-size-fits-all form. So, people on Effexor will be *better* than "normal."

Far more than advertising is involved in the increasing thing-like quality of mania. Mania is technically part of the condition of bipolar disorder, and bipolar disorder is also becoming easier to see, and to desire, in broader groups of people. For example, the diagnosis is increasing in prevalence among people who would have been seen as psychologically unremarkable not long ago. *New York Magazine*'s cover story, "Are You Bipolar?" wonders if "mild bipolar disorder may be to this decade what depression was to the nineties," thanks to new drugs and an expanding definition.[49]

8.3. Framed photograph obtained as a gift at the 2000 American Psychiatry Association meeting. After the author's photo was taken at the meeting, it was digitally inserted into the scene of an overcrowded phone booth and labeled with the advertising slogan for Effexor, an antidepressant. Courtesy of Emily Martin, 2000.

But when do ordinary peaks and valleys become "pathological"?[50] The author of the article, Vanessa Grigoriadis, herself diagnosed with mild bipolar disorder, contrasts her condition with classic mania, where you "book a first-class ticket to Paris and spend $30,000 in one weekend at the Plaza Athénée. Or look on amazed, or terrified, as the sunlight metamorphoses into a band of descending seraphim. Or systematically begin to date all 525,003 men in your Friendster personal network." In her own case, she simply felt "smarter, funnier, cooler, prettier, *better* than I had before. I had fabulous concentration, was undistracted by any edge of competition or envy, and found that I could function easily on five or six hours of sleep. I went out to parties often, dressed in tight fuchsia tops and barely there miniskirts. No one was saying no to me; 'no' was not an acceptable answer." Grigoriadis interviewed a psychiatrist, Frank Miller, on the Upper East Side in New York City who described a hypothetical patient: she "comes in a little more dressed up, a woman maybe in a dress that's too short, a lipstick too widely applied, a kind of spontaneity, a spunkiness that you've just never seen before. It only lasts for a week, and then all of a sudden, they're depressed." Miller describes the diagnosis this way: "That person could easily be reconceptualized as a bipolar individual, although that is the totality of the hypomania that you'd see: four or five days, quite subtle, and not recognized by family, friends, or colleagues as evidence of anything extreme. But there it is: a third mood, so to speak." What is noteworthy about this article is not Miller's diagnosis—a similar form of bipolar disorder is in the DSM under the heading "Bipolar II": depression alternating with hypomania. What is noteworthy is the news coverage of the topic and what Grigoriadis says next.[51] For her, this "third mood" is "heightened experience—a drug you want more of. . . . This can seem to be your best self, the state of self-actualization that one prays to get to with self-exploration, therapy, and medication, but for many remains just out of reach."[52] Both Grigoriadis and Miller suggest bipolarity might be a distinctively New York City phenomenon, the frenetic urban pace attracting bipolar people there in the first place (much as Tom Wolfe described Atlanta in *A Man in Full*), while provoking other people to manifest bipolarity for the first time.

8.4. A 2004 cover of *New York Magazine* illustrates an article about the wide dissemination of mild bipolar disorder with a woman who is smiling and crying at the same time. © 2004 *New York Magazine*. All rights reserved. Reprinted by permission. Photo by Andrew Eccles/JBGPhoto.com.

The category bipolar is also being increasingly extended to young people. Another cover story appeared in *Time Magazine* under the title "Young and Bipolar."[53] The increasing tendency to identify bipolar disorder in young people, and to medicate them for it, is the subject of controversy, to be sure.[54] But the age of onset of bipolar disorder is sliding downward, and young bipolars are, like adults, being charged with the creative burden.[55] *Time* prints a sidebar of photographs titled "Manic Genius," including the usual suspects, Edgar Allan Poe, Vincent van Gogh, Ernest Hemingway, and so on. But *Time* adds a new, young manic: Kurt Cobain, who "took his band Nirvana to the pinnacle . . . but then took his life at the age of 27."[56] Other major mass media publications have picked up the theme: the *Saturday Evening Post* ran an article called "The Challenge of Being Young, Creative, and Bipolar," featuring the author, Lizzy Simon, whose book, *Detour*, describes her life with bipolar disorder after being diagnosed at the age of seventeen. Simon's MTV special, Web site, and public appearances are also part of the increasing salience of bipolar disorder in the self-understanding and perhaps even self-fashioning of young people.[57] The major patient advocacy organization for adult mood disorders, the DBSA, has joined with a new foundation, the Child and Adolescent Bipolar Foundation, to mount a Web art exhibition of pictures painted by children with mood disorders, some as young as six.[58]

What forces are pushing this expansion? Judging from the Celexa posters at the APA, the marketers and advertisers hired by the drug companies were aiming for an increasingly general understanding of depression so that anyone could imagine being in Celexa's picture frame. But there is also another force in play, which is the desire (by marketers, advertisers, and manufacturers) to make consumers aware that particular drugs target specific conditions. For example, more and more drugs, formerly used as antiseizure medications (Lamictal and Depakote) or antipsychotic medications (Zyprexa), have gained FDA approval to claim that they are effective for bipolar disorder. Bipolar disorder then becomes the focus of advertisements designed to send consumers to doctors in search of a particular drug. In Zyprexa's case, the occasion inspired a television ad featuring a woman who shopped and worked frenetically all day long, and then exuberantly splashed her living room wall with red paint in the evening. The voice-over encouraged the viewer to "tell your doctor about your ups as well as your downs," so that you can be medicated with Zyprexa for bipolar disorder instead of with an antidepressant. In the fall of 2005 a new drug for bipolar disorder hit the market. Abilify, from Bristol-Myers Squibb, was ushered into public awareness by means of full-page, full-color ads that ran in the front section of the *New York Times* over several weeks. The ad was directed to the consumer: "You've been up and down, with mood swings and relapses. You may have also been misunderstood or misdiagnosed for years before being properly treated. . . . Abilify may be able to help. . . . Ask your doctor or healthcare professional if ABI-LIFY is right for you."[59]

As a capstone of all these developments, psychiatrists have been publishing books that connect not only New Yorkers but all Americans with hypomania.[60] In *Exuberance*, Kay Jamison sets the tone. The first European immigrants to the New World brought with them an "improbable optimism," as well as ingenuity and vigor. Of these immigrants, only those with the most enthusiasm, possessing "a stupendous energy" and will, undertook to cross the mountains and prairies of the continent. In the westward crossing, "exuberance came into its own—needed and selected for—as a vital feature in the American character."[61] In *The Hypomanic Edge: The Link between (a Little) Craziness and (a Lot of) Success in America*, the psychologist John Gartner surmises with Jamison that the ancestors of contemporary Americans tended to be hypomanic—energetic and optimistic. Because of its strong genetic component, hypomania has come to make up a significant part not just of American character but also of the "American temperament."[62] In his *American Mania: When More Is Not Enough*, Peter Whybrow sees a darker side of American mania. He thinks the biologically wired drive for pleasure and success that fuels mania makes people neglect more satisfying relationships with other people.[63]

These three books manage to make mania seem more like a thing in two ways. They see exuberance, hypomania, and mania as states that existed in the same form and manifested the same behaviors in earlier historical periods as they do today. They make this claim plausible by attaching exuberance, hypomania, and mania to material processes that would be unchanged over time: the forces of selection (Jamison), the operation of genes (Gartner), or the wiring of the brain (Whybrow). These claims might seem like the essence of contemporary scientific practice. Scientists trace a mental illness to its cause in the brain (opening the hope for a cure, or at least improvement) and describe the social consequences of the illness, sometimes good and sometimes bad. I want to raise questions about what this practice leaves out: if the experiences that sent immigrants to the New World included poverty, famine, religious persecution, and much more besides, did their "energies" have the same meaning as the "energies" of those who later explored the continent or speculated on Wall Street? I suggest it would be misleading to even describe these "energies" with the same term.

Finding grounds for resisting the thing-ness of mania takes us back to John. He told us, "we have seen some vistas" and they should be neither "exalted nor put down." Peter Whybrow insists that "there is no difference except the context" between genius and derangement. Both statements are different ways of saying that the way manic states are experienced and the effects they have in the world are not fixed. There is no "thing" called mania that is, apart from its context, invariably on the side of heaven or hell, exaltation or despair. The import of manic experiences depends on when they happen, to whom, in juxtaposition to what events and the presence of what persons. In these respects, mania is no different from any other state of mind that exists only through being experienced. Whatever the physical substrate underneath mania, whether it is in the genes or the brain or both, mania is also an experience, constituted, as are all human experiences, by its context and by social imagination that is historically specific.[64]

Understanding Mania and Manic Depression in Their Contexts

Ironically, the contemporary fashion of identifying famous people from the past as manic depressive may also contribute to making mania appear to be a stable thing. One motive for reinterpreting the past as Jamison does is to shed a salutary light over a diagnosis that shadows many people with stigma. But describing what people experienced in past eras using contemporary terms can be problematic. Can the behavior of people in a time before the category "manic depression" existed be used as evidence that the condition existed then? In *Rewriting the Soul*, Ian Hacking explores this question for the case of multiple personality disorder (MPD). Hacking builds his case using Elizabeth Anscombe's account of intentional actions, which I introduced in chapter 5. Anscombe was arguing against the commonsense view of an intention as composed of an action plus an interior mental state. Looking at the ways we speak of an action as done "intentionally," she concluded that "intention" in everyday language means something done as an action of a whole person, a moral agent, "under a description."[65] The relevant description would include the past and present social contexts relevant to the person as much as his or her interior states.

To turn to Hacking's study, in descriptions of MPD until the 1980s, there was more than one person inside the individual, and these persons were so independent that they might actively struggle for control. Under these older descriptions, it would be appropriate to speak of intentional action on the part of each person who made up the multiple because each had enough integrity and wholeness to have intentions.[66] But in some more recent accounts of multiplicity, under the rubric of disassociative identity disorder, the switch among personalities is involuntary, and hence the criteria for speaking of intentionality are not present in the same way. Hacking suggests that new forms of description made new kinds of intentional action possible. Since the kinds of intentional action that are possible at a given time depend on the particular cultural assumptions that are contained in the languages available for describing action, these new kinds of intentional actions would not have been open to a person lacking those descriptions.[67] To elide the difference between the kind of intentionality in the older "aware" multiple and the new "unconscious" multiple would be as absurd as saying two distinct languages are just the same.[68] Instead of one unitary condition, MPD, there are minimally two, one organized around an older notion of intentionality, and one introducing new, and not fully realized, forms of intentionality.

Hacking might find Jamison's historical work troubling. When Jamison redescribes artists and musicians who lived in earlier centuries as "manic depressive," she means that something in their physical bodies, their particular genetic makeup, the formation of their brains, or all of these, conspired to cause their singular behavior: their mood swings, as well as their periods of creativity and fallowness. However, on the phenomenal level, Jamison might agree that Schumann, Van Gogh, and the other nineteenth-century artists she identifies could not have *experienced* their lives as manic depressives because the cultural work that eventually created the linguistic and social category of manic depression had not yet come into being. Whether or not genes or brains could determine Schumann's or Van Gogh's behavior, what their behavior meant to them would have to lie in the structures of meaning contemporary with them, and manic depression was not yet an available category of thought.[69] Nonetheless, there were certainly similar ways of thinking in the nineteenth century that did link artistic creativity with some kind of madness, often called melancholia. My point is that the contemporary conception of manic depression was not available then, with the specific features of mania that I have been outlining: its celebration in a wide variety of cultural contexts, its ability to be optimized by means of drugs, and its association with motivation and productivity.

I must stress that the wish to find manic depression as a thing-like entity in the distant past extends far beyond Jamison's work. Ron Chernow, the author of the recent biography of Alexander Hamilton, appearing on *Washington Journal* on CSPAN, responded to a caller from Winter Haven, Florida, who had asked, "The way you describe Hamilton, it sounds as though he had great energy, he was very charismatic, he was smart, he wrote the *Federalist Papers* at the same time as he practiced law, he had a real quick mind and was probably a good lawyer—could he have been bipolar?" Chernow replied,

> It's funny you ask that. The very first speech I gave on the book was to a group of doctors in New York and I was talking about these extreme mood swings. . . . Hamilton who had absolutely superb judgment 90 percent of the time, had absolutely atrocious judgment the

remaining 10 percent of the time. As I finished the speech, of the doctors in the audience there was a contingent of psychiatrists who rushed up to the podium and in one voice they said, "Narcissistic or bipolar disorder! We've seen many Manhattan types like this in a clinical setting." I deliberately refrained (as somebody doing an eighteenth-century biography) from introducing modern psychoanalytic jargon into an eighteenth-century narrative where I think it would be very, very jarring and intrusive but it has struck me since the book has come out from people who are trained in psychology or psychiatry how frequently the terms "narcissism" and "bipolar" come up so maybe there is some truth to it.[70]

The "truth" to it is how easy it is to see Hamilton's style of acting and being in the world as another form of the "thing" that is contemporary bipolar disorder.

The importance of Hacking's analysis goes beyond correcting anachronisms. What is at stake is whether we understand intentional human action as gaining its meaning in an interior, hidden, and thus socially inaccessible space, or out in the light of social experience. Anscombe worked in a Wittgensteinian mode to move intentionality out from the private interiority of the mind into the space of social interaction, where meaning in language is constituted.[71] Wittgenstein conveyed this message through many homely examples.

I tell someone: "I'm going to whistle you the theme," . . . it is my intention to whistle it, and I already know what I am going to whistle.

It is my intention to whistle this theme: have I then already, in some sense, whistled it in thought?"[72]

One would like to ask: "Would someone who could look into your mind have been able to see that you *meant* to say *that*?"

Suppose I had written my intention down on a slip of paper, then someone else could have read it there. And can I imagine that he might in some way have found it out *more surely* than that? Certainly not.[73]

The point is that intentionality resides in the whole complex of events, from the inception of the notion to the execution of the action. We decide whether someone had a certain intention, not by referring to some event or template in the mind, but by whether his or her gestures, postures, words, and actions fit with a socially defined notion of being about to whistle a tune or meaning to say something. Sometimes a mental event (whistling the tune or saying the words in one's head) might precede the action, and sometimes not, but in any case, that interior event could not constitute a final criterion for whether someone was intending to whistle or meaning to speak.

Seeing that manic or depressed behavior gets its meaning from the social context in which it is done is important. People living under the description of manic depression or any other mental illness are automatically demoted to less than fully human personhood by virtue of their putative "irrationality." Encouraging a sense that their actions, like anyone's, gain their sense from the entire social context, instead of by reference to an internal process, mental or physical, is my goal. This is one way even those who come to think of their serotonin as out of balance can feel they are (and can be taken for) worthy persons and moral agents. Writing down one's intention to whistle is as sure a way to communicate one's intention as anything one might think! Of course not every action can be understood as having sense, no matter how broad the social context we consider. But I think far more actions of the "irrational" sort can be understood—can be recognized as familiar—than we have realized. In the absence of a robust sense of how actions take their meaning from the social context, no amount of positive revaluing of mania will restore full personhood to those living under the description of manic depression.

CHAPTER NINE

Manic Markets

> As a physician I know that we cannot distinguish
> sharply between normality and abnormality. The
> abnormal is often only an enhancement of the
> normal. It is also known that both normality and
> abnormality often have identical social effects.
>
> —Ludwig Fleck, *Genesis and Development*
> *of a Scientific Fact*

In the world of financial markets, commentators on the economy often speak of alternation between extreme highs and lows as a disease, and sometimes describe it as a form of "manic depression." But in practice, for the adept, such volatility can act as a resource, because the volatility provides profit-taking possibilities for those who can anticipate when the market will shift either way. Mania's interstitial position between mood (floating, changeable feelings in the psyche) and motivation (organized, goal-directed behavior) is crucial for understanding why the "manic" artist or CEO seems to function well in the corporate world of the twenty-first century, but a "manic market" is a harbinger of disaster.

Links between Individuals and Markets

Denizens of Wall Street describe a feedback loop between the state of the market and the moods of stockbrokers. A study by a clinical psychologist was reported in the financial news: "It should come as no surprise that many stockbrokers are as depressed as Internet share prices. . . . Retail brokers, after all, play a key role in attracting the new money that helps push up share prices. When they feel down, the volume of sales calls they make to potential investors can fall by as much as half. In essence, the market becomes sad."[1] The author of the study, Alden Cass, noticed a change in a former fellow student who had joined a Wall Street brokerage. " 'Over six months, this guy was starting to sound an awful lot like my patients,' Mr. Cass recalls. What he found amazed him. Predictably, many brokers showed manic symptoms [during market highs]. They slept little. They had delusions of grandeur. They took excessive risks, spending recklessly and abusing drugs. 'They could do no wrong. That was the mindset,' says Mr. Cass." During market lows, "Mr. Cass found that 23 percent of his sample tested positive for clinical depression compared with 7 percent of men as a whole."

The Securities Industry Association held a seminar with Mr. Cass and colleagues from his hospital (St. Lukes-Roosevelt) to discuss depression among Wall Street brokers and how to minimize it. But during discussion, instead of asking about depression, the brokers hounded a panelist, former J. P. Morgan Chase strategist Doug Cliggott, for investment tips: "Sadly, the event may have done more harm than good . . . Mr. Cliggott put on his best bedside manner, then told them he expected the Nasdaq index to fall below 1,000 points by the end of the year." The brokers' manic energy prevented them from facing the market consequences of depression.

Acting at a slightly greater distance and with more effect is the feedback loop between the moods of those in powerful positions in the business community and the stock market. Commentators fear that a plunge into a depressed mood among businessmen in corporate America and on Wall Street can lead them to take actions that will depress the stock market: "For once, that overused depression-era cliché of Franklin D. Roosevelt's—'We have nothing to fear but fear itself'— is absolutely right. The economy is healthy, inflation non-existent, financial excess of late 1990s is over, the dollar is buoyant. Yet to judge by the thousands of job cuts since Sept. 11, American businessmen have suddenly lost their nerve. And fear is starting to spread to American consumers, who have always been more level-headed than the manic-depressives in corporate boardrooms and on Wall Street."[2] Disordered moods are dangerously contagious.

Acting at a still greater distance, and perhaps with still greater force, are aggregate measures of moods in the general population, measures we often take to be an everyday indication of the economy's health. Calculations such as the Consumer Confidence Index result in figures we understand to stand for the mood of the mass of people as a homogenized consuming force. Consumers en masse can be confident and exuberant or anxious and depressed. Their moods affect the market, even as their moods are affected by the market. As the economist Paul Samuelson explains,

> Now, millions of Americans calibrate their wealth and well-being, at least in part, by the market. The market's fall must affect the economy, social attitudes and national politics, but because the situation is new, no one can say just how much. The biggest danger is a corrosion of consumer confidence and buying, which have buoyed the economy. . . . Despite a hazy future, the past offers valuable lessons. A recent one is this: *mood matters.*
>
> The stock market got wildly overvalued—making its ultimate fall unavoidable—because Americans became hypnotized by silly stories of the Internet and the New Economy. There arose a senseless and stubborn optimism that justified otherwise-crazy stock prices. For a while, the optimism was self-fulfilling. Stocks rose, people spent and businesses invested. The boom began to implode once it became clear that much new corporate investment was squandered. It went into dot-coms or surplus telecom networks. Now, the danger is a swing to a stubborn and senseless pessimism. That, too, could become self-fulfilling. People dump stocks, even though prices now are more reasonable than two years ago.[3]

Samuelson is concerned with moods in the U.S. economy, but others are concerned with moods on a worldwide scale. Reflecting the salience of global markets, the consulting firm RoperASW issued a "Mood of the World" survey in 2003, which was based on a study of 30,000 consumers in thirty countries.[4] While I could not afford to purchase the full report on my research budget, the press coverage suggested that it links optimism and confidence to consumers' proclivity to spend, and pessimism and anxiety to their reluctance to spend.[5] In a more jocular vein, a Web site with a sardonic tone offers the "World Mood Chart," which allows visitors to record their moods and can tabulate thousands of individual entries a day: "Chart your personal mood against that of the world and find out if you are happier or unhappier than the planetary norm."[6] Until they ran into technical difficulties, the site owners plotted the Dow Jones Industrial Average against the world mood average each day.[7]

"Mood matters," as Samuelson says. But do moods matter in different ways in individuals and in the market? The structures of feeling at very different levels—the individual and the stock market—seem homologous to us in some ways and different in others. To begin with the homologies, it is often said that in the market, highs depend on investors' faith in the future of the country and the economy; lows are caused by their fear of the difficult times of the past. Individual mood states are similar, as the psychiatrist Leston Havens explains, "In depression, the future is lost, and the past becomes fixed, immovable, bad, the place of irredeemable mistakes. In contrast, [in mania] the past can be lost as one soars maniacally into an unreal future."[8] Evidently, in manias of both markets and individuals, time seems to speed up and in depressions time seems to slow down.[9] In *American Sucker*, an account of his life while investing in the market in 2000, the film critic David Denby writes,

> In this boom period, you have the illusion that if you can just grab hold of the flying coattails of the New Economy investments you have the chance of getting rich very quickly. My new urgency is driven by greed; I am talking in Internet time. . . . Wealth, much more than ever, seems a function of quickness. The market is a kind of crass metaphysical whip that hastens the annihilation of the passing moment: there is only the next instant, and the next, rushing toward you, and in the Internet age an ideally informed person would never sleep at all but would trade the markets and chase news and rumors through the links twenty-four hours a day.[10]

In the individual as in the market, highs go naturally with speed, energy, and activity, and in the kind of society we inhabit, these states often mean vigorous circulation of our chief token of value: money.

As in the market, individual manias have long been associated with putting everything possible into rapid circulation. In mania, a person will throw objects, gifts, money, or commodities in motion between people and set people in motion in relation to other people. It is as if an individual generates a miniature economic system all by herself. In her memoir, *The Man of Jasmine*, Unica Zürn described her state of mind just before she entered the mental hospital of Wittenau. In the manic phase, she made everything around her circulate rapidly; she circulated so rapidly, she lifted off the earth.

> Whenever she [Zürn is speaking of herself] enters a shop to purchase something, she leaves behind far more money than her purchase costs, and departs the shop with the words: "Happy birthday and many happy returns." Naturally the people in the shops are enchanted. And from now on she encounters one large smile wherever she goes. She also starts to walk in a completely new way: very fast and incredibly nimble. It seems to her as if she were floating two centimetres above the pavement—she's flying![11]

In his memoir, published in 2002, Andy Behrman describes his manic state as "working ridiculously long hours, earning plenty of money, and spending it as quickly as I make it."

> All of this gives me an amazing sense of power and control—and tremendous elation. When I get my salary or hefty commissions, I sometimes cash the large checks so I can have the money in my hands. I love paying the bills and the tabs—especially in cash, for the attention it gets me from salespeople, waiters, and even dinner partners. I'm crazy when it comes to the sight and touch of money. When I go to the bank, I withdraw $5,000 from my account in $20 and $50 bills; the look and feel of so much money give me a jolt and a great sense of security . . . losing control during a shopping spree is probably the ultimate high for me now; it causes a strange sense of panic, a near blackout state. My heart races—I'm nervous, I'm frightened, I'm pressured, I'm stressed. My body becomes numb and tingly, and everything around me is spinning and I feel like I'm going to pass out, but there's a force inside driving me forward.[12]

Similarly, money manager James J. Cramer gives elaborate descriptions of the extreme speed at which his life ran in 1997: "I've always been a manic guy. Not manic depressive, just manic. Fired up. Ready. Everybody in the business knew I was shot out of a cannon each morning." He would be jumping out of bed at 3:30 a.m.; filing a piece online for TheStreet.com by 4:15 a.m.; writing another piece while being driven to New York City at 5 a.m.; trading overseas by 5:30 a.m.; appearing on *Good Morning America* at 8 a.m.; writing another piece in the car on the way back to Wall Street at 8:30 a.m.; planning investment strategy for the day at 9:15 a.m.; and trading at the opening bell of the stock market at 9:30 a.m.[13]

Learning to Be Manic

The similarities between manic individuals and markets explains why corporations could think of deliberately cultivating manic states in their employees. As part of the research for my last book, I participated in a form of outdoor education for the members of a Fortune 500 corporation, in which 22,000 employees from upper management all the way to line workers were trained through exercises on a demanding ropes course (including some on a high wire) to become flexible, agile, and fearless. The goal of the employee training, which was subcontracted by the corporation to a small firm, was to enable workers to adjust rapidly to continuously changing conditions, especially if (or rather *when*) they were downsized. I summarized the continuous adaptation to change sought from these exercises as "flexibility."

Similar employee training firms have now begun to reach for something a little different: one, which I will call the Joule Company, is running training sessions intended to generate high-energy experiences. One course of training is organized along the lines of a scavenger hunt. The hunt will, according to the company's brochure, lead to a "riotous release of energy." When the company founder (whose official title is chief energizing officer) allowed me to work on a hunt as a staff member, I learned that encouraging people to experiment with unconventional behavior releases this energy. Teams win points in the exercise by carrying out daring or (for some) embarrassing stunts as a group: singing a love song to a stranger, borrowing a store mannequin, riding in a FedEx truck, shampooing their own hair (all at the same time) in a beauty salon, borrowing someone's official employee ID card, sneaking a dog into a hotel, and so on. Sometimes the public is mystified or annoyed by these activities. A news article interviewed a local merchant about the group: " 'It's a bunch of crazy people,' says an irate florist at a Newbury Street flower shop, apologizing to a customer after the Yellow team interrupts the flow of business by posing for a photograph with a floral arrangement in her shop (worth 40 points in the scavenger hunt)."[14] But far more often, the company has found, local shopkeepers approve, saying in effect, "it was actually entertaining for my customers—the highlight of our day."

But the company has designed the hunt to produce specific effects. The company founder explained that the hunt is one of their most popular offerings, especially among the many pharmaceutical clients they have.

> It really gets people making decisions together; it gets people showing more of their personality. They come through this powerful shared experience together and because it's in public, there is a positive pressure of stretching outside your comfort zone . . . of doing things that are a little nerve-racking to some and more comfortable for others. You have this powerful, shared experience where people have cracked open their armor and they've put some of their guts out on the table. They've opened themselves up in new ways, they've laughed equally, they've got stories to tell, going forward. . . . So you're willing to look at that person differently—you're willing to say, "Wow, this is sort of a normal guy who's just here like I am, trying to protect his livelihood or his turf the way I am." So it's not a panacea . . . but it's a lubricant, it's a catalyst, and it's an opportunity.
>
> We actually will put our programs out there in a spectrum for the clients, saying [about the hunt], that this will produce the *biggest* high. The hunt will take people as a group and raise the energy level, the excitement, the laughter, the pump up . . . this particular program, the hunt, actually takes a group the highest.

Participating in the market can also induce mania.[15] In a *New Yorker* article from 2000, the "money issue," David Denby writes of his obses-

9.1. Joule Company trainees have found a store mannequin that will get them points in the scavenger hunt. Reproduced with permission.

sive goal to win a million dollars on the stock market by the year's end. He speaks of himself and others around him having become a "speed freak," a "nut," "driven by the tempo of the market, the pulsing, darting flow of money around the globe"; of "[t]he New Economy . . . producing a New Man who in imitation of the economy itself, is going through wrenching changes in the way he lives, works, buys and interacts with other people." He feels "electrified and jubilant," in the midst of a wild investment culture, an "overstimulated climate," a "feverish mentality,"

9.2. Joule Company trainees earn scavenger hunt points by singing to a passerby in Cambridge. Reproduced with permission.

a mood of "bounding, thriving conviviality," intoxicating eagerness, in short, in mania; possessed of a "new kind of personality," "whose character has the liquid properties of cash."[16]

A pictorial representation of this mood appeared in a 2000 ad for Dynegy, an energy company that was expanding at the time. The ad copy appeared opposite a photograph of a man in a dramatic pose, his mouth stretched wide, his hair wild, his arms up, his fists clenched, his body under extreme tension: the ad copy read, "Surfing 60-footers at Waimea/speed climbing El Capitan/teaming across multiple disciplines to implement a cost-efficient yet flexible gas supply model/saving municipalities a bundle (whatever gets those endorphins going)." Business success is portrayed as a form of extreme sports, pursued with fanatic dedication and a driven energy.[17]

One goal of these calls for mania is to stimulate creativity. Yet the creativity desired in the business world is of a particular kind. Take an article in the *Harvard Business Review* titled "The Weird Rules of Creativity."[18] What is desirable about "weird creativity" is its immense activity, monumental productivity, risk taking, and innovation: "Creativity is a function of the *quantity* of work produced."[19] Here creativity is fueled not by cognition but by the raw force of emotion—we might say it is fueled by animal spirits. Weird creativity is fostered not by rational management but by "shifting the rational approach 180 degrees," as Steve Jobs does with what he calls his "reality distortion field." Because this notion of creativity taps into emotional forces, it can be seen as the opposite of "rational." But at the same time, recalling my discussion of the social conformity of mania and depression in the introduction, this notion of creativity *conforms*: it conforms to the demands of productivity as measured by the market.

Mania in the Market

Early in the twentieth century, writing soon after the Depression, John Maynard Keynes explained in no uncertain terms the importance of primitive emotions for the healthy functioning of markets.

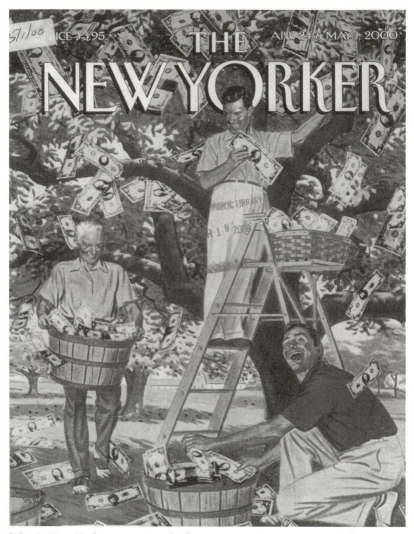

9.3. A *New Yorker* cover in which money grows on trees and three men, one with a manic grin, collect it in baskets. Reprinted with permission. *New Yorker*, April 24 and May 1, 2000. Illustration by Winston Smith, courtesy of the *New Yorker*, Condé Nast Publications Inc.

Most, probably, of our decisions to do something positive, the full consequences of which will be drawn out over many days to come, can only be taken as a result of animal spirits—of a spontaneous urge to action rather than inaction, and not as the outcome of a weighted average of quantitative benefits multiplied by quantitative probabilities. . . . Thus if the animal spirits are dimmed and the spontaneous optimism falters, leaving us to depend on nothing but mathematical expectations, enterprise will fade and die;—though fears of loss may have a basis no more reasonable than hopes of profits had before.[20]

Drawing on his understanding of Descartes, Keynes believed that people would make positive decisions when they were influenced by the spontaneous optimism of fiery animal spirits, and that they would fall into inaction when they felt fear in the wake of the animal spirits' departure.[21] He clearly implies that both optimistic and pessimistic calculations of benefit and loss might be equally reasonable: what differs most crucially is the psychological mood of the investor.[22]

In the decades since Keynes, references to the importance of animal spirits in stock markets have not been uncommon.[23] Often mania, with its driven, exaggerated energy, stands in for Keynes's animal spirits. William Grieder's *One World Ready or Not: The Manic Logic of Global Capitalism* is filled with references to "manic capital," depression, and the calamitous consequences of both. As owners of capital and financial markets become more powerful, their search for ever higher returns becomes increasingly abstracted from social concerns and the practical realities of the market. They plunge forward optimistically into a period of manic investing until a panic or crash intervenes.[24]

Language that describes market cycles as manic depression is rampant in press reports. The drop and rapid recovery of the stock exchange in October 1997 was described as a mood disorder: "If Wall Street were a person we'd think he was mentally ill;"[25] "The stock market was displaying classic signs of manic depression."[26] Similarly, during market swings in 1998, the *Los Angeles Times* quoted a stock analyst: "I've never seen anything like it, it's astounding. . . . The market is hyper, manic-depressive."[27] The *Atlanta Journal and Constitution* referred to a "manic-depressive period in the market—a first quarter with 'manic' gains and a second quarter with 'depressive' losses."[28] An Arizona paper weighed in, "In a manic-depressive economy where elation has been the prevailing mood, a whiff of fear is wafting not just through Wall Street but also through the rarefied air in technology-company cubicles and office suites [of Silicon Valley]."[29] Summing it all up was an ad for Netscape that juxtaposed young people, eyes dilated, arms stretched up, dancing at a rave, and traders bidding on the floor of the stock exchange.

As the ups and downs continued into 1999, James J. Cramer was quoted in the *New York Times*: "'This market needs a double dose of Zyprexa [an antipsychotic now prescribed for manic depression] with some lithium laced in,' he wrote in a TheStreet.com column. 'It has to stop the manic-depressive behavior before it drives us all crazy.'"[30] Looking back on this period in a review of Cramer's 2002 book, David Denby reflects that investment strategies during the late 1990s "seem to have been designed for manic personalities."[31] Indeed, Cramer is explicitly called "manic" in Howard Kurtz's book *The Fortune Tellers*, a judgment Cramer embraces: "I am a hard-driving, manic, emotional wild man who fights with everybody and craves respect."[32] Not surprisingly, Cramer's CNBC show, *Mad Money*, features his manic style.

In 1934, the economist Benjamin Graham invented a character called Mr. Market, and described his moody ups and downs in *The Intelligent Investor*. Drawing on this character, James Grant published a book in 1993 describing his experience as an Internet investment advisor with the task of minding "the mood swings of Mr. Market, the personification of all investors—a manic-depressive who gets wildly excited about stocks one day and deeply pessimistic the next." In its review of Grant's book, the *Washington Post* commented, "Sure, mood swings offer good opportunities to score in the market—but it's hard to tell when Mr. Market's feelings might be justified. Analysts who have said for the past four years that Mr. Market is crazy now look crazy themselves."[33] Others dismissed the manic depressive analogy and its implications, even as they gave it new life: in "Mr. Market is a Manic-Depressive Idiot," Bill Mann of the *Motley Fool* argued that tracking the short-term movements of one's stocks (which exposes the ups and downs of the market) is a mistake because "doing so hands

9.4. An ad for Netscape juxtaposes young people dancing frenetically at a party with traders on the floor of the stock market. Copyright Netscape Communications Corporation, 2006. All rights reserved. Netscape and the Netscape logo are registered trademarks of Netscape in the United States and other countries.

over psychological power to an irrational source." He argued instead that we should look at the market as a combination of myriad individual choices, some rational, some not, rather than grant it a personified and mythical status.[34]

As the term "bipolar disorder" became popular in the psychological realm, a *Wall Street Journal* writer picked it up in 2000: "We now have what I would call a 'bipolar' economy. It's manic in the technology sector, with the tech-heavy Nasdaq rocketing past 5,000 last week and up 112 percent in the past 12 months. But it's increasingly depressive in the other sectors we lump together as the 'Old Economy'. . . . The doctor who must treat this strange bipolar economy is Alan Greenspan. So far the Fed chairman has seemed more worried about the manic phase than the depressive."[35] John Heilman, author of a book on Silicon Valley, was interviewed on NPR's *Weekend Edition* in the context of the courts' challenge to Microsoft's monopoly practices: "It's almost like we've kind of entered this sort of period, in the media, at least, of sort of a collective bipolar disorder . . . you get these kind of manic-depressive swings from one side to the other."

Beginning with Alan Greenspan's use of the term in 1996, business commentators in the following years frequently linked "irrational exuberance" to Keynes's more old-fashioned words on emotions and the market. *Barclays Capital* described "irrational exuberance" as a phenomenon that periodically inflates the value of the market "beyond any limit that might be justified by rational expectations, [and] is no more than an extreme representation of our 'Animal Spirits,' without which, in Keynes's words, 'enterprise will fade and die.'"[36] Other accounts, written in a more sanguine mood, also invoked Keynes: in October 2001, *Business Week* correspondent Christopher Farrell asked whether investors are "irrationally exuberant" given that despite all the threats of the last month, stock values were already above their pre–September 11 level. He argued, "Investors aren't suffering from delusion, a speculative frenzy, false consciousness, or some other distressing form of mass mania." Instead they are expressing an important wellspring of economic growth, risk taking, what economist John Maynard Keynes called "the animal spirits of capitalism."[37]

In 2002, patience with the bipolar market began to wear thin. *Business 2.0* complained

> Bipolar disorder. Is that the problem? High as a weather balloon in one session, deep in the Dauphon's dungeon in the next. Or it is paranoia, perhaps? The stock market has certainly been distracted by a Babel of nagging voices—suspicious that inflation or a slowdown in corporate profits or a tech burnout or all of the above are out to destroy it. A quick read of the Diagnostic and Statistical Manual of Mental Disorders (DSM-IV) fails to pinpoint the malady. But I still suspect that most of its problems are in its head. My message to the stock market, as the immortal Cher once said: "Snap out of it."[38]

Here the diagnosis of bipolar disorder is considered alongside paranoia and both are dismissed as malingering, excuses that businessmen should stop giving.[39]

Clearly, the connection between mania and the market is more than metaphorical. This is a moment in which manic depression and the economic order have become linked through structures of feeling. There are fascinating homologies to be sure, which is part of the reason for the efflorescence of attention in the media. As I noted in chapter 1, people living under the description of manic depression feel gripped by an inevitable force—their exhilaration will inevitably be followed by despair—and this feeling resonates with the sense that market swings are also inevitable. But structures of feeling do more than highlight homologies, because when people notice them, things happen in the world: people can change their minds about what a condition means, alter their self-perception, or take different kinds of action. Much signifying and political work is done when cultural linkages between a mental illness and an economic system catch public attention. A new aesthetic attached to a new kind of person can emerge, but so also can new possibilities for promoting or curtailing the workings of an economic system.

Although manic energy is often celebrated in the case of individual CEOs or traders, an excess of manic energy in the market is usually a cause for concern. One of the ways manic depression, the psychological condition, is good to "think with" when it comes to manic depression, the market condition, is this: manic depression, the psychological condition, is part of a system of moods that oscillate. Depression will be followed inevitably by mania and mania by depression. This gives manic depression its regenerative character (a sign of power) and its self-limiting character (a sign of control). Regenerating power and self-limiting control are both characteristics a healthy market would be glad to have.

Emotion in the Market

Significant attention (usually tinged with fear and caution) is now being devoted to patterns of emotional volatility in markets of the past. Mike Dash revisits the classic mania for tulips in Holland in the seventeenth century.[40] He sees this mania as a kind of disease, a virus, that spread by means of the emotions of greed and love of beauty.[41] Andrew Tobias reissued a new edition of the nineteenth-century *Extraordinary Popular Delusions and the Madness of Crowds* in 1980. Tobias's introduction recommends the book as a caution against following the madness of crowds, as encouragement to buck the crowd, and as a way to become wealthy.[42] Charles Kindleberger's *Manias, Panics, and Crashes* was published in three editions from 1978 to 1996. It documents how frequent manic markets have been in the past and warns that market manias risk causing financial crisis and panic that may spread through many markets near and far.[43] Kindleberger argues that market mania "connotes a loss of touch with reality or rationality, even something close to mass hysteria or insanity." He contends that manias and panics are "associated on occasion with general irrationality or mob psychology."[44] Yet he is perplexed because this irrationality is not addressed by economic theory or the social sciences generally, which assume that "men are rational." He wonders how the two views can be reconciled, warning that we ignore the irrational at the heart of economic cycles at our peril.[45]

Excess emotion in the market looks dangerous to Kindleberger, but he might agree with the architects of modern markets that some emotion is necessarily part of economic activity. Long before Keynes, in the eighteenth century Condorcet and Adam Smith saw economic life as imbued with feelings. In the 1770s and 1780s, commercial judgments were thought to be "a combination of reasons and sentiments." Entrepreneurs should be men of "imagination" and "passion" more than of "sober reason and experience," entranced by the "golden dreams" of mining, empire, and capital investment.[46] However, emotions in the market could get out of control. Booms and busts in the value of public stock were regarded with dismay and fear. Seen as feeding on itself and without moral limit, the market, a pathologically unstable force, placed "politics at the mercy of a self-generated hysteria (in the full sexist sense)."[47] Many political and philosophical efforts were exerted to throw a net of rational control (refinement and politeness) over the eighteenth-century "economic man." The historian John Pocock argues that eighteenth-century markets were seen as "female." The market was an "effeminate being wrestling with his own passions and hysterias and with interior and exterior forces let loose by his fantasies and appetites, and symbolised by such archetypically female goddesses of disorder as Fortune, Luxury, and most recently Credit herself."[48] The goddess Fortuna was often depicted standing on a ball or a globe to signify her instability.

By the nineteenth century, the kinds of emotions associated with a well-functioning market were more explicitly defined and began to shift their gendered alignments. In northeastern America, according to historian John Corrigan's research into the business culture of the time, "Economic downturns were understood to be the product of overexcitement of the market. When speculation became 'frenzied,' when managers departed from sound standards of regulation of investment, the market in a burst of activity overheated, burning itself out and collapsing." The hope was that just enough capital could be fed to the market to reach its peak performance, without allowing it to tumble out of control.[49] The lives of businessmen were supposed to reflect the moderation and cyclicity that lay under the workings of the market: "[T]oo much emotion was as bad as too little emotion in a businessman."[50]

After a serious crash in 1857, which was accompanied by many businessmen's suicides, a Businessman's Revival was held as a public display of emotion "grounded in an understanding of emotion as a valuable commodity that could be exchanged for various other things." The revival was based on a "feminized Christianity that valued emotional religion." However, the revival complemented its emphasis on feminine emotion with additional emphasis on the "masculine qualities of initiative, courage, daring, and speaking one's mind."[51] The revival focused on the issue of how businessmen's emotions could be *regulated* in order to keep them from boiling over and creating an overstimulated market.

> Far from causing an outbreak of religious enthusiasm, the crash in fact influenced the nascent revival toward stricter controls of emotional expression in religious gatherings . . . the language of the revival focused on highly scripted performances of emotion in which expression was constrained by specific regulations about the interval of public prayer (three to five minutes), the form of petitioning (make specific requests), and the duration of meetings (one hour, so businessmen could return to work and immediately take up their duties).[52]

Unlike earlier revivals, mid-century revivals were attended by large numbers of men. There were widespread accounts of men weeping, laughing, and making other displays of emotion. This behavior must have been unusual because at the time, men were not "particularly emotional creatures." In general in the nineteenth century, it was women who normally expressed emotion and nurtured it in their families. At mid-century revivals, women did not necessarily become less emotional, but men clearly became more so.[53]

These historical examples echo the gendered reversal described above: ideas about the scary "female" instability of eighteenth-century markets were giving way. By the nineteenth century, the American "economic man" had become firmly masculine.[54] The wild, passionate "female" energy that fueled the speculative economics of the eighteenth century gave way to the more controlled masculine energy of the nineteenth- and early twentieth-century robber barons and industrial Titans, but much of their Titanic energy was still provided by emotion.

A Few Manic Heroes, Past and Present

Recently, a number of historical and contemporary figures have been held up as exemplars of the manic style. They succeed as entrepreneurs because they are regarded as enterprising, risk taking, and creative. They come from all the major corridors of power in which entrepreneurial energy is at a premium: politics, scientific exploration, entertainment, business, and organized crime. In its section on manic depression, a major textbook in introductory psychology inserted a new sidebar in the 1995 edition. Above a photograph of Theodore Roosevelt, the caption reads: "There is evidence that Theodore Roosevelt was a manic-depressive, and that his mania contributed to his political success." Teddy Roosevelt has also come in for other kinds of attention in recent years, including the second volume of a major biography and a PBS documentary, *TR: The Story of Theodore Roosevelt*.[55] The reviewer of the documentary in *Newsday* notes that he was "volatile and voluble," "the most manic president in American history," a "hyperactive eccentric president."[56]

Attending to another kind of leadership, in 2002 PBS ran an episode of *Nova* about the early twentieth-century Antarctic explorer Ernest Shackleton. The documentary, "Shackleton's Voyage of Endurance," described Shackleton as "inordinately ambitious," with "a huge amount of energy," a man whose "sheer willpower and personal magnetism made him an irresistible leader." He had "some force of character, some flame that burns within a man. You can't learn it. You can't develop it. It's something you radiate. He had this."[57] By happenstance or echoing patterns in the Zeitgeist, many other productions about Shackleton appeared around this time: an exhibition at the American Museum of Natural History (1999), a giant-screen PBS movie, *Shackleton's Antarctic Adventure* (2001), and an A&E miniseries, *Shackleton* (2002). While descriptions in these films stop short of calling Shackleton "manic," reviewers referred to his "wild optimism" and his "manic determination."[58] Stephanie Capparell at the *Wall Street Journal* wondered what was fueling such intense interest, and dubbed it "Shackleton-Mania."[59] Later she coauthored a book that attests to the inspiration Shackleton has been to business leaders, among them James Cramer, and promotes him as a model for others because of his optimism even in the face of disaster.[60]

In a similar revisiting of mania in the past, Larissa MacFarquhar reviews a classic text: "[W]hen [George Gilder's] *Wealth and Poverty* was first published [in 1981], Gilder's depiction of the irrational entrepreneur was considered quite eccentric, but in the intervening twenty years it has become conventional wisdom." Gilder despises materialism as well as rationality and calculation: "Genius, to him, is to be found in intuitive, irrational leaps; in flashes of insight whose origins cannot be traced; in risks so bold that their outcomes cannot possibly be predicted." For human creativity to flourish, minds must remain open to "chance, intuition and mystery."[61] A more approving, even exuberant, description of the merits of irrationality could not be had, unless it were a special issue of *Time* magazine, "Builders and Titans," which presented biographies of the most powerful business leaders during the last one hundred years. A section called "Crazy and in Charge" was devoted to successful leaders whose "craziness"—from eccentricity to "mental illness"—led them to excel in the marketplace.[62]

Numerous well-known contemporary larger-than-life leaders and CEOs have been described as manics. Karl Rove, advisor to George W. Bush, Jeff Taylor, founder and CEO of Monster.com, and Steve Jobs, founder and CEO of Apple Inc., are among them.[63] Entering their company more recently, Dov Charney, CEO of the innovative company American Apparel, is said to be "passionate to the point of mania," leaving the impression that "he might just burst into flames at any moment."[64]

A manic style is an asset not only in legitimate business, but also in the mafia, at least in fiction. The powerful mob boss Tony Soprano from the HBO series *The Sopranos*, struggles to optimize his manic energy and eliminate his depression (as well as his panic attacks) with therapy and medication. In episode 12 of the first season, Tony's psychiatrist signaled her diagnosis of him as manic depressive by prescribing lithium (alongside the Prozac he was already taking). At the time, Tony was submerged in a deep depression, apparently because he had had to sanction the murder of Pussy, a close friend, who had betrayed the organization by wire tapping for the FBI. Ominously, we see Tony open his bathroom medicine cabinet to reveal two prescription bottles labeled "Prozac" and "lithium." He empties both bottles into his mouth and waits to die. Tony is rescued, and after he recovers, although the terms "manic depression" or "bipolar disorder" are never explicitly mentioned, we are left wondering what intensely driven profit scheme he will launch next.

Is mania only valuable for men? Certainly, most "manic" figures described in the mass media are men. In college and university lectures where I have introduced this material, the only women whom audiences ever suggested as candidates were Martha Stewart and Oprah Winfrey. Other audience members were quick to disagree with these suggestions, objecting that Martha Stewart is too rigid and controlling to be included, and Oprah Winfrey is too empathic and kind. I suspect that with mania as a sign of power, as with other such signs, women fall on the twin horns of an old dilemma: if they attempt to wear the signs of power, they lose their ability to be women; if they are really women, they cannot effectively wear the signs of power. Martha Stewart is an instructive case study of this double-bind. In a review of Christopher Byron's *Martha, Inc.*, Anne Kingston attributes Stewart's corporate success to Wall Street's mistaken belief that she was a "woman."

> What she had done was nothing short of amazing: she played the needs of one corporation off against another and then staged an end run around the traditional sources of capital, namely the banks. No one had done it before in media. And Stewart got away with it precisely because the suits around her confused the personal with the corporate Martha Stewart. They thought they were dealing with the mythic Betty Crocker. The fact that Stewart's business is domesticity confuses the matter further, because domestic carries with it associations of servility and unflagging graciousness, qualities Stewart doesn't possess.[65]

But a Betty Crocker could not bring off such financial success, Kingston concluded. In reality, Stewart was a "man": "She was a harridan with her husband . . . she doesn't like children; allegedly she treated her daughter, Alexis, with contempt, and elected to get a hysterectomy in her child-bearing years. . . . She's not a nurturer. Her employees are terrified of her." Only after describing her as temperamentally, emotionally, and physically a "non-woman" did Kingston make the move to include Stewart in the category of powerful manics. Citing Byron's book, Kingston said, "Just before her IPO, she tried to sue the *National Enquirer* for suggesting she was mentally ill." But then she added, "What Byron fails to mention is that manic depression is not unusual in the executive suite, particularly among visionary entrepreneurs." On this account, Stewart achieves manic style, but at the cost of losing her womanhood entirely.

This suggests that today Fortuna—symbol of eighteenth-century market instability—might better be called "Fortunus": powerful masculine figures enact the attributes of the market rather than keeping the market separate and under firm control. The emergence of men who—in a sense—personify the traditionally "female" market brings a lot of unease. There are those in the financial world today—called "contrarian"—who disparaged the 1990s stock market as dangerously inflated and urged a high degree of caution in "minding Mr. Market." They specifically cite the dangerous "female" properties of the market, who is always—like a woman—changing his mind.[66] Financial reports, such as Thestandard.com, also disparaged the fluctuating market for its female characteristics: "The market must be a woman—entitled to change its mind. It closed the day down for the week—its first negative week in a month—but not before first rising, then falling and then rising again."[67]

Fear, perhaps from feeling the consequences of markets unleashed from control, accompanies these shifting frameworks. Perhaps fear could serve as a wedge that would allow us to see things we normally repress. Decrying the dominance of free market ideology today and our inability to conceptualize alternatives, the geographer David Harvey comments sardonically that the usual view in the United States pits "the supreme rationality of the market versus the silly irrationality of anything else."[68] But perhaps the irrationality of the market and what you have to do and be to succeed in it has been forced into the open as a result of policies in the United States beginning in the 1980s that have given markets free reign over more spheres of life. These policies—loosely termed "neoliberal"—fueled investment in the stock market and, in turn, set off a spiral of corporate mergers, layoffs, technological investment, increased profits, and higher stock prices. All this was achieved at the cost of job loss, wage stagnation, and a widening gap between rich and poor—each with its price tag of misery. Perhaps it is hard not to see anymore that "rational choice" contains within it "irrational" choice: it is irrational to promote the well-being of society through means that are sure to damage and impoverish many of its most vulnerable members. Fear might also arise from the prospect that even more dire consequences will surely flow from the hallmark of the neoliberal regimes that are now ascendant, extending the operation of untrammeled self-regulating markets to every imaginable sphere: education, social security, health care, and the environment, just for a start. Neoliberal policies in the United States and elsewhere have deliberately cultivated practices that bolster market mechanisms and entrepreneurial competition, attempting to remove all impediments to their operation.[69] They have aimed to anchor the entrepreneurial form in the very heart of society and make it universal.[70] Is it any wonder, as the economist Karl Polanyi warned long ago, that we fear the unrestrained operation of self-regulating markets, which could annihilate "the human and natural substance of society," physically destroy man, and transform "his surroundings into a wilderness"?[71]

Manic Affinity

If we step back a moment to the days when industrial capitalism was emerging in the United States, we can gain deeper insight into the affinity between mania and powerful contemporary entrepreneurs. As Max Weber showed, modernity put into motion a relentless process in which almost all aspects of work and life were "rationalized." Although the standards of precision, speed, and efficiency associated with rationalization penetrated more and more deeply into institutions, their penetration was never complete. Weber made an analogy to division in mathematics: "The calculation of consistent rationalism has not easily come out even with nothing left over."[72] Some of the "leftovers" hide in "irrational presuppositions" that are accepted as given and incorporated unseen into daily life.[73] Other "leftovers" hide within the "vocational imperative," the passion and energy associated with an individual's calling. Before the emergence of capitalism, in Weber's view, a vocation could emerge from a calling for religion or a passion for meaningful work. But in capitalism, the passion and energy of the vocation would become predominantly linked to the universalized standards of rational capital production: "[W]e are all as it were conscripted as unconsenting participants in a universalized vocational culture, our horizons limited to the rationalized, endless, and inwardly meaningless certainties of vocational humanity."[74] What passion is left becomes "stripped of its religious and ethical meaning," and usually finds a place only in association with "purely mundane passions, which often actually give it the character of sport."[75] Thus, in capitalism the vocation is "stripped of its structures of meaning."[76]

For Weber, the development of capitalism depended on the emergence of a new kind of person with an unprecedented degree of engagement with work. On the one hand, there was willingness to restrain desire as a form of asceticism; on the other there was willingness to impose and tolerate "increased rigor in the supervision of labor, new marketing methods, a new willingness to adapt to the demands of different customers, large turnover and low prices, and reinvestment of profits in the business."[77] These developments led to intensified competition among firms, in which "whoever did not rise had to decline." Weber, following Marx, saw the capitalistic economy as an encompassing world that appears to individuals and firms as "an unalterable order of things." Insofar as they participate in the market, firms and individuals must conform to the rules of the system. Anyone who does not adapt to these rules will eventually be eliminated from the market or thrown out of a job.[78] Those with a calling for this kind of work needed "temperate self-control," "clarity of vision and energy," and "vigor for overcoming the innumerable oppositions." Above all, however, the entrepreneur needed the capacity for an "endlessly more intensive rate of work." He needed to be poised and daring but, more important, strongly disciplined and devoted to his work.[79]

In Weber's description, the capitalist entrepreneur is a pale reflection of the man with a true vocation. As we know, the term "mania" straddles the concepts of mood and motivation. The more mania drifts toward "motivation," the more aptly it fits the rational "male" elements of capitalist firms. The more it drifts toward "mood" the more aptly it fits the unpredictable and irrational "female" emotional elements present in the same capitalist firms. The optimum condition would be just enough unexpected manic ingredients to leaven the deadly control that rationalization requires. Weber himself described this desirable mix. He thought that the danger in all modern work, whether scientific, entrepreneurial, or artistic, is that one might work hard but never have a valuable idea.[80] He wrote that being "truly creative" requires that one brood and search at one's desk with a passionate inner devotion[81] in hopes that one might happen upon the kind of frenzy that Plato described as "mania."[82] As I have already pointed out, the problem with looking to the mania of manic depression for true creativity is that it is tightly bound to social conventions—it is likely to be innovative only in terms the market can value.

A Few Fallen Heroes

The entrepreneur departs from the pattern of manic depression because he is (ideally) always manic, never depressed. Some manic entrepreneurs might have manic depression that is well managed by drugs or therapy or both; others might rely on family or business associates to protect them from the damaging effects of fluctuating moods. Ronald Fieve suggests in *Moodswing* that among affluent families, manic behaviors such as compulsive spending and traveling sprees are "less noticed and in some instances . . . almost a normal style absorbed within the family pattern."[83] In any case, the wealthy and powerful can depend on access to material resources, which are far less available to others. The sociological literature contains eloquent statistical studies of the disparities in health and mental health care in the United States that run along lines of race, class, and gender. My field research was not designed to contribute further statistics to these studies, but it can shed light on the experience of moods in a range of current economic settings.

In support groups, people sometimes directly linked mood states to finances. At a meeting in the inland part of Orange County, Jim was serving as facilitator but nonetheless talked extensively about himself. His manner was energetic and animated. He talked continuously in a way that did not admit interruption, with an intense expression and dramatic hand gestures. His face—bright eyes, ruddy cheeks, and dimples—was wreathed in smiles, but all the while he was talking about his profound depression while living alone in a rented room.

> I was a nuclear engineer who worked for a major defense company near here until six years ago. Then I froze at work one day. The company was laying off workers—they had already laid off more than 4,000 engineers. But I beat them to it. I sat there for six hours catatonic, just holding on to a pencil in my hand and staring down at my desk. That is how security found me. The doctor wrote a report and they couldn't do anything about it, so I got on disability. After this my family fell apart, they didn't like living without money. . . . Ever since then I have been living in one room, my own psychiatric ward, and I am a recluse. Some days I don't get out of bed, in fact days go by that way. Except to pee, of course. I eat one meal a day at most, chicken from Kentucky Fried Chicken, and only part of the meal at that. Lots of Cheese Curls and orange soda. I am just sleeping in bed, hour after hour . . . I can't work. My doctor says my serotonin levels are minuscule, nonexistent. This town has a big aircraft manufacturing complex, and they have also recently laid off 6,100 workers. These people came into work one day and were told they had two weeks' notice. If you were to walk down Main Street, you would walk over many bodies of dead engineers.

Jim used the language of emotional depression to describe his suffering in the wake of national and global economic depression and its effects on him and his family. He "beat them to it" in the sense that he became physically and emotionally "frozen" before his job and his earnings were frozen.

On the other end of the mood scale, which Jim has not experienced lately, there can be equally devastating relationships between moods and economics. When people described these relationships in support groups, their tone could sometimes be humorously bittersweet, as expressed in these three statements, from three different West Coast support groups.

[Michelle said that her $5,000 SSI (Supplemental Security Income) check had just arrived.] There is something about an SSI check that brings on a mania. One time I spent $2,000 of it on a fancy pager with a five-year contract, Chanel makeup, shoes, gifts, etcetera. Those people at the mall know it when they see a manic depressive coming.

Mike: I like women and falling in love is a lot like mania. You feel upbeat, optimistic, elated, and excited, but then I eventually go into a depression, and the relationships don't last. I can go through a lot of money when hypomanic, especially in relation to women, going out, buying dinner, giving the ice cream girl $100. I bought a $35,000 boat last year, which sank. But I lived on it for a while before it sank.

Richard: My psychiatry residency was interrupted by this illness. I went on a cross-country trip, spending money like crazy, with my wife and children in the car. I went up to a house, and, as I remember it, I just touched the door and the chain broke. I went in and said, "Sorry I broke your chain." I was arrested for breaking and entering and did jail time.

But more often, the experience of manic behavior is no joking matter because it is economically devastating. The market's immense capacity to absorb investment acts as a lure to a person in a manic frame of mind. As Kay Jamison comments, "Unfortunately for manics anyway, mania is a natural extension of the economy."[84] Gert was a successful businessman I met at a DMDA conference who worked in the family business before being "felled by manic depression." His father encouraged his mania, his energy, and his enthusiasm. Gert speculated in gold. He would read an investor's report and just get an intuition that gold was going up. He would spend a lot of money: once he bought five gold funds for a total of $100,000, but "the pattern was I would make $5,000 and then lose $25,000."

Peter was a successful businessman, in development, public relations, and marketing. He was taking lithium, but when he was about to move to California his doctor said he could stop taking it. In California he had a five-year contract with a Japanese company to develop a golf course. Even though he didn't know a thing about golf, he did it successfully, and in only four years. This enabled him to go for a year without pay and no need to work. Then things started to fall apart. He was footloose with money, and he bought and sold a couple of houses. Now he has only the big office with a gorgeous view of the ocean, and no business. His wife is filing for divorce and his son says he cannot work with him. He wishes the doctor in Texas had not allowed him to go off lithium. One of his former business associates agreed to help him run an antique sale to raise funds from items in his house: "The guy put signs all over the area saying, 'Antique Sale to benefit the mentally ill.' Now my son is mortified at school — there is such stigma that now none of my former business associates will even return my phone calls."

Wendy can't tolerate any of the mood stabilizers. She has tried them all and either they do nothing or they have terrible side effects like making her hair fall out. She has to take an antipsychotic because otherwise she thinks people will think she comes from another planet. Until her diagnosis several years ago, she was a high-functioning real estate broker. Her cycle fit the real estate cycle very well because it enabled her to work like a maniac in spring and summer and then slow way down in fall and winter. She was very successful. There was a saying in the office: "If Wendy can't sell something, she will buy it." She described her fall.

> When I fell apart, I had built up my assets and I owned a large apartment building. I lost it all in the hospital. Now my goal is only to own a modest house. I am worried because I am so good at convincing others to go along with my wild, grandiose schemes. I can sweep you up with enthusiasm because I really believe in the scheme and that it is good for you. I am a professional salesperson after all, and positive thinking is a large part of that. My boyfriend has gone along

in the past, and now I have pleaded with him to resist. He objects that "it is *so* hard!" What I do is pile one financial obligation up on another until the weight sends me into crisis. I have to keep all the tenants in order, deal with loans, mortgages, all of them so precarious and delicately balanced they threaten to collapse. The growing debt eventually causes *me* to collapse.

The Edge

Accounts like these could help us understand the pain people feel as a result of mania or depression, especially when they are economically disadvantaged. It is equally important to understand how those who cause suffering in others, directly or indirectly, experience inflicting pain on others. Recently, some anthropological researchers have begun to ask how people in positions of power tolerate knowing that their actions may cause others to suffer. For example, in her Wall Street fieldwork, Karen Ho focuses on investment bankers, who, as a condition of their jobs today, not only bring about much suffering for employees of other firms by requiring them to downsize frequently, but also feel the pain of downsizing themselves. One question in her research is how the bankers tolerate knowledge of this double-edged sword, or how they remain to some degree unconscious of it.[85]

In his research in a nuclear weapons facility, Hugh Gusterson inquired how the scientists there tolerated the knowledge that they were making weapons with the capacity to maim and destroy untold numbers of people. Gusterson argued that widespread use of numeric measures of human pain and suffering blunts visceral knowledge by means of the clean coldness of abstraction. Numeric measures can serve to "drive another person's pain from awareness so that the doctor can get on with his or her task of applying scientific rules and logic to the objectified signs of another person's pain without the pain itself getting in the way."[86] Might there be a connection between the hyperenergized, manic state cultivated by traders, bankers, and other executives, and their awareness of suffering? Is there something about being manic that allows you to ignore your own suffering or the suffering you cause others?

In his *100 Years of Psychiatry*, Kraepelin speaks of the use of painful cures for mania in earlier centuries.[87] Since manias would drive a patient to a "higher plane," deliberately inflicting pain on a patient would force him to "descend from his ethereal perch" and "re-enter the husk." Part of what is appealing about the state of mania today is a numbness to pain, something that has been a part of the social life of its "disease picture" for a long time.[88] Why would this be? As I have pointed out before, manic depression is a condition in which mania and depression are mutually entailed. If, on the psychodynamic view, mania is produced as a defense against the suffering of depression, then the very point of mania is to avoid the experience of one's own suffering. Perhaps it is not too great a leap to suggest that experiencing mania can inure a person to the pain of others as well as one's own. Being inured to pain in the present or oblivious to the inevitability of future pain might be as necessary for consumers on a manic buying spree as for CEOs manically generating profitable ideas. Being on a manic "higher plane" may work well to blind one to the kind of painful consequences caused by corporate CEO decisions to merge, downsize, relocate, or subcontract at the expense of their employees.

On the opposite end of the mood scale, in depression, people feel pain so intensely that they sometimes try to escape through suicide. As mania becomes more and more a separate "thing" that can be managed by drugs, what happens to its dark twin, depression? One marketing campaign for a manic depression drug, a form of sustained-release lithium, placed depression over an "edge." "Dancing on the Edge: An Intimate Look at a Bipolar Life," was a display from the 2000 APA exhibit for Scios. Scios's theme for the drug, "Dancing on the Edge," featured large photos on displays that led viewers through the story. This was what happened to a college guy who was wild but in the top 10 percent of his class and got a dream job. In the corporation, he was both terrific Tim, the wonder boy, and terrible Tim, who was fired, jumped from job to job, and got a divorce. He had a catastrophic manic episode, which really scared him. Upon treatment, he got a new small apartment and a new job. Then came the "end game": the display showed a picture of a pistol, pills, a razor, and rope. He felt the "tedious grasp of normalcy" and experienced agitation and anger that he had lost his edge, then became full of ecstatic plans about his return to the good old days. Confronted about his compliance in taking his medication, he took off, attempted suicide, but failed. The last display read:

> I'm so brilliant.
> I'm so confident.
> I'm so successful.
> I'm so attractive.
> I'm so rich.
> I wish I was dead.

It may seem impossible for such opposites to coexist in the same person, but they do. They coexist in the two photographs of Ted Turner in the *Saturday Evening Post*, which show him vibrant with power. The caption under the photographs ends on a fearful note: "Turner's father, like Hemingway's, committed suicide." This raises the implied question: will Turner end his life by suicide as Hemingway did? Poised between the mania that enabled his financial success and the depression that threatens him, Turner is often depicted as a tragic figure. *Time* reported that he prevailed over the "dark legacy of his father" in a life that has been a struggle to master his intense fear of dying in midlife, as his father did. He was convinced that through some "cyclical inevitability" he was doomed to lose whatever he had.[89] A long essay appeared in *The New Yorker* shortly after Turner lost his position at AOL Time Warner, describing his fall from invincibility. The essay ended with Turner in a restaurant quoting Thomas Macaulay's "Horatius" from memory: "And how can man die better / Than facing fearful odds, / For the ashes of his fathers, / And the temples of his gods."[90] The excesses in Turner as capitalist and as yacht captain seem necessary for his success, but his excesses are inextricably connected to the possibility of his suicide. His exuberance burns brighter under the shadow of apprehension. (As the Ted Turner caption hints, the risk of dying by suicide among those diagnosed with manic depression is high.[91]) "Dancing on the Edge" is gripping because it brings together the dancer's lively beauty with his position on the edge of death. To live under

9.5. "Dancing on the Edge," an exhibit at the 2000 American Psychiatric Association meeting. The exhibit advertises Scios Inc., maker of Eskalith, CR, a sustained-release form of lithium used to treat manic depression. Through a number of displays like this one, it tells the story of a young man who plunges from success to despair because of his manic depression. He is helped by medication but becomes suicidal when he refuses to take it. Photo by Emily Martin, 2000.

the description of manic depression is to live and die simultaneously, as if the condition foretells one's possible (even likely) suicide. This is a kind of living death, and it is surrounded by an aura of fear and intense fascination.[92]

· · ·

In part 2 we have taken a route through mania in manic depression and mania in the market, and we have seen that both forms are infused with fear and desire. Although the mania of manic depression and the mania of manic markets are certainly not the same thing, they do both operate on an edge. We might think of the "edge" as a "break" in the smooth public presentation of manic depression, a break that points to things that are either suppressed or beyond expression in language.[93] For the manic male entrepreneur or CEO, the edge might lie near the specter of terrible loss. As the imperative to become the kind of person who can succeed in extremely competitive and unpredictable circumstances has intensified, the prospect of failure has become more frightening. The times are bringing greater knowledge of what capitalism entails and greater fear of what it may require of people. Business entrepreneurs are often called upon to ignore such fear, to continue taking risks even at the risk of social or even physical death. A recent issue of the Economist.com quizzes its readers: John Maynard Keynes referred to "animal spirits" when describing what? Answer: The naïve optimism that inspires entrepreneurs. Explanation: Keynes said that for entrepreneurs, thanks to animal spirits, "the thought of ultimate loss which often overtakes pioneers, as experience undoubtedly tells us and them, is put aside as a healthy man puts aside the expectation of death."[94] But can fears continue to be put aside no matter how great they are?

In an idealized, exuberant, manic state, a person is exalted, above the mundane, not likely to take notice of the ordinary. What is repressed in the image of dancing on the edge, and lies underneath the incitement for a manic leadership style, is that the destruction of lives, occupations, and livelihoods, not to mention communities, environments, and firms, which are a routine part of survival in the economy, can be ignored. In an ethereal but numbed state, a person is less likely to look over the edge and more likely to keep up his "animal spirits" unfalteringly, "without which, in Keynes' words, 'enterprise will fade and die.'"[95]

There are some signs that "the edge" may now be poised above a deeper abyss. Some scholars have argued that terrorist acts by suicide bombers shifted the American cultural imagination in a particular way: what most grabs public attention now is a person who risks or sacrifices his life for a cause. *What* cause matters less than the person's willingness to give up his life in an act of excessive commitment. To be willing to die for a cause one must be excessively alive: extremes of living and dying seem inextricably linked. The official American response to terrorism—starting a war—pits Americans dying for a cause against terrorists dying for a cause, and by implication shows that Americans are as excessively alive as the terrorists are, or so it would seem in such a cultural scenario.[96] The person with a manic leadership style and the person with manic depression both look over an edge into violence: their superabundance of life means they are always risking death, if not for themselves, for other people. Living on the edge of death in a time when national leaders demand that we demonstrate an excess of life makes the manic person seem precisely in tune with what all Americans are now called upon to be.

The Bipolar Condition

Tell me a story.
In this century, and moment, of mania,
Tell me a story.
Make it a story of great distances, and starlight.
The name of the story will be Time,
But you must not pronounce its name.
Tell me a story of deep delight.

—Robert Penn Warren, "Tell Me a Story"

I t can be terrifying to face the darkness around forms of madness like manic depression. A person living under the description of manic depression is a threat to the conception of American personhood that has prevailed for centuries: a person with a central controlling principle based on the will, who is owner of himself and acts out of individual intention and desire toward rational ends. Manic depression, with its strong emotional cycles and multiplicity that interrupts the unitary individual, would indeed be a genuine threat to such a fragile understanding of personhood. But on another view, one I have promoted in this book, everyone's personhood—rational, irrational, or somewhere in between—is less built upon a unitary concept, fragile or not, than made up of a dense web of social connections with others. Even "mad" manic depressives, denizens of the irrational, are capable of being social persons. Even they can spark self-reflective, sometimes creative, and occasionally scintillating social interactions when connected to others in contexts like support groups. Even when connecting to those more powerful than they, as in medical rounds, the "mad" can actively wrestle with the terms used to define them. When taking drugs, they spin a complicated web of filaments between themselves and the drugs, composed of ambivalence and fear, determination and hope. When some filaments break, they spin others, or perhaps they do not.

When the "darkness" of irrationality is considered in a social frame, it becomes a complex, in-between form composed of darkness and light at the same time. Robin Williams and his zany comedy, Dr. Morrison and his bow tie mania, entrepreneurs, explorers, and politicians with manic styles slip back and forth across the line between the rational and irrational. Just as important, when the "lightness" of rationality is looked at with a social lens, it also becomes a complex, in-between form composed of darkness and light at the same time. The manic and depressive swings of the market, the double-voiced pedagogy of the teaching video, and the skull and crossbones on the bottle of medicine in Janssen's virtual world all escape the strict definition of rationality.

Sometimes people living under the description of manic depression find their social webs inadequate to support life, and they fall into the abyss. Or perhaps they jump. Sometimes the safety net of a drug like lithium is enough to allow them to continue "living on the edge." But often it is not. Sometimes even people who do not live under the description of any psychiatric disorder also wonder whether society's social webs are adequate to support life.[1] There are no shortages of unspeakable horrors in the world we live in today. Is it only because I too am "mad" that I frequently contemplate the abyss? Is it possible to value contemplation of the abyss without condoning suicide? Will the use of drugs to optimize mania and eliminate depression allow us to contemplate the abyss without jumping into it?

In his dystopian novel *Brave New World*, Aldous Huxley portrays a dose of the ubiquitous drug *soma* as something that would raise an impenetrable wall between the "actual universe" and the mind.[2] The good citizen Lenina asks the rebel Bernard "why you don't take *soma* when you have these dreadful ideas of yours. You'd forget all about them. And instead of feeling miserable, you'd be jolly. So jolly."[3] In contrast to this picture, I have argued that the drugs of today are meant to ease the social withdrawal of depression and the social extravagance of mania without putting any particular emotion in place. But even though drugs promise no specific content, they do promise personal development. Will the pharmaceutically enhanced person become inwardly turned, even narcissistically self-absorbed, and inured to the needs of others? Or will the person develop richer social relationships? These questions might be appropriate for me to raise, but they are hard for me to answer, participating as I am in whatever effects my multiple psychotropic drugs might be having.

Sometimes the contemporary cultural premium placed on the glory of mania's energy and the self-regenerative quality of the bipolar cycle of moods and motivations becomes a kind of safety net that, because it gives social value to a psychological condition, allows the "mad" to continue living. Ironically, it is the extremes to which the social fabric in the contemporary United States is being subjected, brought about by an environment in which powerful forces are pushing all social relationships to be mediated through the market, that places the animal spirits of the market and the energies of manic depression at a premium. Perhaps there is poetic justice when social value is finally conferred on an "irrational" condition, manic depression, only when the social fabric has been subjected to such "irrational" distortions.

David Denby's exuberance over trying to win a million dollars on the stock market by year's end occurred at a time when the headiest days of growth and profit taking of the 1990s were already in the past and people were expressing anxiety about the economy at every turn. Since then, after September 11 and the entrenchment of a neoliberal regime, experiences of fear and anxiety have struck people in the United States in new ways. Fears of a general collapse of the economy or destruction of a region of the country—these fears are as serious as the fears of personal obliteration that some people living under the description of manic depression have expressed in the pages above. Will these new experiences at the level of the whole country extinguish the cultural potency and charisma of mania and manic markets? In the shock of recent terrorist attacks, new doubts about survival have arisen. Shortly after the attacks in the United States in 2001, there were expressions of doubt that U.S. capitalism could continue in the same form: "It is hard to predict the effect a prolonged campaign against terrorism will have on a form of capitalism built around risk-taking, technological advances, lightning fast reactions and a willingness to let goods money and people move freely."[4] The nation was attacked in its "central nervous system," which is sure to remain "jittery, if not depressed." The effect of the attack was felt more acutely precisely because of our economy's strength: "Technology has allowed businesses, investors, and consumers to spot change even as it is occurring and to respond almost instantaneously. Such speed is usually a good thing. But sometimes, Mr. Greenspan has suggested, it blows our economic circuits."[5]

From among my interlocutors there were efforts to join hands across the divide between the "mentally ill" manic and the Wall Street manic: a newsletter for manic-depressive people described how "the terrorists" who attacked on September 11 know what bipolar people have found out through long experience: "Our brains are fragile as glass, delicate as timepieces, and reliable as the operating systems on home computers. No one is immune. Because we who suffer from depression or Bipolar are among the most vulnerable, we are effectively on the front lines in this new war on terrorism . . . over the years our brains have been through the equivalent of countless Omaha Beach landings. We're seasoned."[6] At about the same time, however, there were tales of precedent-setting heroism in "carrying on regardless": Bradley Jack, the head of Lehman Brothers' investment banking division, "was so keen to get back to work that he hired a bus to drive himself and his colleagues back to New York from a conference in San Francisco. The bus stopped for just one sit-down meal, at a steak house in Nebraska, and on his return Mr. Jack commandeered the entire Manhattan Sheraton hotel for use as temporary offices."[7]

There are other signs that the hyperenergized, competitive fearlessness expressed and extolled in the cultural symbols I have been discussing will actually be intensified: an op-ed in the *New York Times* characterized the post–September 11 era as "a new century and moment of mania," after a line in the Robert Penn Warren poem, "Tell Me a Story," excerpted in this chapter's epigraph.[8] As early as a few weeks after the terrorist attacks on New York, market forecasters noted "bursts of cheer," "a babbling brook of glad tidings," and a "shamefully upbeat" Alan Greenspan.[9] We have entered, they say, a "post-mania mania in the stock market."[10] In the next couple of years, the fierce competition in the air was reflected in advertisements for corporations and for institutions of higher education that made overt references to

Darwinian-style survival of the fittest. Workers and students were exhorted to evolve or be killed off.[11]

Pessimism and fear, while pervasive in the lives of people trying to keep body and soul together in the American workforce, seldom receive a sympathetic ear from those who set the national drumbeat calling forth the optimistic American spirit.[12] On the eve of the 2004 election, those who expressed somber thoughts were accused of being pessimistic or depressed, found morally culpable, and even unpatriotic. Neoconservative spokesmen like David Brooks were almost eager to articulate the belief that individual *will* can determine both mood and wealth. In an editorial in the *New York Times*, Brooks derided liberal assumptions that more money would reduce poverty rates as outmoded and wrong. Liberals, he said, wrongly assume that "economic forces determine culture and shape behavior. . . . In reality, culture shapes economics. A person's behavior determines his or her economic destiny. If people live in an environment that fosters industriousness, sobriety, fidelity, punctuality and dependability, they will thrive. But the Great Society welfare system encouraged or enabled bad behavior, and popular culture glamorizes irresponsibility."[13] Even as Brooks blamed people on welfare for their poverty, and for the character traits he believes cause their poverty, he extolled and held up as a model the "manic energy" that drove the leadership of Teddy Roosevelt.[14] One could not wish for a more concise description of how neoliberal ways of imagining human sociality valorize the intense motivation of manic states.

Brooks ignores the powerful structural forces flowing from an economic system that *requires* a certain degree of unemployment and that systematically de-skills and underpays work. He ignores the effects of persistent racist, classist, and sexist attitudes on the part of employers, police, educators, and bureaucrats, among others. He ignores the factors that weigh heavily against poor women and people of color: lack of universal health insurance, lack of a living wage, lack of adequate childcare, lack of adequate free education, and lack of adequate elder care, among other things. However, there is a certain fit between his claims and the claim discussed in chapter 7 that those remaining on the welfare rolls might suffer from depression. For Brooks, the cause of "bad behavior" is popular culture and the welfare system itself; for advocates of screening for depression in TANF offices, the cause is states of the brain. Both views fail to contend adequately with the impact of poverty and its attendant constraints.

These social ills constitute hidden damage, damage that, though it may be displaced onto others, returns to plague social life. Max Weber looked to a guardian "daemon" who he imagined could "hold the fibers of our lives" in order to call forth our passion for a vocation in the face of deadening rationalization.[15] "Daemons" were the good guardian spirits of Greek and Roman times, the *eudaemons*, whose name is also given to the Greek word "eudaemonia," for human flourishing.[16] However, eudaemons necessarily came along with bad daemons, *cacodaemons*, who created all manner of mischief. This potent combination of beneficence and malignance at play together might be preferable as a guiding image to the blandly smiling faces in pharmaceutical ads. For surely beneficence and malignance are both at play in the contemporary world, at every level.

Race and Gender Revisited

The structural constraints entailed in cultural concepts of race, class, and gender are hard for Brooks to see, but they are also hard for even the most passionate advocates of mental health to see. An enlightened surgeon general, David Satcher, made improvements in mental health a priority of his administration, and appeared in my fieldwork, much to the delight of many of my interlocutors, by giving a speech at the 2000 meetings of the DMDA. His speech accompanied the publication of the supplement to his report, which dealt in its entirety with mental health in the United States.[17] The dominant model operating in the supplement is that there is something concrete and real in the world and (increasingly in the brain) that corresponds one to one with the major psychiatric diagnoses. Identifying this real thing, in the brains, say, of patients, is the proper first step to getting them the right treatment. Identifying "observer bias" and removing it will clear the way to more frequently correct diagnosis. But there are at least three troubling aspects of this view. First, what if the categories into which psychiatry divides disorders themselves already have cultural assumptions embedded in them, not fixed for all time but, as I have sketched for mood disorders, changing with the times? Second, what if our only route to the real is always through linguistic categories that are necessarily saturated with culturally constituted sets of meanings? Third, what if the interests of product-centered pharmaceutical corporations dovetail with seeing psychological states as physical states, extricable from social context? If so, can a pharmacogenomics specific to race or gender be far behind? If any of these conditions were to hold, the job of removing the effects of racialized or gendered perceptions becomes far more difficult. My object in saying this is not to create a cloud of pessimism over the endeavor of the supplement. It is to ask whether the problem of differential treatment for mental illness by race, class, or gender can be addressed without going much farther to eliminate the social factors the supplement identifies and then tries to correct for—poverty and racist or sexist attitudes? Will making medicines available to African Americans or to poor women who suffer more stress due to poverty and discrimination provide something we want to call a solution, let alone a cure?

Optimizing Moods

I have explored how the domain of interior psychic states is being made visible in particular ways and how it is being selectively harnessed for culturally specific purposes. Many people in the United States consider the domain of emotions to be essential for fueling innovation and creativity. But not just any form of emotion will do. Moods are important, but for this practical use, they need to be optimized. Optimizing moods means eliminating depression, and eliminating the extreme mania in mania, leaving only heightened motivation. The notion of optimizing moods means requiring them to go up and down as required by the economy. This kind of fantasy is not new. The goal of controlling a human being remotely was the hallmark of the very earliest development of psychotropic drugs. In the 1960s, the plan to control the administration of drugs to spacemen was explicit. As the sociologist Jackie Orr has shown, if the stress of space flight caused undesirable psychological states, "they suggested the possible administration of pharmaceutical drugs via remote control from earth."[18] In the present, we are no longer dealing with men in space, but exhortations to control moods in relation to system stresses are still around. The neoliberal columnist William Safire said on December 3, 2003, that the recent good economic news was the "bursting out of animal spirits . . . the breath of life . . . made famous by John Maynard Keynes." He cautioned: to avoid a repeat of the late 1990s, we should not "let invaluable animal spirits get the better of" our judgment.[19]

The desire for remote control of emotional states cannot be confined to post–World War II paranoia. Advertisers and marketers invest major amounts of research in figuring out what mood the population is in and what tone their products should aim for. Roper, a major firm that writes expensive reports used by pharmaceutical marketers, published an immediate response to September 11 and the stress it caused the population. The Roper Report warned marketers to avoid "wigged-out characters" like the manic guy who appeared in a "long-running campaign for an electronics chain that featured an 'insane' hard-sell salesman." They recommended that "stoic characters" should be used instead.

An even more explicit message once again came from David Brooks. In a 2003 article in the *New York Times Magazine*, he stressed the need for a new national mood. Because the "CEO superheroes of the 90s . . . will not supply the capitalist face of the age," he called for a return to the "Lincolnian virtue of simplicity and humility," "the staid but unexciting bourgeois virtues," the "slow, steady, boring accumulation of accomplishments and money."[20] Brooks's argument was that the "creativity ethic" of the 1990s needed to give way to the work ethic, which makes wealth acceptable. The work ethic is based on a belief in social mobility, the idea that anyone who works hard can get rich. Social mobility, in turn, is "the very essence of justice, because each person's destiny is somehow related to the amount of talent and effort he or she pours into life."[21] In Brooks's vision, belief in social mobility reduces class conflict because each person is building his or her own fortune without taking anything from the fortunes of others.

Brooks is trying to turn down the emotional temperature just a bit, but he is surely not trying to abolish emotion and moods altogether. Imagine what would happen to the markets if emotion vanished. Could a consumer society go on with consumers who felt neither happy nor sad, who neither desired anything nor felt the lack of anything? When our moods are disordered, we may have too much or too little sociality, but either would be preferable, from the point of view of markets, to socially disconnected emotional flatness. But if social conditions are such that the possibilities for emotions are reduced and conditions for disconnection are enhanced (in part because of the structural forces Brooks tries to ignore), then emotion itself, perceived as the vital spirit of the economy, might be seen as a valuable but endangered resource. Brooks is imagining identifying, measuring, moderating, in short managing this scarce resource, not eliminating it.

I am arguing that emotion is both selectively flattened (recall the Roper Report's stoic characters or David Brooks's work ethic) and incited (recall the Joule Company's manic hunt or Shackleton's mania) in these times. Capacities within a disorder understood as an excess of emotion have come to be a valuable terrain for product development. Our individual responsibility comes to involve monitoring our moods in detail with a watchful eye for the changing possibilities of pharmaceutical optimization. Within the cycle of bipolar disorder, the much-vaunted creativity of mania turns out to be a kind of intense motivation, conforming to the demand for great productivity. For all that mania has been associated with the creativity of great artists, inventors, and politicians of our times, the form of mania being extolled for entrepreneurs today is *conforming* rather than *creative*. As mentioned above, this mania is only innovative in ways the market can value. Echoing contemporary demands for relentless productivity, this sort of mania leads to conformity to the demands of the market, which in turn amplifies reigning neoliberal social norms, narrow and inhuman as they are.[22]

The End of Madness?

Michel Foucault referred to madness as the absence of the work of reason, the absence of work that endlessly shores up a historically specific definition of what reason is. Without the work it takes to achieve that definition of reason, "madness" arises. As Michel Serres explicates Foucault's point, "There is no madman but he in whom work sleeps, he who forgets to create it."[23] As long as Western culture imagines madness as the opposite of reason, it makes madness a fearful prospect. But Foucault also wondered whether there would come a time when Western culture would no longer define itself in distinction to the realm of the mad, the land of unreason.[24] He thought this would mark the end of Western culture's passionate relationship to madness, because madness would no longer serve to represent the culture's deepest fears: of becoming like the "other" who lacks reason. What could cause madness as we know it to disappear? Foucault suggested two possibilities: first, precise pharmacological control of all mental symptoms and second, rigorous definition of behavioral deviations accompanied by methods of neutralization.[25] With these methods in place, the formerly "mad" would be thoroughly brought into the "work" of reason, and "madness" as we formerly understood it would be gone. However, no matter how far technical means of control of mental illness were able to go, Foucault thought that "madness" in some form would continue. This would be true as long as humanity depended on the feared "other" to define who is fully human and who is not. The two possibilities that Foucault thought could cause the end of madness are already at play around us: precise pharmacological control of mood disorders is being offered through increasingly complex combinations of psychotropic drugs; rigorous definition of deviations is being accomplished by detailed mood charting and the compilation of statistics mood charts make possible. We have yet to see how far these methods will go. In this book, at a time when "madness" still exists as the feared "other" of reason, I have detailed how we cannot, however we may fear madness, escape it. We circle around it and into it. We are less "*at a distance* from madness than *within distance* of it."[26]

Short of doing away with the category of "madness," would such an enlarged role for pharmacological agents cure us?[27] Would the suffering often attendant on living under the description of manic depression be eased? The many testimonials in this book, including my own, make it plain that these agents ease suffering. A cure, however, is another matter. A cure implies healing, and healing would have to address not just people's experience, crucial as that is. Healing would have to address the strong but not invincible barriers to our ability to flourish, as individuals and as part of collectivities. Those barriers are erected around race (think of Keith Burton's "I am not crazy" or Ms. Miller's "I ain't gonna mess with it backwards"), gender (think of Marie Cardinal's descent into madness or Martha Stewart's imprisonment in a double-bind), and class (think of welfare clients being screened for depression or the many people without access to health care), to name a few. The effect of all these barriers is intensified when "mental illness" comes into the picture. Unless these barriers are removed, no amount of psychotropic drugs, however soothing, will heal "mental illness."[28]

At the same time, one goal of this book has been to show why the irrationality of those with emotional disorders, their ability to be emotionally extreme, is being treated as a resource, an economic resource for those in a position to take advantage of it in the right way. Those Americans who can are being encouraged to optimize extreme moods by filling out a chart or taking on board the managing presence of a drug. Paradoxically, participating in charting and medication means by definition that one needs management. A great many people are including themselves in such practices. Whose moods then are still in order? The line between the irrational and the rational is in motion. Whatever new ways of being social are emerging, they are emerging onto terrain where the line between the rational and irrational is shifting. We are all irrational (have disordered moods); we are all rational (even manic depressive people can chart their moods.)

In the early chapters of this book the inhabitants of the land of unreason were given a chance to speak: I described them as people whose words and acts were animated by a consciousness of their condition. Seeing them this way is particularly important, given that the domain of the irrational has so often been seen as a harrowing space that is inhabited by those who do not enjoy the full status of persons. As the poet C. E. Chaffin wrote in "Manic-Depression," a poem that traces his movement from imprisonment in depression to release in mania,[29]

The sun rises, stone walls dissolve.
I clench a marigold in my teeth
and tango on the flaming grass.
The soil beneath is black with crematory ash.
I pray the lawn is thick enough
to hide the darkness I dance over.

The shadows cast across this country from time to time—the shadow of death or of profound loss—contain something Americans need to remember. In the specific social world we inhabit, a world harnessed to the harsh realities of increasingly unfettered capitalism and turning between the poles of emotion and anxiety, mania and depression, the dance contains darkness. People living under the description of manic depression have keen experience of this insight; indeed, they cannot avoid it. They cannot help wondering whether the dance will ever be incandescent enough, the lawn thick enough, to banish the darkness. This perspective, as much as the wild energy of mania, is the essential resource contained in manic depression.

Appendix

Guide to Medical Terms

A number of names of drugs and psychiatric conditions are used in this book. Tables 1 and 2 serve as a guide to the main types of diagnoses and drugs I mention.

TABLE 1
Psychiatric Diagnoses

Diagnosis	Category	Brief Definition
bipolar disorder (manic depression)	mood disorder	Extreme mood swings from elevated to depressed
bipolar 1 (or I)	mood disorder	Full-blown mania alternating with depression
bipolar 2 (or II)	mood disorder	Elevated moods are less extreme than full-blown mania. They are described as "hypomania" and they alternate with depression
major (unipolar) depression	mood disorder	Severe and prolonged depressed mood
schizophrenia	psychosis	May include distorted thinking, hallucinations, emotional flatness, apathy
schizoaffective disorder	psychosis	Includes some of the symptoms of bipolar disorder and some of schizophrenia

TABLE 2
Drug Names, Types, and Uses

Brand	Generic Name	Type	Some Common Uses
Ambien	Zolpidem	hypnotic	insomnia
Ativan	Lorazepam	anxiolytic	anxiety
Buspar	Buspirone	anxiolytic	anxiety; depression
Celexa	Citalopram	SSRI	depression
Depakote	Valproic acid	anticonvulsant	bipolar disorder; schizophrenia
Dexedrine	Dextroamphetamine	psychostimulant	attention disorders; depression
Effexor	Venlafaxine	atypical antidepressant	depression
Eskalith	Lithium carbonate	mood stabilizer	bipolar disorder
Focalin	Methylphenidate	psychostimulant	attention disorders
Klonopin	Clonazepam	anxiolytic	anxiety
Lamictal	Lamotrigine	anticonvulsant	bipolar disorder; depression
Lexapro	Escitalopram oxalate	SSRI	depression
Mellaril	Thioridazine	antipsychotic	schizophrenia; schizoaffective disorder
Neurontin	Gabapentin	anticonvulsant	bipolar disorder
Paxil	Paroxetine	SSRI	depression; obsessive compulsive disorder; panic disorder
Prozac	Fluoxetine	SSRI	depression
Risperdal	Risperidone	antipsychotic	schizophrenia; schizoaffective disorder
Ritalin	Methylphenidate	psychostimulant	attention disorders
Seroquel	Quetiapine	antipsychotic	schizophrenia
Tegretol	Carbamazepine	anticonvulsant	bipolar disorder
Topamax	Topiramate	anticonvulsant	bipolar disorder
Trazodone	Desyrel	atypical antidepressant	depression
Wellbutrin	Bupropion	atypical antidepressant	depression; bipolar disorder
Zoloft	Sertraline	SSRI	depression; obsessive compulsive disorder; panic disorder
Zyprexa	Olanzapine	antipsychotic	schizophrenia; schizoaffective and bipolar disorder

TABLE 3

Twelve-Month Prevalence* of Mood Disorders (International), 2001–2003 WHO Survey

United States	9.6
Colombia	6.8
Mexico	4.8
Lebanon	6.6
Nigeria	0.8
Japan	3.1
Beijing	2.5
Shanghai	1.7

Source: NIMH, *The Numbers Count.*

* The proportion of individuals who manifest the disorder over one year.

TABLE 4

Twelve-Month Prevalence of Mood Disorders and Schizophrenia (U.S.), 2001 NIMH Study

Depressive disorders	9.5
Bipolar disorder	1.2
Schizophrenia	1.1

Source: NIMH, *The Numbers Count.*

TABLE 5

Comparison of Number of Uses of the Terms "Bipolar Disorder" and "Manic Depression," 1960–2002

Date	Term: Bipolar	Term: Manic Depression
1960–69	0	0
1970–79	0	0
1980–89	130	174
1990–99	1,579	1,534
2000–2002	1,306	457

Source: ProQuest All Newspapers Index. The search was done on March 17, 2003.

TABLE 6

References to the Phrase "Survival of the Fittest," Averages for Five-Year Intervals

1980–84	4.8
1985–89	30
1990–94	56.2
1995–99	102
2000–2004	115

Source: ProQuest, Basic Search, Multiple Databases, for the years 1980–2004. The search was done on February 24, 2005.

Notes

Preface

1. About twenty years ago, I shifted the focus of my research from ethnographic studies of Chinese villages in Taiwan to ethnographic studies on the popular culture of medicine and biology in the United States. In the ensuing years I wrote about women's experiences of reproduction, as well as popular and scientific understandings of HIV and AIDS. Martin, *Flexible Bodies*; Martin, *The Woman in the Body*.

2. James Baldwin found the gargoyles of Chartres "obscene, inescapable . . . seeming to say that God and the devil can never be divorced" (*Notes of a Native Son*, 174).

3. Although delusions like this are often associated with the diagnosis of schizophrenia, they are also cited in psychiatric definitions of manic depression in standard reference works like the American Psychiatric Association's *Diagnostic and Statistical Manual of Mental Disorders* (DSM). In this book, I will gradually open to scrutiny standard medical terms and definitions such as those that appear in the DSM.

4. Weismantel, *Cholas and Pishtacos*, 8.

5. Baldwin, *Notes of a Native Son*, 174, 61.

6. Ibid., 155, 74–75.

7. A burning issue among these students was that they were forced to take a year's leave upon diagnosis. They would be readmitted if they could show they had been productive during the year away, a condition that some found rather contradictory. Years later the issue would be taken up in the media around concern about litigation over student suicides. See Arenson, "Worried Colleges Step up Efforts over Suicide."

Introduction

1. McCoy, "Cramer's Real-Time 'Real Money' Shows Land in Local Radio."

2. Schonfeld, "Second Act for Manic CEO."

3. Brink, "CEO Sufferings Trickle Down."

4. Boodman, "Going to Extremes."

5. There are widely accessible books describing the basic psychological elements that make emotions contagious. See Goleman, *Emotional Intelligence*; Hatfield, Cacioppo, and Rapson, *Emotional Contagion*; Kotter, *Leading Change*. There are also articles in magazines for parents that detail how to prevent the worst moods from spreading between parents and children. See, e.g., Fintushel, "Are Bad *Moods* Catching?"

6. Goleman, Boyatzis, and McKee, "Primal Leadership," 44.

7. See for example DeWitt and Liu, "The Customer Orientation-Loyalty Model"; Howard and Gengler, "Emotional Contagion Effects on Product Attitudes"; Totterdell, *What Is Emotion Management?*

8. The term "affinity" is from Max Weber's phrase, "elective affinity," used, for example, in his introduction to *Sociology of Religion*. Weber was interested in describing the affinities between different social spheres, such as those between Puritan ethics and capitalist business practices in seventeenth-century England. Weber's emphasis was on the ways affinities reinforced each other and therefore could enhance the development of whole systems such as capitalism. For an imaginative exploration of the concept, see Boon, *Affinities and Extremes*.

9. "Men of the Year."

10. "Americans Should Be Glad."

11. Ibid. David Schneider notes that Americans define humans on the basis of their capacity to reason, as opposed to animals' unreason. Schneider, *American Kinship*, 108.

12. Clifford Geertz relates the disquiet of the Balinese cockfight to its ability to "force together . . . diverse realities" that are "normally well-obscured from view" ("Deep Play," 444).

13. Being diagnosed or treated for bipolar disorder threatens admission to the practice of law in some states. The Florida Board of Bar Examiners, for example, requires special explanation if the candidate to the bar has been charged with a criminal offense, demonstrated violent behavior, been addicted to drugs, or "been treated or received a diagnosis during the last 5 years for schizophrenia or other psychotic disorder; bipolar or major depressive mood disorder; drug or alcohol abuse; impulse control disorder, including kleptomania, pyromania, explosive disorder, pathological or compulsive gambling; or paraphilia such as pedophilia, exhibitionism or voyeurism." Hunter, "Letter Requesting Information."

14. Within the vast philosophical literature on this topic, I have benefited in particular from the work of Steven Lukes. See Hollis and Lukes, *Rationality and Relativism*; Lukes, *Liberals and Cannibals.*

15. Berrios, *History of Mental Symptoms*, 291. For Plato and Aristotle, in Berrios's words, "The absence or obliteration of reason led to error and evil with the 'passions' being the main source of perturbation and chaos" (291). "In Greek culture, affective excitement culminating in irrationality was considered as a common mechanism of insanity" (292).

16. Dodds, *The Greeks and the Irrational*, 185.

17. Butterfield, "This Way Madness Lies," 14.

18. This is a characteristic of Florida law. Based on what is known as the M'Naughten rule, a defendant must be shown to have no understanding of the difference between right and wrong in order to use the insanity defense. As of 1998, twenty-two states used a version of the M'Naughten rule, and twenty-six used a version of the American Law Institute model insanity defense statute, which allowed a softening of the M'Naughten rule.

19. Butterfield, "This Way Madness Lies," 14.

20. In the eighteenth century, by John Locke's definition, the mad were *capable* of rational thought, but they started from the wrong assumptions. According to Locke, "[M]admen do not appear to me to have lost the faculty of reasoning . . . but having joined some ideas very wrongly, they mistake them for truths; and they err as men do that argue right from wrong principles" (*An Essay Concerning Human Understanding*, 1:209–10). Alice Faye Redd's case shows us how far we have diverged from Locke's view. Both the judge and the press agreed that her mental illness (her madness) entailed a *diminished capacity* for rational thought. In her study of the history of colonization in Hawaii, Sally Merry clarifies the role of the law in conferring the status of a rational person: "Law allocates rationality and adulthood when it designates who can vote for whom, who can run for political office, and who can be a citizen. Those given identity within the law as citizens and deemed capable of contractual relationships were defined as rational and civilized; others were labeled irrational, animalistic and dangerous" ("Law and Identity in an American Colony," 149).

21. Kraepelin, *Manic-Depressive Insanity and Paranoia.*

22. Martha Nussbaum's discussion of the role of emotions in the law, connected to Western traditions derived from Aristotle, illuminates how the law is better equipped to handle more ordinary emotional states (*Hiding from Humanity*, 23ff.).

23. Conrad, *Heart of Darkness*.

24. Luhrmann, *Of Two Minds*, 270.

25. Styron, *Darkness Visible*.

26. These dichotomies have been described as characteristic of people of the modern era, who, bolstered by the power of Western science and capitalist expansion, operated by a "constitution" that abjured hybrids that fell in between. To moderns, "hybrids present the horror that must be avoided at all costs by a ceaseless, even maniacal purification." Latour, *We Have Never Been Modern*, 112.

27. Estimates of the prevalence of bipolar disorder are complicated because studies use different units of measurement and different criteria for what counts as bipolar disorder. The common estimate that in the United States 1 percent of the population has bipolar disorder is being challenged by new studies that argue for a higher figure, at least 5 percent. See Akiskal et al., "Re-Evaluating the Prevalence of and Diagnostic Composition within the Broad Clinical Spectrum of Bipolar Disorders." Table 3 (see appendix) shows some published (international) comparative statistics using a twelve-month prevalence—the proportion of individuals who manifest the condition over one year. Table 4 (see appendix) shows statistics for twelve-month prevalence in the United States.

28. Bateson, *Steps to an Ecology of Mind*, 137–38.

29. In her perceptive ethnography of atherosclerosis, Annemarie Mol prefers to speak of enactment rather than performance to capture the ways diagnoses and treatment come into being. For her case, performance would raise too many possibilities: the existence of a stage and a backstage, the question of success or failure, and the issue of effects beyond the performance. For my case, where the attribution of rationality is at stake, these are exactly the possibilities I want to raise. Mol, *The Body Multiple*, 32–33.

30. Joyce, *The Rule of Freedom*, 41.

31. A perceptive account of the "style of thought" of biological psychiatry in historical context is in Rose, "The Neurochemical Self and Its Anomalies."

32. On a popular rendition of the neural location of emotions, see Blakeslee, "Humanity? Maybe It's in the Wiring." For MRIs illustrating a "murderer's brain" and the brain of a depressed person, see Carter, *Mapping the Mind*, 92, 99. Joseph Dumit has done an important ethnographic study of how MRIs are understood and function culturally. See his *Picturing Personhood*.

33. Tierney, "Using MRI Machines," A17.

34. Jamison, *An Unquiet Mind*, 191.

35. Hinshaw, *The Years of Silence Are Past*, 132.

36. Although during my fieldwork there was a major breakthrough in neuroscience, demonstrating for the first time that learning enables the adult mammalian brain to grow new neurons, this experimental finding had not yet had an impact on people's general sense of their mind's capacity. See Gould et al., "Neurogenesis in Adulthood." For a review of the impact of this work, see Gould and Gross, "Neurogenesis in Adult Mammals."

37. Some of the best-known books written by doctors to educate the public about mood disorders do not reduce the cause of mood disorders to the physical realm. They manage this by discussing a wide range of contributing factors, from social environment to family history. See Torrey and Knable, *Surviving Manic Depression*; Mondimore, *Bipolar Disorder*.

38. For a discussion of how methodological variation between studies makes it difficult to determine the prevalence of mood disorders comparatively, see Waraich et al., "Prevalence and Incidence Studies of Mood Disorders."

39. A kind interlocutor from the industry allowed me this glimpse. I describe the circumstances in chapter 9.

40. Carey, "Use of Antipsychotics by the Young Rose Fivefold."

41. Light and Lexchin, "The International War on Cheap Drugs."

42. Landers, "Waiting for Prozac."

43. See McClay, *The Masterless*; Cushman, *Constructing the Self*.

44. Gamwell and Tomes, "The Asylum in Antebellum America."

45. Burton, *The Anatomy of Melancholy*, 9.

46. See MacDonald, *Mystical Bedlam*, 9–10. This book provides a detailed discussion about the disjunction in the seventeenth and eighteenth centuries between supernatural accounts of madness preferred by religious believers and secular accounts preferred by physicians who relied on their increasing understanding of physical science.

47. Screech, "Good Madness in Christendom."

48. Rather, "The Six-Things Non-Natural."

49. Berrios, *History of Mental Symptoms*.

50. Roy Porter gives a lucid overview of this chapter in the history of madness (*Madness*, 56–61).

51. See chapter 9 of Watson, *Basic Writings in the History of Psychology*. which discusses one of the founders of faculty psychology, Christian von

Wolff, and his division of the faculties of the mind into "knowing" on the one hand and "feeling and desire" on the other. S. Alexander Rippa traces the influence of faculty psychology on specifically American educational theories (*Education in a Free Society*, 217–19).

52. The clinical usefulness of the intellectual view of madness had already been challenged early in the century by Pinel, Prichard, and Heinroth, as described in Berrios, *History of Mental Symptoms*, 294. Generally in the nineteenth century, physical explanations of mental illness were dominant, in England at any rate. Andrew Scull's trenchant account makes this plain (*Social Order/Mental Disorder*, 24–27). But the details were far from clear. Allan Young explains the debates in the mid-nineteenth century over whether faculties were properly found in the brain, the mind, or were best abandoned (*The Harmony of Illusions*).

53. Berrios, *History of Mental Symptoms*, 295.

54. Darwin wrote that "the main difficulty in elucidating emotions consists in the fact that the major part is due to historical antecedents registered in the susceptible organisms, but little to individual acquisitions. No experience of the individual can account for the strength or the direction of feeling" (quoted in Berrios, *History of Mental Symptoms*, 296). In this Darwin echoed Herbert Spencer, who held that "the doctrine maintained by some philosophers, that all the desires, all the sentiments, are generated by the experiences of the individual, is so glaringly at variance with hosts of facts, that I cannot but wonder how any one [*sic*] should ever have entertained it." Quoted in R. Young, *Mind, Brain and Adaptation in the Nineteenth Century*, 182–83. See also Browne, "Darwin and the Face of Madness."

55. Berrios, *History of Mental Symptoms*, 298.

56. Ibid., 298–99.

57. Berrios, *History of Mental Symptoms*, 298.

58. Berrios has questioned how central Kraepelin's concern with the affective realm was. Kraepelin's distinction between dementia praecox and manic depression "appears to be based on a distinction between thinking and affect, respectively." But alongside his criteria for the prognosis of manic depression, heredity involved only the "presence of excitement or inhibition." "As far as this writer has been able to determine, nowhere did Kraepelin say that manic-depressive insanity was a *primary disorder* of affect" (Berrios, *History of Mental Symptoms*, 297).

59. Berrios, *History of Mental Symptoms*, 297. Contemporaneous with abstract schemes for classifying mental disorders were rich qualitative descriptions of the specifically emotional side of the emerging categories of

mental illness. In Karl Jaspers's account, the manic fairly flies off the page: "The massive associations at his disposal come spontaneously and uncalled for. They make him witty and sparkling; they also make it impossible for him to maintain any determining tendency and render him at the same time superficial and confused. Physically and mentally he feels that he is extremely healthy and strong. He thinks his abilities are outstanding. With unfailing optimism the patient will contemplate all things around him, the whole world and his own future in the rosiest of lights. Everything is as bright and happy as can be. His ideas and thoughts all agree on this point most harmoniously; to any other idea he is wholly inaccessible" (*General Psychopathology*, 2:596). Kraepelin wrote that the depressed patient "cannot collect his thoughts or pull himself together; his thoughts are as if paralysed, they are immobile. His head feels heavy, quite stupid, as if a board were pushed in front of it, everything is confused. He is no longer able to perceive, or to follow the train of thought of a book or a conversation, he feels weary, enervated, inattentive, inwardly empty; he has no memory, he has no longer command of knowledge formerly familiar to him, he must consider a long time about simple things, he calculates wrongly, makes contradictory statements, does not find words, cannot construct sentences correctly" (*Manic-Depressive Insanity and Paranoia*, 75).

60. Goodwin and Jamison, *Manic-Depressive Illness*, 61.

61. Freud, "Mourning and Melancholia," 161. When Freud's ideas took hold in the United States, they were in the guise of the ego psychology developed by his daughter, Anna Freud. With few exceptions, American psychoanalysts were identified with ego psychology from the 1940s to the 1960s. Thereafter, this psychoanalytic approach lost ground to new forms of therapy focused on group dynamics and individual identity, on the one hand, and to new research in the neurological sciences, on the other. Zaretsky, *Secrets of the Soul*, 333–35.

62. Freud, *The Ego and the Id*, 54–55. Current scholarship has taken Freud's ideas in a number of productive directions. Juliana Schiesari gives a detailed reading of how melancholia is gendered in Renaissance literature (*The Gendering of Melancholia*). *Loss: The Politics of Mourning*, by Eng and Kazanjian, provides a set of case studies of the role of melancholia and mourning in history and politics.

63. Klein, "A Contribution to the Psychogenesis of Manic-Depressive States." See also the work D. W. Winnicott did to develop Klein's theories on the depressive position and the manic defense ("The Manic Defense"). Mabel Blake Cohen et al. provide a useful overview of Freud's, Klein's,

and other psychoanalysts' work on mania and depression ("An Intensive Study of Twelve Cases of Manic-Depressive Psychosis").

64. I read all accounts of mania contained in the *New York Times* using ProQuest's Historical Newspapers index, which covers the years 1851–2001.

65. "Mania Kills Man by Push on Elevated."

66. Staff Correspondent, "Mrs. Fosdick Kills 2 Children and Self."

67. "Chemistry of Insanity."

68. Lawrence, "New Vistas Opened for Chemical Approach to the Treatment of Mental Illness"; Lawrence, "Chemical's Cure of Insane Is Seen."

69. "TV Review: 'Manhattan' Series in Debut on Channel 2."

70. "Main Types of Mental Disorder Explained for the Red Cross."

71. R. Prescott, "Food Consumption, Prices, and Expenditures, 1960–81."

72. Jayson, *Mania*, 214.

73. Jewell, "Ruskin's Life Explains His Works."

74. Ibid.

75. O. Prescott, "Books of the Times."

76. "Leonard Woolf Is Dead at 88."

77. Finkelstein, "Lithium Therapy."

78. L. Brown, "Lithium Use in 'Maude,' Medical Issue."

79. The film is in the History of Medicine collection in the National Library of Medicine. In expressing these views, Fieve tapped into an older clinical tradition in which, writing in technical publications, doctors had for some time been associating manic depression with worldly success. In 1926 Ernst Kretschmer wrote, "In our material there are many excellent examples, where hypomanics, who must certainly be reckoned to the buoyant group, have had astonishing and lasting success in certain walks of life, e.g., merchants, speakers, journalists, etc., and are regarded with great respect by their colleagues. Their positive peculiarities are their tireless energy for, and enjoyment in, their work, their temperament, sharpness, élan, daring, lovableness, adaptability, free unshackled natures, skill in the handling of men, richness of ideas, eloquence, and an astonishingly clear eye for the right moment" (*Physique and Character*, 131).

80. Bentley, "Man's Despair, and Hope."

81. Jamison et al., "Clouds and Silver Linings."

82. Jamison, *Touched with Fire*, 267–70.

83. "Display Ad 52—No Title."

84. Jamison, "Manic-Depressive Illness and Creativity," 63.

85. Goodwin and Jamison, *Manic-Depressive Illness*.

86. Similar concerts were also organized by Jamison in St. Louis and Washington, DC.

87. There are too many to cite here, but *Bipolar Disorder for Dummies*, published in 2005 by Fink and Kraynak, indicates how far the term had come into everyday use.

88. http://www.dbsalliance.org/NameChange.html. See table 5 in the appendix.

89. Wolfe, *A Man in Full*, 195. Wolfe may be alluding to Ted Turner's important role in Atlanta business and his association with bipolar disorder.

90. Jamison, *An Unquiet Mind*, 182.

91. Ibid., 181.

92. Ibid., 182.

93. Harry Stack Sullivan's work contributed to this effort. Without minimizing its specific features, Sullivan argued that "schizophrenic phenomenology" required "for its complete exposition nothing different in essential quality from the elements of commonplace human life" (*Schizophrenia as a Human Process*, 200). More boldly, he also asserted, "I am convinced that in the schizophrenic processes and in the preliminaries of schizophrenic illness—so common among adolescents who are having trouble in their social adjustments—can be seen, in almost laboratory simplicity, glimpses which will combine as a mosaic that explains many more than half of the adult personalities that one encounters" (201–2). Thanks to Amy Smiley for steering me to this point.

94. "The New Jobs: What They Are, What They Pay." As one example of these changes, the Sparrows Point plant of Bethlehem Steel had been an important source of economic security for Baltimore's working class since the early 1900s. After World War II, the plant reached its peak employment of 35,000 workers: union wages supported second- or third-generation steelworkers in middle-class lifestyles. Because of steel imports, the plant workforce was reduced to 8,000 by the mid-1980s (Putting Baltimore's People First, *Putting Baltimore's People First*). In October 2001, Bethlehem Steel filed for bankruptcy, by then supporting a workforce of only 4,000 ("U.S. Steel Losing the Game"). In January 2003, with a workforce of 3,200, management approved the sale of the company to International Steel Group and was expected to lay off 1,000 of the remaining

workers ("End Arrives for Bethlehem Steel"). Statistics from the Bureau of Labor Statistics of the U.S. Department of Labor show the dramatic fall in manufacturing jobs and rise in service jobs for the Baltimore metropolitan region, a decline that continued into the period 1995–2005 (Bureau of Labor Statistics, "State and Area Employment, Hours, and Earnings").

95. Harvey, *The Condition of Postmodernity*.

96. For example, during my fieldwork, the University of California at Irvine's College of Medicine held an evening symposium for the general public called "Human Brain Research for the Layman." An audience of several hundred crammed in, filling all seats as well as the stairways and standing room at the rear of the auditorium to listen to highly technical illustrated talks from twelve brain scientists and psychiatrists at UCI. The speakers focused on brain-imaging techniques and later mingled with the crowd over punch and cookies.

97. The term "post-suburban" has been defined as "vast urbanized areas for which the concept of urban dominance is becoming obsolete. These areas constitute a settlement-space form that is poly-nucleated, functionally dispersed, culturally fragmented, yet hierarchically organized, and that extends for tens and even hundreds of miles . . . They are neither suburbs nor satellite cities; rather, they are fully urbanized and independent spaces that are not dominated by any central city." Gottdiener and Kephart, "The Multinucleated Metropolitan Region," 34.

98. See Attention! in the sample issue of *Culture Matters*, a general interest magazine for cultural anthropology, http://www.nyu.edu/fas/ihpk/CultureMatters/index2.htm (accessed October 4, 2006).

99. McGarry and Joye, U.S. Census, New Jersey; Southern New Jersey Regional Developments, "Southern New Jersey Regional Developments." More significant than the number of pharmaceuticals in New Jersey is that the headquarters of three of the top four drug companies in worldwide sales are located in the state. Morrow, "Smithkline and American Home Are Talking of Huge Drug Merger."

CHAPTER 1

1. For anthropologists, the classic source on the concept of personhood is Mauss, "A Category of the Human Mind."

2. Macpherson, *The Political Theory of Possessive Individualism*, 3. Atwood Gaines specifies that the prevailing conception of personhood in

the United States has its roots in northern European, German Protestant culture. This concept stresses the person's autonomy from other persons and control over the self ("From DSM-I to III-R," 11).

3. Marilyn Strathern, building on a comparison with Melanesian concepts of personhood, describes the contemporary person in Euro-American culture as an agent in whom intention, located within, is the cause of his action. The person is "a carrier, so to speak, not of persons but of the self, and intention and cause are thereby 'expressed' in the fulfillment of his or her wishes" ("Disembodied Choice," 73). Alain Ehrenberg puts the contemporary French version of this tradition in a nutshell: "L'action aujourd'-hui s'est individualisée. Elle n'a alors d'autre source que l'agent qui l'accomplit et dont il est le seul responsible. L'initiative des individus passé au premier plan des critères qui mesurent la valeur de la personne" (Nowadays, action has acquired a wholly individual significance. The origin of an action is its agent; he alone is responsible. Of all the criteria one might use to judge a person's merit, initiative is foremost.) Translation by Amy Smiley. Ehrenberg, *La fatigue d'être soi*, 198.

4. Freud, "Mourning and Melancholia," 163–64. Elias Canetti described mania as a "paroxysm of desire" by analogy to the hunter's quest for prey (*Crowds and Power*, 347).

5. James, "Census of Hallucinations."

6. Napier, *Foreign Bodies*, 163.

7. Whyte, *The Organization Man*.

8. Walkerdine, "Beyond Developmentalism?" 455.

9. Turkle, *Life on the Screen*, 179. The ideal person of the time embodied in many ways what both Marx and Weber described as "rationality." For Weber, economic rationality involved application of the best technical means and quantitative calculation to efficiently reach one's ends; for Marx, it was necessary to detail the ideal principles of rational markets capitalism espoused—free and equal exchange among autonomous agents—to see the ways in which in practice they were anything but rational. See Baran and Sweezy, *Monopoly Capital*, 338.

10. Whyte, *The Organization Man*, 408.

11. Lunbeck, *The Psychiatric Persuasion*, 68–69.

12. Stearns, *American Cool*, 53. Susan Buck-Morss shows the importance of the cognitive deadening of the factory system, written about so vividly by Walter Benjamin, for the new "human sensorium" of modernity, which is both overstimulated and, as a result, numbed ("The City as Dreamworld and Catastrophe," 8).

13. K. Newman, *Falling from Grace*. See also Harrison and Bluestone, *The Great U-Turn*.

14. See table 6 in the appendix.

15. See Nohria and Berkley, "The Virtual Organization," for one description of how perceptions of time and space are changed by electronic communication.

16. Turkle, *Life on the Screen*.

17. The classic analysis of this process is Foucault, *Discipline and Punish*. For an insightful social history of the asylum, see Rothman, *The Discovery of the Asylum*.

18. McClellan, "No Degree, and No Way Back to the Middle."

19. For a compelling review of Marx's description of how, under capitalism, people's personalities must take on a fluid and open form as they learn to strive for constant change, see Berman, *All That Is Solid Melts into Air*. Since Marx's time, the extent and scale of the development ideal have increased. In the realm of health, for example, people are contending with a series of new ideas about healthy bodies: bodies, which, like the new corporations, are exhorted to become lean, agile, and quick, so that they can adjust to new and frightening pathogens. Health now seems to result not from such measures as state-mandated vaccinations offered on a mass scale by central governments, but from the preventive maintenance each individual carries out in accord with a specific, tailor-made program of health, diet, exercise, and stress-reduction techniques.

20. This way of thinking has also gained a religious tone. Bill McKibben points out that although the majority of Americans believe that the adage "God helps those who help themselves" appears in the Bible, "this uber-American idea, a notion at the core of our current individualist politics and culture . . . was in fact uttered by Ben Franklin" ("The Christian Paradox," 31).

21. For the history and development of neoliberal ideas and policies, see Harvey, *A Brief History of Neoliberalism*; Strathern, "Enterprising Kinship"; Rouse, "Thinking through Transnationalism."

22. Norris, "Greenspan Era Taught People to Gamble."

23. Nineteen percent of Americans, according to a 1996 poll, are self-employed, freelance, or sequential temporary workers (Saltzman, "How to Prosper in the You, Inc. Age," 71). Numbers of these categories of workers are difficult to come by because they are not counted separately in standard Department of Labor statistics. For recent estimates of the numbers of freelance workers, see Teicher, "Freelancing in Your Future?"

24. Saltzman, "How to Prosper in the You, Inc. Age," 71.

25. Pulley, *Losing Your Job—Reclaiming Your Soul*, 136.

26. For recent anthropological analyses of global processes in relation to culture, see Gupta and Ferguson, "Beyond 'Culture.'" See also Maurer, "Complex Subjects."

27. Postrel, *The Future and Its Enemies*, xv.

28. Ibid., 57.

29. Hembrooke and Gay, "The Laptop and the Lecture."

30. In France, what the social theorist Jacques Donzelot calls "changing people's attitudes to change" has made its appearance through the *legal* right of every worker to "continued retraining [*formation permanente*]": people are thought to *require* an active attitude toward change. Continued retraining "must therefore literally be a continuous process of retraining, from the cradle to the grave, designed to provide the individual with a feeling of autonomy in relation to work, and at work" (Donzelot, "Pleasure in Work," 273).

31. Historically, emotional flexibility has been associated with an increase in the importance of advanced capitalist institutions. In an important study, William Reddy has shown how, in the French case, increasing contractual relations after the Revolution brought about more, not less, emotional flexibility (*The Navigation of Feeling*, 312–14).

32. American Psychiatric Association Task Force on DSM-IV, *Diagnostic and Statistical Manual of Mental Disorders: DSM-IV-TR*, 825.

33. Ibid., 362.

34. This list is slightly simplified and shortened. For the full list of criteria, see American Psychiatric Association Task Force on DSM-IV, *Diagnostic and Statistical Manual of Mental Disorders: DSM-IV-TR*, 356.

35. When I use the pronoun "we" in a general sense, I refer to people who participate in the Western, Euro-American historical tradition and share at least some of its basic assumptions; when I use the term "American," I refer only to residents of the United States.

36. Lutz and Abu-Lughod, *Language and the Politics of Emotion*.

37. Crapanzano, *Hermes' Dilemma and Hamlet's Desire*, 232. C. Lutz shows that among the Ifaluk in the Western Caroline Islands, emotion words are not seen as referents of internal feeling states, but as statements about the relationship between a person and an event involving other people ("The Domain of Emotion Words on Ifaluk").

38. R. Porter, *Madness*, 42.

39. Goodwin and Jamison, *Manic-Depressive Illness*, 58.

40. Quoted in ibid., 59.

41. Kraepelin, *Manic-Depressive Insanity and Paranoia*.

42. Ibid., 24. Mania and depression were "combined into the new concept of alternating, periodic, circular or double-form insanity. This process culminated with Kraepelin's concept of 'manic-depressive insanity' which included most forms of affective disorder under the same umbrella" (Berrios, *History of Mental Symptoms*, 298–99).

43. Kraepelin, *Manic-Depressive Insanity and Paranoia*, 5–74.

44. Ibid., 2.

45. Ibid., 24.

46. Ibid., 2. Emphasis in original.

47. Contemporary discussions of categories in successive versions of the DSM focus on the differences and similarities between unipolar affective illness (involving only depression) and bipolar affective disorders. They also focus on how to classify the widely varying degrees of mania and depression in individuals (involving alternation between varying degrees of depression and mania). Goodwin and Jamison, *Manic-Depressive Illness*, 70.

48. For the complexities of defining emotion in psychology, see Ekman and Davidson, *The Nature of Emotion*. A useful review of the issues from a neurologist is LeDoux, "Emotion: Clues from the Brain." For ethnographic accounts that founded the contemporary inquiry into the social meaning of emotions, see Lutz and Abu-Lughod, *Language and the Politics of Emotion*; Lutz and White, "The Anthropology of Emotions"; M. Rosaldo, *Knowledge and Passion*; R. Rosaldo, "Grief and a Headhunter's Rage"; R. Solomon, "Getting Angry." There is support for the endeavor in other fields as well. The philosopher Errol Bedford argued in a classic paper that emotion concepts are not only psychological but have to be understood in the context of a wide range of social relationships, institutions, and concepts ("Emotions"). See also Harré, *Physical Being*; and S. Williams, *Emotion and Social Theory*.

49. Crapanzano, *Hermes' Dilemma and Hamlet's Desire*, 232.

50. Ibid., 235.

51. Drawing on his expertise in developmental psychology, William Reddy argues that emotional expressions (he calls them emotives), like performatives, change the world because they change the speaker and his or her feelings (*The Navigation of Feeling*, 96–111).

52. Geertz, "Religion as a Cultural System," 97.

53. The philosopher Gilbert Ryle gives us some markers to follow in the maze of terms used in ordinary English to designate mental states like moods: "Moods . . . monopolize. To say that [a person] is in one mood is . . . to say that he is not in any other. To be in a conversational mood is not to be in a reading, writing or lawn-mowing mood" (*The Concept of Mind*, 99). But to say that moods monopolize is not to say they are all equally intense. As I mentioned, Clifford Geertz stresses the variation in intensity among mood states, some of which can "go nowhere."

54. Geertz, "Religion as a Cultural System," 96.

55. Ibid., 97.

56. Elizabeth Lunbeck, personal communication, October 2003. Karl Jaspers, writing in 1913, spoke of depressive states as involving a "loss in productivity which may be transient or lasting"; hypomanic states as involving "exceptional productivity, of the richest creativeness" (*General Psychopathology*, 1:217). For historical analysis of the concept of the will in the nineteenth century, see Berrios, "The Psychopathology of Affectivity."

57. E. Sullivan, "Mood in Relation to Performance."

58. Sass, "Affectivity in Schizophrenia."

59. Ibid.

60. Anthropologist Janis Hunter Jenkins's work on schizophrenia speaks directly and perceptively to this issue. She stresses the complexity of emotion in the experience of a person with schizophrenia and the possible role of a disjunction between such a person's facial expression and his or her subjective experience. See Jenkins, "Schizophrenia as a Paradigm Case for Understanding Fundamental Human Processes," 42–44.

61. Quoted in Sass, *Madness and Modernism*, 50.

62. Ibid., 26.

63. Writing in 1926, Sophus Thalbitzer described this watershed, which his own work on manic depression had helped bring about, as follows: "The fact that the disorders of mood have hitherto not been much used to throw light on normal emotional life is due to a great extent to the relatively new classification of the mood-psychoses as an independent, clearly defined group of diseases. This does not mean that the great changes in emotional life which appear in almost all forms of mental disease, had hitherto been overlooked; but the dividing line had not been clearly and consciously drawn between the mental diseases in which the abnormal mood for the main part is secondary in relation to the primary changes in the intellectual

sphere (hallucinations and illusions), and the mental disorders in which the distortion of mood in one direction or the other is the essential factor" (*Emotion and Insanity*, 41).

64. T. Lutz, *American Nervousness, 1903*, 4. In another evocative description, neurasthenia "embodied a new anxious sensibility of the excitable subject as symptom, mirror, and source of worldly forces; suddenly, both the self and the surrounding world seemed at once diffuse, weightless, floating, and unreal, weighted down with symptoms, haunted, immobilized, and excessively sensory and concrete" (Harding and Stewart, "Anxieties of Influence," 258). The neurasthenic's "paralysis of will, his sense that he was no longer able to plunge into 'the vital currents of life,' his feeling that life had become somehow unreal" amounted to a feeling of "inner emptiness" that was nonetheless harnessed to an imperative to produce. At its beginning, neurasthenia was a disease of the male subject, the one who was thought to suffer most from the pressures of urban society, the demands of competition in the business world, and the pressure to succeed. Showalter, *The Female Malady*, 174.

65. Lears, "From Salvation to Self-Realization," 7–9.

66. G. Lakoff, *Moral Politics*, 65.

67. Goldstein, "Butching up for Victory," 13.

68. An important area that needs research is the reaction to extreme states like mania in other parts of the world system. There is certainly no one thing that could be called mania in other cultures. But recent ethnographic studies of the disposition of authorities toward extreme experiences akin to mania make some tentative comparisons possible. On the periphery of the global system, under postcolonial conditions, manic-like states are anything but valued by the dominant sectors. For example, Nancy Chen describes how in China, *falungong*, a spiritual and physical practice that taps into vital energy, has been recently denounced by the state and by leading scientists as a cult that promoted superstition and disorder, the antithesis of rational knowledge (*Breathing Spaces*, 177). Faced with tensions between its desire for centralized order and the forces of market liberalism, falungong's unregulated and unbridled energy was seen as a threat. State regulation tried to force it into either a sanctioned arena—state-sponsored sport-like events—or a deviant area—mental illness (186). For another, in Good and Subandi's account of a Javanese woman's psychosis, we glean some hints about how extreme states are regarded in Indonesia. As we know from Benedict Anderson's work, the "idea of power" in Java is

a mysterious, divine energy that permeates the universe. The "entire cosmos [is] suffused by a formless, constantly creative energy" (*Imagined Communities*, 7). But the potency of the self is constituted by spiritual practices that enhance restraint and refinement in language, sentiment, and behavior, correlated with social status (Keeler, "Shame and Stage Fright in Java"). The break with decorum that can come with psychosis is experienced as profoundly embarrassing because it threatens the place of the self in the status hierarchy. The psychotic person may also be seen as in touch with the omnipresent divine energy of the universe but insufficiently potent to handle it without being harmed. See Good and Subandi, "Experiences of Psychosis in Javanese Culture."

69. Comaroff and Comaroff, "Millennial Capitalism," 10.

CHAPTER 2

1. Sass, *The Paradoxes of Delusion*, 21.

2. Kraepelin, *Manic-Depressive Insanity and Paranoia*, 61, emphasis added. A manic-depressive's mistaken identities can "appear to be more an amusing game in which the patient takes pleasure, partially conscious of the arbitrariness of the designation. That occurs especially at the decline of excitement, when the wrong designations are still adhered to, while from the other conduct and occasional utterances of the patient it is evident that he is quite clear about his place of residence and the people round him" (Kraepelin, *Manic-Depressive Insanity and Paranoia*, 7).

3. Rather than tape recording, I often took notes on the spot and then wrote a full account as soon as possible, although all of the interviews I did with pharmaceutical personnel and most of the interviews I did with heads of organizations were tape recorded. In quoted interviews, an ellipsis indicates a pause; in quoted written materials, an ellipsis indicates an omission. I have not constructed composite quotations out of statements made by more than one person. All personal names are pseudonyms, except for those of my academic colleagues and authors speaking about their published work.

4. William Burroughs describes the dress style of the Wild Boys in this way: "[T]here are Bowery suits that appear to be stained with urine and vomit which on closer inspection turn out to be intricate embroideries of fine gold thread . . . it is the double take and many carry it much further to as many as six takes." Quoted in Hebdige, *Subculture*, 24.

5. Bauman, "Verbal Art as Performance," 305.

6. Judith Butler's work has been central in formulating the position that gender is not a role enacted by or expressing a preexisting interior self. Rather gender is an effect of performative acts: "Gender must be understood as the mundane way in which bodily gestures, movements, and enactments of various kinds constitute the illusion of an abiding gendered self" ("Performative Acts and Gender Constitution," 519). Butler's theory of gender identity also has a performative aspect. In her theory, feminine and masculine dispositions are formed as the effect of the prohibition against same-sexed desire. The child's love for his or her same-sexed parent is forbidden on two grounds: first, homosexual desire is forbidden, and second, parent-child desire is forbidden through the incest taboo. Therefore, the child inevitably experiences the loss of his or her same-sexed parent as an object of desire. Following Freud's analysis of melancholia, Butler argues that an object of desire that is lost but cannot be mourned leads to identification with that object. The result is that the child identifies with the lost same-sex parent and incorporates that parent's gender identity— and becomes—a male or female person (*Gender Trouble,* 63–64). Thus the child's gender identity arises performatively (as an effect of) a set of intimate relationships. There is a very rich literature in anthropology on performance (as opposed to performativity) as it plays a part in rituals. A useful collection of essays that focuses on the ways performance can be efficacious in rituals of healing is Laderman and Roseman, *The Performance of Healing.*

7. Sally and Leslie Swartz analyze an interview with a woman in a psychiatric hospital for a manic breakdown. They find that the woman uses "metacommentary"—she refers to the ongoing talk in the interview—and they argue that this makes her apparently unintelligible discourse coherent (Swartz and Swartz, "Talk about Talk").

8. Peggy Phelan, personal communication, March 15, 1999.

9. Fidler, *Affective Disorders.*

10. I do not know how widely these simulations are used, but they are listed in a variety of catalogues of teaching materials on the Web. Charles Nuckolls describes how dramatic enactments were used for teaching in one medical school with such success that plans were made to produce and market them to other medical schools (*Culture,* 209–10). Less formal versions of these scenes were enacted many times in the course of my observations of psychiatric training. In impromptu skits, more advanced students or residents would be designated the roles of patient and doctor

to illustrate to less advanced students the salient behaviors and how they might be treated. One of these teaching sessions was recorded by the film crew of the television series *Hopkins 24/7*, aired by ABC. The segment did not make it into the ABC series, but was included by an HBO production made from the unused footage in a series called *Nurses*.

11. Mischer, "An Evening with Robin Williams."

12. Holtzman, Shenton, and Solovay, "Quality of Thought Disorder in Differential Diagnosis," 379. This study differentiated thought disorders in manic-depressive and schizophrenic patients by analyzing their tape-recorded verbal responses to the Rorschach Test.

13. Kraepelin, *Manic-Depressive Insanity and Paranoia*, 27.

14. Cushman, *Constructing the Self*, 92, 97. In a trenchant critique, Atwood Gaines argues that the prevalent U.S. "cultural ideal of a controlled, rational self" is embodied in the DSM's assumptions about what a mental disorder is ("From DSM-I to III-R," 13).

15. Le Bon, *The Crowd*, 12. Plotz provides many literary examples of how crowds were feared in England (*The Crowd*).

16. Such associations between crowds and irrational behavior persist today, as in an assessment of the exemplary rational behavior of passengers and crew after an airplane crash in Toronto: "One survivor of the Air France crash in Toronto on Tuesday described the 'panic' of his fellow passengers. Yet these people had just evacuated a burning plane in about two minutes. While they had had critical help from the plane's crew members, those trained professionals were busy assisting people with limited mobility, not providing psychotherapy. Thus what the passenger observed was clearly not 'panic' in the sense of an unthinking crowd acting irrationally and abandoning the norms of civilized behavior. Indeed, it was the exact opposite. The Air France evacuation required an extraordinary degree of social coordination—which emerged among a group of strangers with virtually no time to prepare" (Fischhoff, "A Hero in Every Aisle Seat").

17. Dr. Sagar Parikh of the Bipolar Clinic at Clarke Institute in Toronto used the phrase "riding the tiger" to describe this. Tillson, "The CEO's Disease," 31.

18. Gay, "PBS' New Film about Theodore Roosevelt Chronicles the Many Sides of a Passionate, Energetic Man."

19. Gaines, "From DSM-I to III-R," 11.

20. Joel Robbins explores the pervasive attachment of anthropologists to "continuity thinking," which leads us to emphasize continuity over discontinuity in the cultural forms we study. He suspects that we privilege

continuity because it is so deeply rooted in our commonsense notions. See his "On the Paradoxes of Global Pentecostalism and the Perils of Continuity Thinking."

21. Jamison, *An Unquiet Mind*, 68.

22. An astute discussion of the role of having an interpretation in coming to conclusions about rationality is in Risjord, *Woodcutters and Witchcraft*, 13–33.

23. I am indebted to Susan Harding for seeing this dimension of my material in relation to her ethnographic work on fundamentalist Christians. See Harding, *The Book of Jerry Falwell*.

24. When I learned from my primatology colleagues at NYU that they call a similar "heads up" signal among nonhuman primates an "eye flash," I adopted the term.

25. Some examples: what are three things wrong with the penis? It has ring around the collar, hangs out with nuts, and lives next to an asshole. Why is the blonde's belly button black and blue after sex? Because her boyfriend's a blonde, too.

26. In *Madness and Modernism*, Louis Sass describes the particular form "meta" communication takes in schizophrenia. Use of irony (a form of inner distance from the self) and even a subtly mocking ironic tone convey the schizophrenic's degree of "meta-awareness," which, Sass argues, is not "congruent with standard conceptions of cognitive breakdown" (113). But Sass also asserts that meta-awareness alone is not sufficient to impart normality to the schizophrenic condition. The burden remains: a "disconcerting awkwardness and rigidity, a lack of free-flowing activity and syntonic social ease" (115). I am positing that the form of meta-awareness that I observed in bipolar support groups is somewhat different than in schizophrenia because it comes about through interpersonal interactions in a social setting. However, in common with Sass's argument, I would agree that meta-awareness alone does not relieve the bipolar condition of its burdens.

27. I am drawing on Mikhail Bakhtin's concept of double-voicing: "In . . . the double-voiced word, the sounding of a second voice is a part of the project of the utterance. In one way or another, for one reason or another, the author makes use 'of someone else's discourse for his own purposes by inserting a new semantic intention into a discourse which already has and which retains, an intention of its own'" (Morson and Emerson, *Mikhail Bakhtin*), 149.

28. This is like what Canetti called the "discharge," "the moment when all who belong to the crowd get rid of their differences and feel equal" (*Crowds and Power*, 17).

29. Bauman, *Verbal Art as Performance*, 11.

30. Ramanujan quoted in Brenneis, "Dramatic Gestures," 230.

31. Ibid., 230, 231.

32. Raymond Williams uses these terms to describe structures of feeling, which are "social experiences *in solution*, as distinct from other social se-mantic formations which have been *precipitated* and are more evidently and more immediately available" (*Marxism and Literature*, 134; emphasis in original).

33. Ginzburg, "Style as Inclusion, Style as Exclusion," 27.

34. Ibid.

35. Ibid., 34–35, 36.

36. "As the poet wrote with his style or pen, and the designer sketched with his style or pencil, the name of the instrument was familiarly used to express the genius and productions of the writer and the artist." Hence the term "style" connoted a connection between "mind and hands." Subse-quently, Hegel and Heinrich Heine both used "style" in connection with a familiar Romantic theme—artistic freedom (Ginzburg, "Style as Inclusion, Style as Exclusion," 35–36).

37. Ibid., 45.

38. Winter, "The Affective Properties of Styles," 67.

39. Ibid., 71–72. In the case of Hebdige, his analysis of style by subcul-tures like punk points to its use to escape the bourgeois norm (*Subcul-ture*). This subculture is interested in: how to refuse (3), detach from the taken for granted (19), disrupt (138), parody (139), and challenge hegemony obliquely in style (17). This subject position is dramatically different from that of my support group companions, who are already, and not necessarily by choice, relegated to the "abnormal." Their problem is how to gain the dignity of membership in humankind without being stul-tified by the "normal."

Stuart Ewen outlines the historical changes by which U.S. consumer society has made style "a cardinal feature of economic life," providing a "vast palette of symbolic meanings" that could be used to assemble a public self. See Ewen, *All Consuming Images*, 248, 79.

40. Michael Silverstein astutely puts his finger on how style is being deployed in U.S. political campaigns: "How does what impresses us as the

very height of *illogic* have a processual 'logic' of its own, such that success-ful politicians' discourse respects this logic? And where can we see these processes at work, where 'issues' get lumped and turned into 'message' — operators available for stylistic fashioning of image? How does a politician fashion 'message' as a kind of magnet for sometimes randomly assembled 'issues' that clump to it like iron filings arrayed in its magnetic field?" (*Talking Politics*, 21).

41. Mendoza-Denton, "Key Terms in Language and Culture," 235–36. Roman Jakobson elegantly analyzes the "pithy style" of the "brief and tena-cious genre," the Russian proverb, identifying phonological and grammati-cal features ("Notes on the Makeup of a Proverb"). See also Jakobson's "Baudelaire's 'Les Chats'" for an analysis of stylistic elements of Baude-laire's "Les Chats" including rhyme, grammar, gender, phonetics, and se-mantics. Thanks to Renato Rosaldo for pointing me to these papers.

42. Jakobson categorized most forms of aphasia into two types, "the met-onymical, concerned with external relations and the metaphorical, involv-ing internal relations. While each of these two types of aphasia tends toward unipolarity, normal verbal behavior is bipolar. But any individual use of language, any verbal style, any trend in verbal art displays a clear predilec-tion either for the metonymical or for the metaphorical device" (*Studies on Child Language and Aphasia*), 48.

43. Jakobson, *On Language*, 130. See also Jakobson, "Two Aspects of Language."

44. I am indebted to James Boon for telling me about Jakobson's work on style at an early point in my writing.

45. Jakobson, *The Framework of Language*, 106.

46. In his characterization of "schizoid style," Louis Sass is working to-ward a similar end. Describing the introverted, isolated person with "a sense of inner dividedness" as "schizoid," Sass differentiates this aspect of a person from the psychotic condition of "schizophrenia." The "schizoid" style is a "general style of character or personality that may be found to any degree and can be present in well-functioning and reasonably healthy persons. It is a style dominated by a certain hypersensitivity and vulnerabil-ity and by detachment from both self and world" (*Madness and Modernism*, 100–101). Efforts to characterize a "style" go in a different direction from efforts to define pathology. Aspects of a style might, by particular criteria, be pathological. But the style can also be apprehended as a manner of being, a certain flavor characteristic of a person's way of going through life:

"A particular style of being [involves] certain temperamental or emotional propensities and a distinct set of characteristic conflicts, concerns, and styles of psychological defense" (102).

47. The art historian E. H. Gombrich finds similar kinds of aesthetic patterning in the work of artists: "The personal accent of the artist is not made up of individual tricks of hand which can be isolated and described. It is again a question of relationships, of the interaction of countless personal reactions, a matter of distribution and sequences which we perceive as a whole without being able to name the elements in combination" (*Art and Illusion*, 65–66). This does not stop us from trying: we cannot suppress "the active mind," the "effort after meaning" because it "cannot be defeated without our world's collapsing into total ambiguity" (395). Gombrich is trying to capture something ineffable about style: we perceive it as a whole without being able to name the elements that are combined or to describe exactly how or when they are combined.

48. Merleau-Ponty, *Phenomenology of Perception*, 143.

49. Ibid., 146.

50. Merleau-Ponty adds in a footnote that "the mechanics of the skeleton cannot, even at the scientific level, account for the distinctive positions and movements of my body" (*Phenomenology of Perception*, 150).

51. Describing the way rules, customs, habits, and learning come together in complex ways in social life, the anthropologist Veena Das cites a vignette from Michael Gilsenan's ethnography about Lebanon. In the story, a young man performed an act of revenge with a style that, as Gilsenan puts it, included an "archetypal" gesture of indifference to his own safety. Das makes an important point that adds to our understanding of style: to become a man, the young hero had to find his own style of performing a heroic act because this individual style, rather than the enactment of a set part, is what called forth the exclamation from his elders, "You have returned a man!" ("Wittgenstein and Anthropology," 177).

52. As Elias Canetti aptly puts it, "[T]he manic's transformations have a tremendous ease about them" (*Crowds and Power*, 347).

53. My argument here is akin to Ann Stoler's account of colonial regimes, whose authority has been thought to rely on the rule of reason. She argues that Dutch rule in Indonesia also relied on the management of affective states, "public moods," and the racial distribution of sentiments. See Stoler, "Affective States."

Chapter 3

1. See Collier, Maurer, and Suárez-Navaz, "Sanctioned Identities." This article deals specifically with the role of Western legal practice in constituting personhood as ownership of the self and its capacities. D. W. Murray cautions against assuming too quickly that all foundational Western concepts posit an autonomous, unitary self. David Hume himself is cited as a philosopher who posited a noncontinuous, fragmentary self. See Murray, "What Is the Western Concept of the Self?"

2. The will played a large role in John Stuart Mill's mid-nineteenth-century writings about human nature. He thought one could only "overcome the potentially vicious force of habit" by exercising the muscles of the will. This was central to the development of the self and of society: some cultures (such as India and others in the east) remained mired in habit or custom and stasis, but the destructive force of custom could be overcome by the exercise of choice. See Joyce, *The Rule of Freedom*, 118–19.

3. Scull, *Social Order/Mental Disorder*, 286–87.

4. Ibid., 88.

5. Ibid., 86.

6. Jasin, "Considering Off Meds."

7. Icarus, "My Pdoc Emasculated Me."

8. Acoftil, "Neurontin Stories?"

9. Gerth and Mills, *From Max Weber*.

Chapter 4

1. The importance of how linguistic categories are used here cannot be overestimated. Susan Gal states the point succinctly: "The notions of dominance and resistance alert us to the idea that the strongest form of power may well be the ability to define social reality, to impose visions of the world. And such visions are inscribed in language and most important enacted in interaction" ("Language, Gender, and Power," 427).

2. This important concept is Mary Louise Pratt's. See her *Imperial Eyes*, 6–7. It has been usefully developed by James Clifford to understand interactions between museum staff and members of native communities about the interpretation and display of objects in the museums' collections. See his *Routes*, 188–219.

3. Luhrmann, *Of Two Minds*, especially 284–90. As part of my field-work, I sat in on many sessions of a class called Analytic Case Conference, which was designed to train medical residents in psychotherapy. The professor who taught this course and I are jointly writing a paper for publication about the pedagogical similarities between training students to do ethnography and training them to do psychotherapy. For accounts of diagnoses and treatments arrived at through interactions among physicians, nurses, and other staff in a psychiatric ward, see Rhodes, *Emptying Beds*. See also Estroff, *Making It Crazy*.

4. *Webster's Revised Unabridged Dictionary.* "A heavy sea in which large waves rise and dash upon the coast without apparent cause" (Oxford English Dictionary online).

5. For brevity, I have omitted some parts of the medical histories presented in rounds. These presentations are only a small part of the process of recording a case. Interviews of patient and family, observations by physicians and staff, discussions and reinterpretation are all involved in producing the written records that make up a case. The anthropologist and psychiatrist Robert Barrett has written a detailed and illuminating analysis of how the case record is produced in an Australian psychiatric hospital. See his *Psychiatric Team and the Social Definition of Schizophrenia*, 107–42.

6. Slavoj Žižek reveals the dynamic in this kind of coercion, calling it, in Lacanian terms, the "impotent gaze." See his *Looking Awry*, 72.

7. Rosenberg, "The Tyranny of Diagnosis," 255.

8. Butler, *Bodies That Matter*, 232.

9. Butler, *The Psychic Life of Power*, 2; Foucault, *The History of Sexuality: Vol. 1*.

10. Butler, *The Psychic Life of Power*, 3, 19.

11. Although I am in sympathy with Butler's account, I argue that the strong linguistic emphasis of her account (as indicated by the linguistic terms in the quotes above) creates this trap unnecessarily. For Butler, it is primarily language whose terms provide the conditions for the possibility of social life. Such an emphasis is appropriate, perhaps, given her focus on the logically necessary conditions for social existence. But here I am aiming for an approach to knowledge formation based on "embedded knowledge" that "cannot be deduced from people's talk." See Mol, *The Body Multiple*, 15.

12. Butler, *Bodies That Matter*, 237.

13. Billig, *Freudian Repression*, 140. See also Cameron and Kulick, "Introduction."

14. Gordon, *Ghostly Matters*, 22, 206.

15. Kulick, "No," 141.

16. Ibid.

17. Ibid.

18. Ibid.

19. In psychiatry, "poor insight" is considered a common characteristic of psychopathology, especially of schizophrenia. An early discussion of the issue is A. Lewis, "The Psychopathology of Insight." Psychologists have explored the effects of insight on patients' compliance with treatment recommendations and on the outcomes of treatment. See David, "Illness and Insight"; David, "Insight and Psychosis."

20. African Americans' experience with medical experimentation in the early twentieth century, such as in the Tuskegee study, justifies Keith Burton's suspicions. In the Tuskegee study, four hundred poor, mostly illiterate black men were enrolled in a study of the natural history of syphilis. Even after penicillin became available as an effective treatment, the study continued so the researchers could observe the effects of late-stage syphilis. The study only ended in 1972 after a leak to the press. Mr. Burton does state three times that he was terrified of the unknown injections. On the history of the Tuskegee study, see Jones, *Bad Blood*. See also Reverby, *Tuskegee's Truths*.

21. Austin, *How to Do Things with Words*, 60. Emphasis in original.

22. Cameron and Kulick would argue that what is being done in all performatives involves the emergence of a subject. See their "Introduction."

23. Austin, *How to Do Things with Words*, 76.

24. Ibid. Emphasis in original.

25. Ahern, "The Problem of Efficacy," 14.

26. Butler, *Bodies That Matter*, 232.

CHAPTER 5

1. Horwitz, *Creating Mental Illness*, 57.

2. Ibid., 60.

3. Ibid., 74.

4. The DSM is required for bureaucratic reasons, but many physicians find it a very imperfect instrument. In my fieldwork, psychiatrists would

informally describe the myriad emotional complexities hidden under the DSM's headings and subheadings in tones of considerable frustration.

5. Latour, *Science in Action*.

6. Horwitz, *Creating Mental Illness*, 57–77, describes in useful detail other factors that influenced the development of DSM-III and its later entrenchment: the role of lay mental health advocacy, increasing development of psychotropic drugs, and increased funds for research into biomedical causes of mental illness.

7. Silverstein and Urban, "The Natural History of Discourse," 1.

8. Rose, *Inventing Our Selves*, 105. Emphasis in original.

9. Ibid.

10. The philosopher Martin Heidegger described the loss of this kind of knowledge as "un-being" or "the abandonment of being." Under the impact of technology in the modern age, he thought that many things come to be seen as resources that can be improved or produced according to machine-like standards of efficiency, losing their connections to contexts of meaning in the process. See Guignon, *The Cambridge Companion to Heidegger*; Heidegger, *The Basic Problems of Phenomenology*.

11. In the Arcades Project, an archive of materials Walter Benjamin collected to elucidate the relationship between the onset of modern commercial developments and culture in nineteenth-century and early twentieth-century Paris, an important theme is the "interior." With the rising importance of the bourgeoisie, novel kinds of domestic architecture and furnishings came into being as domestic life became a secluded shelter from the dangers of the marketplace. In elaborately designed and decorated interiors, new kinds of intimate family life arose. In Benjamin's words, "To live in these interiors was to have woven a dense fabric about oneself, to have secluded oneself within a spider's web, in whose toils world events hang loosely suspended like so many insect bodies sucked dry. From this cavern, one does not like to stir" (*The Arcades Project*, 216). Benjamin refers to the "traces" people left of themselves in these spaces, traces that were left on the surfaces of interior furnishings. Thought about in this light, the proliferation of coverings for furniture—antimacassars—characteristic of the age, can be seen as materials to capture tracings as well as to ward them off. "The interior is not just the universe but also the *étui* [a small, decorated box to hold useful items] of the private individual. To dwell means to leave traces. In the interior, these are accentuated. Coverlets and antimacassars, cases and containers are devised in abundance; in these, the traces

of the most ordinary objects of use are imprinted. In just the same way, the traces of the inhabitant are imprinted in the interior" (9).

12. John Searle, Jacques Derrida, and Judith Butler, among others, have generated a large and contentious literature about the way performatives work. See Searle, *Speech Acts*. (For references to Derrida and Butler, see below.) For anthropological purposes, I think the agreements among these writers are as significant as their differences. For an application to Mayan languages with rich implications for anthropology generally, see Hanks, *Language and Communicative Practices*.

13. Butler, *Excitable Speech*, 51. Emphasis in original.

14. Butler, *Bodies That Matter*, 163, 232.

15. Butler, *Excitable Speech*, 163.

16. Of particular interest to anthropologists, a major burden of Austin's book, and of other work in the orbit of the late Wittgenstein, such as G.E.M. Anscombe's *Intention*, was to question the link between the meaning of language and an "inward and spiritual act," an "inward performance." Indeed Anscombe's volume on intention is centrally a detailed exposition of how "intention" and interior mental performances must be disarticulated: "you cannot take any performance (even an interior performance) as itself an act of intention; for if you describe a performance, the fact that it has taken place is not a proof of intention; words for example may occur in somebody's mind without his meaning them. So intention is never a performance in the mind, though in some matters a performance in the mind which is seriously *meant* may make a difference to the correct account of the man's action — e.g., in embracing someone. But the matters in question are necessarily ones in which outward acts are 'significant' in some way" (*Intention*, 49; emphasis in original). The relentless message of both Anscombe's and Austin's work is that the meaning of linguistic acts is not necessarily connected with interior mental events. Even the meaning of mentalistic terms like "intention" does not necessarily entail an interior mental event. Both theorists seek to ground meaning in social use and context, human activities that are public and conventional, governed by communities of language users.

This argument has been downplayed in the subsequent critique in literary theory. Derrida, for example, in his "Signature Event Context" argues that utterances are performative because they are "citations" of previously established social conventions: "Could a performative utterance succeed if its formulation did not repeat a 'coded' or iterable utterance, or in other words, if the formula I pronounce in order to open a meeting, launch a ship or a marriage were not identifiable as *conforming* with an iterable model, if it were not then identifiable in some way as a 'citation'?" (18). So far this would not find much resistance in Austin's account of performatives. Derrida goes on to assert that his focus on iterability extends performative language to cases where "intention" is not present. He asserts that for Austin "conscious intention would at the very least have to be totally present and immediately transparent to itself and to others, since it is a determining center [*foyer*] of context" (18). Derrida's shift to iterability allows speech acts to be performative even though "the intention animating the utterance will never be through and through present to itself and to its content" (18). Derrida's quarrel with Austin is in part over the role of the "originating will" in the performative: an utterance like "let there be light" brings something into being through the power of a subject's will. In effect, Derrida asserts that any linguistic sign can be detached from the context in which it was produced and inserted, "cited," in another: "Every sign, linguistic or nonlinguistic, spoken or written . . . can be *cited*, put between quotation marks; in so doing it can break with every given context, engendering an infinity of new contexts in a manner which is absolutely illimitable." Derrida loosens the connection Austin wanted to make between performativity and prior social conventions (12). I have found Benjamin Lee's parsing of this argument very helpful. See his *Talking Heads*, 42–65.

17. My research did not delve into the political activities of these organizations, such as the Depression and Related Affective Disorders Association or Depression and Bipolar Support Alliance. Nor did I engage with members of the various organizations within the antipsychiatry or critical psychiatry movements. Outside the United States, a particularly instructive organization is called the Hearing Voices Network. It is an organization of people who "hear voices" in England, Europe, and Australia, which has been described in useful detail in Blackmun, *Hearing Voices*. If one were to think about what it would take for patients to engage vigorously with the terms of medical understanding, a useful comparative case is described by Steven Epstein in *Impure Science*. Epstein chronicles how grassroots publications and treatment activists challenged not only the medical and social services' provision of care for HIV but even the scientific terms in which it was understood. They opened the door to some heretical views of the causation of AIDS and influenced drug development, approval, and pricing.

18. Karp, *Speaking of Sadness*.

19. As the linguistic anthropologist William Hanks puts it, "Where practice approaches break definitively with speech act theory is in their insistence that performative effectiveness does not depend upon the preexistence of conventional speech act types. Instead it is an emergent feature of practice, an unavoidable part of talk under conditions of differential power, authority, and legitimacy" (*Language and Communicative Practices*, 236).

CHAPTER 6

1. The often unspoken assumption that drugs work on the brain is part of the biomedical model of mental illness that is currently pervasive in the United States. The anthropologist T. M. Luhrmann powerfully articulates a concern that seeing mental illnesses as simply biological will leave patients with a lesser sense of worth. In a simple biomedical model, patients with mental illness are found wanting in the moral core where their rational intention resides. If they are incompletely curable, they will be thereafter less than a fully fledged person. This concern is exacerbated when, in the society as a whole, psychiatric illness comes to be understood only in terms of the biomedical model, at the expense of the interactional terms of psychotherapy. See Luhrmann, *Of Two Minds*, 284–85.

2. For reasons of confidentiality, I have assigned pseudonyms to brand-name drugs on whose accounts my interlocutors worked directly.

3. Francomano, "DTC Advertising: A Matter of Perspective"; Holmer, "Direct-to-Consumer Prescription Drug Advertising Builds Bridges between Patients and Physicians." See also Hollon, "Direct-to-Consumer Marketing of Prescription Drugs." This article presents both sides of the debate over whether DTC ads contribute to the public good by informing people of products that can benefit their health, or detract from it by increasing consumption of prescription drugs in ways that do not benefit patients.

4. See "DTC Advertising Spending Increases." Also useful is "Advertising: The Cause of High Drug Costs?" The trade publication *Pharmaceutical Representative* (from which the two above-cited sources are drawn) reported on studies by the National Institute for Health Care Management (NIHCM) Research and Educational Foundation. According to the NIHCM, "Spending on mass media advertising for prescription drugs

reached $1.8 billion in 1999, up from $375 million in 1995. It continued to accelerate in the first four months of 2000, reaching $946 million for the period, 58% more than the $597 million spent during the same four months in 1999" ("DTC Advertising Spending Increases"). Antihistamines took the largest proportion: 10.2 percent of all expenditures on DTC advertising between January and September 2000. See "Spending on Consumer Ads up in 2000."

5. Elsewhere I have discussed the concept of pharmaceutical "side effects" and its impact on patients. See Martin, "The Pharmaceutical Person." Adriana Petryna has shown that the growth in "the number of people participating in and required for pharmaceutical clinical trials has become massive" ("Drug Development and the Ethics of the Globalized Clinical Trial," 5). The side effects Giosa is talking about are discovered through large clinical trials. Many of these new trials are being conducted in low-income countries where people are, therefore, relatively willing to participate in trials for monetary compensation. Moreover, such subjects are much less likely to complain about side effects. Many other forces are also pushing this expansion: the post–World War II boom in production of pharmaceuticals in the United States, the increase in government regulation and oversight of the industry in the United States (including the ban on use of prisoners for clinical trials in the 1970s), and "treatment saturation" in the United States. "Treatment saturation" means that the affluent people in the United States are using so many drugs that drug-drug interactions interfere with the ability to recruit subjects for these trials. Hence, clinical trials have increasingly been conducted outside the United States. For more on clinical trials and other global aspects of pharmaceutical marketing, see Petryna, Lakoff, and Kleinman, *Global Pharmaceuticals*.

6. "Psychotropic Drug Market Grows"; "Prescriptions Soar for Psychotropic Drugs."

7. Pincus et al., "Prescribing Trends in Psychotropic Medications," 526, 529. Figures from 1990 and 1999 are from IMS Health, courtesy of Nikolas Rose.

8. C. Lutz discusses the "inherent irrationality of emotions" in Western cultural categories: their association with danger, chaos, immaturity, vulnerability and lack of control ("Emotion, Thought, and Estrangement," 291–94).

9. Kiki, "James! Help! My Pdoc Doesn't Know about Neurontin."

10. Jamison, Gerner, and Goodwin, "Patient and Physician Attitudes toward Lithium."

11. Jamison, *An Unquiet Mind*, 91–92.

12. Ibid., 6.

13. Marilyn Strathern connects the advantage that is currently gained by specificity in pharmacogenomics to Western cultural concepts of the "whole person" ("The Whole Person and Its Artifacts").

14. "Trying Topamax and Klonopin."

15. "I'm New Heres an Intro [*sic*]."

16. "Cocktail Hour."

17. An employee in a firm to which pharmaceutical companies outsource their publications graciously gave me a password to the forum. The location of the site is confidential.

18. Joseph Dumit gives an illuminating description of the emergence of a notion of "pharmaceutical normalcy," in which health is precarious and can be achieved only through continuous ingestion of multiple drugs. See Dumit, "Drugs for Life."

CHAPTER 7

1. Raymond Williams used the concept of structures of feeling in order to point beyond formal beliefs or systematic world views to some range of meanings that are "actively lived and felt." Structures of feeling involve "impulse, restraint and tone"; they involve "thought as felt and feeling as thought" (*Marxism and Literature*, 132). For Williams, structures of feeling are parts of social experience that are still in process and therefore are not as clearly recognizable as when they are, if they ever are, built into institutions in a formal way. For example, conventionally, early Victorians believed that poverty and debt were caused by deviance and individual failure. Literary figures like Charles Dickens and Emily Brontë developed a new structure of feeling—a sensibility—in their novels by linking poverty and debt to the unequal social order instead. This structure of feeling was communicated through emotional relationships in concrete stories rather than in a general theory, and it lay outside conventional understandings (134).

2. Miklowitz, *The Bipolar Disorder Survival Guide*.

3. Rose, *Inventing Our Selves*, 103.

4. Miller and Goode, *Man and His Body*.

5. This is similar to Bruno Latour's "action at a distance" (*Science in Action*). On accounting schemes, see Miller, "Accounting and Objectivity"; T. Porter, *Trust in Numbers*.

6. The context of this phrase is: "Everything becomes saleable and buyable. The circulation becomes the great social retort into which everything is thrown, to come out again as a gold-crystal. Not even are the bones of saints, and still less are more delicate res sacrosanctae, extra commercium hominum able to withstand this alchemy" (*Capital*, 132).

7. Otniel Dror has done important historical work on the ways emotions became numerically measured by technological devices in the late nineteenth century. When emotion was "numerized," it became knowable scientifically and became positioned inside the language of reason. See Dror, "Counting the Affects."

8. In a wide-ranging review of the history and social effects of the concept of commensuration, Wendy Nelson Espeland and Mitchell L. Stevens trace the first formulation of how commensurability was paired with control, stability, and rationality, while incommensurability was paired with chaos, anxiety, and threat, to Plato's ideas from the fifth and early fourth centuries BC. See Espeland and Stevens, "Commensuration as a Social Process." They draw on Martha Nussbaum's argument that Plato needed to make ethical values commensurate so that they could be ranked. Once people could rank their values, they could make rational choices among them and avoid following the pull of irrational passions. Aristotle, in contrast, questioned the goal of rendering value general and homogenous and preferred to retain the value of things and people for their own sakes. Nussbaum, "Plato on Commensurability and Desire."

9. Kraepelin, *Manic-Depressive Insanity and Paranoia*, 140.

10. Ibid., 149.

11. Hoff, "Kraepelin: Clinical Sections, I," 269.

12. Engstrom, "Kraepelin: Social Section," 294.

13. Berrios and Hauser, "Clinical Sections," 281.

14. Kraepelin, *One Hundred Years of Psychiatry*, 151.

15. Kraepelin, *Manic-Depressive Insanity and Paranoia*, 151.

16. Kraepelin, *Clinical Psychiatry*, 414.

17. Ibid.

18. At one time, the NIMH Web site solicited participation in ongoing NIMH studies of mood disorders.

19. The Mood Tree is not exclusively for children and is not marketed exclusively to parents, but rather to all ages from six years old and up, including adolescents and adults. The different versions have somewhat different terms on the apples.

20. McDonald, *The Judy Moody Mood Journal*.

21. Mohammed, "A Mood Chart System." I am focusing primarily on mood charts that people come upon or seek out on their own. There is another form of mood charting, in use for nearly a decade, used in large-scale studies of the efficacy of medications for mood disorders. In these studies, based on a retrospective or prospective "Life-Chart Method," patients are recruited and enrolled for the specific purpose of having their affective states charted, or learning how to chart them themselves. See Denicoff et al., "Validation of the Prospective NIMH-Life-Chart Method"; bipolar news, "What Is Life Charting?"

22. Mondimore, *Bipolar Disorder*, 222.

23. Sartorius, "Depressive Disorders," 1.

24. The film was produced by the Canadian Broadcasting Company. A copy is held in the History of Medicine Division of the National Library of Medicine.

25. Healy, *The Antidepressant Era*, 76.

26. Tanouye, "Mental Illness: A Rising Workplace Cost."

27. Stewart et al., "Cost of Lost Productive Work Time among U.S. Workers with Depression."

28. The sociologist Alain Ehrenberg traces the historical entailments between depression as an emerging psychiatric category and French concepts of action and inaction. See Ehrenberg, *La fatigue d'être soi*.

29. "Depressed and on Welfare."

30. The actual path walked by patients who take SSRIs, which might begin with relief, progress to tolerance, and end with new modes of actualizing the self, is far more complex than advertisements convey. For an analysis of first-person accounts of this path, see Metzl, *Prozac on the Couch*, 174–94.

31. Kramer, "There's Nothing Deep about Depression."

32. Lewis and the Illinois Leader, *Illinois Launches Compulsory Mental Health Screening for Children and Pregnant Women*; Medical Condition News, "Texas Medication Algorithm Project Guidelines Produce Improvements in Patients with Major Depressive Disorder." For information on other whistle blowers who have filed charges that the pharmaceutical industry used inappropriate means to promote psychotropic drugs, see the Web site of the Alliance for Human Research Protection at http://www.ahrp.org/infomail/04/07/07.php.

33. Sher, *Live the Life You Love*, 54.

34. This is not entirely new. In *White Collar* (1951), C. Wright Mills described how in twentieth-century salesmanship, traits found in creative salesmen were "expropriated": codified and displayed in a controlled way. Quoted in Ewen, *All Consuming Images*.

35. Warren Sussman showed that late nineteenth-century advice books described the self as based on character, moral integrity that could be improved through hard work, moral behavior, and frugality. After the turn of the twentieth century, advice books focused on personality, a quality that one shaped by making oneself attractive to others. Francesca Bordogna analyzes William James's thesis about the temperament and its link to the physiological constitution of the individual in "The Psychology and Physiology of Temperament."

36. Friedman, "What's the Lure of the Edge?" F7.

37. MacLennan, "The Global CNS Therapeutics Markets."

38. I am echoing Pierre Bourdieu's phraseology in *Distinction*. He describes how rationalization in the school system in France replaces "practical schemes of classification" with "explicit, standardized taxonomies." These typologies are deliberately taught and therefore fixed in memory as knowledge that can be "reproduced in virtually identical form by all the agents subjected to its action" (67).

39. This point is made powerfully by Nikolas Rose in a number of important publications. See, for example, Rose, "Becoming Neurochemical Selves," and *Governing the Soul*.

40. Historically, the collection of statistics has played a key role in enabling new regimes of control to arise. For the role of statistics in colonial regimes, see Anderson, *Imagined Communities*. On the "looping effects" of categories of human kinds, see Hacking, "Making up People."

41. Miller, "Accounting and Objectivity," 79.

42. Mohammed, "A Mood Chart System."

43. In an analogous process, when a specific form of labor is transformed through abstraction from something with use value into something with exchange value, it also becomes social. Marx explained how the specific labor of tailoring a coat could become equivalent to the very different specific labor of weaving linen. First, the concrete labor of tailoring becomes "directly identified with undifferentiated human labour," which is measured by labor time. This makes tailoring "identical with any other sort of labour" including the labor of weaving linen. Although tailoring, like all labor that produces commodities, is "the labour of private individuals

. . . yet, at the same time, it ranks as labour directly social in its character. . . . The labour of private individuals takes the form of its opposite, labour directly social in its form" (*Capital*, 1014).

44. "Moral Thermometer."

45. Another version of the thermometer, published as the frontispiece of one of Rush's books, was divided into an upper section titled "Temperance" and a lower one called "Intemperance." Drinking only water and milk would lead to "health, wealth, serenity of mind, reputation, long life and happiness." Drinking anything more potent than strong punch would lead to vices (idleness, quarreling, anarchy), diseases (gout, melancholy, madness), and punishments (debt, hunger, workhouse, jail). Rush, *An Inquiry into the Effects of Ardent Spirits upon the Human Body and Mind*.

46. "Moral Thermometer," 5–6.

CHAPTER 8

1. Thanks to David Harvey for telling me about Keynes's animal spirits.

2. For one example, see Berresem, "Emotions Flattened and Scattered." Others have laid postmodernity's pervasive emotional emptiness at the feet of the social forces of capitalism, which, requiring continuous growth under intense competition and ruthless entrepreneurialism for survival, have made catastrophic job loss a normal experience for increasing numbers of people. Harvey, *The Condition of Postmodernity*.

3. According to Henry Ellenberger's history of psychoanalysis, the metaphor of colonizing the mind has been used before for new psychiatric discoveries. In France, Mesmer (1734–1815) developed an early form of dynamic psychotherapy to replace exorcism. Because his method explored the mind itself rather than exorcising foreign spirits from it, he was compared to Columbus (*Discovery of the Unconscious*, 57). Charcot, the French doctor who displayed and treated hysteria at Salpetriere in the 1880s, used hypnotism to show the symptoms were not produced by lesions of the nervous system. He was called the "Napoleon of neuroses" (95). In her study of Madagascar, Lesley Sharp has used the notion of the colonized mind. See *The Sacrificed Generation*.

4. Sass, *Madness and Modernism*, 80.

5. Kretschmer, *Physique and Character*, 129–30.

6. Sass, *Madness and Modernism*, 4–982.

7. Lunbeck, *The Psychiatric Persuasion*, 146.

8. Kraus, "How Can the Phenomenological-Anthropological Approach Contribute to Diagnosis and Classification in Psychiatry?" 208.

9. Lunbeck, *The Psychiatric Persuasion*, 146.

10. Southard and Jarrett, *The Kingdom of Evils*, 477. Making a virtue of these traits for psychological studies, the German psychologist Sophus Thalbitzer wrote in 1926 that he regarded manic-depressive patients as "the best material for the study of normal processes of feeling." He argued that in manic depression, normal moods and emotions are strongly defined and magnified: "We see them as if under the microscope with each characteristic feature standing out in bold relief; we can observe the mood-psychosis as a natural mood or feeling raises, as it were to a higher power" (*Emotion and Insanity*, 43).

Ernst Kretschmer reiterated Southard's affection for the manic-depressive type: "The individuals in the region of manic-depressive madness are prevailingly sociable, good-natured men, people with whom one can get on well, who understand a joke, and who take life as it comes. They give themselves naturally and openly, and one soon makes friends with them; they have often something soft and warm in their temperaments" (*Physique and Character*, 124).

11. Kraus, "Identity and Psychosis of the Manic-Depressive," 203. In this and the following article, Kraus provides a wealth of references to earlier work in psychology and psychoanalysis on the conformist attitudes of manic-depressive patients (206–7). See Kraus, "Role Performance, Identity Structure and Psychosis in Melancholic and Manic-Depressive Patients." A 1979 study of multigenerational bipolar illness in families also stressed the unrealistic standards of conformity subscribed to in the families studied. See Davenport, "Manic-Depressive Illness," 25.

12. Kraus, "Identity and Psychosis of the Manic-Depressive," 205–6.

13. In his memoir, Andrew Solomon describes the social withdrawal depression brings: "[M]ajor depression has a number of defining factors — mostly having to do with withdrawal, though agitated or atypical depression may have an intense negativity rather than a flattened passivity — and is usually fairly easy to recognize; it deranges sleep, appetites, and energy. It tends to increase sensitivity to rejection, and it may be accompanied by a loss of self-confidence and self-regard" (*The Noonday Demon*, 48).

14. Kretschmer describes further how people react to the mania of a manic depressive: "It is well known that even manics in a state of excitement have usually something childishly good-natured, trustful, and tractable about them, they are far more up to mischief then harsh acts of violence, they seldom make a serious attempt to do anyone any harm; they just flare up all of a sudden but they are soon quiet again; one can seldom take anything they do in bad part. And the pure typical circular depressives

have some soft quality in their moodiness" (*Physique and Character*, 129). The topic is beyond my scope, but it would be instructive to consider the narcissistic elements in mania. Inflated self-esteem is listed as one of the defining terms of mania in the DSM, indicating that there is a family resemblance between mania and narcissism. Research suggests there might well be comorbidity between manic depression and narcissistic personality disorder, as in Crockford and el-Guebaly, "Psychiatric Comorbidity in Pathological Gambling." Considered not just as a bundle of traits but as a loosely integrated style, however, narcissism conveys more of a sense of social isolation and inner emptiness than mania: it might well elicit a lower "empathic index" than mania. For a perceptive account of narcissism as a style, see Johnson, *Humanizing the Narcissistic Style*. For an important study of the history of narcissism as a concept in psychiatry and a cultural preoccupation in the United States, see Lunbeck, *The Americanization of Narcissism*.

15. Sass traces critically and with care the use of this definition of creativity by Kay Jamison and in psychology generally. See Sass, "Schizophrenia, Modernism, and the 'Creative Imagination,'" 59, 65–67.

16. No one has done more than Louis Sass to elucidate the specific phenomenological features of the schizophrenic condition, such as "unworlding." See in particular Sass, *The Paradoxes of Delusion*.

17. Sass, "Schizophrenia, Modernism, and the 'Creative Imagination,'" 70.

18. Gibbons, *Sights Unseen*; Padgett, *A Child of Silence*; Willocks, *Green River Rising*; MTV "True Life: I'm Bipolar," July 2002; PBS special about Lance in the *American Family* series; Duke and Hochman, *A Brilliant Madness*; Graham, *Personal History*; Gray, *Life Interrupted*; Pauley, *Skywriting*.

19. A rough indication of the rise in frequency of mania as a term in ordinary life is a count of the incidence of the term in *the New York Times* from 1870 to 1999. The *New York Times* printed the term "mania" about a thousand times per decade from 1870 to 1979. In the next two decades, the rate increased threefold, to about three thousand times per decade (ProQuest Historical Newspapers index and ProQuest New York Times index).

20. A particularly useful list is provided in the Internet encyclopedia Wikipedia, http://en.wikipedia.org/wiki/List_of_people_believed_to_have _been_affected_by_bipolar_disorder.

21. In my fieldwork with pharmaceutical marketers and representatives, I learned that such gaps are not uncommon. Messages developed at one

point—say by a firm to whom a pharmaceutical corporation subcontracted a marketing account—might be lost by the time the materials and their imagery were in the hands of sales representatives. But at the 2000 APA meeting, another pharmaceutical company, Abbott Laboratories, distributed a special compilation of classical music on a CD as a gift. The CD included music by Beethoven, Tchaikovsky, Mozart, and other composers often listed as artistic geniuses who suffered from manic depression. I spoke at some length with the Abbott representative who gave me a copy of the CD, as we stood surrounded by glowing posters that advertised Depakote's advantages for the treatment of manic depression. Looking at the musicians included on the CD, I asked him if they were included because they had all had manic depression. He looked surprised: not only did he not know, but he said he had never thought of the possibility.

22. Schiff, "Poor Richard's Redemption."

23. Scr Vaas, "The *Post* Investigates Manic-Depression."

24. Busfield and Campling, *Men, Women, and Madness,* 122.

25. Lunbeck, *The Psychiatric Persuasion,* 149. C. Lutz provides a useful overview of the associations between emotions and the female in American culture ("Emotion, Thought, and Estrangement").

26. Lunbeck, *The Psychiatric Persuasion,* 149. Charles Nuckolls writes about nineteenth-century cultural stereotypes of the "independent" male and the "dependent" female that were congruent with and affected the development of other psychiatric diagnoses—the antisocial personality and the histrionic personality ("Toward a Cultural History of the Personality Disorders").

27. Schnog, "Changing Emotions," 99.

28. Lunbeck, *The Psychiatric Persuasion,* 150.

29. Goodwin and Jamison, *Manic-Depressive Illness,* 168.

30. Jamison, *An Unquiet Mind,* 122–23.

31. Ibid., 122.

32. Corrigan, *Business of the Heart,* 243.

33. Ibid., 241–43.

34. Pfister, "Glamorizing the Psychological," 190.

35. Walser, "Deep Jazz," 274.

36. Ibid., 274–75.

37. Cardinal, *The Words to Say It,* 39.

38. Morrison, *Playing in the Dark,* vi, viii.

39. Rack, *Race, Culture, and Mental Disorder,* 113.

40. Ibid., 115, 116.

41. Ibid. Elizabeth Lunbeck's history of early twentieth-century American psychiatry details the relationship between the race theory of the time and psychiatric diagnosis. By and large, these early psychiatrists accepted the notion of racial differences in temperament, but did not use racial differences to impute pathology. Racial stereotypes were used instead to describe individuals—an alcoholic Irishman or a nervous Jew—as normal for their race (*The Psychiatric Persuasion*, 125–26). Baldwin, *Notes of a Native Son*, 53, and Fanon, *Black Skin, White Masks*, 126ff., provide some classic articulations of the cultural link between black men and out-of-control emotion.

42. "Famous People Who Have Suffered from Depression or Manic-Depression." This extensive list includes Jim Carrey but not Eddie Murphy.

43. Jamison, *An Unquiet Mind*, 213.

44. Jamison, *Touched with Fire*, 105.

45. Goodwin and Jamison, *Manic-Depressive Illness*, 23.

46. Jamison, *An Unquiet Mind*, 80.

47. Mark Micale shows how the style of hysterics was extended as an aesthetic form into the theater in late nineteenth-century France ("Discourses of Hysteria in Fin-de-Siècle France," 76–77).

48. This last scenario may not be mere speculation. See Baard, "The Guilt-Free Soldier."

49. Grigoriadis, "Are You Bipolar?"

50. Ibid.

51. For a Canadian news story, see Evenson, "Is 'Soft' Depression Price of Greatness?" This article quotes a Canadian psychiatrist saying that people with hypomania are "highly functioning people. They're effervescent, energetic, optimistic and charismatic. There are people who get lots done; they are oftentimes artistically gifted as well and are major contributors to society."

52. Grigoriadis, "Are You Bipolar?"

53. Kluger, Song, and Simon, "Young and Bipolar."

54. Carlson, "Mania and ADHD," and Klein, Pine, and Klein, "Debate Forum," question the extrapolation of adult criteria onto children. Bowring and Kovacs, "Difficulties in Diagnosing Manic Disorders among Children and Adolescents," 613, raise the difficulty of identifying psychotic thinking in children with active imaginations.

55. One epidemiological study estimates the lifetime prevalence of bipolar disorders among young American adults at 1.6 percent. Jonas et al., "Prevalence of Mood Disorders in a National Sample of Young American Adults."

56. Kluger, Song, and Simon, "Young and Bipolar," 43.

57. Braun, "The Challenge of Being Young, Creative and Bipolar."

58. "The Storm in My Brain."

59. "Treating Bipolar Disorder Takes Understanding," *New York Times*, October 26, A21, October 31, A7, November 1, A15. This ad ran at least eight times between October 26 and December 7, 2005.

60. For some of the press coverage of this genre, termed "a new critical genre that likens society to a mental patient," see Lacher, "In New Book, Professor Sees a 'Mania' in U.S. for Possessions and Status," 7.

61. Jamison, *Exuberance*, 289.

62. Gartner, *The Hypomanic Edge*.

63. Whybrow, *American Mania*.

64. It follows that existing and forthcoming studies of the different meanings given to psychological states and psychotropic drugs across cultures are crucial additions to our understanding of mania and depression in Western societies. For classic studies, see Crapanzano, *Tuhami*; Kleinman, *Social Origins of Distress and Disease*; Levy, *Tahitians*; Wikan, "Public Grace and Private Fears." For recent or forthcoming studies, see Good and DelVecchio-Good, "Why Do the Masses So Easily Run Amok?"; A. Lakoff, *Pharmaceutical Reason*; Wilce, "Madness, Fear, and Control in Bangladesh." See also Michael Oldani's Princeton dissertation, "Filling Scripts."

65. Anscombe, *Intention*; Hacking, *Rewriting the Soul*, 235.

66. Hacking, *Rewriting the Soul*, 237.

67. Ibid.

68. Of course, earlier conceptions of multiplicity also had a history: "[T]he whole language of many selves had been hammered out by generations of romantic poets and novelists, great and small, and also in innumerable broadsheets and feuilletons too ephemeral for general knowledge today" (Hacking, *Rewriting the Soul*, 232).

69. In a more recent publication, Hacking softens his criticism of retroactive diagnosis, still finding it academically incorrect but allowing that it is sometimes nonetheless able to yield insight. People called "fugueurs" (mad travelers) at the end of the nineteenth century may share something with contemporary people who suffer from what is now called "disassociative fugue," for example. See Hacking, *Mad Travelers*, 87.

70. "Ron Chernow, Author *Alexander Hamilton.*"

71. In anthropology there has been only a modest amount of recent interest in the implications of Wittgenstein's thought for the understanding of cultural processes. This interest is not entirely new—Clifford Geertz's work has long been informed by Wittgensteinian understandings—but it is a welcome sign. See Das, "Wittgenstein and Anthropology." Also, Michael Lynch has recently developed some implications of Wittgenstein's views of language for science studies in his "Representation Is Overrated." By the accident of being in graduate school at Cornell during the years when the faculty in the philosophy department were undergoing a kind of conversion experience as they contended with the unpublished writings Wittgenstein left there before his death, I was swept along in their enthusiasm. I took courses from Max Black, Georg Von Wright, and Bruce Goldberg. Many of my early publications were attempts to see anthropological problems, or dissolve them, with the aid of insights I had gained from this work. In returning to these concerns here, I want to signal the richness of Wittgenstein's thought for anthropological accounts of culture.

72. Wittgenstein, *Zettel*, 2e.

73. Ibid., 8e. Emphasis in original.

CHAPTER 9

1. J. Chaffin, "How Brokers with the Blues May Add to Market Miseries."

2. Kaletsky, "War against Terror Can Be Fought on the Spending Front."

3. Samuelson, "For the Economy, Mood Does Matter." Emphasis added.

4. Roper, "Consumers Anxious but Ads Bring Some Comfort."

5. Kaplan, "Study: Consumers Anxious but Ads Bring Some Comfort."

6. World Mood Chart.

7. Up until the fall of 2004, Benrik's chart plotted the world mood against the Dow Jones Industrial Average. The software was not working properly, so that feature was removed (e-mail correspondence, September 4, 2004). The moods of investors are at least as important as the moods of stockbrokers, CEOs, and consumers. In 2003, State Street Associates launched a global investor confidence index that measures the "sentiments" of institutional investors by tracking the percentage of their portfolios that they place in high-risk assets. The basic idea, according to the

firm, is that "the more of their portfolios that professional investors are willing to devote to riskier as opposed to safer investments, the greater their risk appetite or confidence." State Street Investor, "State Street Investor Confidence Index Summary."

8. Havens, *Making Contact*, 21.

9. In Andrew Solomon's eloquent description of the slowing that accompanies depression, "Depression minutes are like dog years, based on some artificial notion of time. I can remember lying frozen in bed, crying because I was too frightened to take a shower, and at the same time knowing that showers are not scary. I kept running through the individual steps in my mind: you turn and put your feet on the floor; you stand; you walk from here to the bathroom; you open the bathroom door; you walk to the edge of the tub; you turn on the water; you step under the water; you rub yourself with soap; you rinse; you step out; you dry yourself; you walk back to the bed. Twelve steps, which sounded to me then as onerous as a tour through the stations of the cross" (*The Noonday Demon*, 52–53).

Karl Jaspers, a brilliant clinician of the twentieth century, describes the immobility of depression in connection with the fear of economic loss: "*Pure depression* is the opposite of this [mania] in every respect. Its central core is formed from an equally unmotivated and profound sadness to which is added a retardation of psychic events, which is as subjectively painful as it is objectively visible. All instinctual activities are subjected to it. The patient does not want to do anything. The reduced impulse to move and do things turns into complete immobility. No decision can be made and no activity begun. Associations are not available. Patients have no ideas. They complain of a complete disruption of memory. They feel their poverty of performance and complain of their inefficiency, lack of emotion and emptiness. They feel profound gloom as a sensation in the chest or body as if it could be laid hold of there. The depth of their melancholy makes them see the world as grim and grey. They look for the unfavourable and unhappy elements in everything. They accuse themselves of much past guile (self-accusations, notions of having sinned). The present has nothing for them (notions of worthlessness) and the future lies horrifyingly before them (notions of poverty, etc.)" (*General Psychopathology*, 2:597).

10. Denby, *American Sucker*, 7–8.

11. Zürn, *The Man of Jasmine and Other Texts*, 43.

12. Behrman, *Electroboy*, 80.

13. Cramer, *Confessions of a Street Addict*, 92, 124.

14. Bandler, "Can Your Workers Carry a Bowling Ball with a Rubber Band?"

15. The theme of deliberately inducing mania has also been picked up at the grassroots level. On the Web site of the Icarus Project, a forum for people living under the description of bipolar disorder, there is a thread within an online discussion forum that is devoted to inducing mania. The discussion covers possible methods—sleep less, increase caffeine, alter diet—interwoven with plenty of caution about trying to induce mania at all. The Icarus Project was founded to "provide a place to discuss and connect around the paradox of 'navigating the space between brilliance and madness.'" The specific link to the discussion thread is http://www.theicarusproject.net/community/discussionboards/viewtopic .php?t=5048.

16. Denby, "The Quarter of Living Dangerously."

17. As depicted impressionistically in the film *Enron* and captured successfully by firms like Thrillseekers Unlimited, corporations are big customers of extreme sports adventures. Friedman, "What's the Lure of the Edge?"

18. Sutton, "The Weird Rules of Creativity."

19. Ibid., 102.

20. Keynes, *The General Theory of Employment, Interest, and Money,* 161–62.

21. Koppl, "Retrospectives: Animal Spirits," describes how animal spirits worked for Keynes; Moggridge, "Correspondence," has the evidence that Keynes was drawing upon Descartes' notions of fiery particles in the blood that move the nerves and muscles.

22. In psychology, there have been careful assessments of what is called "optimistic bias" as it might differ between schizophrenic patients and healthy comparison subjects. Optimistic bias occurs when a person (unrealistically) evaluates his or her likelihood to experience adverse events as lower than others'. In one study, the healthy comparison subjects showed a greater degree of optimistic bias (and therefore a greater degree of unrealistic judgment) than the schizophrenic patients did. See Prentice, Gold, and Carpenter, "Optimistic Bias in the Perception of Personal Risk." I have not been able to locate any comparative study of bipolar patients in a manic phase, but these experimental results could be taken to suggest that "normal" Americans are unrealistically optimistic.

23. See "Mood Swings and Downswings," 2002, Economist.com.

24. Greider, *One World, Ready or Not*, 227–28.
25. Uchitelle, "Confusion as an Economic Indicator," 1.
26. R. Abelson, "A Sudden Breakout of Mad-Bull Disease," C1.
27. Magnier, "Dramatic Surge in Japan's Yen Spurs New Fear."
28. T. Walker, "Market Cools Down While the Weather Heats Up," F1.
29. Gillmor, "High-Tech High-Fliers Get Hit Hard," E1.
30. Kahn, "The Markets: Market Place."
31. Denby, *American Sucker*, 111.
32. Cramer, *Confessions of a Street Addict*.
33. Glassman, "Psyching out Mr. Market."
34. Mann, "Mr. Market Is a Manic-Depressive Idiot."
35. Ignatius, "Our Bipolar Economy."
36. "Barclays Capital Newsletter." Economists such as Richard Thaler or Robert Schiller try to preserve the rationality of markets by seeing the source of markets' irrationality in the irrational emotions of the populace. In *Irrational Exuberance*, Schiller relies on the influence of newspapers and other mass information technology, together with psychological factors such as overconfidence and magical thinking, to explain the contemporary speculative bubble. He sees market highs and lows as inevitable: "We cannot completely protect society from the effects of waves of irrational exuberance or irrational pessimism—emotional reactions that are themselves part of the human condition" (142–43). This work is attracting attention in the mainstream press. The *New York Times* reported on Thaler's approach: "Rejecting the narrow, mechanical *homo economicus* that serves as a basis for neoclassical theory, [Richard] Thaler proposed that most people actually behave like . . . people! They are prone to error, irrationality and emotion, and they act in ways not always consistent with maximizing their own financial well being" (Lowenstein, "Exuberance Is Rational," 68, 70). Thaler's work, called behavioral economics, ties research in behaviorist psychology with economic decisions and judgments. In so far as it is a dissenting view in economics that is gaining currency, one that places irrational emotion at the center of human economic behavior, it is relevant to our changing cultural understanding of the nature and source of irrationality. The awarding of the Nobel Prize to behavioral economist Daniel Kahneman in 2002 has driven an additional wedge into the assumptions of rational choice economics.
37. Farrell, "Capitalism's 'Animal Spirits' Endure."
38. Griffin, "Looking for the Prevailing Wind."

39. From a writer who looks back at the breaking of the mania come some reasons for how things got so irrational: "This mania can only end the way all prior manias have ended—with public distrust of the very professionals that coerced them into the madness in the first place. . . . By its very definition, a mania is a time of widespread hysteria and faulty rationales. However, in order to believe, investors have to be convinced that there is a rational basis to their actions. This can only occur when certain participants are able to devise untruths and cajole the public" (A. Newman, "Pictures of a Stock Market Mania").

40. Dash, *Tulipomania*.

41. Ibid., 217.

42. Tobias, *Extraordinary Popular Delusions and the Madness of Crowds*, x–xi.

43. Kindleberger, *Manias, Panics and Crashes*, 1.

44. Ibid., 23.

45. Ibid., 20. Business writers frequently invoke this set of books to shed light on the contemporary oscillations in market value. Smith, "All's Well That Ends Like Tulip Mania."

46. Both Adam Smith and Condorcet were preoccupied with economic sentiments: "The essential disposition of moral life, for Condorcet as for Smith, is to think oneself into the feelings of other people; to feel sympathy. This is similar, in its reflexiveness, to the disposition of economic life. To think about economic decisions is to think about how other people think." The writings of Smith and Condorcet were concerned with how social order could be assured if individuals made their own decisions in the marketplace without overarching controls from a government. Rothschild, *Economic Sentiments*, 224. For a nuanced discussion of the eighteenth-century emergence of the notion of "interests," a hybrid condition between the "passions" and "reason," see Hirschman, *The Passions and the Interests*, 42–48.

47. Pocock, *Virtue, Commerce, and History*, 112–13.

48. Ibid., 114.

49. Corrigan, *Business of the Heart*, 62.

50. Ibid.

51. Ibid., 229.

52. Ibid., 253–54.

53. Ibid., 128.

54. Pocock, *Virtue, Commerce, and History*, 114.

55. Rosenbaum and Seligman, *Abnormal Psychology*, 403.

56. Gay, "PBS' New Film about Theodore Roosevelt Chronicles the Many Sides of a Passionate, Energetic Man."

57. PBS, *Shackleton's Voyage of Endurance*.

58. Salamon, "Shackleton Marches On."

59. Capparell, "Explorers: Get Ready for Shackleton-Mania."

60. Capparell, "In the Lead."

61. MacFarquhar, "The Gilder Effect," 121–22.

62. Farnham, "Crazy and in Charge." Charles Nuckolls analyzes the categories in the DSM in terms of the premium American culture places on flamboyant self-dramatization as an extreme form of independence (*Culture*, 205–6).

63. Fineman, "Rove at War"; Amelio, *On the Firing Line*; Kitchen, "Using Heels-over-Heads Approach at Conference."

Elsewhere in the global corporate world, too, business leaders are turning up as virile manics. In a news story in the *Canadian Business* magazine, one that was well-known among my fieldwork interlocutors, Pierre Karl Péladeau, CEO of the Montreal-based global communications company Quebecor, was said to have "the CEO's Disease." Péladeau had gone public about his diagnosis of manic depression, and the article placed him in the company of "the most colorful and ambitious business professionals of our times" for whom manic depression had been a "driving force." In addition, he shared a place beside the magazine's "Peers of the Abyss" sidebar, featuring Winston Churchill, Ted Turner, and Canadian business leaders Robert Campeau and Murray Pezim. But when Péladeau first recognized himself in the descriptions of manic depression in Ronald Fieve's book *Moodswing*, he was not pleased. "I hated it; I would have preferred a heart attack. I thought it was a woman's illness" (Tillson, "The CEO's Disease"). Other international magnates seem to revel in the zaniness of their image. Richard Branson, the British founder of the Virgin Group, is called "the flamboyant CEO," (1) who is "charismatic and competitive" with a "skillfully controlled aggressive streak," a "rock and roll businessman," (2) who combines "cunning, naivety [*sic*] and manic competitiveness," (3) and has "manic-looking eyes" (4) and "manic energy" (5). Citations are as follows: (1) Nandwani, "The Flamboyant CEO"; (2) Ligerakis, "The Challenger: Richard Branson"; (3) Rawnsley, "Review of 'Richard Branson; the Inside Story' by Mick Brown"; (4) "No More Branson Nonsense"; (5) Ellen, "Why Richard Branson's Number Is Up."

64. Walker, "Conscience Undercover."

65. Kingston, "Minding Martha's Business."

66. Grant, *Minding Mr. Market*, xxi.

67. Arora, "Market Movers: Mood Swings."

68. Harvey, *Spaces of Hope*, 154.

69. Harvey, *A Brief History of Neoliberalism*.

70. W. Brown, "Neo-Liberalism and the End of Liberal Democracy"; Lemke, "'The Birth of Biopolitics.'"

71. Polanyi, *The Great Transformation*, 3.

72. Gerth and Mills, *From Max Weber*, 281.

73. Walter Benjamin's Arcades Project contains much that develops Weber's insights on this point. Benjamin contested the claim—often mistakenly attributed to Weber—that modernity, bringing the complete triumph of abstract, formal reason in many major institutions and cultural forms, led to the disenchantment of the world. Benjamin thought that even though social and cultural institutions had become rationalized in form, cultural life became reenchanted with irrational content from dream images and mythical figures. He showed that "underneath the surface of increasing systemic rationalization, on an unconscious 'dream' level, the new urban-industrial world had become fully reenchanted. In the modern city, as in the ur-forests of another era, the 'threatening and alluring face' of myth was alive and everywhere. It peered out of wall posters advertising 'toothpaste for giants,' and whispered its presence in the most rationalized urban plans that, 'with their uniform streets and endless rows of buildings, have realized the dreamed-of architecture of the ancients: the labyrinth.' It appeared, prototypically, in the arcades, where 'the commodities are suspended and shoved together in such boundless confusion, that [they appear] like images out of the most incoherent dreams.'" Buck-Morss notes perceptively that Weber actually did appreciate the persistence of the irrational in modern life (*The Dialectics of Seeing*, 254).

74. Gerth and Mills, *From Max Weber*, 88.

75. Ibid., 182.

76. Scaff, *Fleeing the Iron Cage*, 88.

77. Goldman, *Max Weber and Thomas Mann*, 28–29.

78. Weber, *The Protestant Ethic and the Spirit of Capitalism*, 54–55.

79. Ibid., quoted in Goldman, *Max Weber and Thomas Mann*, 29.

80. Gerth and Mills, *From Max Weber*, 136.

81. Weber, *The Protestant Ethic and the Spirit of Capitalism*, 137.

82. Ibid., 136.

83. Fieve, *Moodswing*, 24.

84. Jamison, *An Unquiet Mind*, 74.

85. Ho, "Liquefying Corporations and Communities."

86. Gusterson, *Nuclear Rites*, 111.

87. Kraepelin, *One Hundred Hears of Psychiatry.*

88. Rosenberg, "The Tyranny of Diagnosis," 250.

89. Painton, "The Taming of Ted Turner."

90. Auletta, "The Lost Tycoon."

91. The mortality rate for untreated manic-depressive patients is higher than it is for most types of heart disease and many types of cancer. At least 20 percent of deaths among manic-depressive patients are "secondary to suicide." Goodwin and Jamison, *Manic-Depressive Illness*, 227, 228.

92. In addition, in many cultures, wrongful death, incomplete burial, suicide, and other socially anomalous events in which life and death collide often produce restless ghosts in their wake. See Hertz, *Death and the Right Hand*; Mueggler, *The Age of Wild Ghosts*.

93. In Roland Barthes' terms, this is a "punctum." I am indebted here to Gordon's *Ghostly Matters*.

94. "Pocket Quiz," Diversions, April 7, 2002, available from http://www.economist.com/diversions/pocketquiz.

95. "Barclays Capital Newsletter."

96. Cultural critic Slavoj Žižek explains that to be willing to die for some cause is to have the "very excess of life." This means terrorists are fascinating because they are "more alive" than others and it means the way to defeat terrorists is to become as alive as they are. Under this logic, a war in which American citizens die is the simplest way for the nation to demonstrate its excess of life. Žižek is not condoning terrorism: as Walter Benn Michaels clarifies, "the question of whether we are doing the right thing has been redescribed as the question of whether we are living our lives to the fullest (whether we're as alive as the suicide bombers.)" Žižek, *Welcome to the Desert of the Real*, 103, quoted in Michaels, *The Shape of the Signifier*, 176.

CONCLUSION

1. Psychologists have studied "depressive realism," a pattern in which, under experimental conditions, depressed people judge their control over events more accurately than nondepressed people do (Teasdale and Barnard, *Affect, Cognition and Change*). Recent evidence has complicated

the picture by showing that depressed people take fewer factors into account when assessing their ability to control experimental events. On these findings, depressed people actually make less accurate judgments than those who are not depressed (Msetfi et al., "Depressive Realism and Outcome Density Bias in Contingency Judgments"). These results are intriguing, but the experimental situation (turning on a lightbulb that only works part of the time) is a long way from the larger issues I am considering, such as assessing the quality of social life in the United States.

2. Huxley, *Brave New World*, 78.

3. Ibid., 92.

4. Stevenson, "Aftermath," 4.

5. Ibid.

6. McManamy, *McMan's Depression and Bipolar Weekly*.

7. Clark, "On the Brink of War."

8. New York Times Editorial, "The Best-Selling Post-Mortem."

9. Abelson, "Bad News Bulls."

10. Ibid.

11. In 2003, the New School in New York City ran a public relations campaign on billboards for the continuous education they provide, lest one fall behind in the Darwinist struggle for survival. In 2005 Microsoft rolled out a print and Web media campaign for upgrades to Office 2003. The ads depict dinosaur-headed humans who begin to realize that they have been working in a bygone era left behind by others who have already evolved with the help of the upgrade. See http://www.microsoft.com/office/evolve/default.mspx (accessed June 20, 2005).

12. Greenhouse, "The Mood at Work," provides statistics on the level of anger, pessimism, and anxiety among Americans who are working, in contrast to the characteristic ebullience of the 1990s.

13. Brooks, "More Than Money," A23.

14. Ibid.

15. This passage is often misunderstood because of the misleading translation in the popular "Gerth and Mills" English edition of Weber's writings: "An unsere Arbeit gehen und der 'Forderung des Tages' gerecht warden — menschlich sowohl wie beruflich. Die aber ist schlicht und einfach, wenn jeder den Dämon findet und ihm gehorcht, der seines Lebens Fäden halt" is translated there, "We shall set to work and meet the 'demands of the day,' in human relations as well as in our vocation. This, however, is plain and simple, if each finds and obeys the demon who holds the fibers of his

very life" (Weber, *From Max Weber: Essays in Sociology*, 156). There is a more accurate translation in Weber, *The Vocation Lectures*: "We must go about our work and meet 'the challenges of the day'—both in our human relations and our vocation. But that moral is simple and straightforward if each person finds and obeys the daemon that holds the threads of *his* life" (31; emphasis in original).

16. Martha Nussbaum provides a rich gloss for the Greek concept of eudaimonia (her preferred spelling). Eudaimonia is "human flourishing, a complete human life," and refers to everything a person imbues with intrinsic value (*Upheavals of Thought*, 32).

17. Doris Chang usefully surveys the politics of the process by which the supplement came into being in "An Introduction to the Politics of Science."

18. See Orr, "The Ecstasy of Miscommunication," 161. See also Orr's innovative history and ethnography of "the psychic life of panic" (*Panic Diaries*).

19. Safire, "Beware 'Animal Spirits.'"

20. Brooks, "A Nation of Grinders," 16.

21. Ibid.

22. The subject would take me too far afield, but this description of mania overlaps in some ways with the "pathological narcissist," a personality type that has been described as a radical conformist who paradoxically sees himself as an outlaw. Žižek, *Looking Awry*, 102–3.

23. Serres, "The Geometry of the Incommunicable," 52.

24. Foucault, "Madness, the Absence of Work." In Michel Serres's words, subjects would arise "who can finally speak of their own country, conceive of their own domain" ("The Geometry of the Incommunicable," 51–52). For Foucault, this would alter the "precarious . . . relationship of our culture to this truth about itself, far away and inverted, which it discovers over and over in madness" ("Madness, the Absence of Work," 98).

25. Foucault, "Madness, the Absence of Work," 99.

26. Ibid. Emphasis in original.

27. I am indebted to Jackie Orr for this point.

28. Another way to approach this issue is to work toward a more effective definition of mental illness. Jerome Wakefield develops this approach as a way of clarifying the sometimes muddled definitions of "disorder" and "disability" in the DSM. These definitions are, I would agree, badly in need of clarification, in particular, as Wakefield persuasively argues,

to clarify what "dysfunction" means. The problems that concern me in this book are quite different, however, and would persist no matter how mental illnesses were redefined. As long as "dysfunction" in the definition of mental illness was still connected to irrationality, the social processes I describe—in which the rational and irrational are inextricably intertwined—retain their relevance. For specific analysis of problems with the definition of social phobia, see Wakefield, "Disorder as Harmful Dysfunction." Wakefield, Horwitz, and Schmitz, "Are We Overpathologizing the Socially Anxious?"

29. Chaffin, *Manic Depression*.

References

Abelson, Alan. "Bad News Bulls." March 11, 2002, http://online.wsj.com/barrons (accessed May 1, 2002).

Abelson, Reed. "A Sudden Breakout of Mad-Bull Disease." *New York Times*, November 2, 1997, C1, 12.

Acoftil. "Neurontin Stories?" 2002, alt.support.depression.manic.moderated (accessed July 15, 2003).

"Advertising: The Cause of High Drug Costs? DTC Gets Most of the Blame." Pharmrep.com (Pharmaceutical Representative Magazine). October 1999, http://www.pharmrep.com/xml/9910/991001.asp (accessed July 3, 2003).

Ahern, Emily M. "The Problem of Efficacy: Strong and Weak Illocutionary Acts." *Man* 14, no. 1 (1979): 1–17.

Akiskal, H. S., M. L. Bourgeois, J. Angst, R. Post, H. Moller, and R. Hirschfeld. "Re-Evaluating the Prevalence of and Diagnostic Composition within the Broad Clinical Spectrum of Bipolar Disorders." *Journal of Affective Disorders* 59 Supplement 1 (2000): S5-S30.

Amelio, Gilbert. *On the Firing Line: My 500 Days at Apple*. New York: HarperBusiness, 1998.

American Psychiatric Association Task Force on DSM-IV. *Diagnostic and Statistical Manual of Mental Disorders: DSM-IV-TR*. 4th ed. Washington, DC: American Psychiatric Association, 2000.

"Americans Should Be Glad That the Iowa Process Helped Display Another Side of the Candidate." *Telegraph Herald*, January 26, 2004.

Anderson, Benedict R. O'G. *Imagined Communities: Reflections on the Origin and Spread of Nationalism*. 1983. Rev. and extended ed. New York: Verso, 1991.

Anscombe, G.E.M. *Intention*. Ithaca: Cornell University Press, 1963.

Arenson, Karen. "Worried Colleges Step up Efforts over Suicide." *New York Times*, December 3, 2004, 1, 20.

Arora, Anjali. "Market Movers: Mood Swings." July 21, 2000, http://www.thestandard.com (accessed June 26, 2002).

Auletta, Ken. "The Lost Tycoon." *New Yorker*, April 23, 2001.

Austin, J. L. *How to Do Things with Words*. Trans. J. O. Urmson. New York: Oxford University Press, 1965.

Ayd, Frank J. *Recognizing the Depressed Patient: With Essentials of Management and Treatment*. New York: Grune and Stratton, 1961.

Baard, Erik. "The Guilt-Free Soldier." January 28, 2003, http://www.villagevoice.com/news/0304,baard,41331,1.html

Baldwin, James. *Notes of a Native Son*. Boston: Beacon Press, 1955.

Bandler, James. "Can Your Workers Carry a Bowling Ball with a Rubber Band?" April 12, 2000, http://interactive.wsj.com (accessed April 13, 2000).

Baran, Paul A., and Paul M. Sweezy. *Monopoly Capital: An Essay on the American Economic and Social Order*. New York: Monthly Review, 1966.

"Barclays Capital Newsletter." June 2001, http://www.barclays.com (accessed April, 2002).

Barrett, Robert J. *The Psychiatric Team and the Social Definition of Schizophrenia*. Cambridge: Cambridge University Press, 1996.

Bateson, Gregory. *Steps to an Ecology of Mind*. New York: Ballantine Books, 1972.

Bauman, Richard. "Verbal Art as Performance." *American Anthropologist* 77, no. 2 (1975): 290–311.

———. *Verbal Art as Performance*. Prospect Heights, IL: Waveland Press, 1977.

Bedford, Errol. "Emotions." *Proceedings of the Aristotelian Society* 57 n.s., no. 12 (1957): 281–304.

Behrman, Andy. *Electroboy: A Memoir of Mania*. 1st ed. New York: Random House, 2002.

Benjamin, Walter. *The Arcades Project*. Trans. Howard Eiland and Kevin McLaughlin. Cambridge, MA: Harvard University Press, 1999.

Bentley, Eric. "Man's Despair, and Hope." *New York Times*, September 3, 1977, 10.

Berman, Marshall. *All That Is Solid Melts into Air*. New York: Simon and Schuster, 1982.

Berresem, Hanjo. "Emotions Flattened and Scattered: 'Borderline Syndromes' and 'Multiple Personality Disorders' in Contemporary American Fiction." In *Emotions in Postmodernism*, ed. Gerhard Hoffman and Alfred Hornung, 271–308. Heidelberg: Universitatsverlag C. Winter, 1997.

Berrios, German E. *The History of Mental Symptoms: Descriptive Psychopathology since the Nineteenth Century*. Cambridge: Cambridge University Press, 1996.

———. "The Psychopathology of Affectivity: Conceptual and Historical Aspects." *Psychological Medicine* 15 (1985): 745–58.

Berrios, G. E., and R. Hauser. "Clinical Sections." In *A History of Clinical Psychiatry: The Origin and History of Psychiatric Disorders*, ed. German E. Berrios and Roy Porter, 280–91. New York: New York University Press, 1995.

Billig, Michael. *Freudian Repression: Conversation Creating the Unconscious*. Cambridge: Cambridge University Press, 1999.

bipolar news. "What Is Life Charting?" Last updated December 4, 2002, http://www.bipolarnews.org/Life%20Charting%20Description.htm (accessed June 9, 2003).

Blackmun, Lisa. *Hearing Voices: Embodiment and Experience*. London: Free Association, 2001.

Blakeslee, Sandra. "Humanity? Maybe It's in the Wiring." *New York Times*, December 9, 2003, F1, 4.

Boodman, Sandra G. "Going to Extremes: Experts Question Rise in Pediatric Diagnosis of Bipolar Illness, a Serious Mood Disorder." *Washington Post*, February 15, 2005, 1.

Boon, James A. *Affinities and Extremes: Crisscrossing the Bittersweet Ethnology of East Indies History, Hindu-Balinese Culture, and Indo-European Allure*. Chicago: University of Chicago Press, 1990.

Bordogna, Francesca. "The Psychology and Physiology of Temperament: Pragmatism in Context." *Journal of the History of Behavioral Sciences* 37, no. 1 (2001): 3–25.

Bourdieu, Pierre. *Distinction: A Social Critique of the Judgement of Taste.* Trans. Richard Nice. Cambridge, MA: Harvard University Press, 1990.

Bowring, Margaret Ann, and Maria Kovacs. "Difficulties in Diagnosing Manic Disorders among Children and Adolescents." *Journal of the American Academy of Child and Adolescent Psychiatry* 31, no. 4 (1992): 611–14.

Braun, Wendy. "The Challenge of Being Young, Creative and Bipolar." *Saturday Evening Post*, January/February 2003, 50–55.

Brenneis, Donald. "Dramatic Gestures: The Fiji Indian Pancayat as Therapeutic Event." In *Disentangling: Conflict Discourse in Pacific Societies*, ed. Karen A. Watson-Gegeo and Geoffrey M. White, 214–38. Palo Alto, CA: Stanford University Press, 1990.

Brink, Susan. "CEO Sufferings Trickle Down." *U.S. News & World Report*, September 29, 2003, 60.

Brooks, David. "More Than Money." *New York Times*, March 2, 2004, A23.

———. "A Nation of Grinders." *New York Times Magazine*, June 29, 2003, 14, 16.

Brown, Les. "Lithium Use in 'Maude,' Medical Issue." *New York Times*, January 22, 1976, 52.

Brown, Wendy. "Neo-Liberalism and the End of Liberal Democracy." *Theory and Event* 7, no. 1 (2003): 1–43.

Browne, Janet. "Darwin and the Face of Madness." In *Anatomy of Madness: Essays in the History of Psychiatry*, ed. Roy Porter, W. F. Bynum, and Michael Shepherd, 151–65. London: Tavistock, 1985.

Buck-Morss, Susan. "The City as Dreamworld and Catastrophe." *October* 73 (Summer 1995): 3–26.

———. *The Dialectics of Seeing: Walter Benjamin and the Arcades Project.* Cambridge, MA: MIT Press, 1989.

Bureau of Labor Statistics. "State and Area Employment, Hours, and Earnings." U.S. Department of Labor, http://data.bls.gov/PDQ/servlet/SurveyOutputServlet?series_id=SMS2400000300000001&data_tool=%2522EaG%2522 (accessed August 12, 2005).

Burton, Richard. *The Anatomy of Melancholy.* New York Review of Books Classics Series. New York: New York Review of Books, 2001.

Busfield, Joan, and Jo Campling. *Men, Women, and Madness: Understanding Gender and Mental Disorder.* New York: New York University Press, 1996.

Butler, Judith. *Bodies That Matter: On the Discursive Limits of "Sex."* New York: Routledge, 1993.

———. *Excitable Speech: A Politics of the Performative.* New York: Routledge, 1997.

———. *Gender Trouble: Feminism and the Subversion of Identity.* New York: Routledge, 1990.

———. "Performative Acts and Gender Constitution: An Essay in Phenomenology and Feminist Theory." *Theatre Journal* 49, no. 1 (1988): 519–31.

Butler, Judith. *The Psychic Life of Power: Theories in Subjection.* Stanford: Stanford University Press, 1997.

Butterfield, Fox. "This Way Madness Lies: A Fall from Grace to Prison." *New York Times*, April 21, 1996, 1, 14.

Cameron, Deborah, and Don Kulick. "Introduction: Language and Desire in Theory and Practice." *Language & Communication*, no. 23 (2003): 93–105.

Canetti, Elias. *Crowds and Power.* Trans. Carol Stewart. New York: Farrar, Straus and Giroux, 1960.

Capparell, Stephanie. "Explorers: Get Ready for Shackleton-Mania." *Wall Street Journal*, April 2, 1998, B1.

———. "In the Lead: Shackleton's Techniques for Surviving Antarctica Inspire Business Leaders." *Wall Street Journal*, December 19, 2000, B1.

Cardinal, Marie. *The Words to Say It.* Cambridge, MA: Van Vactor and Goodheart, 1983.

Carey, Benedict. "Use of Antipsychotics by the Young Rose Fivefold." *New York Times*, June 6, 2006, 18.

Carlson, Gabrielle A. "Mania and ADHD: Comorbidity or Confusion." *Journal of Affective Disorders* 51 (1998): 177–87.

Carter, Rita. *Mapping the Mind.* Berkeley: University of California Press, 1999.

Chaffin, C. E. "Manic-Depression." Winter 1997/Spring 1998, http://www.albany.edu/~interfac/if14/c_e_chaffin.html (accessed 2000).

Chaffin, Joshua. "How Brokers with the Blues May Add to Market Miseries: Clinical Depression on Wall Street Can Affect Share Prices." *Financial Times*, March 8, 2002, 20.

Chang, Doris F. "An Introduction to the Politics of Science: Culture, Race, Ethnicity, and the Supplement to the Surgeon General's Report on Mental Health." *Culture, Medicine, and Psychiatry* 27 (2003): 373–83.

"Chemistry of Insanity." *New York Times*, June 11, 1938, 14.

Chen, Nancy N. *Breathing Spaces: Qigong, Psychiatry, and Healing in China.* New York: Columbia University Press, 2003.

Clark, Andrew. "On the Brink of War: Wall Street." *The Guardian*, September 21, 2001.

Clifford, James. *Routes: Travel and Translation in the Late 20th Century.* Cambridge, MA: Harvard University Press, 1997.

"Cocktail Hour." 1998, http://groups.google.com/group/alt.support.depression.manic/browse_thread/thread/ea1f3f35f7fc1813/6baf9cf659040a43?lnk=st&q=anything+but+the+barest+essentials&rnum=3#6baf9cf659040a43 (accessed April 9, 2000).

Cohen, Mabel Blake, Grace Baker, Robert A. Cohen, Frieda Fromm-Reichmann, and Edith V. Weigert. "An Intensive Study of Twelve Cases of Manic-Depressive Psychosis." *Psychiatry* 17 (1954): 103–37.

Collier, Jane F., Bill Maurer, and Liliana Suárez-Navaz. "Sanctioned Identities: Legal Constructions of Modern Personhood." *Identities* 2, no. 1–2 (1995): 1–27.

Comaroff, Jean, and John L. Comaroff. "Millennial Capitalism: First Thoughts on a Second Coming." In *Millennial Capitalism and the Culture of Neoliberalism,* ed. Jean Comaroff and John L. Comaroff, 1–56. Durham: Duke University Press, 2001.

Conrad, Joseph. *Heart of Darkness*. Cambridge, MA: R. Bentley, 1981.

Corrigan, John. *Business of the Heart: Religion and Emotion in the Nineteenth Century*. Berkeley: University of California Press, 2002.

Cramer, James J. *Confessions of a Street Addict*. New York: Simon and Schuster, 2002.

Crapanzano, Vincent. *Hermes' Dilemma and Hamlet's Desire: On the Epistemology of Interpretation*. Cambridge, MA: Harvard University Press, 1992.

———. *Tuhami: Portrait of a Moroccan*. Chicago: University of Chicago Press, 1980.

Crockford, David Neil, and Nady el-Guebaly. "Psychiatric Comorbidity in Pathological Gambling: A Critical Review." *Canadian Journal of Psychiatry* 43 (1998): 43–50.

Cushman, Philip. *Constructing the Self, Constructing America: A Cultural History of Psychotherapy*. Reading, MA: Addison-Wesley, 1995.

Das, Veena. "Wittgenstein and Anthropology." *Annual Review of Anthropology* 27 (1998): 171–95.

Dash, Mike. *Tulipomania: The Story of the World's Most Coveted Flower and the Extraordinary Passions It Aroused*. New York: Random House, 1999.

Davenport, Yolande B. "Manic-Depressive Illness: Psychodynamic Features of Multigenerational Families." *American Journal of Orthopsychiatry* 49, no. 1 (1979): 24–35.

David, A. S. "Illness and Insight." *British Journal of Hospital Medicine* 48, no. 10 (1992): 652–54.

———. "Insight and Psychosis." *British Journal of Psychiatry* 156 (1990): 798–808.

Denby, David. *American Sucker*. Little, Brown, 2004.

———. "The Quarter of Living Dangerously." *New Yorker* 76, no. 9 (2000), http://proquest.umi.com/pqdweb?did=52772385&Fmt=2&clientId=9269&RQT=309&VName=PQD (accessed October 15, 2006).

Denicoff, K. D., G. S. Leverich, W. A. Nolen, A. J. Rush, S. L. McElroy, P. E. Keck, T. Suppes, L. L. Altshuler, R. Kupka, M. A. Frye, J. Hatef, M. A. Brotman, and R. M. Post. "Validation of the Prospective NIMH-Life-Chart Method (NIMH-LCM-P) for Longitudinal Assessment of Bipolar Illness." *Psychological Medicine Med* 30, no. 6 (2000): 1391–97.

"Depressed and on Welfare." *60 Minutes*. CBS News, CBS Worldwide.

Derrida, Jacques. "Signature Event Context." In *Limited Inc.*, 1–24. Evanston, IL: Northwestern University Press, 1988.

DeWitt, T., and Y. Liu. "The Customer Orientation-Loyalty Model: The Role of Emotional Contagion and Rapport in the Service Encounter." *American Marketing Association Conference Proceedings* 13 (2002): 321.

"Display Ad 52—No Title." *New York Times (1857–Current file)*, ProQuest Historical Newspapers, October 3, 1989, C19.

Dodds, E. R. *The Greeks and the Irrational*. Berkeley: University of California Press, 1951.

Donzelot, Jacques. "Pleasure in Work." In *The Foucault Effect: Studies in Governmentality*, ed. Graham Burchell, Colin Gordon, and Peter Miller, 251–80. Chicago: University of Chicago Press, 1991.

Dror, Otniel E. "Counting the Affects: Discoursing in Numbers." *Social Research* 68, no. 2 (2001): 357–78.

"DTC Advertising Spending Increases." Pharmrep.com (Pharmaceutical Representative Magazine). December 2000, http://www.pharmrep.com/xml/0012/001202.asp (accessed July 3, 2003).

Duke, Patty, and Gloria Hochman. *A Brilliant Madness: Living with Manic-Depressive Illness*. New York: Bantam Books, 1992.

Dumit, Joseph. "Drugs for Life." *Molecular Interventions* 2, no. 3 (2002): 124–27.

———. *Picturing Personhood: Brain Scans and Biomedical Identity*. Princeton: Princeton University Press, 2003.

Economist.com. "Diversions." http://www.economist.com/diversions/pocketquiz (accessed October 23, 2005).

Editorial, *New York Times*. "The Best-Selling Post-Mortem." November 1, 2004, 24.

Ehrenberg, Alain. *La fatigue d'être soi: Dépression et société*. Paris: Odile Jacob, 1998.

Ekman, P., and R. Davidson. *The Nature of Emotion: Fundamental Questions*. New York: Oxford University Press, 1994.

Ellen, Barbara. 2000. "Why Richard Branson's Number Is Up." *The Observer*, Guardian Newspapers Limited, http://web.lexis-nexis.com/universe/document?_m=6186b62ed448c79bc6f741cd45c7e44f&_cod (accessed June 26, 2002).

Ellenberger, Henri F. *The Discovery of the Unconscious: The History and Evolution of Dynamic Psychiatry*. New York: Basic Books, 1970.

"End Arrives for Bethlehem Steel." *Baltimore Business Journal*, American City Business Journals. 2003, http://baltimore.bizjournals.com/baltimore/stories/2001/10/29/editorial1.html (accessed January 2, 2005).

Eng, David L., and David Kazanjian, eds. *Loss: The Politics of Mourning*. Berkeley: University of California Press, 2003.

Engstrom, Eric J. "Kraepelin: Social Section." In *A History of Clinical Psychiatry: The Origin and History of Psychiatric Disorders*, ed. German E. Berrios and Roy Porter, 292–301. New York: New York University Press, 1995.

Epstein, Steven. *Impure Science: AIDS, Activism, and the Politics of Knowledge*. Berkeley: University of California Press, 1996.

Espeland, Wendy Nelson, and Mitchell L. Stevens. "Commensuration as a Social Process." *Annual Review of Sociology* 24 (1998): 313–43.

Estroff, Sue E. *Making It Crazy: An Ethnography of Psychiatric Clients in an American Community*. Berkeley: University of California, 1985.

Evenson, Brad. "Is 'Soft' Depression Price of Greatness?: Mild Bipolarity Is Affiliated with Charisma, Creativity." *National Post* (Canada), March 9, 2004, 1.

Ewen, Stuart. *All Consuming Images: The Politics of Style in Contemporary Culture*. New York: Basic Books, 1988.

"Famous People Who Have Suffered from Depression or Manic-Depression." 2005, http://www.geocities.com/coverbridge2k/artsci/famous_people_depression .html (accessed March 12, 2005).

Fanon, Franz. *Black Skin, White Masks*. Trans. Charles Lam Markmann. New York: Grove Press, 1967.

Farnham, Alan. "Crazy and in Charge: Brilliant Tycoons Have Had a Tendency to Get Eccentric, or Worse." *Time* 152, no. 23 (December 7, 1998): 207–8.

Farrell, Christopher. "Capitalism's 'Animal Spirits' Endure." *BusinessWeek*, October 26, 2001.

Fidler, Donald. *Affective Disorders: Mania and Depression*. Chapel Hill, NC: Health Sciences Consortium, 1987. VHS video.

Fieve, Ronald R. *Moodswing: The Third Revolution in Psychiatry*. New York: William Morrow, 1975.

Fineman, Howard. "Rove at War." *Newsweek* 146 (July 25, 2005): 26–34.

Fink, Candida, and Joe Kraynak. *Bipolar Disorder for Dummies*. Indianapolis: Wiley Publishing, 2005.

Finkelstein, B. A. "Lithium Therapy." *New York Times*, January 26, 1969, 21.

Fintushel, Noelle. "Are Bad Moods Catching?" *Parents* 71 (1996): 106–8.

Fischhoff, Baruch. "A Hero in Every Aisle Seat." *New York Times*, August 7, 2005, 13.

Foucault, Michel. *Discipline and Punish: The Birth of the Prison*. New York: Vintage, 1979.

———. *The History of Sexuality: Vol. 1*. New York: Vintage, 1980.

———. "Madness, the Absence of Work." In *Foucault and His Interlocutors*, ed. Arnold I. Davidson, 97–106. Chicago: University of Chicago Press, 1997.

Francomano, Robert M. 2000. "DTC Advertising: A Matter of Perspective." Pharmrep.com (Pharmaceutical Representative Magazine). July 2000, http:// www.pharmrep.com/xml/0007/000713.asp (accessed July 3, 2003).

Freud, Sigmund. *The Ego and the Id*. Trans. Joan Riviere. Ed. James Strachey. New York: W. W. Norton, 1960.

——— "Mourning and Melancholia." In *Collected Papers*, ed. Ernst Jones, 152–70. New York: Basic Books, 1959.

Friedman, Richard A. "What's the Lure of the Edge? The Answer Is All in Their Heads." *New York Times*, June 20, 2005, F7.

Gaines, Atwood. "From DSM-I to III-R; Voices of Self, Mastery and the Other: A Cultural Constructivist Reading of U.S. Psychiatric Classification." *Social Science and Medicine* 35, no. 1 (1992): 3–24.

Gal, Susan. "Language, Gender, and Power: An Anthropological Review." In *Linguistic Anthropology: A Reader*, ed. Alessandro Duranti, 420–30. Malden, MA: Blackwell, 2001.

Gamwell, Lynn, and Nancy Tomes. "The Asylum in Antebellum America: The 1820s to the 1860s." In *Madness in America: Cultural and Medical Perceptions of Mental Illness before 1914*, ed. Lynn Gamwell and Nancy Tomes, 37–117. Ithaca: Cornell University Press, 1995.

Gardiner, Harris. "Debate Resumes on the Safety of Depression's Wonder Drugs." *New York Times*, August 7, 2003, A1.

Gartner, John D. *The Hypomanic Edge: The Link between (a Little) Craziness and (a Lot of) Success in America*. New York: Simon and Schuster, 2005.

Gay, Verne. "PBS' New Film about Theodore Roosevelt Chronicles the Many Sides of a Passionate, Energetic Man." *Newsday*, October 6, 1996, C10.

Geertz, Clifford. "Deep Play: Notes on the Balinese Cockfight." In *The Interpretation of Cultures: Selected Essays*, 412–54. New York: Basic Books, 1973.

———. "Religion as a Cultural System." In *The Interpretation of Cultures: Selected Essays*, 87–125. New York: Basic Books, 1973.

Gerth, H. H., and C. Wright Mills, eds. and trans. *From Max Weber: Essays in Sociology*. New York: Oxford University Press, 1958.

Gibbons, Kaye. *Sights Unseen*. New York: G. P. Putnam's Sons, 1995.

Gillmor, Dan. "High-Tech High-Fliers Get Hit Hard." *Arizona Republic*, September 7, 1998, E1.

Ginzburg, Carlo. "Style as Inclusion, Style as Exclusion." In *Picturing Science, Producing Art*, ed. Caroline A. Jones and Peter Galison, 27–54. New York: Routledge, 1998.

Glassman, James K. "Psyching out Mr. Market." *Washington Post*, February 21, 1999, H1.

Goldman, Harvey. *Max Weber and Thomas Mann: Calling and the Shaping of the Self*. Berkeley: University of California Press, 1988.

Goldstein, Richard. "Butching up for Victory." *The Nation* 278, no. 3 (2004): 11–14.

Goleman, Daniel. *Emotional Intelligence*. New York: Bantam, 1995.

Goleman, Daniel, Richard Boyatzis, and Annie McKee. "Primal Leadership: The Hidden Driver of Great Performance." *Harvard Business Review* 79, no. 11 (2001): 42–51.

Gombrich, E. H. *Art and Illusion: A Study in the Psychology of Pictorial Representation*. Princeton: Princeton University Press, 1969.

Good, Byron J., and Mary-Jo DelVecchio-Good. "Why Do the Masses So Easily Run Amok?" *Latitudes* 5 (June 2001): 10–19.

Good, Byron J., and M. A. Subandi. "Experiences of Psychosis in Javanese Culture: Reflections on a Case of Acute, Recurrent Psychosis in Contemporary Yogyakarta, Indonesia." In *Schizophrenia, Culture, and Subjectivity: The Edge of Experience*, ed. Janis Hunter Jenkins and Robert John Barrett, 167–95. Cambridge: Cambridge University Press, 2004.

Goodwin, Frederick K., and Kay Redfield Jamison. *Manic-Depressive Illness*. New York: Oxford University Press, 1990.

Gordon, Avery F. *Ghostly Matters: Haunting and the Sociological Imagination*. Minneapolis: University of Minnesota Press, 1997.

Gottdiener, M., and George Kephart. "The Multinucleated Metropolitan Region: A Comparative Analysis." In *Postsuburban California: The Transformation of Orange County since World War II*, ed. Rob Kling, Spencer Olin, and Mark Poster, 31–54. Berkeley: University of California Press, 1991.

Gould, Elizabeth, and Charles G. Gross. "Neurogenesis in Adult Mammals: Some Progress and Problems." *Journal of Neuroscience* 22, no. 3 (2002): 619–23.

Gould, E., P. Tanapat, N. B. Hastings, and T. J. Shors. "Neurogenesis in Adulthood: A Possible Role in Learning." *Trends in Cognitive Sciences* 3, no. 5 (1999): 186–92.

Graham, Katharine. *Personal History.* New York: Knopf, 1997.

Grant, James. *Minding Mr. Market: Ten Years on Wall Street with Grant's Interest Investor.* New York: Farrar, Straus and Giroux, 1993.

Gray, Spalding. *Life Interrupted: The Unfinished Monologue.* New York: Crown, 2005.

Greenhouse, Steven. "The Mood at Work: Anger and Anxiety." *New York Times,* October 29, 2002, 1.

Greider, William. *One World, Ready or Not: The Manic Logic of Global Capitalism.* New York: Simon and Schuster, 1997.

Griffin, Jim. "Looking for the Prevailing Wind." May 2000, www.business2.com/articles/mag (accessed July 5, 2003).

Grigoriadis, Vanessa. "Are You Bipolar?" *New York Magazine,* March 8, 2004.

Guignon, Charles, ed. *The Cambridge Companion to Heidegger.* New York: Cambridge University Press, 1993.

Gupta, Akhil, and James Ferguson. "Beyond 'Culture': Space, Identity, and the Politics of Difference." *Cultural Anthropology* 7, no. 1 (1992): 6–23.

Gusterson, Hugh. *Nuclear Rites: A Weapons Laboratory at the End of the Cold War.* Berkeley: University of California Press, 1996.

Hacking, Ian. *Mad Travelers: Reflections on the Reality of Transient Mental Illnesses.* Cambridge, MA: Harvard University Press, 1998.

———. "Making up People." In *Reconstructing Individualism: Autonomy, Individuality, and the Self in Western Thought,* ed. Thomas C. Heller, Morton Sosna, and David E. Wellbery, 222–36. Stanford: Stanford University Press, 1986.

———. *Rewriting the Soul: Multiple Personality and the Sciences of Memory.* Princeton: Princeton University Press, 1995.

Hanks, William F. *Language and Communicative Practices.* Boulder, CO: Westview Press, 1995.

Harding, Susan Friend. *The Book of Jerry Falwell: Fundamentalist Language and Politics.* Princeton: Princeton University Press, 2000.

Harding, Susan, and Kathleen Stewart. "Anxieties of Influence: Conspiracy Theory and Therapeutic Culture in Millennial America." In *Transparency and Conspiracy,* ed. Harry G. West and Todd Sanders, 258–86. Durham: Duke University Press, 2003.

Harré, Rom. *Physical Being: A Theory for a Corporeal Psychology.* Oxford: Basil Blackwell, 1991.

Harrison, Bennett, and Barry Bluestone. *The Great U-Turn.* New York: Basic Books, 1988.

Harvey, David. *A Brief History of Neoliberalism.* Oxford: Oxford University Press, 2005.

Harvey, David. *The Condition of Postmodernity: An Enquiry into the Origins of Social Change*. Oxford: Basil Blackwell, 1989.

———. *Spaces of Hope*. Berkeley: University of California Press, 2000.

Hatfield, Elaine, John T. Cacioppo, and Richard L. Rapson. *Emotional Contagion*. Cambridge: Cambridge University Press, 1994.

Havens, Leston L. *Making Contact: Uses of Language in Psychotherapy*. Cambridge, MA: Harvard University Press, 1986.

Healy, David. *The Antidepressant Era*. Cambridge, MA: Harvard University Press, 1999.

Hebdige, Dick. *Subculture: The Meaning of Style*. London: Routledge, 1979.

Heidegger, Martin. *The Basic Problems of Phenomenology*. Trans. Albert Hofstadter. Bloomington: Indiana University Press, 1982.

Hembrooke, Helene, and Geri Gay. "The Laptop and the Lecture: The Effects of Multitasking in Learning Environments." *Journal of Computing in Higher Education* 15, no. 1 (2003): 1–19.

Hertz, Robert. *Death and the Right Hand*. Glencoe, IL: Free Press, 1960.

Hinshaw, Stephen P. *The Years of Silence Are Past: My Father's Life with Bipolar Disorders*. Cambridge: Cambridge University Press, 2002.

Hirschman, Albert O. *The Passions and the Interests: Political Arguments for Capitalism before Its Triumph*. Princeton: Princeton University Press, 1977.

Ho, Karen. "Liquefying Corporations and Communities: Wall Street World Views and Socioeconomic Transformations in the Post-Industrial U.S." Ph.D. diss., Princeton University, 2003.

Hoff, Paul. "Kraepelin: Clinical Sections, I." In *A History of Clinical Psychiatry*, ed. G. E. Berrios and Roy Porter, 261–79. New York: New York University Press, 1995.

Hollis, Martin, and Steven Lukes. *Rationality and Relativism*. Cambridge, MA: MIT Press, 1982.

Hollon, Matthew F. "Direct-to-Consumer Marketing of Prescription Drugs: Creating Consumer Demand." *Journal of the American Medical Association* 281, no. 4 (1999): 382–84.

Holmer, Alan F. "Direct-to-Consumer Prescription Drug Advertising Builds Bridges between Patients and Physicians." *Journal of the American Medical Association* 281, no. 4 (1999): 380–82.

Holtzman, Phillip S., Martha E. Shenton, and Margie R. Solovay. "Quality of Thought Disorder in Differential Diagnosis." *Schizophrenia Bulletin* 12, no. 3 (1986): 360–81.

Horwitz, Allan V. *Creating Mental Illness*. Chicago: University of Chicago Press, 2002.

Howard, Daniel J., and Charles Gengler. "Emotional Contagion Effects on Product Attitudes." *Journal of Consumer Research* 28, no. 2 (2001): 189–202.

Hunter, Eleanor Mitchell. "Letter Requesting Information on Past Employment of Applicant for Admission to the Bar." Tallahassee: Florida Board of Bar Examiners, 2005.

Huxley, Aldous. *Brave New World*. New York: HarperPerennial, 1946.

"I'm New Heres an Intro [*sic*]." 2002, http://community.livejournal.com/bp_disorder/85520.html (accessed May 26, 2004).

Icarus. "My Pdoc Emasculated Me." 1998, alt.support.depression.manic (accessed July 16, 2000).

Ignatius, David. "Our Bipolar Economy." *Washington Post*, March 12, 2000, 7.

"It's Good but It's Not Bipolar." *New Yorker* 78, no. 28 (2002): 74.

Jakobson, Roman. "Baudelaire's 'Les Chats.'" In *Language in Literature*, ed. Roman Jakobson, 180–97. Cambridge, MA: Belknap Press, 1987.

———. *The Framework of Language*. Ann Arbor: Michigan Slavic Publications. 1980.

———. "Notes on the Makeup of a Proverb." In *Linguistic and Literary Studies*, ed. Edgar C. Polomé, Mohammad Ali Jazayery, and Werner Winter, 83–85. Paris: Mouton, 1979.

———. *On Language*. Cambridge, MA: Harvard University Press, 1990.

———. *Studies on Child Language and Aphasia*. Paris: Mouton, 1971.

———. "Two Aspects of Language and Two Types of Aphasic Disturbances." In *Language in Literature*, ed. Roman Jakobson, 95–114. Cambridge, MA: Harvard University Press, 1987.

James, William. "Census of Hallucinations." In *Essays in Psychical Research*, ed. William James, 56–78. 1889–97. Cambridge, MA: Harvard University Press, 1986.

Jamison, Kay Redfield. *Exuberance*. New York: Knopf, 2004.

———. "Manic-Depressive Illness and Creativity." *Scientific American* 272, no. 2 (February 1995): 62–67.

———. *Touched with Fire: Manic-Depressive Illness and the Artistic Temperament*. New York: Free Press, 1993.

———. *An Unquiet Mind*. New York: Knopf, 1995.

Jamison, Kay R., Robert H. Gerner, and Frederick K. Goodwin. "Patient and Physician Attitudes toward Lithium: Relationship to Compliance." *Archives of General Psychiatry* 36, no. 8 (1979): 866–69.

Jamison, Kay R., Robert H. Gerner, Constance Hammen, and Christine Padesky. "Clouds and Silver Linings: Positive Experiences Associated with Primary Affective Disorders." *American Journal of Psychiatry* 137, no. 2 (1980): 198–202.

Jasin, Victor. "Considering Off Meds . . . Can't Believe I'm Saying This. . . ." 1996, alt.support.depression.manic (accessed July 20, 2000).

Jaspers, Karl. *General Psychopathology*. Trans. J. Hoenig and Marian W. Hamilton. 2 vols. Baltimore: Johns Hopkins University Press, 1959. Reprint, Manchester University Press, 1963; Johns Hopkins University Press, 1997.

Jayson, Lawrence M. *Mania*. New York: Funk and Wagnalls, 1937.

Jenkins, Janis Hunter. "Schizophrenia as a Paradigm Case for Understanding Fundamental Human Processes." In *Schizophrenia, Culture and Subjectivity: The Edge of Experience*, ed. Janis Hunter Jenkins, 29–61. Cambridge: Cambridge University Press, 2004.

Jewell, Edward Alden. "Ruskin's Life Explains His Works: Mr. Wilenski's Penetrating and Impartial Study of the Prophet of Brantwood's Strange Variations in Character." *New York Times*, October 15, 1933, 2.

Johnson, Stephen M. *Humanizing the Narcissistic Style*. New York: W. W. Norton, 1987.

Jonas, B. S., D. Brody, M. Roper, and W. E. Narrow. "Prevalence of Mood Disorders in a National Sample of Young American Adults." *Social Psychiatry and Psychiatric Epidemiology* 38, no. 11 (2003): 618–24.

Jones, James H. *Bad Blood: The Tuskegee Syphilis Experiment*. New York: Free Press, 1981.

Joyce, Patrick. *The Rule of Freedom: Liberalism and the Modern City*. New York: Verso, 2003.

Kahn, Joseph. "The Markets: Market Place; for a Triple Threat, a Less-Than-Stellar Season." *New York Times*, February 25, 1999, 1.

Kaletsky, Anatole. "War against Terror Can Be Fought on the Spending Front." *The Times*, October 30, 2001.

Kaplan, David. "Study: Consumers Anxious but Ads Bring Some Comfort." *Adweek*, April 14, 2003, http://www.adweek.com.

Karp, David A. *Speaking of Sadness: Depression, Disconnection, and the Meanings of Illness*. New York: Oxford University Press, 1996.

Keeler, Ward. "Shame and Stage Fright in Java." *Ethos* 11, no. 3 (1983): 152–65.

Keynes, John Maynard. *The General Theory of Employment, Interest, and Money*. New York: Harcourt, Brace, and World, 1936.

Kiki. "James! Help! My Pdoc Doesn't Know about Neurontin." 1998, alt.support .depression.manic (accessed July 25, 2000).

Kindleberger, Charles P. *Manias, Panics and Crashes: A History of Financial Crises*. New York: John Wiley, 1996.

Kingston, Anne. "Minding Martha's Business." *National Post*, April 12, 2002, 5.

Kitchen, Patricia. "Using Heels-over-Heads Approach at Conference." *Newsday*, November 17, 2000, 80.

Klein, Melanie. "A Contribution to the Psychogenesis of Manic-Depressive States." *International Journal of Psychoanalysis* 16 (1935): 145–74.

Klein, Rachel G., Daniel S. Pine, and Donald F. Klein. "Debate Forum: Negative." *Journal of the American Academy of Child and Adolescent Psychiatry* 37, no. 10 (1998): 1093–95.

Kleinman, Arthur. *Social Origins of Distress and Disease: Depression, Neurasthenia, and Pain in Modern China*. New Haven: Yale University Press, 1986.

Kluger, Jeffrey, Sora Song, and Lizzie Simon. "Young and Bipolar." *Time*, August 19, 2002, 38–51.

Koppl, Roger. "Retrospectives: Animal Spirits." *Journal of Economic Perspectives* 5, no. 3 (1991): 203–10.

Kotter, John P. *Leading Change*. Cambridge, MA: Harvard Business School Press, 1996.

Kraepelin, Emil. *Clinical Psychiatry*. Delmar, NY: Scholars' Facsimiles and Reprints, 1981.

———. *Manic-Depressive Insanity and Paranoia*. 1921. Reprint, Bristol, England: Thoemmes Press, 2002.

————. *One Hundred Years of Psychiatry*. Cambridge, MA: Harvard University Press, 1962.

Kramer, Peter D. *Against Depression*. New York: Viking Penguin, 2005.

————. "There's Nothing Deep about Depression." *New York Times Magazine*, April 17, 2005, 50–57.

Kraus, Alfred. "How Can the Phenomenological-Anthropological Approach Contribute to Diagnosis and Classification in Psychiatry?" In *Nature and Narrative: An Introduction to the New Philosophy of Psychiatry*, ed. Bill Fulford et al., 199–216. Oxford: Oxford University Press, 2003.

————. "Identity and Psychosis of the Manic-Depressive." In *Phenomenology and Psychiatry*, ed. A. J. J. De Konig and F. A. Jenner, 201–16. London: Academic Press, 1982.

————. "Role Performance, Identity Structure and Psychosis in Melancholic and Manic-Depressive Patients." In *Interpersonal Factors in the Origin and Course of Affective Disorders*, ed. Christoph Mundt et al., 31–47. London: Gaskell, 1996.

Kretschmer, E. *Physique and Character: An Investigation of the Nature of Constitution and of the Theory of Temperament*. Trans. W. J. H. Sprott. 2nd rev. and enlarged ed. New York: Harcourt, Brace, 1926.

Kulick, Don. "No." *Language & Communication*, no. 23 (2003): 139–51.

Lacher, Irene. "In New Book, Professor Sees a 'Mania' in U.S. for Possessions and Status." *New York Times*, March 12, 2005, 7, 13.

Laderman, Carol, and Marina Roseman, eds. *The Performance of Healing*. New York: Routledge, 1996.

Lakoff, Andrew. *Pharmaceutical Reason: Knowledge and Value in Global Psychiatry*. Cambridge: Cambridge University Press, 2005.

Lakoff, George. *Moral Politics: What Conservatives Know That Liberals Don't*. Chicago: University of Chicago Press, 1996.

Landers, Peter. "Waiting for Prozac: Drug Firms Push Japan to Change View of Depression." *Wall Street Journal*, October 9, 2002, 1.

Latour, Bruno. *Science in Action: How to Follow Scientists and Engineers through Society*. Cambridge, MA: Harvard University Press, 1987.

————. *We Have Never Been Modern*. Cambridge, MA: Harvard University Press, 1993.

Lawrence, William. "Chemical's Cure of Insane Is Seen." *New York Times*, July 16, 1947, 18.

————. "New Vistas Opened for Chemical Approach to the Treatment of Mental Illness." *New York Times*, December 14, 1947, E9.

Le Bon, Gustave. *The Crowd: A Study of the Popular Mind*. 1896. Reprint, Marietta, GA: Cherokee Publishing, 1982.

Lears, T. J. Jackson. "From Salvation to Self-Realization: Advertising and the Therapeutic Roots of the Consumer Culture, 1880–1930." In *The Culture of Consumption: Critical Essays in American History, 1880–1980*, ed. Richard Wightman Fox and T. J. Jackson Lears, 1–38. New York: Pantheon Books, 1983.

LeDoux, Joseph E. "Emotion: Clues from the Brain." *Annual Review of Psychology* 46 (1995): 209.

Lee, Benjamin. *Talking Heads: Language, Metalanguage and the Semiotics of Subjectivity*. Durham: Duke University Press, 1997.

Lemke, Thomas. "'The Birth of Biopolitics': Michel Foucault's Lecture at the Collège De France on Neo-Liberal Governmentality." *Economy and Society* 30, no. 2 (2001): 190–207.

"Leonard Woolf Is Dead at 88; Led Literary Group in London." *New York Times*, August 15, 1969, 35.

Levy, Robert I. *Tahitians: Mind and Experience in the Society Islands*. Chicago: University of Chicago Press, 1973.

Lewis, A. "The Psychopathology of Insight." *British Journal of Medical Psychology* 14 (1934): 332–48.

Lewis, Laura Dawn, and the Illinois Leader. "Illinois Launches Compulsory Mental Health Screening for Children and Pregnant Women." Couples Company and the Illinois Leader, 2004, http://www.couplescompany.com/Features/Politics/2004/OrwellianPregnancy.pdf (accessed April 24, 2005).

Ligerakis, Maria. "The Challenger: Richard Branson." http://www.bandt.com.au/articles/64/0c009764 (accessed June 27, 2002).

Light, Donald W., and Joel Lexchin. "The International War on Cheap Drugs." *New Doctor* 81 (2004): 1.

Locke, John. *An Essay Concerning Human Understanding, Great Books in Philosophy*. Amherst, NY: Prometheus Books, 1995.

Lowenstein, Roger. "Exuberance Is Rational, or at Least Human." *New York Times Magazine*, February 11, 2001, 68–70.

Luhrmann, T. M. *Of Two Minds: The Growing Disorder in American Psychiatry*. New York: Knopf, 2000.

Lukes, Steven. *Liberals and Cannibals: The Implications of Diversity*. New York: Verso, 2003.

Lunbeck, Elizabeth. *The Americanization of Narcissism*, forthcoming.

———. *The Psychiatric Persuasion: Knowledge, Gender, and Power in Modern America*. Princeton: Princeton University Press, 1994.

Lutz, Catherine. "The Domain of Emotion Words on Ifaluk." In *The Social Construction of Emotions*, ed. Rom Harré, 268–88. London: Basil Blackwell, 1986.

———. "Emotion, Thought, and Estrangement: Emotion as a Cultural Category." *Cultural Anthropology* 1, no. 3 (1986): 287–309.

Lutz, Catherine, and Lila Abu-Lughod. *Language and the Politics of Emotion*. Studies in Emotion and Social Interaction. New York: Cambridge University Press, 1990.

Lutz, Catherine, and Geoffrey White. "The Anthropology of Emotions." *Annual Review of Anthropology* 15 (1986): 405–36.

Lutz, Tom. *American Nervousness, 1903*. Ithaca: Cornell University Press, 1991.

Lynch, Michael. "Representation Is Overrated: Some Critical Remarks about the Use of the Concept of Representation in Science Studies." *Configurations* 2, no. 1 (1994): 137–49.

MacDonald, M. *Mystical Bedlam: Madness, Anxiety, and Healing in Seventeenth-Century England*. Cambridge: Cambridge University Press, 1981.

MacFarquhar, Larissa. "The Gilder Effect." In *The New Gilded Age: The New Yorker Looks at the Culture of Affluence*, ed. David Remnick, 111–24. New York: Random House, 2000.

MacLennan, R. "The Global CNS Therapeutics Markets: An Overview." 2002, http://www.frost.com/prod/serviet/market-insight.pag?docid=IKHA-5ALUC3& ctxht=FomCtx1&ctxixpLink=FomCtx2&ctxixpLabel+FomCtx3 (accessed December 1, 2003).

Macpherson, C. B. *The Political Theory of Possessive Individualism: Hobbes to Locke*. Oxford: Oxford University Press, 1962.

Magnier, Mark. "Dramatic Surge in Japan's Yen Spurs New Fear." *Los Angeles Times*, October 9, 1998, 1.

"Main Types of Mental Disorder Explained for the Red Cross." *New York Times*, March 20, 1944, 12.

"Mania Kills Man by Push on Elevated." *New York Times*, September 27, 1929, 1, 3.

Mann, Bill. "Mr. Market Is a Manic-Depressive Idiot." Motley Fool, http://www.fool.com/news/1999/foth991006.htm (accessed March 5, 2002).

Martin, Emily. *Flexible Bodies: Tracking Immunity in America from the Days of Polio to the Age of AIDS*. Boston: Beacon Press, 1994.

——. "The Pharmaceutical Person." *BioSocieties* 1 (2006): 273–88.

——. *The Woman in the Body: A Cultural Analysis of Reproduction*. Boston: Beacon Press, 1987.

Marx, Karl. *Capital: A Critique of Political Economy*. Ed. Frederick Engels. Vol. 1. 1887. New York: International Publishers, 1967.

Maurer, Bill. "Complex Subjects: Offshore Finance, Complexity Theory and the Dispersion of the Modern." *Socialist Review* 25 (November 1996): 114–45.

Mauss, Marcel. "A Category of the Human Mind: The Notion of Person; the Notion of Self." In *The Category of the Person: Anthropology, Philosophy, History*, ed. Michael Carrithers, Steven Collins, and Steven Lukes, 1–25. 1938. Cambridge: Cambridge University Press, 1985.

McClay, Wilfred M. *The Masterless: Self and Society in Modern America*. Chapel Hill: University of North Carolina Press, 1994.

McClellan, Mark. "No Degree, and No Way Back to the Middle." *New York Times*, May 24, 2005, 15.

McCoy, Adrian. "Cramer's Real-Time 'Real Money' Shows Land in Local Radio." *Knight Ridder Tribune Business News*, March 5, 2006, 1.

McDonald, Megan. *The Judy Moody Mood Journal*. Cambridge, MA: Candlewick Press, 2003.

McGarry, James, and David Joye. U.S. Census, New Jersey, by County; Middlesex-Somerset-Hunterdon Labor Area Review of 1997 and Outlook for 1998. Bureau of Labor Market Information, http://www.wnjpin.state.nj.us /OneStopCareerCenter/laborMarketInformation/lmi08/rolno.htm (accessed July 18, 2000).

McKibben, Bill. "The Christian Paradox." *Harpers* 311, no. 1863 (2005): 31–37.

McManamy, John. *McMan's Depression and Bipolar Weekly*, September 18, 2001.

Medical Condition News. "Texas Medication Algorithm Project Guidelines Produce Improvements in Patients with Major Depressive Disorder." News-Medical.Net, 2004, http://www.news-medical.net/?id=3084 (accessed April 24, 2005).

"Men of the Year." *GQ*, November 1998, 395–425.

Mendoza-Denton, Norma. "Key Terms in Language and Culture." In *Key Terms in Language and Culture*, ed. Alessandro Duranti, 235–37. New York: Blackwell, 2001.

Merleau-Ponty, M. *Phenomenology of Perception*. London: Routledge, 1962.

Merry, Sally Engle. "Law and Identity in an American Colony." In *Law & Empire in the Pacific: Fiji and Hawaii*, ed. Sally Engle Merry and Donald Brenneis, 123–52. Santa Fe: School of American Research Press, 2004.

Metzl, Jonathan. *Prozac on the Couch: Prescribing Gender in the Era of Wonder Drugs*. Durham: Duke University Press, 2003.

Micale, Mark S. "Discourses of Hysteria in Fin-de-Siècle France." In *The Mind of Modernism: Medicine, Psychology, and the Cultural Arts in Europe and America, 1880–1940*, ed. Mark S. Micale, 71–92. Stanford: Stanford University Press, 2004.

Michaels, Walter Benn. *The Shape of the Signifier: 1967 to the End of History*. Princeton: Princeton University Press, 2004.

Miklowitz, David Jay. *The Bipolar Disorder Survival Guide: What You and Your Family Need to Know*. New York: Guilford Press, 2002.

Miller, Benjamin F., and Ruth Goode. *Man and His Body*. New York: Simon and Schuster, 1960.

Miller, Peter. "Accounting and Objectivity: The Invention of Calculating Selves and Calculable Spaces." *Annals of Scholarship* 9, nos. 1–2 (1992): 61–86.

Mischer, Don. "An Evening with Robin Williams (Live and Uncensored)." *60 Minutes*, 1983.

Moggridge, D. E. "Correspondence." *Journal of Economic Perspectives* 6, no. 3 (1992): 207–12.

Mohammed, Jinnah R. "A Mood Chart System: Livingmanicdepressive—a Bipolar and Depression Website." http://www.livingmanicdepressive.com/D_030.html (accessed April 18, 2003).

Mol, Annemarie. *The Body Multiple: Ontology in Medical Practice*. Durham: Duke University Press, 2002.

Mondimore, Francis. *Bipolar Disorder: A Guide for Parents and Families*. Baltimore: Johns Hopkins University Press, 1999.

"Moral Thermometer." *Journal of Health and Recreation* 4, no. 1 (1833): 5.

Morrison, Toni. *Playing in the Dark: Whiteness and the Literary Imagination*. New York: Random House, 1993.

Morrow, David. "Smithkline and American Home Are Talking of Huge Drug Merger." *New York Times*, January 21, 1998, 1, 5.

Morson, Gary Saul, and Caryl Emerson. *Mikhail Bakhtin: Creation of a Prosaics*. Stanford: Stanford University Press, 1990.

Msetfi, Rachel M., Robin A. Murphy, Jane Simpson, and Diana E. Kornbrot. "Depressive Realism and Outcome Density Bias in Contingency Judgments: The

Effect of the Context and Intertrial Interval." *Journal of Experimental Psychology: General* 134, no. 1 (2005): 10–22.

Mueggler, Erik. *The Age of Wild Ghosts: Memory, Violence, and Place in Southwest China*. Berkeley: University of California Press, 2001.

Murray, D. W. "What Is the Western Concept of the Self? On Forgetting David Hume." *Ethos* 21, no. 1 (1993): 3–23.

Nandwani, Deepali. "The Flamboyant CEO." http://www.entertainment.sify.com/content/weekendstory.asp?news_code_num=173&lang_cod (accessed June 27, 2002).

Napier, A. David. *Foreign Bodies: Performance, Art, and Symbolic Anthropology*. Berkeley: University of California Press, 1992.

"The New Jobs: What They Are, What They Pay." *New York Times*, January 4, 1998, 14.

Newman, Alan M. "Pictures of a Stock Market Mania: The Inside Truth." March 3, 2002, http://www.cross-currents.net/charts.htm (accessed April 4, 2002).

Newman, Katherine. *Falling from Grace: The Experience of Downward Mobility in the American Middle Class*. New York: Free Press, 1988.

NIMH. *The Numbers Count: Mental Disorders in America*. 2001, http://www.nimh.nih.gov/publicat/numbers.cfm (accessed August 12, 2005).

"No More Branson Nonsense." *The Scotsman*, September 9, 1998, 17.

Nohria, Nitin, and James D. Berkley. "The Virtual Organization: Bureaucracy, Technology, and the Implosion of Control." In *The Post-Bureaucratic Organization: New Perspectives on Organizational Change*, ed. Charles Heckscher and Anne Donnellon, 108–28. Thousand Oaks, CA: Sage, 1994.

Norris, Floyd. "Greenspan Era Taught People to Gamble." *New York Times*, July 22, 2005, 1.

Nuckolls, Charles W. *Culture: A Problem That Cannot Be Solved*. Madison: University of Wisconsin Press, 1998.

———. "Toward a Cultural History of the Personality Disorders." *Social Science and Medicine* 35, no. 1 (1992): 37–47.

Nussbaum, Martha. *Hiding from Humanity: Disgust, Shame, and the Law*. Princeton: Princeton University Press, 2004.

———. "Plato on Commensurability and Desire." *Proceedings of the Aristotelian Society* 58 (supplemental) (1984): 55–80.

———. *Upheavals of Thought: The Intelligence of Emotions*. Cambridge: Cambridge University Press, 2001.

Oldani, Michael. "Filling Scripts: A Multi-Sited Ethnography of Pharmaceutical Sales Practices, Psychiatric Prescribing, and Phamily Life in North America." Ph.D. diss., Princeton University, 2006.

Orr, Jackie. "The Ecstasy of Miscommunication: Cyberpsychiatry and Mental Disease." In *Doing Science and Culture*, ed. Roddey Reid and Sharon Traweek, 151–76. New York: Routledge, 2000.

———. *Panic Diaries: A Genealogy of Panic Disorder*. Durham: Duke University Press, 2006.

Padgett, Abigail. *A Child of Silence*. New York: Mysterious Press, 1993.

Painton, Priscilla. "The Taming of Ted Turner." *Time* 139 (January 6, 1992): 34–40.

Pauley, Jane. *Skywriting: A Life out of the Blue*. New York: Random House, 2004.

PBS. *Shackleton's Voyage of Endurance: Transcript*. Public Broadcasting System, 2002.

Petryna, Adriana. "Drug Development and the Ethics of the Globalized Clinical Trial." *Occasional Papers, School of Social Science, Institute for Advanced Study* 22 (2005): 1–21.

Petryna, Adriana, Andrew Lakoff, and Arthur Kleinman, eds. *Global Pharmaceuticals: Ethics, Markets, Practices*. Durham: Duke University Press, 2006.

Pfister, Joel. "Glamorizing the Psychological: The Politics of the Performances of Modern Psychological Identities." In *Inventing the Psychological: Toward a Cultural History of Emotional Life in America*, ed. Joel Pfister and Nancy Schnog, 167–216. New Haven: Yale University Press, 1997.

Pincus, Harold Alan, Terri L. Tanielian, Steven C. Marcus, Mark Ofson, Deborah A. Zarin, James Thompson, and Julie Magno Zito. "Prescribing Trends in Psychotropic Medications: Primary Care, Psychiatry, and Other Medical Specialties." *Journal of the American Medical Association* 279, no. 7 (1998): 526–31.

Plotz, John. *The Crowd: British Literature and Public Politics*. Berkeley: University of California Press, 2000.

Pocock, J. G. A. *Virtue, Commerce, and History*. New York: Cambridge University Press, 1985.

Polanyi, Karl. *The Great Transformation*. New York: Farrar and Rinehart, 1944.

Porter, Roy. *Madness: A Brief History*. New York: Oxford University Press, 2002.

Porter, Theodore M. *Trust in Numbers: The Pursuit of Objectivity in Science and Public Life*. Princeton: Princeton University Press, 1995.

Postrel, Virginia. *The Future and Its Enemies: The Growing Conflict over Creativity, Enterprise, and Progress*. New York: Free Press, 1998.

Pratt, Mary Louise. *Imperial Eyes: Travel Writing and Transculturation*. New York: Routledge, 1992.

Prentice, Kristen J., James M. Gold, and William T. Carpenter, Jr. "Optimistic Bias in the Perception of Personal Risk: Patterns in Schizophrenia." *American Journal of Psychiatry* 162, no. 3 (2005): 507–12.

Prescott, Orville. "Books of the Times." *New York Times*, September 15, 1947, 15.

Prescott, Richard. "Food Consumption, Prices, and Expenditures, 1960–81." Washington, DC: Economic Research Service, U.S. Department of Agriculture, November 1982.

"Prescriptions Soar for Psychotropic Drugs." Pharmrep.com (Pharmaceutical Representative Magazine). May 1998, http://www.pharmrep.com/xml/9505/950506.asp (accessed July 3, 2003).

"Psychotropic Drug Market Grows." Pharmrep.com (Pharmaceutical Representative Magazine). April 1997, http://www.pharmrep.com/xml/9704/970410.asp (accessed July 3, 2003).

Pulley, Mary Lynn. *Losing Your Job—Reclaiming Your Soul*. San Francisco: Jossey-Bass, 1997.

Putting Baltimore's People First. *Putting Baltimore's People First: Keys to Responsible Economic Development of Our City*. Baltimore: AFL-CIO, 2004.

Rack, Philip. *Race, Culture, and Mental Disorder*. London: Tavistock Publications, 1982.

Ramanujan, A. K. "Indian Poetics: Dramatic Criticism." In *The Literature of India: An Introduction*, ed. Edward C. Dimock, Jr., et al., 397–408. Chicago: University of Chicago Press, 1974.

Rather, L. J. "The Six-Things Non-Natural: A Note on the Origins and Fate of a Doctrine and a Phrase." *Clio Medica* 3 (1968): 337–47.

Rawnsley, Andrew. "Review of 'Richard Branson: The Inside Story' by Mick Brown." *The Guardian*, April 29, 1988.

Reddy, William M. *The Navigation of Feeling: A Framework for the History of Emotions*. Cambridge: Cambridge University Press, 2001.

Reverby, Susan. *Tuskegee's Truths: Rethinking the Tuskegee Syphilis Study*. Studies in Social Medicine. Chapel Hill: University of North Carolina Press, 2000.

Rhodes, Lorna A. *Emptying Beds: The Work of an Emergency Psychiatric Unit*. Berkeley: University of California Press, 1991.

Rippa, S. Alexander. *Education in a Free Society: An American History*. New York: Longman, 1980.

Risjord, Mark W. *Woodcutters and Witchcraft: Rationality and Interpretive Change in the Social Sciences*. Albany: SUNY Press, 2000.

Robbins, Joel. "On the Paradoxes of Global Pentecostalism and the Perils of Continuity Thinking." *Religion* 33, no. 2 (2003): 221–31.

"Ron Chernow, Author, *Alexander Hamilton*." *Washington Journal*, CSPAN, June 18, 2004.

Roper. "Consumers Anxious but Ads Bring Some Comfort." 2003, http://www.roperasw.com/newsroom/news/n0304005.html (accessed March 15, 2003).

Rosaldo, Michelle Z. *Knowledge and Passion: Ilongot Notions of Self and Social Life*. Cambridge: Cambridge University Press, 1980.

Rosaldo, Renato. *Grief and a Headhunter's Rage: On the Cultural Force of Emotions*. Ed. Edward M. Bruner. Vol. 42: *Text, Play, and Story: The Construction and Reconstruction of Self and Society: Proceedings of the American Ethnological Society, 1983*. American Ethnological Society, 1984.

Rose, Nikolas. "Becoming Neurochemical Selves." In *Biotechnology, Commerce and Civil Society*, ed. Nico Stehr. New Brunswick, NJ: Transaction Press, 2004.
———. *Governing the Soul: The Shaping of the Private Self*. London: Routledge, 1989.
———. *Inventing Our Selves: Psychology, Power and Personhood*. Cambridge: Cambridge University Press, 1998.
———. "The Neurochemical Self and Its Anomalies." In *Risk and Morality*, ed. Richard V. Ericson and Aaron Doyle, 407–37. Toronto: University of Toronto Press, 2003.

Rosenbaum, David L., and Martin E. Seligman, eds. *Abnormal Psychology*. New York: W. W. Norton, 1995.

Rosenberg, Charles E. "The Tyranny of Diagnosis: Specific Entities and Individual Experience." *Milbank Quarterly* 80, no. 2 (2002): 237–60.

Rothman, David J. *The Discovery of the Asylum: Social Order and Disorder in the New Republic*. New York: Little, Brown, 1990.

Rothschild, Emma. *Economic Sentiments: Adam Smith, Condorcet, and the Enlightenment*. Cambridge, MA: Harvard University Press, 2001.

Rouse, Roger. "Thinking through Transnationalism: Notes on the Cultural Politics of Class Relations in the Contemporary United States." *Public Culture* 7, no. 2 (1995): 353–402.

Rush, Benjamin. *An Inquiry into the Effects of Ardent Spirits upon the Human Body and Mind*. New York: Cornelius David, 1811.

Ryle, Gilbert. *The Concept of Mind*. London: Hutchinson, 1949.

Safire, William. "Beware 'Animal Spirits.'" *New York Times*, December 3, 2003, A31.

Salamon, Julie. "Shackleton Marches On." *New York Times*, March 26, 2002, 1.

Saltzman, A. "How to Prosper in the You, Inc. Age." *U.S. News & World Report* 121, no. 17 (1996): 66–79.

Samuelson, Robert J. "For the Economy, Mood Does Matter." *San Diego Union-Tribune*, July 24, 2002, B8.

Sartorius, Norman. "Depressive Disorders: A Major Public Health Problem." In *Mood Disorders: The World's Major Public Health Problem*, ed. Frank J. Ayd, 1–8. Baltimore: Ayd Medical Communications, 1978.

Sass, Louis. "Affectivity in Schizophrenia: A Phenomenological Perspective." *Journal of Consciousness Studies* 11 (2004): 127–47.

———. *Madness and Modernism: Insanity in the Light of Modern Art, Literature, and Thought*. Cambridge, MA: Harvard University Press, 1992.

———. *The Paradoxes of Delusion: Wittgenstein, Schreber, and the Schizophrenic Mind*. Ithaca: Cornell University Press, 1994.

———. "Schizophrenia, Modernism, and the 'Creative Imagination': On Creativity and Psychopathology." *Creativity Research Journal* 13, no. 1 (2000): 55–74.

Scaff, Lawrence A. *Fleeing the Iron Cage: Culture, Politics, and Modernity in the Thought of Max Weber*. Berkeley: University of California Press, 1989.

Schiesari, Juliana. *The Gendering of Melancholia: Feminism, Psychoanalysis, and the Symbolics of Loss in Renaissance Literature*. Ithaca: Cornell University Press, 1992.

Schiff, Stacey. "Poor Richard's Redemption." *New York Times*, January 17, 2006, 19.

Schiller, Robert J. *Irrational Exuberance*. Princeton: Princeton University Press, 2000.

Schneider, David. *American Kinship: A Cultural Account*. Englewood Cliffs, NJ: Prentice Hall, 1968.

Schnog, Nancy. "Changing Emotions: Moods and the Nineteenth-Century American Woman Writer." In *Inventing the Psychological: Toward a Cultural History of Emotional Life in America*, ed. Joel Pfister and Nancy Schnog, 84–109. New Haven: Yale University Press, 1997.

Schonfeld, Erick. "Second Act for Manic CEO." *Business 2.0*, September 2002.

Screech, M. A. "Good Madness in Christendom." In *The Anatomy of Madness: Essays in the History of Psychiatry*, ed. Roy Porter, W. F. Bynum, and Michael Shepherd, 25–39. London: Tavistock Publications, 1985.

Scull, Andrew. *Social Order/Mental Disorder: Anglo-American Psychiatry in Historical Perspective*. Berkeley: University of California Press, 1989.

Searle, John R. *Speech Acts: An Essay in the Philosophy of Language*. London: Cambridge University Press, 1969.

Ser Vaas, Cory. "The *Post* Investigates Manic-Depression." *Saturday Evening Post* 268 (March/April 1996): 46.

Serres, Michel. "The Geometry of the Incommunicable: Madness." In *Foucault and His Interlocutors*, ed. Arnold I. Davidson, 36–56. Chicago: University of Chicago Press, 1997.

Sharp, Lesley Alexandra. *The Sacrificed Generation: Youth, History, and the Colonized Mind in Madagascar*. Berkeley: University of California Press, 2002.

Sher, Barbara. *Live the Life You Love*. New York: Random House, 1997.

Showalter, Elaine. *The Female Malady: Women, Madness and English Culture, 1830–1980*. New York: Pantheon, 1985.

Silverstein, Michael. *Talking Politics: The Substance of Style from Abe To "W."* Chicago: Prickly Paradigm Press, 2003.

Silverstein, Michael, and Greg Urban. "The Natural History of Discourse." In *Natural Histories of Discourse*, ed. Michael Silverstein and Greg Urban, 1–17. Chicago: University of Chicago Press, 1996.

Smith, Nancy deWolf. "All's Well That Ends Like Tulip Mania." *Wall Street Journal*, April 4, 2000.

Solomon, Andrew. *The Noonday Demon: An Atlas of Depression*. New York: Scribner, 2001.

Solomon, Robert C. "Getting Angry: The Jamesian Theory of Emotion in Anthropology." In *Culture Theory: Essays on Mind, Self, Emotion*, ed. Richard A. Shweder and Robert Levine. Cambridge: Cambridge University Press, 1984.

Southard, E. E., and Mary C. Jarrett. *The Kingdom of Evils*. New York: Macmillan, 1922.

Southern New Jersey Regional Developments. "Southern New Jersey Regional Developments." http://www.wnjpin.state.nj.us/OneStopCareerCenter/LaborMarketInformation/lmi08/empecoso.htm (accessed July 18, 2000).

"Spending on Consumer Ads up in 2000." Pharmrep.com (Pharmaceutical Representative Magazine). May 2001, http://www.pharmrep.com/xml/0105/010502.asp (accessed July 3, 2003).

Staff Correspondent. "Mrs. Fosdick Kills 2 Children and Self." *New York Times*, April 5, 1932, 1, 4.

State Street Investor. "State Street Investor Confidence Index Summary." 2005, http://www.statestreet.com/industry_insights/investor_confidence_index/summary.pdf (accessed October 1, 2005).

Stearns, Peter. *American Cool: Constructing a Twentieth-Century Emotional Style.* New York: New York University Press, 2001.

Stevenson, Richard W. "Aftermath: The Prospect of a War without a Wartime Boom." *New York Times,* September 23, 2001, 4.

Stewart, Walter F., Judith A. Ricci, Elsbeth Chee, Steven R. Hahn, and David Morganstein. "Cost of Lost Productive Work Time among U.S. Workers with Depression." *Journal of the American Medical Association* 289, no. 23 (2003): 3135–44.

Stoler, Ann Laura. "Affective States." In *A Companion to the Anthropology of Politics,* ed. David Nugent and Joan Vincent. Malden, MA: Blackwell, 2004.

"The Storm in My Brain: Kids and Mood Disorders" (Bipolar Disorder and Depression). DBSA, http://dbsalliance.org/pdf/storm.pdf (accessed August 15, 2005).

Strathern, Marilyn. "Disembodied Choice." In *Other Intentions: Cultural Contexts and the Attribution of Inner States,* ed. Lawrence Rosen, 69–89. Santa Fe: School of American Research Press, 1995.

———. "Enterprising Kinship: Consumer Choice and the New Reproductive Technologies." *Cambridge Anthropology* 14, no. 1 (1990): 1–12.

———. "The Whole Person and Its Artifacts." *Annual Review of Anthropology* 33 (2004): 1–19.

Styron, William. *Darkness Visible: A Memoir of Madness.* New York: Random House, 1990.

Sullivan, Elizabeth Teresa. *Mood in Relation to Performance.* Vol. 53: *Archives of Psychology.* New York: Johnson Associates, 1922.

Sullivan, Harry Stack. *Schizophrenia as a Human Process.* New York: W. W. Norton, 1962.

Sutton, Robert I. "The Weird Rules of Creativity." *Harvard Business Review* 79 (2001): 94–107.

Swartz, Sally, and Leslie Swartz. "Talk about Talk: Metacommentary and Context in the Analysis of Psychotic Discourse." *Culture, Medicine, and Psychiatry* 11 (1987): 395–416.

Tanouye, Elyse. "Mental Illness: A Rising Workplace Cost—One Form, Depression, Takes $70 Billion Toll Annually; Bank One Intervenes Early." *Wall Street Journal,* June 13, 2001, B1.

Teasdale, J. D., and P. J. Barnard. *Affect, Cognition and Change: Remodelling Depressive Thought.* Hillsdale, NJ: Erlbaum, 1993.

Teicher, Stacy A. "Freelancing in Your Future?: Rise of Independent Workers Highlights Challenges Facing Today's U.S. Labor Market." *Christian Science Monitor,* August 2, 2004, 14.

Thalbitzer, Sophus. *Emotion and Insanity.* International Library of Psychology. New York: Harcourt, 1926.

Tierney, John. "Using MRI Machines to See Partisanship on the Brain." *New York Times,* April 20, 2004, A1, 17.

Tillson, Tamsen. "The CEO's Disease." *Canadian Business* 69, no. 3 (1996): 26–31.

Tobias, Andrew. *Extraordinary Popular Delusions and the Madness of Crowds*. New York: Three Rivers Press, 1980.

Torrey, E. Fuller, and Michael B. Knable. *Surviving Manic Depression: A Manual on Bipolar Disorder for Patients, Families, and Providers*. New York: Basic Books, 2002.

Totterdell, Dr. Peter. "What Is Emotion Management?" Institute of Work Psychology, http://www.shef.ac.uk/~iwp/publications/whatis/emotion_management.pdf (accessed July 16, 2003).

"Trying Topamax and Klonopin." 2002, http://groups.google.com/group/alt.support .depression.manic/browse_thread/thread/6ea994194578e39f/5e841c6a5e841c6a 5d2bbe91?q=after+getting+sun+blisters&rnum=1#5e841c6a5d2bbe9 (accessed November 7, 2003).

Turkle, Sherry. *Life on the Screen: Identity in the Age of the Internet*. New York: Simon and Schuster, 1995.

"TV Review: 'Manhattan' Series in Debut on Channel 2." *New York Times*, March 12, 1960, 43.

Uchitelle, Louis. "Confusion as an Economic Indicator." *New York Times*, November 2, 1997, 1, 6.

"U.S. Steel Losing the Game." *Baltimore Business Journal*, American City Business Journals. 2001, http://baltimore.bizjournals.com/baltimore/stories/2001/10/29/ editorial1.html (accessed January 2, 2005).

Wakefield, Jerome C. "Disorder as Harmful Dysfunction: A Conceptual Critique of DSM-III-R's Definition of Mental Disorder." *Psychological Review* 99, no. 2 (1992): 232–47.

Wakefield, Jerome C., Allan Horwitz, and Mark F. Schmitz. "Are We Overpathologizing the Socially Anxious? Social Phobia from a Harmful Dysfunction Perspective." *Canadian Journal of Psychiatry* 50, no. 6 (2005): 317.

Walker, Rob. "Conscience Undercover." *New York Times Magazine*, August 1, 2004, 18.

Walker, Tom. "Market Cools Down While the Weather Heats Up." *Atlanta Journal and Constitution*, July 1, 1998, F1.

Walkerdine, Valerie. "Beyond Developmentalism?" *Theory and Psychology* 3, no. 4 (1993): 451–69.

Walser, Robert. "Deep Jazz: Notes on Interiority, Race, and Criticism." In *Inventing the Psychological: Toward a Cultural History of Emotional Life in America*, ed. Joel Pfister and Nancy Schnog, 271–96. New Haven: Yale University Press, 1997.

Waraich, P., E. M. Goldner, J. M. Somers, and L. Hsu. "Prevalence and Incidence Studies of Mood Disorders: A Systematic Review of the Literature." *Canadian Journal of Psychiatry* 49, no. 2 (2004): 124–38.

Watson, Robert Irving. *Basic Writings in the History of Psychology*. New York: Oxford University Press, 1979.

Weber, Max. *From Max Weber: Essays in Sociology*. Ed. and trans. H. H. Gerth and C. Wright Mills. 1946. New York: Oxford University Press, 1958.

———. *The Protestant Ethic and the Spirit of Capitalism*. Trans. Talcott Parsons. New York: Scribner, 1958.

Weber, Max. *The Sociology of Religion*. Boston: Beacon Press, 1993.

———. *The Vocation Lectures*. Trans. Rodney Livingstone. Ed. David Owen and Tracy B. Strong. Indianapolis: Hackett Publishing, 2004.

Webster's Revised Unabridged Dictionary. Ed. Noah Porter. Springfield, MA: C. & G. Merriam, 1913.

Weismantel, Mary. *Cholas and Pishtacos*. Chicago: University of Chicago Press, 2001.

Whybrow, Peter C. *American Mania: When More Is Not Enough*. New York: W. W. Norton, 2005.

Whyte, William H. *The Organization Man*. New York: Simon and Schuster, 1956.

Wikan, Unni. "Public Grace and Private Fears." *Ethos* 15, no. 4 (December 1987): 337–65.

Wilce, Jim. "Madness, Fear, and Control in Bangladesh: Clashing Bodies of Power/Knowledge." *Medical Anthropological Quarterly* 18, no. 3 (2004): 357–75.

Williams, Raymond. *Marxism and Literature*. Oxford: Oxford University Press, 1977.

Williams, Simon J. *Emotion and Social Theory: Corporeal Reflections on the (Ir)Rational*. Thousand Oaks, CA: Sage, 2001.

Willocks, Tim. *Green River Rising*. London: J. Cape, 1994.

Winnicott, D. W. "The Manic Defense." In *Through Pediatrics to Psychoanalysis: Collected Papers*, 129–44. New York: Brunner/Mazel, 1992.

Winter, Irene J. "The Affective Properties of Styles: An Inquiry into Analytical Process and the Inscription of Meaning in Art History." In *Picturing Science, Producing Art*, ed. Caroline Jones and Peter Gallison, 55–77. New York: Routledge, 1998.

Wittgenstein, Ludwig. *Zettel*. Berkeley: University of California Press, 1967.

Wolfe, Tom. *A Man in Full*. New York: Farrar, Straus Giroux, 1998.

World Mood Chart. 2004, http://www.thiswebsitewillchangeyourlife.com/content/mood.asp (accessed October 1, 2006).

Young, Allan. *The Harmony of Illusions: Inventing Post-Traumatic Stress Disorder*. Princeton: Princeton University Press, 1995.

Young, Robert M. *Mind, Brain and Adaptation in the Nineteenth Century: Cerebral Localization and Its Biological Context from Gall to Ferrier*. Oxford: Clarendon, 1970.

Zaretsky, Eli. *Secrets of the Soul: A Social and Cultural History of Psychoanalysis*. New York: Knopf, 2004.

Žižek, Slavoj. *Looking Awry: An Introduction to Jacques Lacan through Popular Culture*. Cambridge, MA: MIT Press, 1991.

———. *Welcome to the Desert of the Real*. New York: Wooster Press, 2001.

Zürn, Unica. *The Man of Jasmine and Other Texts*. London: Atlas Press, 1994.

Index